BISON
BOOKS

RIVER CITY EMPIRE
Tom Dennison's Omaha

Orville D. Menard

Foreword to the Bison Books edition
by Laurie Smith Camp

With a new introduction by the author

UNIVERSITY OF NEBRASKA PRESS
LINCOLN AND LONDON

First Nebraska paperback printing: 2013

Library of Congress Cataloging-in-Publication Data
Menard, Orville D.
[Political bossism in mid-America]
River City Empire: Tom Dennison's Omaha / Orville D. Menard; foreword to the Bison
Books edition by Laurie Smith Camp; with a new introduction by the author.
pages cm
Includes bibliographical references and index.
ISBN 978-0-8032-4833-5 (pbk.: alk. paper)
1. Political corruption—Nebraska—Omaha—History—20th century.
2. Omaha (Neb.)—Politics and government.
3. Dennison, Tom, 1859–1934. I. Title.
JS1251.8.M46 2013
320.809782254—dc23   2013029665

Foreword

"Ladies and Gentlemen, you are about to see a story of murder, greed, corruption, violence, exploitation, adultery, and treachery—all those things we hold dear to our hearts."

This opening line from the Broadway musical *Chicago* could be used to describe the book by Orville D. Menard that you are about to read. But *Chicago* is a fictional account of Prohibition-era corruption in the Midwest. Professor Menard's book is true. *Chicago* is a comedy. Professor Menard's book may make you smile as you reflect on the eternal foibles of human nature, but it will make you cringe as you learn how a city can lose its integrity and its very soul.

If you enjoyed the Ken Burns series *Prohibition*; if you were riveted to the screen watching Tom Hanks in *Road to Perdition*; if you are fascinated by J. Edgar Hoover, his G-men, and the denizens of the underworld they brought to justice, then this book is for you. It tells the story of some of the most colorful and exciting characters of Omaha's past. It describes some of Omaha's proudest moments and its most shameful. It tells a story of murder, greed, corruption, violence, exploitation, treachery, collaboration, acquiescence, and willful blindness. In some ways, it is a "how to" book for those who want to build a political machine linked to a crime syndicate. But it also tells a story of heroism: the mayor who nearly sacrificed his life standing up to a lynch mob four thousand strong, the honest public servants who risked their lives to bring members of the crime syndicate to justice, journalists who reported the truth, and reformers who never gave up. Used wisely, this is a "how to" book for those who want to ensure that political bossism never takes root in American cities again.

For me, it's personal. This book records a history I *do* hold dear to my heart.

In 1898, when my grandparents were still courting, Omaha was a model, magical city that hosted the Trans Mississippi Exposition—a world's fair that welcomed 2.6 million visitors and inspired L. Frank Baum to write *The Wizard of Oz*. The city's future was as bright as the thousands of new-fangled incandescent lights that illuminated the Exposition's Grand Court.

In 1900 my grandparents operated a grocery store at 1403 Douglas Street, next door to Omaha's Budweiser Saloon. Husbands and fathers who spent all their earnings in Omaha gambling houses, saloons, and other places of adult entertainment came to the store for groceries—on credit. My grandfather was a Scottish immigrant with a staunch Calvinist upbringing. So if the sinner seemed repentant and could recite a verse from the Bible, the family got groceries. In 1903 my grandparents closed their store, deeply in debt, and for the next thirty years became an integral part of Omaha's reform movement. The reformers had one mission: to break the back of the political machine and crime syndicate run by Tom Dennison, the enigmatic man who controlled Omaha's City Hall, police force, and vice enterprises, operating quietly from the back of the Budweiser Saloon.

The reformers made progress. They declared a victory when their candidates gained control of Omaha's City Hall in 1918. Then, on September 28, 1919, Omaha saw its darkest day. Professor Menard describes in chilling detail how a lynch mob gathered force, losing all sense of honor and humanity. My grandfather was at the Douglas County Courthouse on that fateful Sunday night, trying to save the files of the clerk of the district court as the mob set fire after fire and slashed the hoses of the firefighters. No one could save the human target of the mob's mission. In a Pulitzer Prize–winning editorial following the riot, the *Omaha World-Herald* said Omaha was operating under the rule of the "wolf pack." Tom Dennison's nickname was the "Old Gray Wolf." At the next election, Dennison's machine was in control of Omaha's City Hall once again.

In 1929 my grandfather and his oldest son were admitted to the Nebraska bar on the same day. My father, Edson Smith, began work as an assistant U.S. attorney, responsible for enforcement of America's "great experiment"—Prohibition. He drafted a code of etiquette for officers investigating Prohibition violations, to ensure that there would be a clear difference between law enforcers and law violators and that the constitutional rights of all suspects would be respected. On August 5, 1932, he filed a grand jury indictment against Tom Dennison, Dennison's chief partner-in-vice Billy Nesselhous, and fifty-seven of their associates for 168 acts of conspiracy to violate the National Prohibition Act. A jury trial began in October and for months drew the attention of news media nationwide. The trial concluded with an unusual twist, but it brought an end to the Dennison-Nesselhous enterprises. Political bossism in Omaha was dead in 1933—long before many other American cities were freed of such an affliction.

Sixty years later, a few months after my father's death, Professor Menard's compelling book about the Dennison era and the federal conspiracy trial was published. I read the book and learned a history of my quiet hometown—and my modest father— that I never knew. The book (and Professor Menard's popular speaking engagements complete with costumed Dennison role-play) provoked discussion about the era. Some people wondered whether a political boss was really such a bad thing. After all, Dennison ensured that Omaha was independent of the powerful crime syndicates that controlled nearby Kansas City and Chicago. With Dennison in charge, Omahans had a "go-to guy" when they needed to negotiate with the criminal underworld. A benevolent dictatorship is an efficient form of government, and Dennison was a man who could be very benevolent and highly efficient.

After reading the book, you will make your own judgment about the costs and benefits of political bossism. My view is biased. Since 2001 I have served as a federal district judge. I preside over conspiracy trials involving drug kingpins, human trafficking, money laundering, extortion, bribery, and fraud. But crime syndicates no longer control American city halls and police departments. In the United States, the era of the political boss linked to the underworld has faded. From my vantage, we must never return to that era, and we must help societies abroad understand that the best way to govern is through fair elections and the rule of law.

On New Year's Eve 2009, I attended a gathering at a neighbor's home and saw a gray-haired man with dark-rimmed eyeglasses and bushy eyebrows sitting quietly in a corner. I sat next to him and said, "I want to tell you something. For many years, I presented workshops on management ethics. For good examples, I told anecdotes about *your* management style. For bad examples, I told stories about Tom Dennison." I didn't expect the man to recognize Dennison's name, but he became animated and said, "Oh, I know all about Dennison! I live in the house that was owned by Dennison's bagman, Billy Nesselhous! I think Billy hid his treasure in there somewhere, and I'm still looking for it!" I asked if he would like a copy of Professor Menard's book about Tom Dennison, and he said yes. When I tried to buy a copy, it was out of print, so I gave Mr. Buffett my copy. He later told me he read it cover to cover and enjoyed it very much.

I told Professor Menard his book must not be allowed to remain out of print. It tells a story from which timeless lessons should be drawn. The book is entertaining, but it is entertainment with a purpose.

Ladies and Gentlemen, please take your seats. The curtain is about to rise.

Laurie Smith Camp
Chief Judge
United States District Court
District of Nebraska

River City Empire (originally published in 1989 as *Political Bossism in Mid-America*) explores political machine politics in Omaha, Nebraska, over some thirty years. Several items of new information now compel an update. Recent material prompts a review of the "Cowboy Mayor's" 1877 gunfight in Texas, his own version versus an eyewitness account. Ever since Omaha's 1919 Courthouse Riot, the alleged victim's name has been spelled Loebeck, but the accurate spelling is Loeback. Lynched Will Brown's physical condition has frequently been described by anonymous sources as preventing him from attacking anyone. The origin of the descriptions has now been identified.

"Cowboy Jim" Dahlman Leaves Texas

Omaha's "perpetual mayor," Jim Dahlman, was well known for his honesty. His explanation of why he left Texas was accepted for years. Believing he had killed Charley Bree in a street gunfight in 1877, Dahlman fled to northwest Nebraska. An interview with a "Texas old-timer" tells another story, casting Dahlman not as having a gunfight but in darkness shooting a good man.

In a 1910 newspaper interview, Dahlman told of his leaving Texas for Nebraska. Dahlman said he was about twenty when he shot his brother-in-law, Charley Bree, who was abusing his sister. One evening they met in a street in Youkam, Texas. According to Dahlman, Bree fired first and missed him; Dahlman then fired. His bullet hit Bree in the forehead, and he "dropped like lead." The young cowboy thought he had killed Bree and "lost no time in getting out of there," arriving under the name Jim Murray in Nebraska. In years to come he became a community leader and regional political figure. A pending marriage prompted the desire to clear his name, and he asked a friend to check with authorities in Texas to find out whether he was still wanted for murder. The response was "no" as Bree had not died, "although he needed killing."

"An old settler," C. C. Koerth, in a 1910 interview in a San Antonio newspaper, had a different description of the gunfight. Asked if he remembered the shooting between Dahlman and Bree, Koerth answered "yes," that it was near his house and he remembered it. Two heavily armed men, J. C. Dahlman and "Bud" Seekers, rode into town one afternoon, looking for lodging. About midnight Koerth saw Bree leaning against a tree when Dahlman and Seekers appeared. Three shots rang out, the first two missing Bree but the third hitting him in the head. He had drawn his pistol but fell without shooting back. A bleeding Bree arrived at Koerth's back door saying, "They have murdered me."

Unmentioned in either interview was that Dahlman had been indicted in Texas for cattle rustling in 1877 (the charge was dismissed five years later). Perhaps Texas Rangers having papers for his arrest was another inducement for Dahlman to leave the state. Dahlman later paid a five-hundred-dollar fine for breaking bond; cleared of legal problems, he resumed his name and married. His desire to clear his name was perhaps also influenced by an increasing interest in politics and wanting to preempt any electoral rumors or problems.

In Nebraska Dahlman turned his life around, becoming a trusted cowhand who became Omaha's "perpetual mayor." Koerth was a druggist who lived in Yoakum for twelve years, respected by the town's inhabitants. Dahlman described Bree as shiftless and no more than an outlaw. Koerth remembered a good man shot in a cowardly midnight assault. There is no question that Dahlman shot Bree, but whose version is true, the gunfighter's claim of defending his sister or the account of an eyewitness? Whichever one is believed, Dahlman became a lawman, a friend of William Jennings Bryan, and a popular mayor known as "Honest Jim."

Agnes Loeback (Loebeck)

Omaha's newspapers on September 26, 1919, reported that white Agnes Loebeck was the victim of an alleged midnight assault by a black man, later identified as William Brown. Tempers in the white community flared, and on Sunday the 28th a crowd headed for the Douglas County Courthouse, where Brown was incarcerated. Late in the afternoon the crowd became a mob, set fire to the courthouse, and seized and lynched Brown. In the following days the press repeatedly referred to Agnes Loebeck, and in future articles and other references her last name invariably was spelled Loebeck. That inaccurate spelling became standard for years to come.

At the conclusion of a Workshop on the Riot in 2005, at the Douglas County Historical Society in Omaha, Nebraska, a young woman told the speaker that her family genealogy revealed that Agnes was her great aunt, whose name was actually spelled Loeback. Further research confirmed Loeback as accurate.

Harrison J. Pinkett

As noted above, Will Brown was accused of rape, arrested, incarcerated, and lynched in September 1919. Reports soon circulated that Brown was innocent because he was physically in capable of committing the crime. Others disputed that description as unwarranted because he was said to have been employed in a lumber yard, a packing house, and as a coal hauler, all requiring physical fitness.

Reports of Brown's frailties for years continued to call into question his being Agnes's attacker. A physical examination by an unidentified person concluded Brown was "too twisted by rheumatism to assault anyone." An unidentified *Omaha World-Herald* reporter claimed he interviewed Brown in jail and confirmed his crippled condition. A similar *Lincoln Journal* article claimed that Brown's condition ruled out his attacking Agnes and her companion Milton Hoffman. George Leighton, in his *Five Cities*, states that a lawyer examined Brown and "found the man badly twisted with rheumatism and wondered how anyone in such a condition could have assaulted anyone." The name of the lawyer was never reported by Leighton or any of the other commentators.

During a 1938 WPA Writers' Project, Harrison J. Pinkett revealed he had met with the jailed Brown, and his comments on his condition were thereafter reported but without attribution. Pinkett was the first African American admitted to the bar of the U.S. Supreme Court and the first university-trained African American attorney to open an office in Omaha. A transcript of the interview recorded that Mr. Pinkett "definitely states that it would have been impossible for him [Brown] to attack anyone." His words were ignored by the masses intent on lynching Brown but became the standard anonymous reference in accounts of the riot. His identity was lost for seventy-two years, until his remarks came to light in the long forgotten WPA interview.

Dedicated To My Greatest Teachers

Paul Beck
Duane Hill
Lane Lancaster
Virgene McBride
Raphael Zariski

Mr. Dennison is a Republican and a very prominent and influential one in city, state and national politics. In fact he has the reputation of being the most powerful Republican political factor in Omaha, but while he has the means of putting scores of his friends in office, he has persistently refused to run for an office of any kind himself, preferring to be a private in the ranks of his army.

--Addison E. Sheldon

Dennison is the one outstanding political boss of this town, who has ruled with an iron hand for the greater part of the past twenty-five or thirty years.

--James C. Kinsler

The Dennison machine directly or indirectly goes into every home in the city with its influence. They have directors in every big corporation, they belong to all of the churches and lodges and add respectability to the organization.

--Roy N. Towl

Contents

A section of illustrations follows page 130.

Preface

During the first third of the twentieth century Omaha, Nebraska, was under boss rule. Here, similar to growing cities elsewhere in America during these years, a political machine was central to the inhabitants' lives. Whether an Omahan was high on the social ladder or occupied a far lesser place, the machine was prepared to exercise its capacity to punish or to reward--the essence of power. A newly arrived immigrant looking for a job or a worker in need of food or coal turned to the machine. A firm seeking privileges from city hall turned to the machine. Able to function only with police toleration, underworld figures turned to the machine. For over thirty years the man who controlled Omaha's political machine was Thomas Dennison. In the post-World War II world, the city gained a reputation as a conservative, rather lifeless and noncosmopolitan place. But from the turn of the century to the 1930s it was renowned as a wide-open bootlegging and gambling center. Himself once a professional gambler, Dennison presided over these activities and manipulated local government to the benefit of his numerous constituencies.

There have been many studies of political bosses, but most have dealt with larger cities than Omaha. As a middle size community, Omaha provides an opportunity to explore bossism in a smaller, perhaps more representative environment of the United States. Richard C. Wade, editor of an urban life in America series, has noted that the nation's urbanization was not confined to the Chicagos and Detroits, but also included the St. Pauls, Denvers, and Omahas. "As a railroad center and a meat-packing center it [Omaha] felt the weight of the industrial giants of our age; as an expanding city it offered a broad base of opportunities." Among them was politics.

In Omaha, as in so many other cities, a political boss emerged, presiding over a political machine which stands as a test case of its counterparts elsewhere. Thomas Dennison and his organization are the focal points in the pages to follow, exploring and probing machine poli-

xix

tics in his city. Generally these will be familiar to students of boss politics because there was great similarity among its practitioners. Less well known, however, is the inside "how" of their methods. Winning elections, serving legitimate and illegitimate business associates, and administering justice--boss style--are herein not merely mentioned but given a complete accounting.

Scholars will find in Dennison's middle size city confirmation of several theses of bossism, and affirmation of two aspects of machine politics seldom noted. While much has been written about the factors which led to decline of the bosses, little attention has centered on the deliberate use of the courtroom by reformers not for judicial remedy but for political ends. Many a boss's reign was broken in a court although conviction seldom resulted. However, a jury's guilty verdict was more than likely not the machine opponents' purpose, but negative publicity with an eye to the next election. Other forces may have been already at work to weaken the bosses, but the *coup de grace* was delivered by a judicial branch turned to for political purpose.

Second, little has been said about the failure of almost all political machines to provide for systems of succession. Fearing for their power, machine leaders were reluctant to suggest they might be replaced. Consequently they ruled as indispensable men, their authority personal and untransferable. When they left the scene their structures left with them, denied the opportunity to adapt to changing circumstances. In New York and Chicago institutionalized means of conveying power did become part of their machines' gears and cogs and their lengthly life span was not therefore dependent on any particular figure. Omaha was part of the more familiar pattern: court revelations the seed for political defeat, and a very personalized machine.

A history of Omaha is not provided here, for such an endeavor is beyond the intent or purpose. Rather, one aspect is the focus--machine politics in Omaha from 1900 to 1933, portraying how a machine operated, describing an era which helped to shape our political lives. With that in mind, the work's organization is topical instead of chronological; the concern is power and the various ways a boss employed it, and how an entire city was enrolled in its exercise. Throughout, although the time-honored term "political machine" is adhered to, the cold, impersonal image conveyed by such an analogy is rejected as not really descriptive of reality. Animated, living entities of great complexity, the organizations which once dominated America's cities were more akin to a species, a political organism, than to interlocking metalic parts. It is the former notion of life filled, survival seeking bodies that pervades my examination of the Dennison era.

While there is a vast literature on bossism the bosses themselves seldom left anything in writing. Theirs was an oral command world. North Dakota's Alexander McKenzie, a lesser known boss, summed up for his kind the necessity to communicate directly: "Never write a letter--walk across the state if necessary, but never write a letter. Sure, what you say goes up in smoke, but what you *write* is before you always." Public documents provide some assistance in studying bossism, in Dennison's case court records particularly, and newspapers are a valuable source for any student of any boss. Dennison's close associates left neither memoirs nor autobiographies and a biography written about James Dahlman, Omaha's "perpetual mayor" during the Dennison years, fails even to mention Dennison's name. However, one of Dennison's assistants did write a series of letters which were saved by two of his correspondents. Tom Crawford, feeling double-crossed, wrote to his fellow anti-Dennisonites, detailing machine operations. As citations will demonstrate, these letters proved to be a major source. They were used with caution given Crawford's antipathy to Dennison, but in conjunction with other data proved reliable.

Much of that other data is a result of interviews, an indispensable method for gathering information on such a topic. I am indebted to the persons who shared their vivid memories with me, and understanding of the many who refused, usually on grounds of not wanting to implicate themselves or heirs in bygone questionable activities. Most of those interviewed were willing to be acknowledged for their contributions; several were not and agreed to talk with me only on condition of anonymity. When drawing upon information from an anonymous contributor, no citation or reference will be provided, other than a broad comment such as occupation. With this in mind, I appreciate T. Harry Williams's comment that "Some academic readers may object to the introduction of unidentified sources, but the practice is sometimes necessary in taking testimony from living persons."

I wish to acknowledge and thank for their help the library staffs of the University of Nebraska at Omaha, the Western History Collection of Denver, Colorado's, Public Library, the Library of Leadville, Colorado, the National Archives and Records Service, and the Nebraska State Historical Society. Grateful acknowledgment is extended to all who assisted me in Chadron, Nebraska's, City Hall, in Nebraska's Dawes and Douglas County Courthouses, and in the office of the Clerk of the District Court, Montgomery County, Red Oak, Iowa.

I owe persons interviewed particular thanks because their recollections provide a dimension impossible to grasp through the written word. Public acknowledgment is due those who chose not to remain anonymous, all of Omaha unless otherwise noted: Fred Boien, Bertha Calloway, Dorothy M. Cathers, Herman J. Creal, A.P. Deutsch of Wickenburg, Arizona, Alice Dennison, John C. Duggan of Jackson, Nebraska, Frank L. Frost, Jerry Gordon, Anton Kurtz, Charles Martin, William "Billy" Maher, William R. Milner, William Dean Noyes, and Louis J. Pruch. The late Dr. John Ragan (Tom Dennison's grandson, who spent an afternoon sharing recollections of his grandfather and of the home they shared at 72nd and Military Streets), Pearl Reilly, W.B. Quiqley of Valentine, Nebraska, Jack D. Ringwalt, Wray Scott, Edward Shafton, Edson Smith, Olga J. Strimple, William H. Thompson, Ralph P. Walsh of Willis, Nebraska, Ned Williams, Joel H. Wright, and W.W. Zerbe.

A research grant from the University Research Committee of the University of Nebraska at Omaha and a Professional Development Leave provided by the University made possible time devoted solely to research on Omaha's machine. Thanks also to Harl A. Dalstrom and Jerold Simmons, both of UNO's History Department. Professor Dalstrom has been a source of support and suggestions for several years, given his grasp of Nebraska's and Omaha's past. Key comments on the manuscript relating to organization and points of emphasis were provided by Professor Simmons, abetting efforts toward clarity and focus. Colleagues in the Department of Political Science, especially Joong-Gun Chung, Kent Kirwan, and Bernard Kolasa have provided encouragement and advice while demonstrating great patience with my turning many a conversation to Tom Dennison. Great thanks also to Joyce Crockett and Roger M. Hubbard of Campus Computing at UNO for their generous assistance in the final stages of manuscript preparation. I am also indebted to the Nebraska State Historical Society, and the National Cowboy Hall of Fame for permission to incorporate in revised form my articles which appeared in the Winter, 1987, issues of *Nebraska History* and *Persimmon Hill*.

But most of all I am grateful to my wife Darlene. With understanding rather than complaint she has shared our home with Dennison for years, and the research finally taking form as a book can be attributed to her. Any shortcomings in the result can be attributed to me.

A description of Omaha's political machine is the culmination of all the assistance provided. The goal has been to understand, not judge--to enlighten, not condemn. Total truth about Dennison and his city may not be found here, but the effort may at least suggest that *"Se non e vero, e ben trovato."* (Even if it's not true, it's believable.)

Orville D. Menard

CHAPTER I

Formation

*He was one of the most hated, feared, obeyed
and picturesque personalities ever to live in Omaha.*
--Nathan Nielsen

They combined generosity with a capacity and readiness for violence. They possessed organizational and leadership gifts, but resorted to manipulation and fraud. They were corrupt and corrupting, yet their followers extolled their honesty and took their word as bond. They bent the law to their purposes and selectively had it enforced, nonetheless are remembered for having controlled corruption and crime thus "keeping the lid on." They were needed, but outlived their usefulness. They were the city bosses.

Political life today in American cities exhibits reaction to their years of power and their influence remains among us: nonpartisan elections, merit systems, careful bidding systems, an abiding distrust of district elections, voter registration, the secret ballot, the conviction that the answer to "politics" is proper structure and administrative efficiency to resolve municipal problems. Throughout the land candidates for office laud their own electoral organization while charging their opponents with heading a machine. The bosses are largely gone from the scene, but we are the inheritors of their political estates.

Late in the fall of 1932 one of them was embroiled in a trial for conspiracy to violate the federal prohibition act. For a month the prosecution laid before jurors in court and the city's citizens through newspaper coverage, a torrent of evidence and testimony revealing purported involvements of his political machine in underworld activities. Fifty-nine individuals had been cited in the indictment, but by the time the legal action's central figure took the stand, only sixteen remained on trial because of judge directed not guilty verdicts and mistrial.

1

On November 15, 1932, the "Old Man" took the stand. Thomas Dennison, Omaha, Nebraska's, political boss since the turn of the century, prime target of the prosecution and anti-machine forces in the city, now faced not only the jury but the citizens of what electorally was once securely his city. Opponents, repeatedly defeated when challenging Dennison through traditional political channels, had turned to the courts as the means to discredit him and subsequently achieve victory at the polls.

An imposing figure was on the witness stand; despite his advanced years Dennison was still firmly upright and power long exercised remained obvious in his bearing. His frequently noted "steely blue eyes" viewed the audience through spectacles, and the habitual smile, narrow and whimsical as sometimes described, was more narrow and less whimsical. Dennison's hands were broad and thick fingered, his left ring finger supporting a large gem. Reminders of a youth on the road as a laborer in the west were summoned by his broad shoulders, six foot height, and two hundred pounds. The left ear looked cauliflowered, but while Dennison had ample opportunity to develop that ear in fights (a nickname as a young man was "Pick Handle" Tom), it was due to skin cancer developed in later years. Although he was known to stutter slightly when under stress, there was no stuttering during his testimony. Tastefully and immaculately dressed as usual, Dennison appeared little different from contemporaries in the business and professional world: dark suit with curving watch chain over lower part of the vest.

Yet it was clear that Dennison had aged for his hands were discolored and one reporter wrote the accused was palsied. He had suffered a slight stroke on Christmas day in 1927, another in June of the trial year, and an extension for health reasons had been requested by his attorneys. However, the request was denied on the basis of government rebuttals that the accused had recently been seen in public as usual. Whatever his actual health, it was clear the long used title of "Old Man" now also served as a description. From the witness stand he was able to survey the courtroom, his prosecuting opponents, his co-defendant associates, and trace a colorful lifetime, leading from Nebraska and Iowa farmland, to the faro tables of the West, to power as a city boss.

In 1860 John and Anna Dennison moved their family from Delhi, Iowa (in the eastern part of the state some thirty-five miles west of Dubuque), to the northeast corner of Nebraska in Dakota County. Both parents were Irish immigrants (he at age sixteen), John's birthplace being County Limerick, and Anna's County Tyrone. They had met in New Orleans, and shortly after their marriage moved to Iowa. Four years before their arrival in Nebraska, Father Jeremiah Trecy had established a colony on the west bank of the Missouri River, about a mile and a half from the present site of Jackson, Nebraska. Father Trecy brought with him from Garryowner Parish, near Dubuque, sixty people, mostly Irish immigrants, and eighteen ox-drawn wagons. In June 1856 the colony named its site St. John's in honor of St. John the Baptist, and for the next two years the new settlement, the first Catholic Parish in Nebraska, thrived, growing to two hundred by 1858.

Here the Dennisons arrived two years later, bringing with them their infant son Thomas, born in Iowa on October 26, 1858.[1] Typical of the times and locale, Tom was not baptized until December of 1861, when a circuit Priest administered the rite. (Father Trecy had gone to Washington, D.C., in 1860 to seek permission to establish an Indian mission; the Civil War started while he was there and he became a chaplain, never to return to Jackson.) Thomas Dennison had no middle name, for as he explained when he became a grandfather, "No old time Irishman ever had a middle name. Middle names were reserved for kings and princes."[2]

In the early 1860s, the residents of St. John's moved away from the Missouri's banks as the river increasingly threatened them. Jackson was founded and St. John's ceased to exist in 1866, except in memory, with the Dennisons by now living in the new and predominately Irish community. For two hundred dollars, Tom's father in 1869 bought eighty acres of land just west of Jackson, and for sixty dollars added a little over forty-four more nine years later, land he farmed until his death, which followed his second wife's by but four days, on April 10, 1905. Two years later Tom released any claim to the land to his brother John for the sum of $1,500.[3]

John and Anna had eight children, Thomas being the third eldest. When he was eight years old his mother died, and his formal schooling likely ended not too much later. (See Appendix.) By the time he was a teenager he was spending his days as an area farm laborer. Hiring out locally, for the next several years he never strayed far from Jackson, mentioning with pride when reminiscing his having won the corn husking championship of Mills County, Iowa, in 1872 while serving as a farm hand for Simpson Finnell. Widower John Dennison remarried in 1878, adding to his own eight children the eight of Irish born widow Mary Mullen.[4] According to a family joke, the large frame house on the farm became overcrowded: "That put the Dennisons on the road."[5]

The exact date of Tom's leaving home is unclear, but was in the late 1870s. Whatever the timing and motivation, he headed west, a tall and powerfully built young man, his size and strength finding companions in the jobs they were called upon to fulfill during Dennison's wanderings. He was a blacksmith in Kansas, chopped wood in Colorado for a year, labored as a railroader in New Mexico, and as a prospector in New Mexico, Montana, and Colorado. A rugged individual, he became a bouncer "in a couple of pretty bad . . . saloons where you could get killed on a job like that," and proved to be a bad shot in an attempted robbery. Dennison once told how he and a friend, Tom Farrell, had gone to a miner's shack in Kokomo, Colorado (not far from Leadville), where they had heard a large amount of money was stashed. They threw open the door and unloaded their forty-fours at the sleeping man's bunk. "We only succeeded in hitting the _ _ _ _ _ [sic] in the toe," recalled Dennison. "We did not succeed in getting his money."[6]

His travels gave him the opportunity to learn lessons not available in Jackson, and he proved a quick and ready pupil, becoming especially knowledgeable in games of chance--he emerged a professional gambler. A later associate explained the circumstances which led Dennison to lay aside his picks and shovels and move from field camps to boom towns and gambling halls.[7]

> After months of arduous labor to sink a deep mine shaft, the youth awoke one morning to discover that the hole had filled with water. Swearing that he would never do another days work as long as he lived, Dennison began a colorful career as an intimate of

4

some of the most notorious western gaming rendezvous of the later decades of the nineteenth century.

During those years, Tom Dennison, professional gambler, became a familiar figure, part owner, or partner in a number of gambling halls. His first work in his acquired trade, according to Dennison, was in 1883 at the Texas House, one of Leadville, Colorado's, most celebrated establishments in a city noted for its numerous gambling halls. He became a floorman the next year, and in 1885 acquired one-fourth interest in the thriving business. In the spring of 1886 he sold out his Texas House holding and bought into The Opera House, also in Leadville, selling out in turn in the fall and moving to Denver.

In Colorado's capital city, he became associated with the Arcade, like the Texas House a preeminent and well known gathering place for gamblers. For a time he traveled between Leadville and Denver, then went on to Butte, Montana, where he worked at The Board of Trade, before going on to Ogden, Utah, and a partnership in two gambling houses. Dennison came to Omaha for two or three months in 1889, later recalling that during that time he had been in the gambling business, the policy business, and bought and sold horses.[8]

After his short Omaha stay, he returned to Montana, spending a year at Helena's The Capital, two years in Butte, and then six months at Henry Hines's Place in Salt Lake City, Utah. During his ten years of gambler travels, he also spent time in Aspen, Colorado, at a place called Our Corner, and dealt faro in San Diego, being an expert "in a square game."[9] The places Dennison chose to associate with as a gentleman gambler were noted for their lavishness and offered the very best in food and drink in addition to their gambling rooms.

Dennison was but one of a host of immigrants when he arrived in Leadville, the silver boom town, incorporated in February 1878. News of the discovery that the area's "black sand" was lead carbonate filled with silver had spread rapidly and widely, and wealth seekers crossed the mountains to share in the riches of Lake County. Daily came hundreds, some seeking to find silver while others arrived to share in or relieve them of their new found wealth--if

5

found. "They walked in over Mosquito Pass, rode Spotswood and McClelland's stages, drove teams and wagons and rode horseback. By 1880, some 30,000 people called Leadville home."[10] Three years later Dennison came to the booming city of saloons and gambling halls, where shootings and violence were more common than uncommon in the ten thousand foot elevation city. A six month record of deaths in 1881 from other than natural causes showed that in that year, between March 1 and September 7, forty-seven individuals either committed suicide, had fatal accidents, died from unknown causes, or, in the case of seventeen of the deceased, "died with their boots on" as a result of gun shot wounds.[11] Meanwhile booze flowed, cards were dealt, roulette wheels twirled, and dice rolled, providing revenue for the city as well as for successful players. Saloon licenses, gambler fees, and prostitution fines were counted on for over half of the city's revenues in the mid-1880s.[12]

When Dennison joined the staff of the Texas House, the place was young but already famous. Samuel Harlan and J.H.F. Chapman were Dennison's employers, their home state providing the name for the lavish setting of their games of chance. Standing on the east side of Harrison Avenue (number 216), the two story building was entitled to claim a place in the first rank in a city noted "for the number and elegance of its club houses."[13] In the Texas House Dennison and others enjoyed furnishings carefully selected to satisfy and nurture temperaments oriented to quality. The first floor was divided into two large rooms, the front one being the barroom entered through two large walnut and glass doors. Flanked by paneled glass, the bar, stocked with the finest quality liquors, covered the length of one wall. Faro and roulette players went on to the rear of the first floor, where "strict and unwavering honesty is the watchword, and all who sit down at the tables, have the satisfaction of knowing that they are among gentlemen."[14]

A lushly carpeted stairway climbed to the second floor's beautifully papered and frescoed hallway, highlighted by brilliant lighting. Doors opened into several rooms, the first two becoming one when folding walnut doors were drawn back. In these rooms, as throughout the building, good taste and the money available to satisfy it were obvious. Soft Brussels carpets, elegant curtains, richly upholstered chairs and settees invited players to rest and relax in prosperous surroundings. Next came the office of Harlan and Chapman, dominated by a massive black walnut desk, with other furniture appropriate to the setting. The second floor's rear apartment was divided into two parts by a rich curtain, the smaller section offering a table laden with a variety of foods for hungry gamblers. On the other side of the curtain were walls bordered with shades of gold, with full length mirrors reflecting the various games and gamblers, winning and losing in the Texas House's main gaming room.

Early in December of 1882, the Texas House caught fire; the entire second floor was destroyed, and only the bar and a cigar stand were survivors on the first. Harlan and Chapman set to the task of rebuilding immediately, and some six weeks later, on January 17, 1883, opened the doors to their faithfully restored and reborn Texas House. In other events the month of the fire, and earlier that year, Leadville's dual nature as both a dangerous place to reside and one striving for gracious and refined living was apparent. Irish poet and dramatist Oscar Wilde had lectured in April to a full house at the Tabor Opera House, but most recalled from his trip to the "silver city" a sign in Pap Wyman's saloon: "Please do not shoot the pianist. He is doing his best."[15] Several months later, on Christmas night, a shooting completed a days drinking between two men, with one of them killed for making remarks insulting to the other's wife. Given the provocation, exoneration was secured by the killer. Two days later, another gunfight resulted in death when a gambler settled a frequently argued debt with a faro dealer. But the season was being celebrated in more traditional style in Leadville's houses of worship. At the Church of the Sacred Heart, for example, on Christmas morning a flutist, a violinist, and choir of eight provided a classical program, their finale being *Adeste Fidelis*.

Large parties were also part of the scene, one of the grandest thrown by seven young businessmen who had the chef of Leadville's finest hotel, the Clarendon, prepare their banquet. Chef La Pierce offered to hosts and guests fried oysters on toast, stuffed turkey with chestnuts, roast suckling pig, roast California quail, Mumm's Extra Dry, imported cigars, and cigarettes and bon bons.[16] In high living, wide-open, thriving Leadville, Tom Dennison spent

7

his mid-twenties, honing his professional skills, meeting scores of individuals similarly seeking wealth, and making contacts which were to lead him into other gambling houses in several states in years to come. These skills and contacts, further developed, became part of the man who ultimately ended up in Omaha, "a classy gambler, who didn't deal with roughnecks." Also part of him was a familiarity with violence and vice combined with appreciation for quality and finer things.

Dennison left Leadville in 1886, going down to Denver in the fall to become part of the Arcade. Why he left Leadville is unknown. A gambling crackdown did not come to the city until 1888-89, and in 1886 the houses were doing well. Ownership of the Texas House had changed during Dennison's years there, but as a gradual turnover implying no sudden changes in personnel.[17] At age twenty-seven, after four years in the same location, it may just be that Tom decided he had been there long enough. Perhaps not coincidentally, Charles O. Pierson, one of the proprietors of the Texas House during two of Dennison's years there, left Leadville about the same time he did, and in 1887 was listed as a partner in Denver's Arcade Club Rooms. Dennison's Denver base became the Arcade, again associating himself with a renowned and expensively appointed gambling house, and with Pierson. A few years later they moved on to Omaha, where Dennison and Pierson worked together in 1894 at the appropriately named Denver, a saloon providing opportunities for "sportsmen," with Pierson as proprietor and Dennison as manager.[18]

Dennison's arrival at the Arcade on Larimer street was during "those free and easy days in the early days of the commonwealth when gambling ran wide-open, dance halls flourished and saloons were made without keyholes, because they were never closed."[19] Being Denver's prime gambling spot, the Arcade, it was said, really did not need a street number because everyone knew where it was (it was at 1613). Although gambling was the fundamental reason for the Arcade's existence, it was unnecessary to leave the premises to eat, drink, or sleep for all were well provided. "The inner man was well cared for" by its owners, "while experts were attending to the depletion of the thousands of corpulent wallets that went into the establishment never to come out."[20]

8

The first structure on the lot, then on the city's outskirts, was a frame house built in the 1860s by A.H. Miles, which he rented to Mr. and Mrs. George C. Breed in 1870 after growth had created a street too noisy for his taste. Experienced in the catering business, the Breeds opened a restaurant and ran it for several years, then went to Pueblo leaving the site to James Fisher, a butcher. He built a two story brick building, where on the first floor John Elitch Jr., established a reputation for quality cuisine, adding to his fame later with Denver's Elitch's Gardens.

Ownership of the building passed through several hands in subsequent years, with the first floor sustaining its fine dining, and the second in the course of those years becoming the Arcade Club Rooms, where those "corpulent" wallets were skillfully thinned.[21] Famous names of the "Queen City's" gambling world populated the upper floor as owners or players. Ed Chase, a Denver showman who operated a variety theatre in the 1870s, the Cricket, later acquiring the Progressive and the Palace, bought into the Arcade's gambling business in the eighties. He decided the old building needed replacing, but feared losing the second floor's profits if he closed down for reconstruction. The problem was resolved by having gambling go "merrily on while masons and carpenters raised the new walls about the old."[22]

A close friend of Dennison's, Vaso L. Chucovich, took over the Arcade in 1900. Like Dennison, Chucovich had traveled widely in the west as a young man and the Yugoslavian immigrant, who came to the U.S. in 1877 when he was nineteen years old, soon was impressed "by the way money could be lost--and made--by cultivating the soft greenness of a gambling table."[23] Chucovich prospered at the Arcade and brought to it a certain prestige, for he was an associate of local political power Robert Speer.[24] Chucovich was not only a valued contact for Dennison in Denver, but also a trusted family companion. A grandson of the "Old Man" fondly remembered "Uncle Chuck's" visits to the Dennison home in Omaha, and his serving as a chaperon for trips, including one to Europe.[25]

Before the Arcade closed its gambling wheels and tab-

9

les in 1910, it was host to hordes of eager players, many of them famous and flamboyant: "Bat" Masterson, "Soapy" Smith, and "Dead-Eye Dick" to mention but a few. During a game at the Arcade, "Dead-Eye" drew his ivory handled revolver and warned that if there was any more cheating he would kill the culprit. "I ain't mentioning any names," he declared, "but I'll shoot his other eye out."[26] "Soapy" Smith, a shell game artist and con man who was an Arcade regular, became upset when Chase installed a nickelodeon in the early days of electricity. The mechanical music detracted "Soapy" from his drinking and gambling, and he liked to jam the machine with nickels hammered out of shape with his gun butt. One night, losses and the detested music combined to urge "Soapy" to use the other end of his colt, and he and his brother shot up the place.[27]

Charles Pierson, one of the part-owners while Dennison was with the Arcade, had made his fortune during Leadville's boom days, and in addition to buying a one-third interest in the Denver gambling house, had paid $75,000 for a ranch near Aspen. One evening, Charlie decided to break the house and then take over a neighboring gambling place, The Murphy House. He went in with $10,000, bought two chips for his money, bet $3,000 and lost; then he used his second chip for a $7,000 wager and lost that too. In two plays and two wrong numbers his stake was gone. Undaunted, he invited everyone to the bar and the next morning paid a $1,500 liquor bill.[28]

During a later renowned spree of drinking and gambling, Pierson lost not only his money but also his property and share in the Arcade, all in forty-eight hours.[29] He started by going through the money he had in his pockets, some $10,000, then had the funds in the Arcade's safe divided into three parts. Taking his third he proceeded to lose it as his losing streak picked up momentum. Then he sold his ranch, wagered the sum received--and lost it. Finally, he put up his share of the Arcade; a turn of a card proved Pierson's luck unchanged. In those forty-eight hours Charlie Pierson went from wealthy man to man penniless.[30]

The Arcade of "Soapy" Smith, "Dead-Eye" Dick, and Tom Dennison witnessed scores of shootings and thousands of dollars changing hands in the second floor gambling rooms.

10

But the first floor restaurant was reputed as Denver's best, exhalted in a newspaper of the day as a "Palatial Restaurant" and "one of the grandest epicurean retreats to be found in the United States."[31] Denver's worthies and visiting dignitaries dined there, while those with other tastes to satisfy spent their hours with the second floor games (the "gentle people" and the "hard faction" as one observer divided the Arcade's clientele).[32] Entering the Arcade, guests passed under its identifying saloon sign trademark--a backward "S." Once inside they were surrounded by opulence and craftsmanship, obvious in hand carved solid mahogany reflected in French plate glass mirrors. The thirty foot bar was not in itself exceptional except for the quantity and quality of alcohol served there as some celebrated and others mourned, the house with neutrality benefiting from the bar bills of winners and losers alike. Ed Chase had a leaded glass skylight installed over the bar, its centerpiece being a large tiger, the cost to Chase--or his customers--being some $1,000.

In spaces between mirrors on the walls there hung oil paintings "from the hands of masters," some mirrors and art works illuminated by a chandelier worth six hundred dollars, others by ornate, gold-filled lighting fixtures. Along one wall there stood a huge wall clock, then valued at several hundred dollars, in a solid mahogany frame. In these lavish surroundings one could savor one of Elitch's steaks in the first floor dining room, or go to the upper floor for drinking and gaming.[33] Roulette fanciers gathered on the east side of the Club Rooms, about one-third of the building's length from Larimer Street, while the poker players' table was halfway between the roulette wheels and Larimer. Near windows overlooking the street, crap players rolled the dice, and opposite them a policy wheel was spinning out its winners and losers.[34] In these surroundings Tom Dennison spent his Denver years, leaving them in 1888 or 1889 for gambling halls in Montana and Utah.

In 1892 the thirty-four year old Dennison came to Omaha, home for the rest of his life. Why he decided to settle in Omaha is unknown. George Leighton of *Harper's* reported that Dennison was reputedly the representative of a gambling syndicate. According to Leighton, when Dennison arrived in Omaha he deposited $75,000 in a bank--with instructions to its president that $50,000 was for use as the banker desired. Dennison thereby became a favored figure, we are told, and rival gamblers began having difficulties with the authorities, difficulties he was spared.[35] Another suggestion is that he was induced to come to Omaha by Edward Rosewater, a prominent and politically influential newspaperman in search of a political protege. In any case, Dennison must have been attracted to Omaha by its reputation as a wide-open town, where professional gamblers with skills, knowledge, and contacts were able to lead a profitable and largely undisturbed existence, especially if those contacts were extended into the city's political circles. Dennison's reason for choosing Omaha as his place of business, be it games of chance or politics or both, may reside in the memory that he "knew how to deal the cards," that Omaha was an "open town, a gamblin' town, and that was right up Tom's alley."[36]

The man with the "cold and penetrating steely blue eyes," wearing the "narrow, whimsical smile," wanderer from Nebraska's farms to the most famed and luxurious gambling halls in Colorado, had by now established traits which henceforth were associated with the name of Tom Dennison. Occasionally there was a glint in those eyes, lightening his handsome but hard features. Surrounded by drinkers and smokers, Dennison sometimes had a cigar or cigarette, but as for liquor by his own words he "never drank." He cautioned that a head unfogged by beer or whiskey was essential for gambling--either at a card table or in the game of politics. During his years as a political power, he informed anyone who had the temerity to appear in his office smelling of booze there would be no discussion that day.

Dennison was "a weatherbeaten type," according to an attorney who became an opposition leader: "he might have passed as an old sailor. He had a cauliflower ear, an ear that had been injured someway; looked like it had been through a meat grinder." Skin cancer not injury explains the ear's appearance, but Dennison in his younger years had ample opportunities to nourish a cauliflower ear. He once told about an argument he had with a "tough" in Leadville, hearing the next day the character was looking for him, gun or knife in hand. Walking down Leadville's main street, Dennison saw the armed man coming his way. "I grabbed the first thing I could think of," Tom recalled. In those days of miners, stores had pick handles standing out in front and Dennison took one in hand, hit the fellow on the head and "darn near killed him." Thus did Dennison earn the title of "Pick-Handle" Tom.[37]

He was a loner, caring little for what people thought or said about him, his smile and serenity above the political battles. In bearing, he was "a perfect gentleman. His eyes, I mean, the expression, it would be interesting if you could just have a movie of this sort of thing. I have no way of describing the expression in his face," mused one who knew him. "His eyes, his strange smile, his manners; its something that was just, well--perhaps the only man in the world that could really act like that would be Tom Dennison."[38] Shunning profanity, he was a softspoken man committed to brevity, slightly turning away from his listener when he did speak. Preferring to answer questions rather than lead a conversation, the "Old Man" offered few opportunities to gain much insight into his thoughts. Although he spoke little and quietly, when he did speak others listened carefully and acted quickly.

Conservatively and fashionably dressed, he always carried a cane, adorned a finger with an onyx and gold ring, and a diamond stickpin was carefully placed just above the "v" of his vest. Ostentatious in neither dress nor manner, he was a man who preferred to avoid as much as possible any public or limelight role. In later years when Omaha's business establishment threw an annual party for Dennison's organization (machine to its detractors), when called upon to speak he either refused or slightly stuttered a very few words. His years of playing faro and other games had taught him the value of shielding his emotions, and his associates discerned little from his face. Dennison was a gracious host on social occasions, and a guest at one his gatherings recalls that "Boss Tom" was "most of all a good listener and never missed anything that was said--I got the impression if he were sitting in a high stake poker game and a larger bet was made he would show no emotion."[39]

There was a lighter side to the "Old Man," and his wit served as a foil to inquisitive reporters. Unable to come to agreement for the hiring of a new business manager, the Omaha Board of Education one evening in 1926 was taking a third ballot on the question. One of the members facetiously cast his ballot for Thomas Dennison, to the merriment of

13

some board members and chagrin of others. When Dennison was told of the vote cast for him, he advised that "I could save the board some money if they had picked me. Whom did they make it?" Told the board adjourned after that third ballot, Dennison observed "Then I have another chance at it."[40] When asked in 1925 whether Omaha had a political boss, Dennison said "no," adding that to have a boss a city needs an organization like Tammany Hall. But the only political organization he knew of in Omaha was the Committee of 5000 (a reform group formed to oppose Dennison). "Perhaps," said Omaha's boss, "I had better say five and three ciphers."[41]

Pragmatism was a major weapon in Dennison's political armory, and similar to bosses in other cities partisanship was of little consequence in forming political alliances. Although himself a Republican and in his earlier political years supportive of Republican candidates (Omaha was then Republican), he did not allow party labels to stand as an obstacle to his interests. If a Democratic candidate appeared more inclined than a Republican rival to provide protection for Dennison's gambling enterprises, the machine's third ward was delivered to the Democrat. James Dahlman, mayor during most of the Dennison years, was a leading Democrat in city and state politics. Dennison was unperturbed by Dahlman's party preference, much more impressed by his ability to win votes and willingness to cooperate with the organization.

Hardly oriented toward temperance as social policy, Dennison nonetheless in 1913 was supportive of the Anti-Saloon League-Ministerial Union. Both Dennison and the Union were in favor of reducing the number of saloons in Omaha by half, and the reformers, according to the *World-Herald*, were willing to "mix their eggs with Tom Dennison's eggs and let him carry the basket." The crucial issue, of course, was deciding which half to close, a power Dennison thought attractive enough to warrant his temporary alliance. Carrying "the basket" meant to him the capacity to order bars of enemies closed.[42]

Generally placid and reserved, Dennison was nonetheless capable of quick anger and then disagreeing with everybody. Oncoming ire was forecast by stuttering and the word then spread: "Be careful, the 'Old Man' is stuttering." Such outbursts were confined to Dennison's office, however, and the general image was of the taciturn, self-controlled boss. He had a great fondness for animals, and Omahans walking downtown by his office were accustomed to seeing him out in front on the sidewalk feeding the pigeons. Concern and love of animals revealed itself in later years with establishment of the White Eagle Kennels, where the political boss raised champion wirehaired terriers, a breed characterized by intelligence and a lively, fun seeking disposition. Pride in his dogs led to one area of conversation that Dennison delighted in, and "at dog shows in all parts of the country, his pedigreed pets won blue ribbons and a grand championship was also his."[43]

A little over a year after coming to Omaha, Dennison married Ada Provost on September 11, 1893, tall and brown haired, daughter of Charles Provost, a newspaper editor in Omaha's neighbor city across the Missouri, Council Bluffs. Two sons born to Tom and "Pet" (his nickname for Ada), died in infancy, and daughter Francis became the object of indulgent parents. As a father, Dennison sharply separated his private and professional lives and Ada and Francis were kept distant from the daily activities which provided them a comfortable life. Among young Francis's youthful possessions was a "put and take" top, an item then popular among teenagers. Hers, however, was made of gold and dangled from the neck chain she wore. For the most part, the Dennison's wealth was not flaunted, and although it was obvious parents and daughter were well off, theirs was an unobstrusive lifestyle. The women's distance from Tom's role in Omaha was such that a frequent bridge playing friend with Ada and Francis recalls that "In all those conversations, I can never remember politics being mentioned."[44]

Yet the outside world and its threats to Dennison were apparent to the family. Dennison's daughter and her husband, Vernon R. Ragan, lived with him on his estate at 72nd Street and Military in his later years (Ada died in 1922), and one of their sons recalled greeting the chauffeur driven automobile at day's end, with grandfather in the back seat, submachine gun lying across his lap. The estate grounds, some eight and one-half acres, were surrounded by a six foot high cyclone fence, floodlit at night by throwing one switch from the house, and tresspassers discovered that Dennison kept not only wirehaired terriers, but also larger guard dogs.[45] Amplifying the childhood memory is a report filed with Roy Towl, a determined Dennison opponent, by an informant at the police station during the same early 1930s time period. Towl was instructed to check the department's machine guns, with the expectation of finding that the chief of police, then John "Gentleman Jack" Pszanowski, had loaned such a weapon to Dennison through Harry Buford, Dennison's chauffeur and a lieutenant on the force.[46] Despite the obvious physical reminders of a threatened existence, Dennison attempted otherwise to isolate his family from his political life and controversies. When the situation warranted, one arousing adverse and contentious publicity, Dennison would send the family on a trip, and "Uncle Chuck" from Denver might be called upon as an escort.

After eight years as a widower, Dennison suddenly remarried in October 1930. His bride was a seventeen year old Omahan, very pretty Nevajo Truman, who gave her age as twenty-one for the marriage ceremony in Crown Point, Indiana. She later commented she gave a false age because Dennison thought it would be better if her true age was not provided. The young woman admitted to having been attracted to the seventy-two year old Dennison because he was well known and glamorous in her eyes. He called her "his little girl," or "Bright Eyes," or his "Queen." But the marriage was short-lived and in 1933 Nevajo filed for divorce. For almost all of their three married years she stayed with her mother on Country Club Boulevard, living with Dennison only the first three months of the marriage. Sometimes he dropped by the County Club home for lunch or an afternoon nap, but that was the extent of their relationship. "Cruelty many times and without provocation" was given as cause for the divorce suit, which was granted uncontested. According to Nevajo, there was really not much to it: "We just agreed to disagree, that's all."[47] She attempted to be recognized by the court as special administratrix of his estate when he died a year later (he died intestate), filing as his widow; however, daughter Francis ultimately won the appointment.[48]

Dennison aroused strong emotions in both enemies and friends. To those who admired him, he was revered as a man of boundless generosity whose word was bond, and surviving associates displayed a sense of unwavering loyalty and unstinting admiration. Machine welfare activities were well

16

known, and stories spread about the "Old Man" personally
doling out money from his office to the needy and to charities. One young man, a worker in a cleaners, became a hundred dollars richer thanks to Mr. Dennison. Having the job
of checking pockets in suits sent in for cleaning, the
employee found some crumpled bills: one $1,000 bill, two
$500s, and six $100s. He rushed to an official of the establishment, and the tailor's tag was checked--Dennison.
He was immediately called, but knew nothing about sending
any suits to the cleaners. Francis was asked about the
matter, and "yes," she had sent some cleaning to the firm.
"A fellow paid me an old debt," explained Dennison, and
then he asked who found the money. "Give him a $100."[49]

An organization maxim extolled Dennison's word "as
being good as gold." Often he asserted the most important
thing in a person's life was his word; once Dennison's was
given "you could lay book on it." Potential candidates
sought his aid, and when he agreed to back them, gratified
office seekers left his office, confident the "Old Man" was
going to deliver votes their way. There are suggestions,
however, that Dennison's commitments may not have been as
binding as loyalists recall, and that some of his affirma-
tions were in fact carefully disguised ploys to keep the
myth intact. On occasion, a candidate promised assistance
by Dennison discovered the organization in fact failed to
rally to his cause. A complaint to Dennison was explained
away by the "Old Man's" declaring he had told Billy (right-
hand man William Nesselhous) to handle the matter and apparently Billy had let him down. Nesselhous, concerned with
other matters and absolutely loyal to Dennison, was content
to bear the guilt and Dennison's reputation was unimpaired.

Dennison's less than total fulfillment of all his
promises is further suggested by Tom Crawford's recollection that many times, present with Dennison in his private
office, he heard the "Old Man" deal with loyal campaign
workers who came in to receive their rewards. Asked what
kind of work they desired, they indicated perhaps a department of city government. With the job seeker in the office,
Dennison dutifully called the appropriate commissioner to
request a place for the loyalist, adding the supporter was
on the way over to claim the job. Turning to the satisfied
applicant, Dennison pointed out he had done all in his
power, now it was up to the boys in city hall. When the

17

applicant was gone, avers Crawford, Dennison called the commissioner back to tell him to stall the fellow along. "I must tell them something when they come to see me . . . pat him on the shoulder as he has some friends and we do not want to make him mad at us." Other times positions were indeed forthcoming but only on a temporary basis--nonetheless a job was delivered and the "Old Man's" word was preserved.[50]

Family members recall his strong allegiance to his kin, and a fund maintained in an Omaha bank to be drawn upon by a brother or sister whenever needed. A tale of Jim Dennison's move to Oklahoma and problems there as a newcomer is shared to depict Tom's devotion to his relatives. Whenever Jim went out on the road with his wagon and horses he was stopped by a neighboring Oklahoman, threatened, and warned there was no room for an Irishman from the north in Oklahoma. Tiring of the abuse, Jim wrote and asked Tom to come and help him. He soon appeared, and the brothers went forth, Tom keeping low in the wagon. When the bully stopped them and began his harangue, Tom jumped out and gave him a "tremendous licking," followed by a promise that unless he left Jim alone there would be another beating, but even tougher. "That settled Jim's troubles."[51]

Something of a person's character may be disclosed in their remarks about the world around them, in a few words telling us a great deal about their perception of both self and others. For Dennison, a person's measure was to be on the square with him: "A man might be a safe-blower, a former convict or what not so long as he was not a 'double-crosser'." He confessed that "I like dogs. They're honest and don't try to double-cross you." In his office the walls carried pictures of his family, boxers, dogs, horses, and deceased local politicians. "Some of those old-timers were not my friends," he mused of the last named. "But they were men. Give me a man, even if he is an enemy."

He believed that some people by nature are good, some bad, and no amount of lawmaking was going to alter that basic fact. Furthermore, he saw legislation as self limiting, since "Laws that people don't believe in can't be enforced if whole armies tried it. There are so many laws," he added, "that people are either lawbreakers or hypocrites. For my part, I hate a damn hypocrite." In his judgment some of those statutes were illadvised because "People are always getting excited about the little things, like minor lawbreaking and misdemeanors." Not surprisingly he considered efforts to curtail gambling misplaced: "A dinky crap game or pennyante poker causes a hell of a racket. But the stock market gambling was all right."[52]

Dennison had a series of slogans providing operational guidance, including "Promise everything, but give nothing." The way to handle challengers was to "Keep your opposition answering you and they will have little time to attack you," or "Keep your opposition defending themselves, and in this way, they have little time to be framing you." The means to create and maintain control over people? "Keep them broke--keep them trying to get even--keep them eating out of your hand and then you can keep them in line."[53]

During his many years in Omaha, Dennison had several offices, one of the earliest being in the rear of the Budweiser Saloon at 1409 Douglas Street. People from all walks of life gathered there, politicians, businessmen, gamblers, visitors both reputable and disreputable from other cities. "For a saloon," a *World-Herald* editorial informed its readers, "it is a remarkably quiet, genteel sort of place. Loud and boisterous talk is seldom heard there."[54] Prohibition made it necessary to abandon the Budweiser (prohibition was adopted in Nebraska in 1917), and Dennison moved around the corner into the Karbach Block, having an office for several years at 209 South 15th Street in the Bankers Savings and Loan Building.

He opened another very private office on South 15th at number 317, above the Cornhusker Cigar Store, dividing his time between two offices. To visit Dennison in his office above the Cornhusker, the more secretive one, a prospective visitor crossed the cigar store to a door watched over by former prizefighter Jimmy Lee. If he allowed the individual to pass, a wire service room was entered where Rosie O'Toole was busy taking bets. Then the path led downstairs where another former fighter, Chip Lee, directed the visitor to stairs on the right leading up to Dennison's office. Austerity was the decor and lights were kept low, except for one bright one beaming on the visitor's chair which was placed directly in front of Dennison's desk. Since the desk was on a platform about a foot high the Boss was always looking down upon his guest, seated beneath the bright light. A large safe was also in the room, and Dennison provided a banking service for individuals who for one reason or another preferred dealing with him rather than one of the nearby more traditional banks.[55] Perhaps the caller was a fugitive with stolen goods seeking to "bank" his goods temporarily. Or it might be an out-of-town visitor concerned about carrying large amounts of cash. Tom asked few questions and provided security and secrecy.

When Dennison arrived in Omaha he carried with him his physical and frontier ruggedness, a taste for finer things and extensive contacts, particularly among persons willing to challenge laws proscribing games of chance. Quotations by him or attributed to him suggest he also brought with him traits to be further honed in city politics: a mind suspicious of others, manipulative and duplicitous, but ready to reward those who earned his regard as being on the square. The law seems to have been something of a nuisance, or at least lawmakers were prone to legislate in the wrong areas, without regard to the probable ineffectuality of their efforts considering human nature. As he saw it:[56]

> A town is what the people want it to be, and . . . raiding crews can't change what people want. Omaha has always been one of the cleanest towns on the map. But if it were snow white, and everybody went to church, and drank nothing but milk, and quit smoking and chewing, and quit chasing women, still the reformers would howl.

In 1892 the gambler of the Texas House and the Arcade came to Omaha, formed and prepared to become Dennison, city boss, given the appropriate conditions and opportunities.

NOTES

Chapter I

[1]Three times Dennison gave his year of birth as 1859; see *Red Oak Weekly Express*, June 2, 1905, *Omaha Daily News*, April 18, 1907, hereafter cited as ODN, and on the witness stand in November 1932, he gave his age as seventy-three, thus born in 1859; *Omaha World-Herald*, morning edition, November 16, 1932, hereafter cited as MOW-H. For the 1858 birth date see Colorado Census, 1885, National Archives Microfilm, No. M158, Contents Jefferson, Lake, and La Platte Counties; U.S. Bureau of the Census, *Census Schedule Dakota County, Nebraska, 1860*. His gravestone, in Omaha's Forest Lawn Cemetery, is engraved 1858-1934. Alice Dennison's family bible shows her father's birthday (Tom's younger brother) as November 6, 1859. See also John Kyle Davis, "The Gray Wolf: Tom Dennison of Omaha," *Nebraska History*, 58 (Spring, 1979), p. 48, fn. 1.

[2]St. Patrick's, Jackson, Nebraska, Combined Record, July, 1858 to February, 1867, p. 23. For Dennison's quote on lack of a middle name see *Omaha World-Herald*, evening edition, November 10, 1923, hereafter cited as EOW-H.

[3]Nebraska, Dakota County Deed Book, Book H; and Nebraska, Dakota County Deed Book, Book L. The land remains under the Dennison family name in the agricultural real estate assessment record. On Tom selling to John see Nebraska, Dakota County Deed Record, Book 30, p. 626.

[4]Interview with Alice Dennison, daughter of John W. Dennison, Tom's brother, conducted by Orville D. Menard, October 3, 1979, Omaha, Nebraska. The Dennison children and their location as listed in 1931: James, Hyne, Oklahoma; Patrick F., Omaha; Thomas, Omaha; John W., Omaha; Stephen, Cincinnati, Ohio; Alice, wife of Henry Kendricks, Columbus, Ohio; Margaret, wife of James Walsh, Dickson County, Nebraska; and Anna, widow of James Wilson, Omaha. As listed in Addison E. Sheldon, *Nebraska: The Land and the People* (3 vols.; Chicago: The Lewis Publishing Co., 1931), II, 183. (Note: Sheldon incorrectly lists "Welsh" instead of "Walsh.")

[5]Interview with John C. Duggan and Ralph P. Walsh, conducted by Orville D. Menard, September 28, 1979, Willis, Nebraska. Walsh's grandfather was John, Tom's father.

[6]*Ibid.* Sherman Morris (alias Frank Shercliffe), testified during a libel suit that Dennison had told him the story of the unsuccessful robbery. See ODN, April 18, 1907, and EOW-H, April 18, 1907.

[7]Letter, Tom Crawford to Roy Towl, January 3, 1933, attached summary of proposed book "The Power House," Nebraska State Historical Society, Roy Towl papers, MS 3534, Box 1, Folder 1933, Jan-Apr., City Hall. Hereafter cited as Towl papers.

[8]ODN, April 17, 18, 1907.

[9]EOW-H, April 16, 1907. On Dennison's travels and associations see

also ODN, April 17, 1907; MOW-H, February 15, 1934; Nathan Nielsen, "Wrecking Ball Brings Back Memories of the 'Gray Wolf'," *Sunday World-Herald*, May 9, 1965, p. 22-B; Sheldon, *Nebraska: The Land and the People*, p. 183.

[10]Edward Blair and E. Richard Churchill, *Everybody Came to Leadville* (Gunnison, Colorado: B & B Printers, 1971), pp. 3-4.

[11]Sherill Warford, *Verdict: Guilty as Charged, Leadville Justice* (Leadville: Silver City Printing Co., 1977), pp. 17-18.

[12]Record, Leadville City Council, November 17, 1885-July 16, 1889, p. 104 and p. 47.

[13]*Leadville Chronicle Annual, 1882*, p. 17.

[14]*Ibid.*

[15]Blair and Churchill, *Everybody Came to Leadville*, pp. 25-26.

[16]Don and Jean Griswold, "Leadville: A City of Contrast," Article LII, *The Herald Democrat*, December 23, 1966.

[17]Proprietors of the Texas House during Dennison's time in Leadville: 1881-1882, Samuel Harlan and J.H.F. Chapman; 1883, Chapman; 1884-85, C.O. Pierson Co. (Charles O. Pierson, C.K. Simpson, B.C. Youngson); 1886, Pierson C.O. & Co. (C.O. Pierson, Cornelius Featherly). See Ballenger & Richards, *Annual Leadville City Directory* (Leadville: Ballenger & Richards), appropriate years. Of Pierson's partner Featherly, we are told he "was a debonair little fellow with a soft, slender hand like that of a school girl. He was known among gamblers as a mechanic which meant one so adept at cards that he could work the faro box to suit his requirements when there was a big play on the table and in this graceful way he made great stakes come his way." "The Notorious Texas House," *Field and Farm*, #1750 (August 20, 1919), p. 8.

[18]Corbett & Ballenger's *Fifteenth Annual Denver City Directory for 1887* (Denver: Corbett & Ballenger, 1887). On Pierson and Dennison connection in Omaha see EOW-H, February 27, 1894.

[19]*The Denver Post*, November 10, 1918.

[20]*The Denver Times*, November 9, 1919.

[21]On the Arcade's history see *The Denver Republican*, March 7, 1890; "Reminiscences," *Field and Farm*, IX (March 22, 1890), p. 6.

[22]*The Denver Post*, December 20, 1933; see also *Rocky Mountain News*, March 17, 1946.

[23]*Rocky Mountain News*, March 17, 1946; see also *The Denver Republican*, July 18, 1900, and *The Denver Post*, December 20, 1933.

[24]*The Denver Times*, February 19, 1900; see also *The Denver Times*, February 17, 1900.

[25]Interview with John Ragan, conducted by Orville D. Menard, September 22, 1979, Omaha, Nebraska.

[26]*Rocky Mountain News*, March 17, 1946.

[27]Dial Scott, *Saloons of Denver* (Fort Collins, Colorado: The Old Army Press, 1973), p. 41.

[28]*The Denver Post*, April 1, 1928.

[29]*The Denver Times*, November 9, 1918.

[30]*Ibid.*

[31]*The Denver Republican*, February 1, 1891.

[32]Scott, *Saloons of Denver*, pp. 40-41.

[33]*The Denver Post*, November 10, 1918, and December 20, 1933;   see

also *The Denver Times*, November 11, 1918.

[34]Second floor description from *The Denver Times*, February 16, 1900.

[35]George Leighton, *Five Cities: the Story of Their Youth* (New York: Harper & Bros., 1939), p. 194.

[36]Duggan/Walsh interview.

[37]Interview with William Maher, conducted by Orville D. Menard, October 23, 1979, Omaha, Nebraska.

[38]Interview with Jerry Gordon, conducted by Orville D. Menard, June 20, 1979, Omaha, Nebraska.

[39]Letter from A.P. Deutsch, Wickenburg, Arizona, to Orville D. Menard, August 1980.

[40]EOW-H, August 3, 1926.

[41]ODN, November 21, 1925.

[42]MOW-H, April 29, 1913.

[43]MOW-H, February 15, 1934.

[44]Interview with Olga J. Strimple, conducted by Orville D. Menard, August 10, 1979, Omaha, Nebraska.

[45]Ragan interview.

[46]"Report on Paul Sutton," dated May 23-24, 1931, no signature, Towl papers, Box 1, Folder 1931, May-August, City Hall.

[47]EOW-H, August 22, 1933.

[48]Dennison Probate, County Court, Douglas County, Nebraska, In re Estate of Thomas Dennison, #21861, Fee Book 48, page 296, Special.

[49]EOW-H, February 6, 1930.

[50]Letter, Tom Crawford to Roy N. Towl, April 21, 1932, Nebraska State Historical Society, Christian A. Sorensen papers, MS 2951, Box 35, Folder 65. Hereafter cited as Sorensen papers.

[51]Alice Dennison interview and Duggan/Walsh interview.

[52]First quotation from MOW-H, February 15, 1934, the others from Nielsen, "Wrecking Ball Brings Back Memories." See the article by Florian Newbranch, "Dennison is Serene," EOW-H, January 2, 1930, the source of many of the quotations in the foregoing articles.

[53]Source of the quotations in the order given: Letter, Tom Crawford to Roy Towl, April 21, 1932, Sorensen papers, Box 35, Folder 65; letter, Murphy (Crawford's alias) to Cora Marling, April 15, 1932, Sorensen papers, Box 35, Folder 66; letter, Murphy to E.D. O'Sullivan, March 31, 1932, Sorensen papers, Box 35, Folder 65; letter, Crawford to Irving Stalmaster, September 17, 1932, Sorensen papers, Box 39, Folder 191.

[54]EOW-H, January 14, 1914.

[55]Letter, Towl to Harold D. Wilson, Deputy Prohibition Administrator, Omaha, February 3, 1932, Towl papers, Box 1, Folder 1932, Febr., City Hall; and interview with William Zerbe conducted by Orville D. Menard, July 18, 1979, Omaha, Nebraska.

[56]Nielsen, "Wrecking Ball Brings Back Memories."

CHAPTER II

Penetration

*If you want to find a rogue's rookery,
go to Omaha.*
--Kansas City Newspaper, 1873

Dennison's profession lured him into politics, for in order to apply his gambler skills it was necessary to penetrate political circles and secure protection from too zealous application of the law. Not only was he impelled toward seeking political influence by his trade, a common phenomenon among individuals operating on the law's margins or beyond, but conditions were favorable to his transition from professional gambler to political boss. Already common in Omaha's newspapers through the 1890s were the words "political machine," but the complex organism that was going to dominate in coming years remained in large measure to be further refined. Dennison undertook the task after establishing himself as "King Gambler"; like Plunkett of America's oldest political machine, Tammany Hall, he saw his opportunities and "took 'em." Waiting for him was a community nurturing the foundations of bossism, amassing services to be performed, offering the building blocks for a political machine.

The men who ran the machines, men like Tom Dennison, were complete pragmatists, owing their position to skills rather than ancestry, often sharing the lower class origins of their faithful river ward voters. They mastered the art of political organization and shrewdly manipulated the tools of power--reward and punishment. Guided by the goals of achieving and sustaining political control, the bosses were willing to embrace all elements of society to satisfy their urge for power. No person or group was excluded from their alliances for they sought support wherever they could find it, hampered by neither notions of social or economic distinctions nor ideological baggage to define friends and

25

foes. As has been said, the bosses had but seven principles: five loaves and two fishes. A machine's priorities are evident in the response of a county officer appearing before a New York legislative committee in the early 1880s. When asked whether he performed his public duties faithfully, he answered he did so whenever they did not interfere with his political duties, which included "fixing" primaries and bailing out friends who had legal problems.[1]

The machines were marvels of heterogeneity, capitalizing upon the ethnic, social, and economic differences of their faithful followers. Utopian visions and philosophizing about the nature of the state were alien to them. Rather, the bosses offered favors, promised and delivered not according to feudalistic notions of *noblesse oblige* but as a reward for services rendered. Businessmen, down-and-outers, underworld figures, ethnic groups, American born or immigrant, professionals as well as laborers were welcome in the machine's roomy mansion. *Quid pro quo* was emblazoned on the boss's coat of political arms, and all that was requested in return for favors was loyal service--measured in money or votes, the raw materials of power.[2]

As political machines spread across the United States in response to urbanization and changing needs they assumed a distinctive pattern and shared attributes. They were hierarchical organizations in a familiar pyramidal structure of power, with leaders and led bound in a system of mutual obligations. Power was not, however, a quality possessed solely by the boss, to be disbursed or used as he might autocratically determine, but was shared in varying degrees with members of the organization and with outside associates whose cooperation was deemed essential. Individuals with sources of strength among ethnic compatriots or possessing some other power base within their wards, businessmen and professionals exercising influence in the community by virtue of wealth or position, all had to be attended to by the boss and placed limits on his power as he fashioned accommodations and compromises.[3]

As these were achieved a facade of harmony and unity was created, but threats were ever present from internal challengers or outside reform minded opponents. To sustain control, the boss sought to impose discipline through rewards and punishments, doled out carefully and in proportion to contribution or challenge. Rewards took the form of pay offs, which varied from cash, to jobs and services, to contracts, to arrangements with city officialdom for protection from undue interference in the pursuit of profit-- be that pursuit by large firm, peddler, or prostitute. Punishments likewise differed, ranging from denial of the above, to administrative and police harassment, to ostracism and exile, and sometimes brute force.

Recognizing needs other than the material, the bosses provided a sense of belonging to persons adrift in new surroundings. A focus for loyalties and recognition was available, particularly significant for peoples recently uprooted and generally denied these comforts by well established societal stratifications.[4] Elites were the preserve of white Northern European protestants, while the late nineteenth-century immigrants were largely uneducated peasant Catholics from Ireland or Southern or Eastern Europe. Unwelcome except as low level laborers, these new Americans turned to a political boss who was waiting and willing to help them. His price was taken by those called upon to pay as really quite cheap. Nothing more than a vote.[5]

Funding for the machine's vote buying came from both the upperworld and underworld business communities. In need of governmental assistance in order to maximize their profits, they were willing to help cover "campaign expenses." Compliant enterprises, small or large, wholesaler or retailer, railroad or utility, gambler or prostitute facilitated their operations by purchasing governmental cooperation and protection. Who was to benefit from tax breaks, easements, rights of way, inspections and licenses, contracts for city services (what firms to provide gasoline for municipal vehicles, what grocery to supply the fire houses, what printer to take care of governmental forms), which laws to enforce rigorously or without rigor were questions whose answers were for sale. Whether an eminent pillar of society's elite, a corner grocer, a lower ward gambler or a madam, all sought favor with the boss for the favors he was able to arrange. As the city power broker, the boss accepted tribute (cash and services) and bestowed his special services in return. He was the middleman between his business associates, whether legally or illegally engaged, and those in public office.

In the reciprocal relationships of machine politics, the boss needed the legitimate businessmen just as they depended upon him. An observation of Mr. Dooley's offers a succinct appraisal of the machine/business relationship:[6]

> It seem to me that 'th on'y thing to do is keep pollyticians an' the business men apart. They seem to have a bad infloonce on eah other. Whiniver I see an alderman an' a banker walkin' down th' street together I know th' Recordn' angel will have to ordher another bottle iv ink.

Those passing appropriate ordinances, funneling public business to the deserving, and overseeing the citizens' morality--city councilmen and other useful holders of responsible posts--were not in a position personally to contract for their services. The boss spared them and their respectable customers, seeking benefits resulting from the public officials attending or not attending to diligent fulfillment of their oaths, the embarrassment of questionable direct contacts. A middleman was also required by individuals making their living from illegal activities.[7] Despite the market for its services, the underworld confronted city ordinances and state statutes proscribing meeting the demand. Since the legal obstacles most often were solidly in place thanks to civic sentiment, they were dealt with by stratagem. Campaign contributions to the machine by unlawful enterprises purchased exemption from laws designed to interfere with their operations. Law enforcement was selectively applied against those enterprising individuals who failed to respond to machine requests for donations.

Sustained by financial aid and faithful voters, the machine constantly attended to the electoral process in order to bind its beneficiaries to it and have them voting properly in city hall and county courthouse. Accountability of elected office holders took on new meaning in the sanctum of machine headquarters. Controlling these individuals, or at least influencing them as much as possible according to the machine's strength, the boss sought implementation of public policy so as to satisfy his many constituencies. Overall the strategy was to "keep the lid on," molding a stable environment for business activity with an emphasis on curbing unwelcome challengers (undesirable competition, organized labor). Resulting corruption in the form of patronage, bribery, shakedowns, graft, and fraud was basic to the organization's operation. A machine managed these activities to benefit itself and its business partners, systemizing them to infuse order where otherwise chaos would have prevailed among those seeking governmental favors. Controlled corruption was the result.

Similarly, crime was controlled to the same ends as corruption, that is, avoid ruinous competition and enhance profits. *Sub rosa* regulation of criminal activities replaced overt law enforcement, thus crime was controlled but not from city hall. Underworld figures and activities functioned under the watchful eye of the machine's lieutenants, and transgressors of the boss's edicts relating to underworld division of the market or failure to meet financial obligations at headquarters brought swift retribution, often in the form of exile. Incoming thieves, pickpockets, gamblers, and others intending to break the official laws in a city were given a visa as it were by the boss, enabling them to reside and operate, stipulating conditions and subject to rapid revocation. The result was controlled crime.

Although it was once popular to assail the business community for its role in machine politics, Lincoln Steffens aptly pointed out that it was not businessmen who were "the root of all evil." Big and small merchants, utility or railroad, saloon or bordello all sought what Steffens perceived as the true root of the evil--special privileges. For a price privileges were dispensed through the machine by city government: leniency or stringency in application of city ordinances, police protection or harassment, tax breaks, contracts, these and more resulting from purchase of privilege with the boss as middleman.[8]

Political machines were creatures of the cities, their electoral base usually concentrated in the river wards and lower class districts. Their influence, however, extended city wide because of business community allies and friendly office holders. Although it was not uncommon for the county where the city dwelled to succumb to machine politics, a state wide machine was a rarity. How much and whether state government intervened in a boss's jurisdiction were continuing concerns given the unitary relationship existing between state and local governments. Even with home rule charters, cities are ultimately under state jurisdiction, and state legislatures may grant or withdraw powers or create structures for their underlings as the majority in the state capital building may determine. Consequently, the bosses had a cogent reason for not attempting to expand their power base beyond local borders and challenging those in a position to do them harm.

Given the United States' federal system, machines were historically beyond the scope of national jurisdiction, Washington's concern directed toward the shared power relationship between itself and state governments. Cities were there for states to supervise. However, as the national government's perception of its responsibilities expanded in the 1930s and therewith its powers, bosses discovered the new player had tremendous resources to use for or against them. Those finding favor with the White House prospered, while those who became liabilities or embarrassments confronted opponents securing assistance from Washington. Lukewarm relationships or neglect were also a price of White House displeasure and politically damaging.[9]

It is a time honored convention to refer to the political systems which once dominated America's cities as political machines, as has been followed here and will continue to be because the term is so entrenched. An image of assembly line efficiency, of parts and gears meshing in prescribed and repetitive patterns is evoked by machine politics. Given such a prototype, it is little wonder that social scientists have concentrated on disassembling the so-called machines in the quest for understanding their parts, connections, functions, and malfunctions. Conceiving the boss's organization as a machine also simplified the reformer's task. If a political machine was mismanaging the city and its government was malfunctioning, then obviously restructuring was necessitated. New parts or retooling to replace the outmoded or defective were called for to assure smooth and efficient government. Institutional tinkering resulted. Commission and city manager forms of municipal governance, merit plans and civil service, contract bidding, voter registration and secret ballots, nonpartisanship, long ballots, at-large elections, and democracy through recall, initiative, and referendum were heralded and introduced as new mechanisms designed to produce corruption free, that is, boss free municipal administration.

However, the machines proved to be adaptable creatures--unlike mechanical machines--and in several cases learned to live with and even prosper amid the reformer's creations. It is not the intention here to explore the life span of political machines, but to suggest that the industrial machine analogy oversimplified a very complicated development in American political history. Impersonality and lifelessness are qualilties of a machine, but the organizations that dominated urban politics for so many years can scarcely be characterized as impersonal or lifeless. Their growth, maturity, and passing are matters of great complexity, reminding us of the interdependence of social, economic, and political change. Engines and sophisticated equipment are also intricate in their design and structure, but as Eric L. McKitrick has aptly noted the engine's complexity renders it vulnerable because removal or destruction of key parts will immobilize it. But reformers discovered that political machines drew strength from their diversity and possessed an amazing capacity for regeneration and adaptability.

Pursuing the point, McKitrick said of the political machine that "its very complexity, the very functional autonomy of so many of its parts, makes it more like an organism."[10] Recognizing the political machine as an organism, composed of living cells and organs, functionally performing their own missions but dependent one upon another, conveys the life filled, interdependent vitality that the word "machine" denies. Considering political machines as organisms directs attention to the multifaceted environments which gave them birth and subsequently sustained them. It leads to exploration of the reciprocal relationship between the machines and their surroundings, and the efforts exerted to prosper and ensure viability in the political survival enterprise. It reminds us societal change is driven by a host of factors, and thereby a broader perspective for appreciation of the machines' appearance, dominance, and ultimately becoming political dinosaurs. A 1930s student of bossism leads the way: "For the politician is, above all else, a child of his environment even though he is one of the factors that help fashion and maintain that environment."[11] Not unAmerican was the political boss and his machine--they evolved in America not as mutants but as children of their time.

Developments of the nineteenth century created propitious conditions for Dennison's political career in Omaha. Factors beckoning bossism here as elsewhere were certain attitudes, institutions, and needs, combining into a "spirit of the times" capable of transforming city government. Growth of the cities, industrialization, and Andrew Jackson's political heritage opened wide the door to politics for men like Thomas Dennison, making possible their grasping and holding power. People traditionally acknowledged as the political elite, the gentry of the early nineteenth century, withdrew from local governance in the wake of the common man's emergence and Jacksonian Democracy. Formerly a gentleman's obligation to be fulfilled along with other social responsibilities, with respect the reward, politics had acquired a disreputable flavor as professional politicians made their appearance, spending full time in organizing the electorate and providing services, dependent upon electoral outcomes for their livelihood. The gentry had retreated and possessors of new wealth, the industrialists, were too busy with their commercial enterprises for time consuming political activity. Abjuring political activism, they harbored no sense of civic obligation to impel entreaties for votes. Commerce seized their imaginations and to it they devoted their prodigious energies and talents. They abdicated local public office incumbency and chores of political organization to a rising breed they cooperated with to mutual advantage.

Too busy amassing wealth to engage in daily political activity themselves, the entrepreneurs nonetheless contributed a spirit that helped energize the new urban politicians. The industrialists were ambitious fortune hunters, shrewd individuals, both generous and ruthless, avid in demanding loyalty and harsh in confrontations with competitors. These attributes merged with the frontier heritage of pragmatism, opportunism, and individualism. When the combination was applied to the business of politics, a formidable generation of professional politicians was the consequence.[12]

Transformation in attitudes toward local office and attendant changed ethos is inherent in two remarks widely separate in time and place: "Back in 1835," in New York City, "Chancellor James Kent, voice of the native aristocracy, had explained that 'the office of assistant alderman could be pleasant and desirable to persons of leisure, of intelligence, and of disinterested zeal for the wise and just regulation of the public concerns of the city.'" A transformed view of the local politicians' sense of duty appears in the musing of an old Chicago precinct captain upon the incarceration of a colleague: "I don't understand that. How can they send him to jail for taking money? Why do they think he became an alderman in the first place? That's like putting a priest away for praying."[13]

Jackson's spoils system, the long ballot, and male mass suffrage also helped ripen conditions for bossism. Upon taking office, "Old Hickory" was little disposed to sustain the traditional practice of relatively small turnover in administrative personnel. The people's voice was now to be heard not only in elective offices, but also in the corridors of power populated by appointed officers. Keeping those governing faithful to their responsibilities meant holding all of them accountable to the people. Therefore, whenever voters saw fit to fire incumbents and hire a new team of rulers, it was only proper that their voice reach into the bureaucracy with partisan dismissals and appointments by the newly elected. Democratic in tone (anyone is eligible, rotation in office according to popular will), the spoils system flourished as the bosses turned it into an instrument of power. By marshalling their dependent voters, they gained influence over elected officials and thereby over jobs in the public sector. Patronage thus ensured and at machine disposal became a key source of boss favors, a prized reward for service to the organization. The spoils system was guided by the maxim that "In politics it is assumed that a man is trained for any place in the public service he can get."[14] Securing a place meant earning it by fighting political battles on the winning side.

Similarly the long ballot was converted to machine ends, like the spoils system democratic in inspiration but similarly subject to manipulation for partisan purposes. Advocates of the long ballot argued that public officials should be accountable to the led. Therefore all of them should be elected, the lesser in rank as well as the highest, for only via the ballot box might they be held responsible for deeds and misdeeds. As more and more offices were added to the ballot the longer and longer it became--to the delight of the bosses. Voter apathy, ignorance, and loyalty to the machine delivered local officialdom, where voter interest was least and the machine's greatest, into the bosses' hands. Following the instructions of organization workers, lower ward voters faithfully cast their ballots for dozens of positions far down on the list, to them inconsequential, turning the long ballot into an instrument ensuring safe seats for machine favored candidates.

Given the American mass suffrage system, taking advantage of the long ballot and capturing offices in city hall and county courthouse was dependent upon delivering blocks of votes. Once again the times stood ready to promote bossism; potential electors were in abundance to vote properly--and often--for meager reward. Thousands of city residents confronted minimal levels of existence: they needed shelter, food, fuel, and employment. The machines came to the rescue, distributing aid and providing some measure of security. Moreover, latter day immigrants, differing in language, culture, and religion from the settled Northern European protestants, needed an agent for explanations and assimilation, a friend able to untangle legal complications and guide them through the labyrinth of city regulations. They had left behind their families, disconnected themselves from their native communities, social surroundings, and friendships, and were anxious to find replacements in the new land. The boss gladly charged to the rescue, offering the immigrants and down-and-outers assistance both physical and nonmaterial. He became provider of food, fuel, and jobs, a spokesman in city hall's bureaucracy, a grantor of recognition to those who worked for him and his candidates. He made them all feel welcome in his rooms and saloons where city politics were discussed. Loyality in return was expected and votes extracted.

All did not equally share in the machine's largess, but comprehensiveness was neither possible nor a goal. What was necessary, and accomplished, was to reach many and then let stories of the boss's generosity spread and generate additional loyalty and support. Assistance to one person or family had repercussions well beyond the immediate number. Sometimes aid was "secretly" delivered, headquarters depending upon a few well planted words by a ward worker to have it soon widely known that the kindly unknown benefactor was indeed the "Old Man."[15] The fact that jobs provided were menial, welfare received spasmodic, and recognition granted limited was overlooked in the wonder these gifts were bestowed at all. And by granting them, the boss assisted his business clientele by inhibiting worker unrest.[16] In addition, by virtue of the machine's socialization role in standing for and promoting the American way (free enterprise, opportunity, and assimilation rather than separation), it contributed to deterring the growth of a politically viable Social Democratic party in the United States.

Thanks to America's suffrage system, hordes of males, and later females, had access to the ballot box, a privilege the bosses hugely appreciated even if the newly enfranchised did not. Whether from rural United States or foreign nation, immigrants went to polling places although the action's significance may not have accompanied them. Busy just trying to survive, descendants of autocratic cultures where the very notion of voting was alien, the newcomers learned the vote was a valuable commodity when traded for assistance. Political bosses and their machines aided and organized the mass of voters, delivered it on election day, and gained influence over city decision makers, or now more accurately, decision ratifiers.

As urban areas grew in population, physical growth and government functions mushroomed. The rush was on for new buildings and life's amenities as the cities confronted booming demands for services. Fire and police protection, street and sidewalk improvements and expansion, garbage collection and sewers, utilities, public transportation, and a myriad of other metropolitan needs demanded action from local officials. City hall's doors led to the chambers where contracts for city projects were let, franchises were decided upon, licenses were secured, and security from too stringent enforcement of building codes might be obtained. Sundry other benefits were available to place recipients beyond harm's way. Succinctly stated, the growth of the city "opened up for the municipal politician a new El Dorado."[17] In order to grasp opportunities and share in the profits that tempted, people sought advantages where they could and with whom they could. That came to mean the political boss, the broker who, for a fee, saw to it that proper decisions and actions were forthcoming from city hall.

But why resort to a boss, why not deal directly with decision makers? Once more an environmental characteristic contributed to the emergence of machine politics, combining with all the others in results now familiar. An attempt to find *the* decision maker in an American city was an exercise in frustration, since Americans in their fear of centralized power and faith in decentralization had rendered their cities studies in fragmentation and thus irresponsibility. To thwart ambitious governors the governed turned to institutional methods of obstruction and delay, discerned as the price of liberty. But in a nation rapidly expanding, building, and industrializing, ferreting out the individual or body capable of making a decision was imperative. Americans' predisposition against centralized power meant cities were unable to respond effectively to problems as decision seekers became entwined in overlapping boards and commissions. They watched with a sense of helplessness as mayors and city councils inconclusively grappled with one another, while county and state governments vied for their shares in city nondecision making.

Springing from this fragmented environment was the necessity for someone able to provide answers and secure quick results. Lincoln Steffens's recollection of a conversation with Tammany's Richard Croker captures the situation. The journalist was asking the politician why there had to be a boss when there already was a mayor and city council when he was interrupted:[18]

> That's why . . . . It's because there's a mayor *and* a city council *and* judges *and*--a hundred other men to deal with. A government is nothing but a business, and you can't do business with a lot of officials, who check and cross one another and who come and go, there this year, out the next. A business man wants to do business with one man, and one who is always there to remember and carry out--the business.

Responding to conditions and needs, the political boss was fashioned, summoned into being to provide the necessary centralization and service as go-between for his numerous clients, drawn from all walks of life, all seeking privileges from city hall.

When Thomas Dennison came to stay, Omaha was only thirty-eight years old, a gateway to the West from its earliest beginnings on the banks of the Missouri River. People involved in or associated with steamboats, horse and mule drawn wagons, and later the railroads crafted its early history. Starting with one log cabin built on July 4, 1854, Omaha had grown by Dennison's arrival into a regional transportation, manufacturing, and livestock center. Paralleling economic growth was a population boom as thousands chose to ignore the advice in a poem printed in *Harper's Magazine* in 1869:[19]

Hast thou ever been in Omaha,
    Where rolls the dark Missouri down,
And four strong horses scarce can draw
    An empty wagon through the town?

Where sand is blown from every mound
    To fill your eyes and throat--
Where all the steamers are aground
    And all the shanties are afloat?

Where whiskey shops the livelong night
    Are vending out their poison juice;
Where men are often *very* tight
    And women deemed a trifle loose?

Where taverns have an anxious quest
    For every corner, shelf and crack;
With half the people going west,
    and *all* the others going back?

Where theaters are all the run,
    And bloody scalpers come to trade;
Where everything is overdone
    And everybody overpaid?

If not, take heed to what I say:
    You'll find it just as I have found it;
And if it lies upon your way,
    For God's sake, reader, *go around it!*

Frank Streamer, likely author of the anonymously published verse, was a wanderer who spent some time in Omaha in the 1860s before moving on to oblivion. Thousands, however, settled in Omaha and the city grew from 16,083 in 1870 to 30,518 ten years later, to over 102,000 by the time Dennison made it his home.[20] Not far removed from its frontier days, Omaha possessed a scrofulous reputation. Twenty years before Dennison's arrival a Kansas City newspaper's readers learned that upriver was a "very cesspool of iniquity," and the editors were "not certain that Omaha is a fit subject for an editorial, but this we know, no better subject for the prayers of a nation can be found."[21]

Freight haulers on land and river, cowboys and stockmen, optimists on the way to gold and silver riches, pessimists on the way back, railroad and packing house laborers, immigrants from afar and from farms, converged in lower downtown Omaha to embellish Omaha's wide-open image. Famous and colorful figures of the era's gambling and con man fraternity added to the scarlet scene, for example "Doc" Baggs whose title was in recognition for quackery, and who strolled the streets under a stovepipe hat, sporting a gold headed cane. "Canada Bill" (William Jones) led a collection of card sharks and con men during the 1870s, once breaking up a prize fight by entering the ring with drawn pistols to point out to the referee one fighter was fouling the other, the one being fouled being the man "Canada Bill" and his men had bet on. Their usual hangout was Harry Clayton's Crystal Saloon, not that the choice was a limited one, because in 1873 there were 132 bars for some 16,000 residents. Faro and three card monte players won and lost at Clayton's, "Dutch Charlie" Klader being one of the faithful.

Matt Harris ran a gambling hall for the city's more affluent and socially recognized citizens, including army officers. The upper class was also welcome at a poker room on Union Block where specially prepared luncheons were served amid expensive furnishings. Less eminent players were not to sully such stately establishments, but Dan Allen warmly greeted them at his popular gambling house in the second story of a building on Pioneer Block. Among the attractions of Allen's place was the convenience of a first floor pawnshop, made even more convenient by a dumb waiter carrying down the valuables of losers and carrying cash up to them--at high interest rates. One of Omaha's most famous madams, Anna Wilson, was Allen's consort for years. In 1907 Anna donated her 9th and Douglas Street bordello, valued at $100,000, to Omaha for use as an emergency hospital, later adding funds for maintenance of her gift to the city. When she died in 1911 (buried next to Dan at Prospect Hill Cemetery), she bequeathed her sizeable estate, a quarter million dollars, to charities and hospitals.

Gamblers also went to Frank Shaw's and Tom Ratfiffe's place over Hornberger's saloon at 1321 Douglas, Shaw cast as a "bold, dashing" figure fond of laying big bets on the roulette wheel. Constituting a social set among their kind, the leading or boss gamblers settled down for afternoon poker games at Dick Wilde's bar. They discussed topics other than dealt hands, however. Politics and gambling were closely linked since the degree of law enforcement imposed--or not imposed--depended upon their influence with city hall. Accordingly, gamblers, saloonkeepers, and bartenders built a political power base in their part of the city, the first ward, later to become the third. [22]

Thanks to political allies, the gambling fraternity and its customers tested one another's skills in a variety of challenges despite laws, both state and local, forbidding their activities. "Offenses Against Chastity, Morality and Decency," a statute passed by the First General Assembly of the Territory of Nebraska, held in Omaha in 1855, included cards, dice, faro, roulette, or any other games played for money. Subsequent legislation by the state of Nebraska, and by Omaha officials under delegated powers, reiterated the bans against gambling. A decade before Dennison's setting up his lottery wheel, city fathers in their concern for civic virtue had by ordinance declared gambling with cards, dice, or "other devices or implements" misdemeanors punishable by a fine of no less than twenty dollars.[23]

In Omaha as in many other communities, a downtown river ward hosted tolerated gambling, saloons open all hours, and prostitution. These wards had greeted the early pioneers as they nestled on the river bottoms. When their original inhabitants prospered they moved to new and loftier neighborhoods, leaving the lower areas to transients and indigent immigrants. Later arrivals rented rooms in cheap tenements, and labored in the warehouses, railroad yards, machine shops, and factories that soon typified these wards of rapidly growing cities. Sharing the streets and alleys with industry, tenements, and labor force were the bars, gambling houses, and red light districts, in Omaha largely concentrated in lower downtown, the third ward of Dennison's era. Its boundaries when he arrived were from the river front and Cass Street west to 15th Street, then south to Jackson, thence east back to the river; by the time Dennison was deeply involved in ward politics the limits were Leavenworth Street on the south, Nicholas on the north, the Missouri River on the east, and 16th Street on the west (Omaha's north-south streets are numbered from the river). Adjustments came in the course of the "Old Man's" long reign, so that by 1930 the third's outlines were Dodge Street to the south, Charles on the north, and following the direction of city growth, 30th Street to the west.

Myriad opportunities were awaiting a man of Dennison's background and talents in lower downtown. But Omaha was much more than one district and its sordid reputation, and the city was demonstrating the results of the previous decade's boom years. At the close of 1892, smelting, the Union Pacific shops, and brewing were its top three industries (distilling was fifth). Omaha's, and Nebraska's, first brewery had been established by Frederick Krug in 1859 at 10th and Farnam. He soon faced competition from the Metz Brothers who entered production two years later, then Gottlieb Storz expanded a small firm started in 1876 to one matching Krug's output of 50,000 barrels annually by 1892. Helping to stock Omaha's by now numerous bars with whiskey and spirits was the Willow Springs Distillery, third largest in the United States with an 1891 production of 2,412,784 gallons.[24]

By 1892 travelers and goods were arriving on the many tracks now leading into the growing railway center; in 1863 the Union Pacific had come to Omaha, soon followed by the Chicago and Northwestern; the Chicago, Rock Island, and Pacific; the St. Joseph and Council Bluffs; and the Chicago, Burlington, and Quincy. A new neighbor, South Omaha, boosted as the "Miracle City," was flourishing, stimulated by the rapidly expanding meat packing industry. A Wyoming cattle baron, Alexander Swan, had the acumen to recognize Omaha's geographical advantages, including not only its central position in the corn belt, but the fact it was five hundred miles closer than Chicago to the western herds. In 1883, Swan organized with local entrepreneurs the first successful stockyards in the Omaha area, the Union Stock Yards Company, buying land for the new enterprise from the Union Pacific. Opening the next year, the Union Stockyards became a magnet for major meat packers who joined several smaller firms who had been operating in the Omaha area for over a decade.

One of these smaller packing plants was owned by the Sheely brothers, Joseph and John, immigrants from Wurttemberg, Germany. They opened their plant in 1881 at 27th and Martha, the location influenced by a city ordinance making it illegal to dump packing house residue within five miles of city hall. Initially the plant area was inhabited by the Irish, but then Poles began moving in, going to work with the Sheelys. Although the packing house burned down in 1886, the nucleus of Poles attracted fellow countrymen and by 1908 the neighborhood, now called Sheely Town, was predominately Polish.[25] But it was large firms lured from Chicago by Omaha's valuable location who built the city into a major meat center, winning for South Omaha third place among the nation's meat packers by 1890. (South Omaha and Omaha remained separate until 1915, when South Omaha was annexed.) Great names of the industry built plants near the Union Stock Yards, with Armour, Cudahy, and Swift the best known and prosperous, and they "contributed more to Omaha's growth, wealth, and importance than any other enterprise."[26]

Railroads, smelter works, packing houses, and the general building of a city required laborers to make reality of the investors' schemes and dreams. Once again Omaha mirrored the national pattern as immigrants joined native-born Americans to provide the necessary sweat and muscle. At the turn of the century U.S. census figures gave Omaha's population as 102,555, of whom 23,552 were foreign born, with an additional native 32,828 whose parents were foreign or mixed foreign and native. Thus near a quarter of Omahans were immigrants in 1900; add to them the children of foreign born or mixed and over half of the population is represented.

Scandinavians were the most numerous of the foreign born (6,710, Swedes leading with 3,968), followed by Germans (5,874), then immigrants from the British Isles (2,168 English, Scots, and Welsh, and 2,164 Irish). Austrians and Russians accounted for 2,763 and 1,228 respectively (Poles were included in the figures for Austria, Russia, and Germany in the 1900 and 1910 countings), with only 449 Italians indicated in the 1900 census. By 1910, when Dennison was well along the way to his long dominion over the city, the population had grown to 124,096, the foreign born totaling 27,068, and children of foreign born or mixed foreign/native parentage numbering 39,595. The foreign born percentage of the population had dropped slightly, but the

41

two categories taken together still accounted for over half of Omahans. Scandinavians continued as the most numerous foreign born, with the Germans and British Isles emigrants remaining second and third. Only the Scandinavians of the top three groups had increased in total number since 1900, but dramatic gains were evident for others as the locus for emigration shifted from Northern Europe to Southern and Eastern.

The number of Russians had more than doubled in the 1900-1910 decade, rising from 1,228 to 2,592, and Austrians went up to 3,414 from 2,763 (recalling that the 1910 census included Poles in the figures for Russia and Austria). Most impressive was the increase among the Italians, surging from less than 500 ten years earlier to 2,361. Given their general peasant origins, and their linguistic, religious, and cultural differences from earlier arrivals, a large pool of potential voters had arrived bearing great need for Dennison's services. A reservoir of people in need of the kinds of assistance at his disposal was well supplied by growing Omaha.

Immigrants from Western and Northern Europe had dispersed widely, but the newcomers clustered among those sharing their language and customs. Various parts of Omaha, especially in the southeast and south, took on ethnic characteristics, and a Little Italy, Bohemia Town, and other nationality neighborhoods joined Sheely Town in providing familiar surroundings for new Omahans. Howard Chudacoff has shown that Omaha did not develop sectors clearly dominated by a particular group during this period, but he points out that pluralities were common, particularly so far as the Italians and Eastern Europeans were concerned. "Thus one could identify a certain district with a certain group because more of that group lived there than anywhere else."[27] Neighborhoods assumed names and features common to the prevalent nationality, and restaurants, groceries, business signs, churches and religious symbols delineated an area's prevailing ethnic heritage. It is still possible to read from these on Omaha's older streets the map of ethnic concentrations and movements.

Ethnic Omaha, as it was forming at Dennison's arrival and as it matured with the great immigrations to come, followed an arc south then southwest from downtown. Little

Italy grew just south of the third ward as Italians and Sicilians laid claim to the area. The language, the grocery stores, the signs on the small businesses made clear that here was Omaha's Italian sector. Thence in an arc southwest, following the railroad tracks and the packing houses came the Czech, Polish, and Bohemian neighborhoods. Going down the south side of Q Street west of 24th (packing houses were on the north) a visitor might have heard Greek spoken for a few years as a Greek community was being founded. But an anti-Greek riot in 1909 largely drove its members out of town,[28] though they left their mark on still visible business signs on the few buildings that remain. A few blocks west the Irish, many of whom arrived as railroad workers then stayed on with the packers, settled on Irish Hill. A little further south, around 36th and X Streets, the early Croatian immigrants' habit of keeping geese provided their district its name--Goose Hollow. Back towards the north and out of South Omaha into the central and western parts of the city (to about 48th Street when Dennison arrived), a largely assimilated and wealthier population resided, for here the Western and Northern Europeans had spread and "Americanized."

On the far side of the downtown district, that is, north of Cass Street, the Jewish community was evident with the the B'nai Jacob Anshe Sholen at 22nd and Cuming. The 1880s had brought a large influx of Eastern European Jews to Omaha, met and assisted by a committee of coreligionists who represented a small but then largely assimilated Jewish community. An identifiable neighborhood of the newly arrived soon appeared, locating between 9th and 13th, Harney to Center Streets.[29] They later moved to the near north side just mentioned, and thence further west, blacks replacing them on the north side as their migration gained great momentum between 1910 and 1920.

Long present in Omaha but small in numbers, most early blacks toiled for the railroads and packing plants, while some 100 established businesses and others became professional people. Approximately 3,400 blacks lived in Omaha in 1900, increasing by only some 1,000 over the next ten years. However, between 1910 and 1920 the black population more than doubled to 10,315 (11,123 in 1930), with the near north side the main concentration, not so much by choice as by constraint. As black Omahans grew in number so did housing advertisements increasingly specifying "for colored families," making it clear that ads for housing without the specification were unavailable to them.[30]

Heading east on Cuming, toward the river, an early Omahan like Dennison came to 16th Street and the third ward's western fringes; a southeasterly turn led into the heart of downtown. Had Dennison been getting acquainted with Omaha in April 1892, he might have ridden on one of Dr. Samuel Mercer's overhead electric wire streetcars which had recently replaced both horse drawn and cable vehicles. Streetlights guided the way after dark, the first twenty installed in 1883 when the Northwest Light and Power Company brought electric lighting to Omaha. A new post office was under construction, Dennison and the building getting started about the same time in Omaha. Taking the entire block between 16th and 17th Streets, and Dodge and Capitol Avenue, when completed the structure was one of the city's most impressive, with its Romanesque architecture, granite stones, imposing columns and arches, all beneath a 190 foot high square tower. Each side of the tower presented a large clock near the top, one for each of the four compass directions, impressively telling time for Omahans throughout the city. Supervisory architect for the job was John Latenser, whose path crossed Dennison's in many a building endeavor in years to come.

Important structures already in place included Hayden Brothers Department Store, the firm's two acres of space contained in two recently completed five story buildings. Within Hayden's the shopper was offered a complete line of goods, from all wool "super" carpeting to a pail of jelly. On the northwest corner of 16th and Douglas Streets stood the recently completed Boston Store of J.L. Brandeis and Sons, four stories of shopping opportunities. The Boston Store burned down in 1894, but a new one twice as large soon replaced it, and in 1906 another Brandeis building appeared on the intersection's southwest corner. Two more recently completed buildings, sources of great civic pride, were the New York Life Building, in red stone rising an imposing ten stories, the top seven in a u-shape giving the appearance of twin towers, and the seven story Bee Building, home of the *Omaha Bee*, pride of Edward Rosewater. A new city hall was rising next to the Bee Building, standing when finished as a castle-like center for city business, complete with tower and turrets. Perhaps Dennison's smile appeared if he mused over words from Mayor R.C. Cushing's June 19, 1890, cornerstone laying speech:[31]

> Within its walls, we trust that no ignoble motive, no corrupt suggestion, may ever find a place, and it may be not only an edifice for the transaction of the city's affairs, but also a temple of integrity, justice, and patriotism.

Although he never held public office and physically he seldom if ever entered the new city hall, Dennison nonetheless was destined long to be present among those who conducted the city's affairs, and also in the Douglas County Courthouse across the street, completed in 1885.

Four years before his arrival, three bank buildings were completed: the First National, the Merchant's National, and the United States National, looking imposing and stolid behind its Corinthian columns. The Omaha National had made an expensive addition in 1889, the Paxton Block completed just the year before. In 1892 the Karbach Building opened, where Dennison years later took an office when prohibition forced him from the rear of the Budweiser Saloon. But not all construction was to house banks and businesses for in search of respectability, aiming to overcome the reputation of a frontier river town fit only for gamblers, drinkers, and general riffraff, Omaha's leaders in the same years decided to bring culture and civilization to their fellow citizens.

In September 1881 Boyd's Opera House was opened at the northeast corner of Farnam and 15th by James E. Boyd, future Nebraska governor. Sold and renamed the Farnam Street Theatre several years later, it was offering Field and Companies' "Famous American Minstrels" when Dennison came to town. Boyd's second effort, the New Theatre, located at 17th and Harney just a couple of blocks from the first, began offering stage productions in 1891. In the spring of 1892 its audiences were enjoying "The Power of the Press," playing in Omaha after a 150 night run in New York. In the Grand Opera House at 15th and Capitol Avenue, 5,000 spectators were treated to a variety of events, including one evening the chance to watch the great John L. Sullivan fight. Built in 1885 as the Exposition Building, the Grand Opera House (the facade carried both names) burned down a decade after opening and Omaha was deprived of its arched doorways and windows housed in and between its several towers, each surmounted by a pyramidal like roof and spire. Customers paid a dime in April 1892 to hear the Royal Quartette, the Johnson Trio, and Irish comedian James Drew.

Elegant hotels received guests and Omahans were particularly proud of the Paxton Hotel at the southwest corner of 14th and Farnam, and the Mercer, a first class, 150 room Hotel at 12th and Howard Streets owned by Samuel D. Mercer. Similar repute was granted the five story, fireproof Millard Hotel at the northeast corner of 13th and Douglas. The Murray, the Brunswick, the Dellone, the Barker, the Merchants, and the Casey Hotels offered less costly lodging. To the finer establishments came a string of distinguished visitors, including Presidents Grant, Hayes, Cleveland, and Harrison. Other guests included Grand Duke Alexis of Russia on his way to a buffalo hunt, and African explorer Henry Stanley on a return visit to Omaha in 1890, where he once had worked. For Thomas Dennison, Omaha two years later was not a stopover but an opportunity. When he surveyed the city it was a bustling place in the midst of growth. Satisfaction for a variety of tastes was available, from zither or tennis clubs to the earthy attractions of lower Douglas Street and Capitol Avenue. For him the choice was the third ward's gambling halls and saloons and soon the politics of his ward.

His move into politics and a broker and centralizing role was facilitated by the typical fragmentation of local government legislated by state lawmakers. The people working in city hall and the courthouse endured over the years frequent bills passed by the Nebraska state legislature altering their governmental structures and powers (a home rule amendment was not added to the constitution until 1912). Paying little heed to the constitution's prohibition against passing local or special laws respecting incorporating cities, towns, and villages, or changing or amending their charters, the legislature created in 1887 the category of metropolitan class for Omaha.[32]

Terms for Omaha's office holders were either one or two years, according to the legislators latest whim. Similarly the numbers, titles, and electoral base of city officials were subject to alteration from Lincoln, with some of them shifting from elected to appointed and back again.

Omaha's first charter provided for nine aldermen elected annually, these becoming councilmen in 1869 with their number doubled, two from each ward taking office in alternate years. Then in 1881 the legislature determined that half of the councilmen should be elected at-large, the other half still by wards, these two groups now elected alternatively. Sometimes voted in, sometimes appointed, the city clerk and engineer were officials never quite certain of how they would gain another term.

In addition to tinkering with terms, electoral base, and size of Omaha's governing bodies, the legislature also over time reduced the mayor's powers, constrained the council's authority through the creation of boards and commissions, and in the process complicated municipal governance. During the city's early years the mayor was chief executive officer and the council's presiding officer with attendant power to vote in case of ties. The presiding officer role was taken from the mayor in 1879, leaving him with a limited veto subject to override (the veto power was bolstered by legislation three years later by giving the mayor an item veto on appropriations). Moreover, the mayor's province in legal issues and law enforcement was reduced. Originally enjoying status as a justice of the peace with both civil and criminal powers, Omaha's mayor was first stripped of civil jurisdiction and later lost his court when in 1869 the state legislature stipulated an elected police judge should take over. The mayor was able to exercise a power traditionally in the hands of chief executives, for two years later an act passed that proved to be especially beneficial to Omahans who had problems with the police during Jim Dahlman's long tenure. Nebraska's lawmakers recognized the mayor's pardon power, one which "Cowboy Jim" delighted in liberally using.

An 1887 statute created a Board of Police and Fire Commissioners, placing control of the fire and police departments in the hands of four members appointed by the governor to four year terms, plus the mayor as an ex-officio member. In addition to responsibility for its two departments (board members were drawn from at least three political parties, and their oath included the provision that political motives would not influence their decisions), the nonpartisan board was granted a power crucially important in Omaha--to grant and supervise liquor licenses.

Several other bodies soon were created to join in the business of governing the city: a Board of Public Works with three members appointed by the mayor; the Board of Health consisting of the mayor, the chairs of designated council committees, and health officials; the Board of Inspection of Buildings, composed of appropriate subordinate city officials; and a Board of Park Commissioners with five members serving five year terms, appointed by a majority of the judges of the district courts. Thus various Omaha officeholders owed their positions to the voters, city officialdom, the governor, or district judges. Victor Rosewater's 1894 assessment appears understated: ". . . with the increasing number of city officers and the increasing complexity of their duties and functions, the responsibility of municipal officers has been altered and shifted."[33]

By all measures, Omaha in the early 1890s was a candidate for a political boss, someone capable of amassing a following, penetrating complexity, and able to get things done by organizing the right people. Thomas Dennison, professional gambler and future machine leader, set up his first policy game in Omaha at 108 So. 14th Street in mid-November of 1892, buying out Charles Koster and Tom Bidderston for $1,300 cash. The next spring for $400 he bought another shop, and brother John joined him in the policy business, the two working together to cover both downtown and South Omaha (East Omaha was soon added). How Dennison spent the months between his arrival and setting up his first policy game is unknown, although there were reports of his generally being seen in the lobby of his hotel or at Sam Sonnenberg's pawn shop.

That he was engaged in wagering during this period is certainly to be expected, and in September 1892 he was one of a number of Omahans who traveled by train to New Orleans for the John L. Sullivan, "Gentleman Jim" Corbett championship prize fight, taking with him some five or six thousand dollars. Dennison bet Corbett would stay ten rounds and won when the challenger came out for the eleventh. (Corbett went on to knock out "The Great John L" in the twenty-first round.) Dennison was a lavish spender on the return ride to Omaha, flashing a large roll of money in the club car, buying drinks repeatedly for his fellow travelers. In addition to the money so freely spent, he had enough to advance a sizeable loan, $1,700, to an associate who had lost on the fight.[34]

A couple of months later, Dennison initiated his policy game in Omaha, his customers buying numbers they hoped
would be drawn from his policy wheel, crowning them winners
for the day. Dennison's wheel looked like a big base drum,
with brass rims, and heads made of glass. Players watched
rubber tubes containing the numbers bet on tumble about as
the wheel spun. When it stopped, through a slot three or
four of these tubes were taken out and slips of paper were
removed from each one. Written on these pieces of paper
were the winning numbers, announced by the wheel operator
who then wrote them on a nearby slate. Buyers of the drawn
numbers now came forward to claim their purse.

Dennison was running his game in 1899 in the Dodge
European Hotel at 111 South 13th Street, patrons entering
his policy room through a door on an alley. A small office
was squeezed into the southwest corner and a few chairs
were scattered about the rest of the room. There was a
counter where bets were placed, and a chalkboard on one
wall for recording the winning numbers. A telephone waited
on the south wall, a private line taken out by Dennison
under the alias of John R. Crowder, for a call from John's
South Omaha office. Discarded nonwinning numbers cluttered
the floor, and for those seeking to improve their chances,
a "dreambook" was available for consultation before buying
another number or numbers. Had you dreamed the night before
of, say, a white horse, a check of the "dream book" under
"white horse" indicated the numbers to buy.

It was unnessary to be present to win because ticket
writers were responsible for contacting players, collecting
their bets, and paying off winners. Dennison's number sellers carried carbon paper tablets and provided duplicates
of all tickets sold; the money collected was due to Dennison an hour and a half before a drawing. Conditions of the
game were spelled out on the back of the policy slips,
revealing much about the relationship between the management and its representatives:[35]

> This is a Mutual Benefit Association and any party wishing to
> contribute to the general fund will not receive a slip from any of
> the agents without this notice on the back of the said slip, as
> the management will not be responsible or hold themselves liable
> for any others. This is only a memorandum of amounts agreed upon,

and is not sold as a ticket of any kind. The holder will do the management a favor by reporting to the main office any neglect on the part of their agent. If the holder of this memorandum should lose same they forfeit all rights or any benefit of said association. Should the agent fail to report to the management or turn over his book in time before the announcement of results the holder of this memorandum is only entitled to the return of his money, according to the rules of the association. Please report if the agents fails to call regularly.

John R. Crowder

In addition to his policy wheel, Dennison had other gambling interests which willy-nilly placed him in the saloon business since gambling and drinking were then near synonymous terms. In a typical saloon, the bar usually occupied the first floor, and the second floor (or basement) hosted the crap, roulette, and card players. Dennison managed old associate Charlie Pierson's Denver Saloon in early 1894, where gambling of course was served in addition to drinks. Between 1900 and 1902 he had from one-fifth to one-third interest in Cliff Cole's, a well known haunt of Omaha's gambling community. Dennison disingenuously remarked in the course of a 1907 libel suit against the *Daily News* that he heard faro and roulette were being played on the second floor at Cole's, but for himself, "I was never upstairs in the place when they were gambling there."[36]

Years later, a former associate charged Dennison with supplementing his income by serving as a fence during his early Omaha days, and also claimed Dennison had pinpointed victims for criminal acquaintances, receiving a cut of the proceeds.[37] In a court deposition, Sherman Morris, alias Frank Shercliffe, claimed he first met Dennison in Salt Lake City where Tom suggested and planned several robberies for Morris to commit. Not all were successful, but a theft from two women Dennison had identified as wealthy in diamonds resulted in $6,000 worth of the jewels being stolen, with Morris receiving one-third of the amount for his troubles. Other crimes allegedly committed at Dennison's inspiration and to his profit were said to have been planned in Omaha in 1892, one carried out in Denver by Morris (a robbery to relieve a blacksmith of a machine he had developed to beat faro), the other a sensational diamond robbery near Missouri Valley, Iowa, just across the river and north of Omaha.

Thirteen years after the diamonds were stolen, Dennison was charged by the state of Iowa with receiving and aiding in the concealment of stolen property. Morris (Shercliffe) had been arrested shortly after the crime, found guilty, and imprisoned in the Iowa state penitentiary at Fort Madison. Dennison expended great effort and money over the next several years to secure Morris a parole, enlisting the support of prominent Omahans to his cause, including Mayor Frank E. Moores, Victor (Edward's son) Rosewater of the *Bee* newspaper, and Chief of Police Martin White. Accompanied to Des Moines by Dennison, the Chief in May 1899 carried a letter to Iowa's governor, signed by Moores and Rosewater, arguing on Morris's behalf. The "Old Man" also used his third ward strength to help reelect Dave M. Mercer to Congress with the intent of securing his assistance in the effort to gain the prisoner's release.

Dennison was said to have felt responsible for the convicted man's imprisonment and wanted to help him out; Morris later stated Dennison visited him several times at Fort Madison, coming under the name of Ed Hogan. Finally the release efforts bore fruit and in November 1900 Iowa Governor L. M. Shaw granted the pardon. Shercliffe, as he was now better known, returned to Omaha, paroled to Douglas County, Nebraska, and moved in with his benefactor for a while.[38] However, a couple years later there was a falling out between the two men and Shercliffe was forced out of Omaha (Shercliffe maintained his former ally accused him of robbing one of his places), thereby breaking his parole. He was soon arrested in Kansas City, shot in the foot in the course of his capture, and escorted back to Fort Madison. There he spoke with fellow convicts about making Dennison pay for every month he had to sit in prison, mentioning he had a hold on Dennison and would force him to pay one hundred dollars for each month of imprisonment.[39]

During Shercliffe's renewed stay at the prison, a Harrison County, Iowa, grand jury indicted Dennison on the receiving and concealing stolen goods charge and the prisoner became the state's star witness. Failing in efforts to have the charges quashed and to prevent extradition, Dennison's attorneys did succeed in gaining a change in venue; thus the trial was held in Red Oak, Iowa, in Montgomery County. Prosecution was led by the county attorney, but he was assisted by special counsel Elmer E. Thomas of Omaha, a fervent Dennison opponent and leading member of the Civic Federation. Explanation for the long delay between the robbery and Dennison's appearance in court--thirteen years--lies in the Civic Federation's political opposition to Dennison. Exhibits were introduced on behalf of the defendant by his attorney charging Thomas with having appeared before the Harrison County grand jury, not as a witness but as a representative of the Civic Federation, urging it to indict Dennison. Thomas, according to the defense, had promised that the Civic Federation and the Jewelers Protective Association of the United States would cover all the county's costs if an indictment was returned.

A grand juror submitted an affidavit supporting Dennison's allegation, substantiating that Thomas had promised to cover all costs, and stating the grand jury subpoenaed witnesses named by the Omahan. No complaint against Dennison had been filed by any resident of the county, the affidavit asserted, and there was no request to investigate the matter except from Thomas. Except for Thomas's promises "The cases would not have been taken up as it was an old case," wrote the juror. Harrison county's auditor reported that he had reviewed the expenditures made for summoning witnesses in the grand jury investigation, and found that only a $1.35 had been spent by Harrison County, the monies in question paid, if at all, by other than the county.[40]

When the trial began on May 23, 1905, the prosecution laid out its version of the robbery, with Shercliffe taking a seat in the train's smoking car when he boarded in Omaha, wearing whiskers as a disguise. Waiting until the train crossed into Iowa, he attacked diamond dealer W.L. Pollock of New York, hitting and shooting him, though not fatally. Tearing open his victim's vest, Shercliffe grabbed the diamonds Pollock was carrying, then pulled the brake rope and jumped off the train. After burying the jewels nearby the robber made his way to Des Moines. Caught and convicted of the crime he was given the seventeen year sentence Dennison labored to reduce through his parole efforts.

The prosecution charged Dennison had seen Pollock's diamonds in Sam Sonnenberg's pawn shop, had even examined them, and learned what train the diamond dealer was going to take to Sioux City. On the witness stand, Shercliffe declared Dennison had urged him to commit the robbery, that he accordingly did so and followed the gambler's instructions to bury the jewels near Missouri Valley. He concluded his testimony by recalling Dennison had sent him a wire in Des Moines with the cryptic message "O.K."[41] The defense rejoined with fifty witnesses on Dennison's behalf, a cross section of Omaha, introducing depositions challenging the state's assertions. All denounced Shercliffe's character and extolled that of the accused. On the trial's eleventh day the verdict was delivered: "We the Jury, find the defendant not guilty." The Civic Federation's effort had failed, both in gaining a conviction and in its attempt to discredit Dennison politically, the latter actually the primary motivation. Under cross-examination, Shercliffe testified Thomas had confided to him that through the trial he "wanted to purify the political conditions in Omaha."[42]

The court test of strength showed the "Old Man" was the stronger--this time. Brief in its duration, the trial was flimsy in evidence, the star witness's character and credibility questionable. Little was learned other than what was widely known: Tom Dennison was an influential gambler. Many years later a lengthly and highly publicized trial held in Omaha against an elderly defendant running out of time had far different consequences. When Thomas took Dennison on in Red Oak, the "Old Man" was just getting started.

In the years just prior to the Pollock case, Dennison had developed a business partnership with Billy Nesselhous, involving slot machines, gambling, and a few horses. They also became associates in the Budweiser Saloon, originally Cliff Cole's, at 1409 Douglas shortly after the turn of the century. Dennison denied having been a partner with Nesselhous in the bar, claiming he but owned the building and Billy rented it.[43] Whatever the bar relationship, Dennison maintained his office and held court in the rear of the building behind the Budweiser.

From early in the century until prohibition set in, here those seeking Dennison's services made their appearance and supplications; here he received his lieutenants, mapped strategies, issued orders, and discussed issues with businessmen from both the legitimate (upperworld) and illegitimate (underworld) communities in his room beyond the bar. As they talked with the "Old Man," visitors were surrounded by walls adorned with autographed photographs of politicians, actors, actresses, jockeys, and race horses. To this room Mayor James Dahlman was one day escorted by two police officers, obviously of a mind it was better to take the inebriated mayor to the Budweiser than to nearby police headquarters. Before falling asleep in a comfortable chair, "Cowboy Jim" announced that Tom Dennison "might run the goddamn town, but he [Dahlman] was the mayor!"

Dennison had a brief flirtation with the retail world in 1900, going into business with Sam Sonnenberg, the downtown pawn broker he had known for several years, in a men's furnishing store on N Street. The venture was short-lived for Tom not long after was citing his business activities as training and racing horses, plus handling his rental properties. At the same time he claimed he had given up gambling in 1902--but not for good as it turned out.[44] During all of Dennison's Omaha years, gambling was illegal. Therefore, from his earliest days in the city to the time he left for good in 1933, it was necessary for Dennison to have political influence to protect himself and his colleagues from enforcement of troublesome laws. His ambition and influence eventually went well beyond politics for protection, as he expanded his range of contacts, interests, and capabilities.

Political organization was not unknown to Omaha's third ward before Dennison's appearance since fellow gamblers, the Big Four, had in 1887 undertaken the task. Charles D. Bibbins from Chicago, H.B. Kennedy who came from Missouri, an Easterner by name of Charles White, and Texan Jack Morrison used their establishment, the Diamond, as a political base of operations. One of Omaha's most expensively equipped gambling houses of the period, the Diamond was in a two story building with an intriguing address for devotees of chance--1313 Douglas Street. On the first floor patrons drank, shot pool, and placed bets on horse races. Faro, roulette, and poker fanciers went to the second floor for their games, to win or lose in plush surroundings.

In the late 1890s the Big Four suddenly left town, leaving record of neither why they left nor of who convinced them they were no longer welcome. Several years later, Alfred Sorenson, long-time Omaha resident and editor of a weekly newspaper, in the course of scorning Dennison's political influence, commented that while the Big Four had been companionable fellows, when they entered into "the governing business they were forced to leave the city."[45] It may be more than coincidental that their departure coincides with Dennison's political emergence. The 1897 mayoral contest pitted Democratic and Peoples Independent candidate Edward Howell against Republican Frank E. Moores. For the first time, Dennison, crowned "King gambling shop bee" by the *World-Herald* (which was supporting Howell) read comments regarding his political involvement in a city election. Now operating his policy shop in an alleyway between Douglas and Dodge Streets between 12th and 14th, Dennison was identified as Moores's right-hand man, offering his support in return for a promise that his gambling interests could carry on unmolested if Moores was victorious.[46] Dennison's friend and ally Edward Rosewater, editor of the *Bee*, likewise placed his significant influence behind Moores, and the Rosewater-Moores-Dennison triad became familiar in Omaha politics for several years.

Howell supporters, according to Rosewater's *Bee*, included a number of "tinhorn" gamblers, Bibbins, White, and Morrison among the most active (no mention of Kennedy). Large contributions to Howell's campaign fund were purportedly made by White and Bibbins to assist the poker playing Howell.[47] Although Dennison was not yet strong enough to deliver the third ward to him, Moores went on to win the election. The Big Four subsequently left Omaha and went their separate ways. Dennison moved into the gap left by his departed colleagues, ambitious, talented, and motivated by his need for protection for himself and his kind. His experiences and contacts in Colorado, his policy shops, his awareness of the consequences of political influence, persuaded him to seek control of power over elected and subsequently appointed officials.[48] As he progressed his business and political competitors in the ward suffered, their establishments increasingly falling victim to law enforcement vigilance and cleanup campaigns. Subjected to harassment and arrest, their customers drained away to the benefit of those cooperating with the "King Gambler."[49] His allies, exempt from police raids and legal interference, satisfied with impunity the demands of Omahans and travelers seeking their illicit wares.

Within three years his position was consolidated and

an editorial in 1900 warned that "Tom Dennison, notorious as the king of the policy shops that have flourished in Omaha under the protection of the Moores's administration, has been and is today the power behind the throne."[50] Dennison used his power to establish his primacy over gambling in the city, determining who could or could not share in the spoils. Sometimes he did not bother to go through the chief of police, but gave orders himself for selective law enforcement directly to patrolmen on their beats.[51] Examples abound of Dennison exerting his authority to advance his monopoly. Runners reported to him one day that a rival policy shop had been set up. The challenger had failed to clear with Dennison; the "King Gambler" first tried to come to terms with the fellow, Charles Alstadt, but without success. Shortly after Alstadt was in Mickey Mullen's saloon and watched two men sell Dennison policy slips in the presence of two detectives. When Alstadt pulled one of his slips out, the detectives arrested him and he spent the night in the police station. Dennison's associates went unmolested by the law enforcers. The next day in police court Alstadt was charged not with gambling, but with vagrancy despite the fact he was proprietor of a hotel in South Omaha. He pleaded not guilty and was released on his own recognizance, mindful of Dennison's capabilities.[52]

Dennison's talents and influential associates made him a force to be reckoned with, and the foundation was well laid for the dawning thirty years of power. "I have got this town fixed so the chief [Donahue] will stand for anything," he told an associate in 1904, the same year one of his children died. Chief Donahue and detectives on the police force appeared at the funeral, and Billy Nesselhous was asked what all those policeman where doing there, was Dennison a stool pigeon? "No," was the reply, "Dennison's got the chief and all these coppers under his thumb."[53] In 1899 an unidentified saloonkeeper confided to a reporter that pressure was being applied on bar owners to urge brewers to exert their influence and help quash a prosecution brought by an independent minded county sheriff against Dennison for gambling. Omaha police were suddenly enforcing a Sunday closing law, ignored for years, to get the saloonkeepers' attention. Mayor Moores and Police Chief Martin White, in an effort to counter the sheriff's action, were informing the owners that strict enforcement would cease as soon as Dennison was cleared. Powerful forces were acknowledged to be backing Dennison, another saloonkeeper declared, including the mayor, the police and fire commissioners, and the police chief. The pressure worked and the case was ultimately dismissed.[54]

Dennison's ward power was brought to bear against Frank Sampson, who attempted to open a new gambling house on lower Douglas in 1902 without having completed arrangements with Dennison, by now the administration's agent in gambling matters. A policeman was posted to stand in front of Sampson's new establishment as soon the door was opened, where he proceeded to stop all before they entered, "ostentatiously" taking down names and addresses in his book. When Police Chief Donahue was asked why the officer was stationed there, he replied he understood there was a case of smallpox inside. A guard was therefore necessary to maintain a quarantine. Donahue did not know whether it was usual to permit people to enter a building where there was a quarantine, but affirmed the policeman would remain at his post until the disease was wiped out. In answer to whether there was any smallpox over at Cliff Cole's, where Dennison then had an interest, the Chief answered, "No, it hasn't broke out there yet." In a matter of days Sampson gave up as his customers vanished, and the officer went on to other law enforcement assignments. Chief Donahue now announced that because he had heard games of chance were available at Sampson's, he had decided to station one of his men there to take down the names of witnesses. He was determined, avowed the conscientious chief of police, to stamp out gambling.[55]

Dennison's path and actions to achieve influence in the third ward are largely unknown, but conditions were proper for someone's emergence, both in general and in particular following the departure of the Big Four. He was able to profit from what was left behind by his predecessors, consolidating his position by organizing the saloonkeepers in the ward into a welfare association, and establishing alliances with breweries in the city. He was also a protege of one of Omaha's most politically astute and powerful men, Edward Rosewater, a matter for the next chapter. The *Daily News* in 1901 proclaimed that smooth Tom Dennison was the man with the brains and pocketbook behind a strong political combination, determining courses of action, fumed the paper, and then financing them to the benefit of himself and those allied with him.[56]

Not only Dennison's fellow Omahans attested to his political clout; so did a noted member of the muckraker fraternity, Josiah Flynt Willard, who came to Omaha the same year to investigate the graft situation. Muckrakers, the band of journalists dedicated to exposing corruption and misconduct in commerce or politics with facts and figures, pursued a goal stated by their most well known member, Lincoln Steffens: "to sound the civic pride of an apparently shameless citizenship," galvanizing it to action and reform.[57] Rankled by their writings, Theodore Roosevelt contributed the sobriquet when he recalled to listeners' attention on April 16, 1906, the muckraker in Bunyan's *Pilgrim's Progress*. Often indispensable, the muckraker, said Roosevelt, nonetheless had to know when to stop raking the muck and look upward toward the celestial crown rather than continually be looking down.[58]

Not yet bearing the title of muckraker, added some five years later, Willard came to Omaha billed as a criminal expert. Carefully observing the world through his gray eyes, Willard was a small man whose life was a combination of high society and time spent on the road with hoboes and tramps. His father was a wealthy newspaper editor, but Josiah, after unsuccessful efforts in higher education in both the U.S. and Europe, had taken to the road for further schooling, gaining a familiarity with the underworld and earning acceptance in its circles. In articles and books he portrayed a world seldom seen by his father's associates or his classmates. Known to his readers as Josiah Flynt Willard, he was "Cigarette" to those he traveled with and wrote about.[59]

Forty-eight hours in Omaha provided him a newspaper story published in a full page spread bearing the provocative title "THE MACHINE IS TRIMMING THIS CITY." He toured Omaha's third ward saloons and streets, talking and listening, and attempted to draw Dennison into a conversation when they met on a corner. Not knowing who Willard was, Dennison at first seemed willing to talk, drawn on by the visitor's evident knowledge of the policy game and other mutual matters of interest. But Dennison was given a warning by an attorney who was with him (Chief Donahue was also along), and he lapsed into silence.

Willard's article reported Dennison to be boss of a wide-open city, a man powerful enough to say what thieves were welcome to come to town, protect them while here, and tell them when they had to leave. "His say goes in this town," wrote Willard, "clear from top to bottom. Why, even Croker in New York isn't a big enough man to order the 'guns' around that way."[60] Protection purchased was proudly boasted by a saloonkeeper. He had license to do anything in Omaha he wanted short of murder, he said, because he had contributed $1,400 to help put the "gang" in office at the last election.

Tom Dennison, private citizen, "King Gambler" and "King of the Grafters," was a key figure in the "machine" and "that organization in political life known from New York to San Francisco, as the body of men who exploit municipal or private gain in a business-like fashion--is 'trimming' the city."[61] As Willard recognized, a "body of men" must be considered. Dennison ruled neither alone nor completely, and several others were also key figures in the organization. They were individuals from Omaha's wealthy and socially respectable elite as well as men far removed from the society pages, the "undercrust" of the city's marginal men. With connections throughout Omaha's social structure, Thomas Dennison had penetrated to the center of political power by the turn of the century, and there he remained for three decades.

Chapter II

[1]James Bryce, *The American Commonwealth* (New York: Macmillan and Co., 1891), II, fn. 1, p. 114.

[2]On the heterogeneous nature of the machines and on their pragmatism see Elmer E. Cornwell Jr., "Bosses, Machines, and Ethnic Groups," in Lee S. Greene, ed., "City Bosses and Political Machines," *The Annals of the American Academy of Political and Social Science*, vol. 353 (May, 1964), pp. 27-39; Mosei Ostrogorski, "The Politicians and the Machine," *Organization of Political Parties*, II, *The United States*, edited and abridged by Seymour Lipsett (New York: Doubleday Anchor Paperbacks, 1964), pp. 179-227. Reprinted in Alexander B. Callow Jr., *American Urban History: An Interpretive Reader with Commentaries* (New York: Oxford University Press, 1969), see pp. 316, 322-323; Edward C. Banfield and James Q. Wilson, *City Politics* (Cambridge: Harvard University Press and M.I.T. Press, 1963), p. 116; Daniel J. Boorstin, *The Americans: The Democratic Experience* (New York: Random House, 1973), pp. 252-261.

[3]See Howard Chudacoff, *The Evolution of American Urban Society* (2nd ed.; Englewood Cliffs, New Jersey: Prentice-Hall Inc., 1981), pp. 144-145; Joel A. Tarr, *A Study in Boss Politics: William Lorimer of Chicago* (Urbana: University of Illinois Press, 1971), p. 4. Useful definitions of political machines are provided in Norman I. Fainstein and Susan S. Fainstein, "The Political Traditions of the City: Machines and Reform," in *Urban Political Movements* (Englewood Cliffs, New Jersey: Prentice-Hall Inc., 1974), pp. 14-15; Fred I. Greenstein, "The Changing Pattern of Urban Party Politics," in Greene, "City Bosses and Political Machines," pp. 3-4.

[4]See Banfield and Wilson, *City Politics*, pp. 115-117; the machine provided the "chief social rallying point" according to Theodore Roosevelt, "Machine Politics in New York City," *The Century Magazine*, XXXIII (November, 1886), pp. 78-79; Daniel Patrick Moynihan, "The Irish of New York," in Lawrence H. Fuchs, ed., *American Ethnic Politics* (New York: Harper Torchbooks, 1968), pp. 77-108; Eric L. McKitrick, "The Study of Corruption," *Political Science Quarterly*, LXXII (December, 1957), pp. 506-507, 511-512; Robert K. Merton, "The Latent Functions of the Machine: A Sociologists View," reprinted from his *Social Theory and Social Structure* in Alexander B. Callow, *The City Boss in America: An Interpretive Reader* (New York: Oxford University Press, 1976), see pp. 25-31; Bruce M. Stave, *The New Deal and the Last Hurrah: Pittsburgh Machine Politics* (Pittsburgh: University of Pittsburgh Press, 1970), pp. 5-6; Tarr, *A Study in Boss Politics*, p. 11; Raymond E. Wolfinger, "The Development and Persistence of Ethnic Voting," *American Political Science Review*, 59 (December, 1965), reprinted in Fuchs, *American Urban*

Politics, pp. 171-172.

[5]On immigrants and voting see Cornwell, "Bosses, Machines, and Ethnic Groups," pp. 27-32; Bryce's view of the matter is expressed in his observation that "The immigrants vote but they are not fit for the suffrage." *The American Commonwealth*, p. 95.

[6]Edward J. Bander, *Mr. Dooley on the Choice of Law* (Charlottesville: The Michie Company, 1963), p. 107. An abundant literature on the boss and the business community exists; especially useful are Lincoln Steffens, *The Shame of the Cities* (New York: Hill and Wang, Inc., 1957), and his *The Autobiography of Lincoln Steffens* (New York: Harcourt, Brace and Company, 1931), pp. 371-417. See also Banfield and Wilson, *City Politics*, pp. 245-246, 261-267, 272-275; Samuel P. Hays, "The Politics of Reform in the Progressive Era," *Pacific Northwest Quarterly*, (October, 1964), reprinted in Callow, *American Urban History*, pp. 434-435; Melvin G. Holli, *Reform in Detroit: Hagen S. Pingree and Urban Politics* (New York: Oxford University Press, 1969), pp. 169-170; Merton, "The Latent Functions of the Machine," pp. 26-27; Ostrogorski, "The Politicians and the Machine," pp. 327-329; Roosevelt, "Machine Politics in New York City," p. 74.

[7]On bosses and the underworld see Harold F. Gosnell, *Machine Politics Chicago Model* (2nd ed.; Chicago: University of Chicago Press, 1968), pp. 42-43; Merton, "The Latent Functions of the Machine," pp. 29-32; Josie Washburn, *The Underworld Sewer* (Omaha: Washburn Publishing Co., 1909), p. 58.

[8]Steffens, *The Autobiography of Lincoln Steffens*, pp. 492-493.

[9]On the federal government and bossism see Lyle W. Dorsett, *Franklin D. Roosevelt and the City Bosses* (Port Washington, New York: Kennikat Press, 1977); see also his *The Pendergast Machine* (New York: Oxford University Press, 1968). Another author provides a "true account of how the Federal Government closed in on Pendergast and rocked his political machine to its foundations." Maurice Milligan, *Missouri Waltz* (New York: Charles Scribner's Sons, 1978), the quotation is from p. 169. For an earlier example of federal involvement in ruining a boss see Walton Bean, *Boss Ruef's San Francisco* (Berkeley and Los Angeles: University of California Press, 1968). See also Warren Moscow, *The Last of the Big Time Bosses* (New York: Stein and Day, 1971), in which President John Kennedy is described as abandoning Carmen de Sapio because of a campaign "doublecross" by a De Sapio lieutenant.

[10]McKitrick, "The Study of Corruption," p. 508.

[11]John T. Salter, *Boss Rule: Portraits in City Politics* (New York: McGraw Hill, 1935), p. 12. See also Ostrogorski, who speaks of American politicians emerging through a process of natural selection in his "The Politicians and the Machine," pp. 301-306; Samuel P. Orth, who calls the party machines "natural products of their time," *The Boss and the Machine* (New Haven: Yale University Press, 1919), pp. 38-39. Greenstein makes a similar observation in his "The Changing Patterns of Urban Politics," p. 5.

[12]See William C. Havard, "From Bossism to Cosmopolitanism in the Relationship of Urban Leadership to State Politics," in Greene, "City Bosses and Political Machines," p. 86; Greenstein, "The Changing Patterns of Urban Politics," p. 3.

[13]Boorstin, *The Americans*, pp. 258-259; Mike Royko, EOW-H, August 1, 1983. On leadership's transition see also Bryce, *The American Commonwealth*, pp. 66-67; Roosevelt, "Machine Politics in New York City," p. 75; Alex Gottfried, "Political Machines," *International Encyclopedia of the Social Sciences* (New York: The Macmillan Co. and Free Press, 1968), p. 249; Chudacoff, *The Evolution of American Urban Society*, pp. 142-144.

[14]Salter, *Boss Rule: Portraits in City Politics*, p. 31.

[15]The bosses would have been "virtually unthinkable without their immigrant clienteles," states Cornwell, "Bosses, Machines and Ethnic Groups," p. 29, see pp. 28-33. See also Stave, *The New Deal and the Last Hurrah*, pp. 5-6; Gottfried, "Political Machines," p. 250; Wolfinger, "The Development and Persistence of Ethnic Voting," pp. 170-172; Boorstin, *The Americans*, pp. 254-255; Tarr, *A Study in Boss Politics*, pp. 10-11; Orth, *The Boss and the Machine*, pp. 61-62, 90; Holli, *Reform in Detroit*, p. 190.

[16]On the machines' conservative impact on workers see Fainstein and Fainstein, "The Political Traditions of the City: Machine and Reform," pp. 18-20.

[17]Orth, *The Boss and the Machine*, p. 59.

[18]Steffens, *The Autobiography of Lincoln Steffens*, p. 236. On fragmentation of government and machines see McKitrick who labels the diffusion of power the "principal" environmental element in his "The Study of Corruption," p. 505; Banfield and Wilson, *City Politics*, pp. 76-84; Boorstin, *The Americans*, pp. 260-261; Bryce, *The American Commonwealth*, pp. 88-92; Chudacoff, *The Evolution of American Urban Society*, p. 142; Cornwell, "Bosses, Machines, and Ethnic Groups," p. 28; Gottfried, "Political Machines," p. 250; Merton, "The Latent Functions of the Political Machine," pp. 24-25; Tarr, *A Study of Boss Politics*, pp. 15-17.

[19]Alfred Sorenson, *The Story of Omaha* (Omaha: Printed by the National Printing Company, 1923), p. 460. Sorenson related that he was told by Dr. Victor H. Coffman that Streamer had written the poem while waiting in the doctor's office. Streamer showed Dr. Coffman the poem who advised that "he ought to publish it"; the verse was duly sent to *Harper's* and it appeared in September 1869. Sorenson discounts that John G. Saxe was author of the piece. *Ibid.*, p. 461.

[20]See Howard Chudacoff, "Where Rolls the Dark Missouri Down," *Nebraska History*, 52 (Spring, 1971), pp. 5, 14. The U.S. Census figures for 1890 show 140,452, but these figures have been challenged as inflated by Edgar Z. Palmer, "The Correctness of the 1890 Census of Population for Nebraska Cities," *Nebraska History*, 32 (December, 1951), pp. 259-268.

[21]Sorenson, *The Story of Omaha*, quoted from an unnamed Kansas City newspaper in 1873, p. 469.

[22]*Ibid.*, see pp. 460-483.

[23]On early gambling legislation see *Laws, Resolutions, and Memorials Passed at the Regular Session of the First General Assembly of the Territory of Nebraska*, Convened at Omaha City, on the 16th Day of January, 1855 (Omaha City, Nebraska Territory: Sherman & Strickland, Territorial Publishers, 1855), pp. 247-248; *The Revised Ordinances of the City of Omaha: also the City Charter, Former Charters of the City and Amendments Thereto: Together with all State Laws Relating to the City* (Omaha: Omaha Steam Book and Job Printing House, 1872), p. 87; *The Revised Ordi-*

nances of the City of Omaha, Nebraska (Omaha: Gibson, Miller & Richardson, 1890), pp. 355-357; *Thomas' Revised Ordinances of the City of Omaha, Nebraska* (Omaha: Klopp & Bartlett Co., 1905), pp. 284-286.

[24]For a description of early brewing and distillery business see James W. Savage and John T. Bell, *History of the City of Omaha Nebraska* (New York and Chicago: Munsell & Company, 1894), reprinted, Evansville, Indiana: Unigraphic Inc., 1976, pp. 506-509.

[25]"Sheely Town Was Rough On Outsiders," EOW-H, April 23, 1976. Sheely Town was bordered on the north by Martha Street and about Frederick on the south, the east and west borders being respectively 26th Street and Hanscom Boulevard.

[26]Sorenson, *The Story of Omaha*, p. 600, and see pp. 610-611; also Savage and Bell, *The History of the City of Omaha Nebraska*, pp. 593-612; Chudacoff, "Where Rolls the Dark Missouri Down," p. 8; Chudacoff, *Mobile Americans: Residential and Social Mobility in Omaha 1870-1972* (New York: Oxford University Press, 1972), p. 15; and Dorothy Devereux Dustin, *Omaha and Douglas County: A Panoramic History* (Woodland Hills, California: Windsor Publications, Inc., 1980), p. 76.

[27]Chudacoff, *Mobile Americans*, p. 82, and see pp. 61-82.

[28]John G. Bitzes, "The Anti-Greek Riot of 1909--South Omaha," unpublished Master's thesis, University of Omaha, 1964.

[29]Jonathan Rosenbaum and Patricia O'Connor-Seger, eds., *Our Story: Recollections of Omaha's Early Jewish Community, 1825-1925*, Omaha Sector of the National Council of Jewish Women, 1981, see pp. 36, 66-74.

[30]See James Harvey Kerns, "Industrial and Business Life of Negroes in Omaha," unpublished Master's thesis, University of Omaha, 1932, pp. 1-5; Chudacoff, *Mobile Americans*, pp. 127, 155; Lawrence Larsen and Barbara J. Cottrell, *The Gate City: A History of Omaha* (Boulder, Colorado: Pruett Publishing Company, 1982), pp. 156-168.

[31]Savage and Bell, *History of the City of Omaha Nebraska*, p. 217.

[32]Section 18, Article III, Nebraska Constitution.

[33]Victor Rosewater, "Municipal Government in Nebraska," *Publications of the State Historical Society* 6 (1894-1895), p. 80, and pp. 76-87.

[34]See testimony of S.G.V. Griswold and deposition of Harry P. Hynds, "The State of Iowa vs. Tom Dennison," The State of Iowa, County of Montgomery, In the District Court for Montgomery County, Documents No. 6122 and 6123, hereafter cited as Documents 6122-6123. See also *Red Oak Weekly Express*, June 9, 1905.

[35]EOW-H, February 27, 1899; see also EOW-H, February 20, 21, 1899.

[36]ODN, April 17, 1907; on Dennison working for Pierson see EOW-H, February 27, 1894.

[37]ODN, April 18, 1907.

[38]ODN, April 25, 1904.

[39]See testimony of Michael Conroy and B.K. Pierce, Documents 6122-6123.

[40]Certified statement of George W. Atkins, auditor of Harrison County, Documents 6122-6123.

[41]*Red Oak Weekly Express*, May 26, 1905.

[42]EOW-H, May 25, 1905. On the political goals of the trial, see Conroy testimony, Documents 6122-6123.

[43]EOW-H, November 16, 1932.

[44]ODN, April 17, 1907.

[45]*The Examiner*, November 2, 1901; Sorenson, *The Story of Omaha*, p. 479; Davis, "The Gray Wolf: Tom Dennison of Omaha," pp. 26-32.

[46]EOW-H, April 15, 1897.

[47]Bee, April 15, 1897.

[48]EOW-H, January 27, 1899; *Sunday World-Herald*, June 23, 1968.

[49]EOW-H, February 24, 1900; MOW-H, February 15, 1934.

[50]EOW-H, February 24, 1900.

[51]*Ibid.*

[52]*Ibid.*

[53]ODN, April 24, 1904; see also EOW-H editorial, February 27, 1899; *The Examiner*, November 2, 1901; ODN, April 16, 1907.

[54]On the gambling charge and its course see EOW-H, January 27, February 1, 2, 3, October 4, 22, 23, 1899; ODN, November 22, 23, 1899; EOW-H, February 24, and March 1, 1900.

[55]ODN, January 23, 24, 1902.

[56]ODN, November 4, 1901.

[57]Steffens, *The Shame of the Cities*, p. 1.

[58]Arthur and Lila Weinberg, eds., *The Muckrakers* (New York: Simon and Schuster, 1961), pp. 56-60; see also Louis Filler, *The Muckrakers* (University Park: The Pennsylvania State University Press, 1968), pp. 4-5, 56, 251-260.

[59]Filler, *The Muckrakers*, pp. 68-79.

[60]Josiah Flynt Willard, "The Machine is Trimming the City," EOW-H, October 28, 1901.

[61]*Ibid.*

CHAPTER III

Association

*. . . all emperors must accept
the company of their peers . . . .*
--David Halberstam

Unlike autocrats ruling in lofty isolation, political
bosses shared power with others. Their authority was dependent upon accommodations with other powerful figures in
their cities, be they respected business and civic leaders,
fellow politicians, or underworld lords. To hold and expand
upon positions of influence the bosses performed an ongoing
deft balancing act among their many clients, all similarly
striving to secure and enhance their own power base and
share of the benefits coming the way of the protected and
powerful.

The interrelated and interdependent nature of plural-
istic cities and machine politics is strikingly obvious in
the web of power relationships emanating from headquarters.
Often have the bosses been identified as power brokers, an
apt characterization of their importance as well as dependence. In a society based upon accountability of public
officials through the ballot box, they themselves were
accountable to those served and with whom power was shared.
Mutual support and mutual dependence were conditions of
existence for boss, businessman, and racketeer. "In the
great cities of the United States," we thus find "the existence of a powerful underworld, with its alliances with
businessmen and machine politicians, may be taken for granted."[1]

The word "alliance" is a reminder that the bosses were
skilled diplomats, employing talents basic to fulfilling
their role as power brokers. To bring together into one
effective system individuals and groups from the lowest to
the highest levels of society, securing rewards and satisfaction to all was an achievement entitling the boss to the

title *"diplomate extraordinaire"* as the necessary promises, compromises, and alliances were forged. The more skillful the diplomacy the more successful the boss. Like his counterparts, Tom Dennison developed a host of allies and alliances, with four names especially significant: a feisty newspaperman of national renown, Edward Rosewater; a businessman of the highest economic and social standing, Frank B. Johnson, a dapper man far from the limelight who sustained a close but secretive alliance with the "Old Man"; Dennison's alter ego and man Friday, William Nesselhous; and colorful Mayor James "Cowboy Jim" Dahlman. Each was a vital part of Omaha's political machine, contributing talents, perspectives, and contacts necessary in combination to flesh out the operation.

A figure all but ignored in studies of machine politics is the business boss. Walter Lippman and Lincoln Steffens grasped the role's importance, and in their travels about the United States carried with them a chart of "corruption of government." Upon arriving in a community all that was required of them was to discover the names appropriate to their template.[2] Prominent thereon was the business boss, conduit between his social and economic counterparts in the legitimate business community and the political boss. Many individuals of high station were reluctant to negotiate directly with the less than highly regarded professional politicians, a task readily assumed by the business boss. Communication was not all one way, however, for through his intermediary role he afforded access to well placed men and organizations otherwise blocked to individuals like low born and lower ward Tom Dennison.

Edward Rosewater had long been an Omaha resident by the time of Dennison's arrival, having established himself as a prominent Republican, editor, man of wealth and power. He forged an alliance with the much younger gambler, one which would advance his own numerous political interests and lay the foundation for the city's long reign of machine politics under his protege, Tom Dennison. Once described "as the best practical politician in Nebraska," Rosewater was a political fighter, a man "who knew the Omaha battlefield better than any living man. He knew its underworld and its upperworld, its captains, its lieutenants, its rank and file."[3]

The knowledgeable Rosewater was identified as the political mentor of Thomas Dennison by a long-time city editor of the *World-Herald* who asserted Dennison was "the creature of the *Bee*," the man Rosewater personally selected to educate in the intricacies of Omaha politics, to be lieutenant and heir to the teacher. Recently arrived from the gambling halls of the West, Dennison was taken in hand and schooled in district organization and the arcane topics of successful political action. The former newspaperman did not know exactly how the two men had come together, but was convinced the connection was well established. Similarly, another individual who knew Dennison and the period well was convinced the "Old Man" owed his Omaha political education to the *Bee's* editor. He went even further to assert that Rosewater was responsible for Dennison's coming to Omaha in the first place, going to Colorado and recruiting the gambler to come to Omaha and enter politics. "I heard this all my life from different sources," recalled William Zerbe, who repeatedly listened to Dennison refer to "my friend Rosewater."[4] Whenever and however initiated and fostered, the two men became political partners.

Soon the press, other than the *Bee*, was repeatedly charging the Rosewater-Dennison-Moores machine with running roughshod in Omaha and polluting politics (Frank E. Moores was mayor from 1897 to his death in office in 1906, the last year of his third term). In the twentieth century's very early years Dennison was a frequent target of diatribes in Joe Polcar's *Daily News*, in Alfred Sorenson's *Examiner* (for some reason referring to Dennison as the "Colonel"), and in the *World-Herald*. The *Bee's* pages, however, were markedly free of any assaults on Tom Dennison. Edward Rosewater died in 1906, but his pupil continued his association with the *Bee* and the family for a time through son Victor who became the paper's managing editor. A Dennison letter to Victor (see Appendix) conveys the casual tone of a communication with one well known, and a private investigator brought into town by Polcar to probe corruption in 1913 reported that Victor and his newspaper were "subservient to and part of the system."[5]

A powerful figure in Nebraska politics, Edward Rosewater's voice and influence had been nationally known, and he "was a confidante to J. Pierpont Morgan and Andrew Carnegie, and to President Benjamin Harrison and William Mc-

Kinley."[6] Thomas Dennison's famous political mentor was an immigrant of Jewish ancestry from the village of Bukovan, some fifty miles south of Prague, nestled in a valley of pines and poplars.[7] Herman Rossenwasser's first wife died after but a year or two of their marriage, and the first born of his second marriage, to Rosalia Kohn, was Edward on January 28, 1841.

Life in Bukovan centered on agriculture, with Herman in addition to caring for a few acres of land also serving as the neighborhood butcher. The boy attended elementary school in nearby villages, and stayed with relatives for one year in Prague while going to a Realschule. Edward's schooling in his homeland soon ended as letters from other relatives who had emigrated to Cleveland in the United States convinced Edward's mother that the family's future appeared brighter in America than with the limited opportunities in the old country. Moreover, forced military service was not far off for Edward, now the eldest of ten children, and the decision was made to leave. Years later Edward could still visualize the "sad and tearful faces of relatives before me and hear the agonizing sobs of mother as she takes a last look at the home in which she had lived since her married life began."[8]

On Christmas Day in 1854 the Rosenwassers landed in New York, beginning the New Year and their life in Cleveland on January 1, 1855. Soon the family name was changed to Rosewater, and the father and two eldest sons went to work. Edward and his brother became peddlers, not too successfully, and in the next three years Edward held several jobs: polishing tin and silver for a wholesale dealer, running errands for a grocer, laboring later in a dry goods store. In 1857 he received his only formal schooling in the United States when he spent three months at Hollister and Feltons's Commercial College, acquiring enough accounting knowledge to earn a position as bookkeeper in a wholesale willow and basket house. The firm went down in the crash of 1857 and Edward, nearing seventeen, was jobless. Along with an unemployed telegrapher friend, James Hamilton Warren, he left Cleveland to try for work in nearby communities. Ingenuity led them to open an employment agency in Sandusky, but they had no better luck in finding jobs for others then for themselves.

Meanwhile, Warren was teaching Rosewater the Morse Code, and on New Years Day, 1859, the tyro telegrapher returned to Cleveland anxious to become a professional. No vacancies existed for a young man with his limited skills, but he received permission from a firm to practice in its depot office. Three months as a volunteer followed, Edward honing his Morse Code abilities, rewarded by securing a job in Oberlin. Soon after he moved on to work briefly in Tennessee, then to a railroad station as telegrapher in Stevenson, Alabama. His introduction to the excitement of politics came during presidential election night in 1860, when he and other operators received instructions to transmit returns from their towns and counties. Consequently Rosewater was placed at the electoral center of Stevenson, witness to the excitement of partisan politics and its passions.

He moved to Nashville in the spring of 1861, but Jefferson Davis's proclamation in August that everyone in Confederate territory had to acknowledge his government within forty days or be considered an alien enemy, plus the severance of all dispatches beyond Louisville on order of Washington, D.C., on the thirtieth of that month, sent Rosewater back north. After a brief period with his family in Cleveland, he joined the Union Army as a telegrapher, assigned subsequently to the headquarters of various generals as fighting progressed. Rosewater was stationed in Washington in 1863, working in the War Department Building (later torn down to make way for a new State, War, and Navy building) at the corner of 17th and Pennsylvania Avenue. His post, on the second story next to the Secretary of War's office, was the nerve center of Union communications. Since there was no telegraph office in the White House, President Lincoln was a frequent visitor to the office, walking to the War Department Building to read dispatches on the war's difficult course.

New Year's Day seems often to have been propitious for Edward Rosewater and January 1, 1863, was no exception. That morning he was handed a message to be dispatched, signed by Lincoln. Over the nation's telegraph lines sped to Americans the words of the Emancipation Proclamation, propelled by the fingers of Edward Rosewater. Attending the President's New Year's Day reception a few hours later, Rosewater observed that among the large number of guests there were no blacks, a "rather singular" situation he thought, reflecting no great notice of the Proclamation.

Proximate to men of power, Rosewater received, thanks to his War Department service, a political education. His was an insider's view, affording opportunities for the able student to accumulate knowledge on the processes of government. "He had his eyes opened," wrote his son, "to the twists and turns of the political shaper and pretender."[9] Political interests stimulated in Stevenson were advanced for Rosewater in Washington, a city with but one reason for existence--politics. In the early fall of 1863 he took his skills and growing political acumen west, summoned by Edward Creighton on the recommendation of one of Rosewater's former telegraphy teachers.

A former Ohio wagon driver, Creighton had plotted the route for an overland magnetic wire system in 1860. Three years later he was serving as its general manager in the Omaha City headquarters, a location advantageous for connecting lines and relays. A shortage of telegraphers in Omaha led Creighton to contact an old associate, Anson Stager, the man who had allowed Rosewater to practice telegraphy in Cleveland several years before, and asked him to recommend someone for chief operator. Stager named his former pupil, who accepted Creighton's forthcoming offer and set off for Omaha in the early fall of 1863.

Traveling by train to St. Joseph, Missouri, Rosewater there transferred to a steamboat to continue the trip to his new home. The steamer *Emilie* departed on September 20, 1863, its passengers anticipating three days on the river to Omaha, some seventy-five miles away. Groundings and other delays, then a broken rudder, convinced Rosewater it was time to abandon the steamer. At Nebraska City he left the *Emilie* and completed his journey by stage coach. Rosewater's arrival preceded by but a couple months that of the Union Pacific Railroad, and he joined fellow Omahans on the banks of the Missouri River at 2:00 p.m. on December 2, 1863, for ground breaking ceremonies. The date marked the beginning of the railway west and Omaha's future as a railroad and stockyards center.

Rosewater did well on his new job and advanced to Omaha's Western Union manager, augmenting his salary by writing newspaper articles and working nights as a book-keeper for the Omaha National Bank. Returning briefly to Cleveland, he married Leah Colman on November 13, 1864. The couple returned immediately to Omaha, home for the rest of their lives, where they raised five children. Political interests grew apace with the family as Rosewater increasingly became politically involved in his community. In the presidential campaign of 1868 he sided with the "regular republicans" of General John M. Thayer, a Nebraska U.S. Senator, their group championing U.S. Grant. With Thayer's term running out, Rosewater feared his reelection would be endangered by another Republican faction which controlled the city's Republican paper, appropriately titled *The Republican*.

Never a man to approach a problem with less than enthusiasm, Rosewater convinced friends to support a new paper for Omaha, and he sought advice from eastern editors in the hiring of a managing editor. "Our Omaha Republican," Rosewater advised the easterners, "is in the hands of corrupt men connected with the Indian and Whisky rings."[10] A daily named *The Tribune*, was the result, with Rosewater serving briefly as its editor until his replacement, hired from Massachusetts, arrived. As he reflected on his experience, a glint appeared in the versatile Rosewater's eye as he confessed that "I felt decidedly flattered by my first editorial experience."[11] He was less sanguine about the fledgling newspaper's future and withdrew from the board of directors (*The Republican* and *The Tribune* merged in March 1871). Soon thereafter he also left the Western Union, taking the job of office manager with the Atlantic and Pacific Telegraph Company. Elected to Nebraska's lower house in 1870, he went on a leave of absence from his new employers to continue his political education at the state level.

During his term he led a successful impeachment against Governor David Butler, and engaged in a struggle for consolidation of the public school system in Omaha (to be governed by a locally elected board of education). Since his consolidation effort was opposed by *The Republican*, Rosewater decided a counter publication of some sort was necessary. In cooperation with another former *Tribune* employee, Harry Geralde, he decided to publish a fly sheet for distribution without charge to Omaha business establishments. In 1871 the first edition was ready, promising its readers the latest telegraphic information, local developments, and advertisements. Rosewater had suggested *The Omaha Punchinelle* for a title, explaining it brought to mind wit and sarcasm. "Why not call it the *Bee*," asked Geralde, "it gives honey and stings, and is the emblem of industry."[12] Geralde's idea was accepted and the new paper had its name.

Now an editor needed to be selected. Rosewater declined the position, telling his colleague he did not want his name to be associated publicly with the new and yet insignificant addition to Omaha's press. When the first *Bee* reached its readers on June 19, 1871, it was with Geralde's name as proprietor and editor. Six weeks later, on July 27, 1871, The *Bee*, until now largely an advertisement and theatrical sheet, was transformed from a handout to a subscription evening journal. Its editor-in-chief was Geralde, and Edward Rosewater was acknowledged as publisher and proprietor. When submitted to the voters in a referendum, Rosewater's school bill was ratified, but amid protests from other papers to the Atlantic and Pacific Telegraph Company about their employee venturing into journalism. He resigned and left telegraphy behind; not long after Geralde moved on and only Edward's name appeared as head of the *Bee*. The politician had his voice.

From this point to his death in 1906, he used it on behalf of an assortment of causes, two of his verbal assaults leading to physical exchanges. A racial comment by a probate judge printed in *The Herald* on July 5, 1873, provoked Rosewater to counter in the *Bee*. Joining the contest, *The Republican* published an article insulting to both Rosewater and blacks and he demanded an apology from A.D. Balcombe, *The Republican's* manager. Balcombe instead published a letter in his paper inviting Rosewater to apply to the proper person to get his fill of satisfaction. In response, Rosewater accosted Balcombe at 14th and Douglas and a fight broke out, Rosewater later claiming victory with some fifteen or twenty blows on his foe with his rawhide whip. Balcombe had a different version, boasting that he wrestled his opponent to the ground and sat on him until others broke up the fight. In any case, Rosewater "not ungrudgingly" paid a police court fine.

In a second fight Rosewater was quite obviously the loser, and for a time it was not sure he would even survive. An article in the the *Bee* in February 1876 made reference to a "colored den" on lower Douglas Street. The owner, Richard D. Curry, through *The Republican* protested the impression given of his establishment, only to have Rosewater answer in his paper that he believed in equality before the law and if Curry's place was a den for gambling and drinking the less said the better. A week later, Curry, a 250 pound former blacksmith, and a man named Smith Coffey encountered Rosewater outside the post office. Heated words were exchanged. Then, while Coffey held him, Curry beat Rosewater with a "lead-loaded slingshot," hollering he was going to kill him for giving his place a bad name. Finally pulled free by passersby, Rosewater was taken to a nearby drugstore for first aid, then home where he spent three weeks in bed, his life in the balance for several days. His condition was so grave that the wooden sidewalk outside his home was covered by carpeting to muffle sounds and police stood guard. Convalescence at home was followed by lengthly recuperation out of town. When Rosewater finally returned to the fray, the dark hair that formerly covered his head was gone, not to return.

Although his appearance changed somewhat, the spirit and political ambition remained undiminished and the campaign of 1876 found the militant editor back in politics. The *Bee* remained a Republican newspaper and in its pages in years to come Rosewater championed the secret ballot, direct primaries, and direct election of U.S. Senators. Rosewater used his paper to argue for regulation of railroads, postal telegraph and postal savings banks, and free and compulsory public schooling. He was an early proponent and strong supporter of what came to be Omaha's spectacular and successful 1898 Trans-Mississippi Exposition.

He opposed, among other things, monopolies, professional labor reformers, annexation of the Philippines, and medical quackery (including a street corner lady dentist who claimed to extract teeth painlessly, while nearby her brass band drowned out the cries of patients), and women's suffrage. His sentiment that politics was not a becoming activity for females earned him a debate at Boyd's Opera House with Susan B. Anthony during the suffragists national convention in Omaha in the fall of 1881. Prohibition he also resisted, not because he favored drinking (he was a near abstainer), but because he thought it was unworkable.

And in election after election Rosewater and his *Bee* lent backing to Republican candidates for local office and his vision of what was best for Omaha. It was these contests that induced Edward Rosewater, wealthy, socially prominent, to ally with a man and men able to deliver the votes capable of transforming his ideas into policy or preventing those he opposed. Rosewater's opinions, channeled through his newspaper, were influential ones, but insufficient in themselves to alter or direct governmental decision making. The editor's ambitions and considered courses of action needed electoral support in order for them to be transformed from Rosewater policy to public policy by officeholders reflecting his views. To that end Rosewater sought out a political boss, a man able to deliver on election day. Differing in class standing and profession, inhabiting different worlds in many ways, business boss and political boss found unity in their desire to manipulate public power to their respective advantage. And the key thereto was the nature of America's electorate at the turn of the century, amenable to benefits the political machine was prompt to provide in exchange for a vote--or in some other way contrive to secure.

Rosewater and Dennison became political allies in the mid-1890s, prominent newspaper man mentor to the gambler from the mining towns of the west. As early as the 1897 city election the *World-Herald* was scoring the *Bee* for shielding Dennison, the "policy shop king," asserting the gambler was right-hand man to Rosewater, furnishing money and serving as the editor's chief lieutenant.[13] In several opposition articles during the local elections three years later, the theme of the Rosewater-Moores-Dennison combination was a familiar one.[14] "Tom Dennison," Omahans were informed one afternoon, "notorious and desperate, is the premier of the kitchen cabinet that is engineering the fortunes of the Rosewater-Moores-Dennison ticket."[15] During the fall campaign for the school board, the *Daily News* warned the Republican ticket had been dictated by the triad, intending to bring even the schools under their machine for personal ends.[16] A deputy county attorney, complaining of the difficulty in securing evidence in Omaha through the police department, referred to the "Dennisonwater" organ of

74

the machine, "formerly known in its more lucid moments as the Omaha Bee . . . ."[17]

During the Pollock diamond theft case in Red Oak, on two occasions the Dennison-Rosewater connection became part of the public record, once directly, once inadvertently. At one point Shercliffe testified that Elmer Thomas had confided that he wanted to use the trial to display Dennison, the thief and gambler, and reveal "what kind of man the mayor, chief of police, and Edward Rosewater were associated with."[18] And when Dennison was on the stand, his attorney, W.J. Connell, after reeling off a number of facts, asked his client in a remarkable slip of tongue: "Now, isn't that so, Mr. Rosewater?"[19] Dennison denied any such alias, and "Rosewater" was stricken from the record and question.

During the summer of 1906 Rosewater pursued nomination for the U.S. Senate. Although he secured all eighty-eight of Omaha's delegates to the Republican party's August state convention, he lost there on the sixth ballot. On the evening of the last day of August, Rosewater went to his beloved Bee Building, entering through a rear door, greeting a fireman and janitress as he passed. They were not surprised to see him since he frequently made such late visits to roam about. The next morning about 10:00 a.m., Judge A.C. Troup opened his chambers in the Bee Building and found Rosewater seated lifeless on a courtroom bench. Apparently the man from Bukovan had entered the chambers, closed the door behind him, sat down, and there "his heart simply stopped," his panama hat "resting lightly on his hand. . . ."[20]

Years after death brought the Edward Rosewater-Tom Dennison relationship to an end, a visitor to the "Old Man's" office looking around the room saw on the walls pictures of people important to him: his late wife Ada, his daughter and two grandsons, Frank Moores, and Edward Rosewater.[21] The student had not forgotten his teacher and the alliance forged so many years before. For a time it appeared Victor and Dennison would sustain it, and a few references were made during the 1909 city election to an attempt to continue the Rosewater-Dennison machine. But seldom thereafter. Victor seemed to concentrate his energies on national politics, a level of no immediate concern to the city's political boss and their worlds had little to share.

Apparently Victor did not savor local politics as his father had, and increased competition from the *World-Herald* added to financial problems at the *Bee*. Victor decided to sell the paper and in 1920 found a buyer in Nelson B. Updike, a wealthy Omaha grian dealer. Updike went on to buy the *Daily News* in 1927, merging it with the *Bee* to publish the *Bee-News*. The Hearst chain bought that paper the next year, and in 1937 the *Bee-News* went out of existence, leaving Omaha with the *World-Herald* as its surviving daily newspaper. Shortly after selling, Victor Rosewater moved to Philadelphia, living there until his death in 1940.[22]

Edward Rosewater's death and his son's apparent disinterest or inability to succeed him meant a key role in Omaha's political machine was going increasingly unplayed--business boss. But where power is to be wielded there soon appears someone able and willing to assume the risks, rewards, and sheer satisfaction of being a power wielder. Rosewater's successor as Omaha's business boss, remaining so throughout the remainder of Dennison's political boss tenure, was Frank B. Johnson, prestigious president of the Omaha Printing Company.

There is no record of how he came to acquire the position, no suggestion as to whether he was a consensus figure among the business elite, nor of the nature of the struggle--if there was one--which crowned him paramount spokesman for the "upperworld" to Tom Dennison. But emerge he did, becoming a very silent partner in the machine, recognized among the politically knowledgeable of the times as one of Omaha's most powerful men. Despite clearly ranking as Omaha's business boss to political boss Tom Dennison, Frank B. Johnson with but a few exceptions succeeded in keeping his name far from public view. Resolutely he kept behind the scenes, his aversion to having his name appear in the newspapers just as resolutely honored, his family's prestige and status in the community accomplices to his invisible political prominence. Even long after his death the press took pains to avoid mentioning his name, alluding instead to his profession and role. In 1965, although Johnson had been gone for twenty-six years, an article referred to Dennison's having had "regular luncheons with a printing company president." Three years later a longtime newspaper-man reminisced about a "prominent business man who acted as sort of a go-between between Dennison and Omaha's business community."[23] As a result of Mr. Johnson's yearning for privacy there is little material available about him, but some suggestion of his scope and personality may be discerned in a poem. A rare exception to his general press invisibility came in 1917, at one and the same time marking the year he achieved enough power to be a target, but not enough to be immune as subsequently he would be.[24]

> If grandma has the asthma or if Fido has a fit,
>> If the worms are in the cabbage patch and raising hek with it,
> And if your next door neighbor throws his garbage in
>> your yard,
> Or the peddler sold you palm-leaf fans and said it was Swiss chard--
>>> See Johnson!
>>> Frank Johnson!
>
> * * *
>
> In the gentle game of politics he is a submarine
>> Who shoots beneath the surface and is very seldom seen,
> And those whom he is boosting and others that he's not
> Are generally satisfied no what matter what their lot
>>> For Johnson,
>>> Frank Johnson,
> Can always make them tickled with the treatment that they got.
>
> * * *

The "submarine" was the son of Samuel R. Johnson, an Indiana native who settled in Rock Bluff, Nebraska, in 1857 after various ventures in Missouri, California, and Iowa. Four years later Frank was born in Rock Bluff, then a thriving river town near today's Plattsmouth, Nebraska. In 1863 the Johnsons moved to Council Bluffs when that Iowa community was chosen to be the link with the railways west. Eventually all the residents of Rock Bluff moved on and the community vanished.

Samuel Johnson opened a wholesale grocery business in his new home, moving it and his family across the river in 1874 to Omaha. Success led Johnson on to other activities and his name became associated with a host of significant developments. He helped build and became president of Omaha's first city waterworks company, adding a few years later presidency of the Cable Tramway Company. He branched out into banking and served as president of the Nebraska National Bank, and as a director of the Commercial National Bank before retiring in 1884 and moving to California.

But Frank remained in Omaha, his family name well known in the city's highest business circles. He took a job as a messenger with the Omaha National Bank when he graduated from Omaha High School and rapidly won promotion to teller. He soon was in the company of the city's most esteemed men, the Creightons and Paxtons for example, and became a member of their poker playing circle. Deciding to try wagering of another sort, he left the bank and formed a commission house which foundered after short-lived prosperity. Various positions followed, some simultaneously, including with the Armour Stockyards Company, Omaha financial institutions, and selling for his father.

He found time for marriage and eloped with Maria A. Reed, daughter of Byron Reed. A premier real estate figure in the city, Reed was an Omaha pioneer who started his career in a small wood frame building. He was eminently successful and joined the small circle of Omaha's most wealthy men. Johnson, coming from considerable family status of his own right, now added the aura of "Reed" with his marriage to Maria. Involved in a bank in Sidney, Nebraska, in 1888, Johnson lost heavily when a cashier, who later committed suicide, embezzled large sums from the bank. The Johnsons returned to Omaha and Frank and Frederick Nye in early 1889 bought a newspaper founded in 1858, *The Republican,* Rosewater's old nemesis.

Their editorial efforts produced a newspaper described as brilliant: "Typographically it was a gem, and editorially it scintillated with wit, sarcasm, philosophy, politics, science, and art."[25] It was exalted as being ten years ahead of the town--which may explain why in nine months it lost $75,000; Nye and Johnson sold the newspaper in October to J.C. Wilcox, with the latter deciding to keep the job printing department. In 1892 Johnson removed the word "Republican" from the Omaha Republican Printing Company, and the Omaha Printing Company was born, the foundation of Frank B. Johnson's fortune as he guided and nourished it to major status.

Success with his printing company made Johnson almost as rich, it has been written, as his father-in-law and he became a skillful player on the Omaha stock market.[26] A man who made friends easily, Johnson was soft-spoken and placid, a peacemaker type rather than bombastic. A strong family man, he was remembered for his kindnesses at home, and the sense of enjoyment revealed when he was able to help someone. His mother-in-law never learned to appreciate his cigar smoking, some ten or twelve a day, but she was gratified when Frank (she always addressed him as Mr. Johnson) finally signed on as a member of Trinity Cathedral.

An editorial cartoon in the fall of 1917 called attention to Johnson's office activities and the fact they were not concentrated on printing. A line of characters under the heading "Frank Johnson's Mail," are depicted outside his office; they are a mixed group: a man on crutches, a black woman, a child, a couple of down-and-outers, but sharing one thing in common--need.[27] In fact individuals from all walks of life were drawn to his office, some seeking his influence in political or police affairs, others requesting employment recommendations, all aware of his importance throughout the city. A few dollars went to "touches" who made their way to his office on a regular basis (remembered from "the old days"), or more generously to business friends who might leave with $15,000.[28] Whatever anticipated returns Johnson placed in his political or financial books, he exacted one promise from his beneficiaries--secrecy. They were not to talk about his assistance. Anyone who violated the trust forfeited any future help.

When, how, and why Johnson became a major political figure in Omaha remains unknown, his sense of secretiveness successfully covering his career. So long as Edward Rosewater was alive he was outside the inner power circle, as seen in an 1895 confrontation when Johnson decided to run for clerk of the district court. During the Douglas County Democratic convention, Johnson secured the nomination for the position but surrendered it a few days later. The *Bee* had charged him with bribery of delegates and editorially remonstrated his business career was scarcely one to provide a basis for public confidence.[29] Johnson's withdrawal resulted not from these charges, claimed the *World-Herald,* but from being "bullied and bought" by Edward Rosewater.

According to the Democratic paper, Johnson was invited to the office of the *Bee's* editor on the Monday afternoon following the Saturday county convention. When the candidate arrived, he was told he had to leave the race because he had bought votes to secure the nomination. If so, responded Johnson, he did nothing different from other aspirants, including those of the citizen's reform movement whose expenses had been picked up by that noble organization.

Rosewater threatened to publish more material on Johnson, but the younger man retaliated he did not care so long as the truth were told. He would be forced out, promised Rosewater, adding that he planned to "blast him and his family," dig through his past, and disgrace him. "I never went after a man that I did not get him and I am going to get you now . . . ."[30] Still Johnson refused to withdraw, announcing as he left he did not intend to be bullied into doing so. That evening and Tuesday morning Rosewater kept busy, Johnson learned, informing members of Johnson's family by marriage, friends, and other associates that Frank was going to be disgraced and they with him unless he conceded the nomination. Finally, on Tuesday afternoon, Johnson was again summoned to Rosewater's office who made an offer: all of his campaign expenses would be refunded if he withdrew. Asked how much money was involved, Johnson replied $2,500. Rosewater protested the amount, but when Johnson pointed out that was the approximate figure the *Bee's* bribery charges against him amounted to, he agreed to provide the sum as soon as Johnson filed his withdrawal. Johnson decided to comply.

Over the next several years Frank Johnson's name is absent from Omaha's political news, the memory of the encounter and the perils of seeking elective office a political lesson well learned. Then, following Rosewater's death and Victor's less than enthusiastic commitment to local politics, the business boss responsibilities sought shoulders sufficiently broad to bear them. They were found on Frank B. Johnson and his long tenure as business boss began shortly before World War I. He was particularly well suited for the position and indeed fits the role to a measure well beyond even Edward Rosewater. Typically the business boss was a quiet partner, valued for his contacts in the reputable realms of finance and commerce. Although Rosewater was a member of the elite and therefore in a position to play the role of mediator, and accorded here the title of business boss, he was untypical of his kind in his flamboyance, never far from the center of publicity and publicly leading many a fray. Johnson, however, with his "submarine" description perfectly fits the profile of the powerful businessman become powerful politically, far from the surface contests for power but strategically crucial.

When Johnson became a force can be approximately judged, the how partially explained by Johnson's several advantages, including his personality. A practical man, he was yet daring when necessary (he had a great fondness for poker), calm and self-possessed. An image of strength emanates from a photographic portrait. In Omaha's business community he was a well known figure, well endowed to play the mediator role. His father's contributions to the city left a heritage to draw upon, as did that of his in-laws, pioneers of stature and wealth further buttressing his influence. His own success lent additional credence to his claim as spokesman for the socially elevated and financially mighty.

But why would a man with all of his advantages decide to commit himself to machine politics? Wealth, standing, influence, all were his and viewed from pre-World War I carried the promise of ever greater successes waiting in the future. In general one can say of political bosses that politics was their path to power and financial gain. Finding other channels blocked by established northern European groups, turn of the century immigrants or their offspring turned to political machines receptive to their talents and aspirations. But the business bosses were already successful men, men like Johnson, enjoying the privileges and comforts that wealth entailed; politics was unnecessary to vertical mobility and acceptance in the larger community. Apparently Frank B. Johnson decided to spend years as a business boss because he enjoyed politics and the sense of power his engagement provided, seeking neither publicity nor fame (few in Omaha today know his name or his place in the machine). Surely opportunities for financial gain were presented to a printing company with access to decisions regarding print contracts in both the public and private sectors. But it was for the power and pleasure of its exercise that "Johnson, Frank Johnson" was lured into politics and thence into the company of Tom Dennison.

Omaha's political machine for most of its years was led by an inner circle triad of Dennison, Billy Nesselhous, and Johnson, the last being the one "who pushed the buttons for them."[31] Often referred to as "the go-between" or the "pipeline," Johnson conferred with the political boss when the "better elements" wanted something done. And it worked in the other direction, since Dennison cleared with Johnson when the "Old Man's" constituencies were pressing him for action. An insurance executive recalled hearing "both at the time and far more recently that the so-called respectable citizen behind the Dennison gang was Frank Johnson of the Omaha Printing Company. I do not have any definite proof, except to say that it was generally the opinion of the so-called better social and business circles of Omaha that this was the case."[32] A Dennison worker is a more direct link, emphatically stating that Johnson and Dennison "were close, very close," adding with crossed fingers to emphasize the point they "were just like that."[33] Together they discussed forthcoming actions and "a lot of times I've heard Johnson himself tell Dennison right cold turkey, 'Tom, I can't sell that.'"[34]

The link between Dennison, Johnson, and the *Bee* came home to a young reporter just after World War I (the newspaper still a voice for the machine under Victor). Summoned to the editor's office the reporter was instructed to go see Frank Johnson and take down whatever he said. Then he was to write the story, "write it down just as he says it. Don't bother to check the facts or talk to anyone else. Mr. Dennison is interested in this story. It is the policy of this paper to print whatever Mr. Dennison or Mr. Johnson wants."[35] He was advised that Johnson would give him some money and he was not to hesitate to accept it for himself. The editor was correct, Johnson gave the reporter fifty dollars, more than his monthly salary at the time.

Printing company owner and political boss met in one another's offices, with Johnson in the earlier days of their relationship usually going to Dennison's behind the Budweiser.[36] After the War, there was apparently no pattern and Dennison sometimes went to Johnson's office a family member recalls. During the investigation resulting in the 1932 conspiracy trial, Dennison's office was under surveillance and a report on activities for March 3 duly noted Frank Johnson arrived at 11:25 a.m., staying only five minutes.[37] When the trial came to pass, throughout its two month course Frank Johnson was never mentioned, sustaining to the end his privileged secrecy.

Dennison and Johnson not only exchanged office visits, they were also in daily contact by telephone. Direct lines were on their desks and every morning Dennison called the printing company president, it was said, "for his daily marching orders."[38] Election day was of particular importance to both of them, of course, and getting out the vote was a shared prime goal. To assure voters made it to the polls, the organization made it a practice to hire all the rental cars available in the city on election day, assigning drivers to cover the wards. Car rental dealers were promptly paid, in cash, by Frank Johnson.[39]

Elections raised questions other than getting the vote out; for example, which candidates should the voters be called upon to endorse? Dennison's promoting Frank Riha for county commissioner one year resulted in a Johnson visit to the "Old Man's" 15th Street office. With Dennison's police officer secretary present, Johnson complained that supporting Riha was a mistake because he was in the printing business. If Riha was elected, Johnson predicted he would want to dictate all the printing and stationery jobs. Admitting Riha had been in several times to see him, Dennison promised his presence on the county commission would make no printing contract difference, and "you will get all that big business all the same."[40] He did not want anything upset Johnson countered, but left Dennison's office assured he had no cause for worry.

An attempt to assess whether Dennison or Johnson was the more powerful is pointless. They were partners, drawn together by their particular qualifications, relying upon one another not out of friendship or common goals but mutual need. Upperworld and underworld, voters and public officials, benefited from the accommodations and shared power their relationship vested upon the city. "Pipeline" and "Broker" are titles assigned to business and political boss, signifying not relative positions of power, but two prime and interdependent parts of a political machine. Henceforth, as Omaha's experience with boss politics is recounted it is Dennison's name that will recur while Frank Johnson's recedes, not because Johnson was insignificant but because of the nature of the topic. Business bosses were deep background figures, and Johnson's tight net of secrecy added a personal quality to enhance the institutional. Johnson's role placed him between his socially respected associates and Tom Dennison. Since businessmen relied upon their spokesman to remain out of public view, there is little to draw his name into the machine's actual operations.

On the illegitimate side of operations, there was another Dennison partner, although less a go-between in function since Dennison's need here for a spokesman was not the same as with Johnson's world. Dennison was not a guest or member of country clubs, a man whose family was featured on the society pages; but in his third ward he knew well "the Dennizens of the Underworld." Here an intermediary was unnecessary and he dealt directly with his lower downtown clients, sharing and understanding their part of the city. William "Billy" Nesselhous's niche in the organization was, nonetheless, in part as a pipeline, especially so far as prostitution was concerned. But his significance went well beyond that assignment, which was only a small portion of Billy's overall place in the organization and in Dennison's life. He was the "Old Man's" alter ego, sharing his innermost secrets, offices (in the 1920s the address for both was the same), and proceeds from their many endeavors. Turn of the century Omaha brought the two gamblers together and in a few years, working closely with his friend and partner, Billy "had reached a stage of importance so that he must be recognized as one of Omaha's most prominent and influential citizens."[41] Yet that assessment was soon forgotten since Nesselhous was content to dwell in Dennison's shadow, secure in the knowledge that "Whatever is Tom's is Billy's, and whatever is Billy's is Tom's."[42]

Born in Fairfield, Iowa, on September 1, 1866, William Nesselhous was the son of a harness maker and blacksmith who had changed the German spelling of Nesselhaus to Nesselhous. The father died while the son was still a child, but before the elder Nesselhous's death Billy met many race track followers and horsemen through his father's work, and developed a fascination with race horses and racing that lasted all his life. Work as a coal hauler became the boy's lot as soon as he was old enough to join the wagon trains between Fairfield and Ottumwa, Iowa, and he gained a step-father with his mother's marriage to Charles Withnell.

About 1885 Billy came with the Withnells to Omaha, and within a few years was known in saloons and on street corners with his shell game. He wore a swallow-tailed coat with a pocket in one tail that contained a dice box and a "stripper" (large roll of bills). Prospering from his street gambling, Nesselhous bought the Turf Saloon, selling it in turn to buy the Budweiser. By now he was in association with Dennison and together they ran a gambling room, laying the financial foundation for their future varied activities. The Budweiser was more than the word "saloon" connotes, for here came people from all classes to conduct business, celebrate, and enjoy the pleasures of a leading Omaha club. Greeting them all, Nesselhous made a wide range of acquaintances, and he was friend and friendly with bartenders, pool hall habitues, prostitutes, bankers, and stock brokers.

He had little formal education, but street life educated him to advanced standing in gambling mathematics. Billy was said to know the percentages of any game of chance, and identified himself as a businessman who relied upon them. Anyone was fair game who entered a Nesselhous backed gambling room, and he was quite pleased to take money from challengers of his carefully calculated odds. Love of horse racing led him to build a large stable of horses and they ran on tracks all over the United States. Three years before his 1937 death he sold or gave away all of his race horses.

Small and wiry in appearance, with a long face usually bearing a wry smile as though indulgent of the world, Nesselhous laid aside his swallow-tail coat to become a dapper dresser with an eye for pretty girls. His lifestyle varied considerably from the "Old Man's"; he loved to throw extravagant parties and played attentive host for machine social occasions. A visiting dignitary of upper or underworld did business with Dennison during the day then was turned over to Billy for the night. The Nesselhous posh suite at 333 Fontenelle Hotel was well known as the address where a drink was readily available despite prohibition, and where other pleasures were industriously attended to.

Although Nesselhous had many friends his activities did not earn him universal appeal: he was once described as having "just grew up out of the sidewalk." While he liked to associate with socialites, he was discreet, mindful his reputation was not one to place him on the social register and he wished to embarrass no one. He never married and was said to have disappointed many women when his will failed to fulfill the extravagant promises he allegedly had made. One of his affairs was with an acrobat and trapeze performer who came to Omaha once a year on tour. When "Dainty Marie," came to town, "Nesselhous would be among the missing."[43]

Unlike Dennison or Johnson, Nesselhous was not renowned as a soft-touch, although his pockets occasionally opened to people, albeit protestingly, he had known a longtime. But one family received gifts from him for years with neither request to him nor complaint from him. Every month for years a Chinese household of eleven children received $25.00 from Nesselhous to help pay for groceries, and Christmas was time for a shower of gifts. They were the grandchildren of a gentleman who had run a restaurant over the Budweiser, prohibition both closing the bar and causing him to lose his business.[44]

One effort to secure funds from Nesselhous for higher education earned a promise to think about it, but his death denied us the opportunity to discover what his decision may have been. In early December 1936, a member of the Board of Regents of the Municipal University of Omaha, an institution less than secure in the financial support it received, approached Nesselhous and suggested he make a contribution to the University. "The boys of Omaha," stated the regent, "have been pretty good to you." Nesselhous replied he had been an angel for about fifteen years; the regent then pressed him with "This would be a good way for you to do something nice for your city." He reminded Nesselhous the University needed $100,000 to enable the school to accept a government grant for a new building. Asking for time to think about it, Nesselhous agreed to meet with a group of regents after the holidays. He died before the meeting could take place, leaving us to wonder whether Nesselhous might have become a benefactor for the University.[45]

There was one part of his life that Nesselhous never

neglected, his mother's well being. He bought her a home in 1925 in an elegant neighborhood, at 5505 Farnam Street. The man who sold Nesselhous the property, George H. Payne, a prominent realtor who had built the house three years before, liked to tell the story about selling it. Meeting in Payne's office in an Omaha bank building to close the deal, Nesselhous presented the selling price in cash. Payne said "no," he could not accept that much money in his office; he would turn the deed over when the money was deposited and credited to his account downstairs in the bank. The men went downstairs and the transaction was accomplished. Nesselhous then turned to the cautious Payne and asked, "Did you think if I got you to take the money upstairs, I'd have a thug take it away from you on the way down?" All over the city he opened charge accounts for his mother, and was delighted when she used one. He visited her every afternoon and called her every evening at nine. When she died, some two and a half years before her son, he left his Fontenelle suite and moved to the Farnam Street home.

The man who looked like "he grew out of a sidewalk" owned other property in Omaha, investing his money in real estate as well as blue chip stocks and bonds (in his mother's name).[46] One of his last ventures was a thoroughbred Belgian horse farm. In 1935 he bought a 240 acre tract on West Dodge, about three-quarter miles west of Boys Town. He imported horses from Belgium and built a farm, a model of efficiency and modernity, with work on a five acre lake nearing completion at the time of his death.[47] Four to five hundred people attended his funeral at St. Andrews Episcopal Church, representative of all segments of Omaha life. Among the mourners that January day were George Brandeis, his name prominent because of the family's department store and buildings, and Joe Dugan, a "hack" driver. Sheriff Joe Hopkins was nearby, as was tough Joseph Potach, "the enforcer," long an associate of Billy and the "Old Man" in the organization. "Whitey the Apple Seller" came to show his respects, as did James English, County Attorney.[48]

The boy from Fairfield, the coal hauler and shell game artist, left an estate that well measured his ventures with Dennison. A summary of his holdings shows he left a little over a million dollars, holdings made possible from the profits of his and Dennison's numerous activities, beginning with their gambling days at the Budweiser and expanding to assorted gambling halls thereafter, from the River-side to the immensely profitable Friar's Club.[49] Known as the businessman of the alliance, Nesselhous seldom exposed his political hand, remaining so successfully in the back-ground that even Dennison lieutenants were unaware of his importance to the "Old Man" and the machine. Dennison val-ued his associate's judgment, a confidence placed in a friend not only for business matters but also political. Machine politics were based upon a system of loyalties and reciprocal benefits, but loyalties sometimes shifted and the successful boss had ever to be on guard for breaks in the ranks. Nesselhous was the man Dennison trusted above all others, knowing he was a constant and loyal ally.

Their relationship divided responsibilities; Dennison functioned as the political organizer, properly called the political boss, while Nesselhous tended to their gambling and other enterprises. Dennison rarely was present at Head-quarters in the evening, but Nesselhous remained on the job, the "Old Man's" agent, keeping an eye on their city. Between the two men there was never a written contract defining their tasks or designating percentages or shares. Their unwritten understanding with one another was suffi-cient and at the end of each month Nesselhous presented Dennison a roll of bills. Dennison the non-drinker had in Nesselhous a colleague who delighted in nights devoted to partying with individuals who warranted entertaining. The taciturn and reserved political boss was balanced by his outgoing associate, Nesselhous playing the role of genial diplomat to the blunt and frank Dennison. Whereas Dennison did not hesitate to rebuke or offend, saying little and expecting to hear little, Nesselhous went along with people and patiently listened to all they had to say. Appearing to agree with them and providing solace, he shortly thereafter reported all to Dennison.[50]

The "Old Man," Frank, and Billy were the inside powers of Omaha's political machine. Their respective talents and contacts combined into a well balanced operation, satisfy-ing to them and to those who depended upon the machine to satisfy their appetites, ambitions, and needs. None of the three held any public office during their long involvement in the city's political life. Dennison was the type of political boss who never ran for a position himself, pre-ferring anonymous manipulation from his dimly lit offices to the campaign glare and publicity centering on candidates. While he avoided the limelight, his two associates did so even more assiduously, remaining well hidden from public view, so much so that many Omahans were unaware of their deep political involvement.

Therefore, a public figure was needed, someone to take center stage and serve the organization's interests while satisfying his own desire for acclaim. Someone to be popular but not power hungry was necessary, a vote getter able to inspire followers but not demand too large a leadership role, one who understood--or could learn--the realities of power swirling around city hall. James Dahlman, a cowboy from Texas turned politician, filled those requirements and served as mayor of the city for twenty-one years. Death removed him in 1930 from the office he was first elected to in 1906, and only once in all those years, in 1918, did the voters fail to return him to city hall.

NOTES

Chapter III

[1]Gosnell, *Machine Politics*, p. 42. On the interrelated nature of upperworld, underworld, and political machines, see Merton, "The Latent Functions of the Machine," pp. 30-32.

[2]Steffens, *The Autobiography of Lincoln Steffens*, p. 596.

[3]Sheldon, *Nebraska: The Land and the People*, I, p. 748.

[4]Zerbe interview, September 16, 1979.

[5]Special Report, Kansas City Investigator CFMP, December 20, 1913, Rosewater Collection, Reel 3, Box 1927, Omaha Public Library. Hereafter cited as Rosewater Collection.

[6]Frank Santiago, "Fighting Editor, Rosewater," EOW-H, August 6, 1975.

[7]Victor Rosewater, "Biography of Edward Rosewater," typescript, Rosewater Collection, Reel 1, Box 1818. Information which follows on Edward Rosewater's life is largely drawn from Victor's biography of his father, unless otherwise noted.

[8]*Ibid.*, p. 5.

[9]*Ibid.*, p. 39.

[10]*Ibid.*, p. 58.

[11]*Ibid.*, p. 59.

[12]*Ibid.*, p. 67.

[13]EOW-H, April 16, 1897.

[14]EOW-H, February 20, 21, 23, 26, 1900.

[15]EOW-H, March 1, 1900.

[16]ODN, October 10, 1901.

[17]EOW-H, July 21, 1902.

[18]EOW-H, May 25, 1905.

[19]EOW-H, June 2, 1905.

[20]Rosewater, "Biography of Edward Rosewater," p. 280.

[21]EOW-H, January 3, 1930.

[22]EOW-H, July 12, 1940.

[23]*Sunday World-Herald*, May 9, 1965; also *Ibid.*, June 23, 1968.

[24]*Sunday World-Herald*, September 30, 1917.

[25]Sorenson, *The Story of Omaha*, p. 432.

[26]B.F. Sylvester, *The West Farnam Story* (Omaha: The Author, 1964), unpaged.

[27]*Sunday World-Herald*, September 30, 1917.

[28]EOW-H, April 6, 1939.

[29]Bee, October 6, 1895.

[30]EOW-H, October 10, 1895.

[31]Interview with Fred Boien, conducted by Orville D. Menard, March 25, 1980, Omaha, Nebraska.

[32]Interview with Jack D. Ringwalt, conducted by Orville D. Menard, August 7, 1979, Omaha, Nebraska. Also Zerbe interview July 7, 1979, on

the "pipeline" role Johnson played.

[33]Maher interview, October 23, 1979.

[34]*Ibid.*

[35]Dick Irving, "Reliable Source," *Omaha* (April, 1978), p. 14. Also Interview with Ned Williams, conducted by Orville D. Menard, August 1, 1979, Council Bluffs, Iowa. Williams was the reporter in question; Gordon interview, June 20, 1979.

[36]Interview with N.L. Refregier, conducted by Orville D. Menard, July 26, 1979; interview with William H. Thompson, conducted by Orville D. Menard, August 8, 1979, Omaha, Nebraska.

[37]Report, "Activities on 15th st, March 3, reported March 4, 1932." Towl papers, Box 1, Folder 1932, March, City Hall.

[38]Robert McMorris, "Like It Was," EOW-H, November 12, 1975.

[39]Zerbe interview, July 16, 1979.

[40]Letter, Tom Crawford to Irvin Stalmaster, September 14, 1932, Sorensen papers, Box 39, Folder 191.

[41]EOW-H, January 17, 1914.

[42]Bee, January 3, 1937; *Sunday World-Herald*, January 3, 1937.

[43]Maher interview, October 30, 1979.

[44]*Sunday World-Herald*, January 3, 1937.

[45]Bee, January 3, 1937.

[46]Nesselhous had a farm in north Omaha near the Florence area where he entertained, giving up the property when he bought the Payne mansion. He also owned land along the Missouri River, south of what is now Eppley Air Field, an area where the river bends and was known as the Hogranch.

[47]Bee, January 3, 1937. The Nesselhous farm here referred to, valued at $48,000, was given in his probate as: the south 1/2 of Northwest quarter, and the Southwest 1/4 of section 14, township 15, range 11, Douglas County. William Nesselhous, Fee Book 53, Page 353, Probate, County Court, Douglas County, Nebraska.

[48]Bee, January 3, 1937.

[49]Nesselhous probate.

[50]In addition to the January 3, 1937, Bee, and W-H, see "Statement of Grace Housky," Taken at office of William Welch at Logan, Iowa, at 8:00 o'clock P.M., June 23, 1932, as given in response to questions asked by Mr. E.D. O'Sullivan, and reported by James M. Johnson, Court Reporter, Omaha, Nebr." Sorensen papers, Box 35, Folder 67.

CHAPTER IV

Association-II

He was conscientiously honest. He was never for sale.
I never asked Dahlman to do a thing that was wrong.
--Thomas Dennison

Omaha's "perpetual mayor" was born in Texas on December 15, 1856, the fourth child in a family of seven. Home was a frontier ranch for his parents, Charles and Mary Dahlman, in De Witt County near Yorktown, some sixty-five miles southeast of San Antonio. Political turmoil in Germany ushered many liberals to America in the 1840s, among them Charles Dahlman. He lived for a time in New Orleans, but moved on to De Witt County in 1845, traveling by sea to Port Lavaca then by wagon to ranch and farm.

Much of the task of raising the family fell upon Mary because her husband was frequently gone buying and selling cattle. Wife and children assumed complete responsibility for running the ranch when Charles went to fight in the Civil War, and "The mayor's memories of his boyhood center chiefly around his mother . . . ."[1] Since there was no public school in the area, Charles Dahlman and other ranchers supported a private school to provide their children education, although school was sporadic and attendance similar on those days when the doors were open. But Jim was an able pupil and adult correspondence reveals a man at ease and competent in his use of the English language. Of his family's educational background, Dahlman claimed "My people were men of letters"; adding, "As well as I can remember, I recall my father saying that some of his ancestors were professors."[2]

At age fifteen Jim ran away from home, explaining years later that one day while plowing a field with his brother he decided a future on the ranch promised nothing but hard work for little in return. The next few years are obscure, Dahlman once saying he fell in with bad company,

93

and later boasting his youth was spent "with a rope in one hand, spurs on my heels and a six-shooter on my hip."[3] Returning home in his later teens a skilled horseman and cowboy, he went to work as a range rider for his father and other ranchers. Although not a large man, Jim was lean and tough, proud of his thick black hair. Leanness stayed with him all of his life, although his hair did not.

When Jim was about twenty an older sister married Charles Bree, a man considered by the new brother-in-law to be a shiftless and outlaw sort. Bree deserted his wife shortly after a child was born to the couple, and Dahlman let it be known he intended to shoot Bree the next time their paths crossed. Cross they did in a small town in Lavaca County, and as Dahlman approached a dance hall he had seen his prey enter, Bree, warned Dahlman was coming, came out with rifle in hand. Bree got in the first shot, never to take another as Dahlman's return bullet struck him in the forehead. He died within a few hours. "If I had not fired," Dahlman explained years later, "Bree would have killed me. As it was it was a miracle I was not hit."[4]

Jim Dahlman, twenty-two years old, fled Texas, leaving immediately for Arkansas where he stayed in hiding for six months. His closest friend, Bennett Irwin, joined him early in 1878 and the two young men set off by train for Omaha. Arriving there in March, they went west on the Union Pacific Railroad as far as Sidney, then headed north by stagecoach for their destination, the E. "Zeke" Newman N-Bar ranch on the Niobrara River at the mouth of Antelope Creek, twelve miles southeast of Gordon, Nebraska. Bennett's brother Billy was a foreman on the N-Bar, one of the largest ranches in the area, and the two Texans, surviving their first Nebraska blizzard en route, were taken on as hands, Dahlman under the alias of Jim Murray.[5]

During the next six years, Murray rose from cowboy to foreman in charge of trail herds, earning the trust and respect of his fellow cowboys and his employer. Just a year after his arrival he participated in a roundup credited with opening Nebraska's sandhills to the cattle industry. Indians were known to be able to survive in the hills' trackless miles, but it was believed neither cattle nor white man could endure their barrenness. When Dull Knife and Little Wolf, leading the flight of the Cheyenne Sioux, fled into the sandhills above Ogallala, the army finally gave up pursuit, considering those hills a greater enemy than the Indians.

But the richness of these lands was discovered in the spring of 1879, when Frank North unveiled their potential in a southern area until then thought dry, but henceforth called the lake country (an area to the west of the Middle Loup, North Loup, and Dismal Rivers). Newman cowboys made a similar discovery in the north about the same time. Dahlman was one of the men sent into the "wasteland" in April in a desperation move to see whether any cattle driven there by a ferocious March blizzard might have survived. In five weeks the Newman hands located their strays, about 8,000 of them, plus another 1,000 without brands, descendants of strays from other years. Far from being starved creatures, the animals were well fed and soon brought a large profit to the N-Bar. When he saw the cattle his men drove back to the ranch, Newman exclaimed "That's cattle country, by God."[6] Dahlman agreed with his boss, commenting in a speech years later, "From that time on the sandhills became one of the favorite cattle ranges of northwest Nebraska. In time ranches were located in the valleys and settlers followed the ranches. The opening of the sandhills dates from the spring of 1879."[7]

Two other memorable drives marked Jim's years with Newman, one leading from Oregon to Montana. Newman's men traveled by train to Oregon to buy the cattle, carrying in a shoe box the $300,000 in cash to pay for them. Because Dahlman brought through alive the highest percentage of the cattle of any foreman, he was presented by the N-Bar's owner a pearl handled revolver, a knife, and a holster belt to carry them.[8] In the fall of 1883, a year and a half after the Oregon effort, Dahlman completed another major drive. This time he came up the Texas trail from a herd roundup in Comanche County, Kansas, to deliver 2,880 head of cattle to the Standing Rock Agency in the Dakota territory.[9]

After the Texas trail drive to supply the Sioux with meat for the winter, Dahlman, upon Newman's recommendation, became the bookkeeper at the Pine Ridge Indian Agency for George F. Blanchard. While Jim had been leading the drive up from Kansas, Blanchard had hired Miss Harriet Abbott, a

Wellesley College student from Winterport, Maine, as tutor to his large family. She had never before been to the West and she and Dahlman, the Texas cowboy taking up his new duties in the early winter, met for the first time. In the spring of 1884 Jim became a brand inspector with the Wyoming Stockman's Association as cattlemen banded together to combat rustlers. The new position took Jim the short distance to Valentine, Nebraska, and the courtship continued. Years afterward, during his last visit to Chadron, he told a crowd at the Dawes County fair grounds about proposing to Harriet:[10]

> She came from Wellesley college, and was a sight for sore eyes. I fell in love, fell hard! We used to ride horseback over the ranch.
> I sure have enjoyed by [sic] visit to the ravines and nooks where we visited in those days and lingered at the spots where I popped the question. There were lots of them where "No" was the answer. But, the one where she answered in the affirmative--ah--that one was the best of them all.

In December Jim and Harriet married at Union, Iowa, where the bride's sister lived.[11] He had returned to Texas before the wedding to clear himself of charges in the Bree killing, and the newly wed Dahlmans quickly settled in Nebraska.[12] Although politics later called Jim many times out of the state, Nebraska henceforth was the Dahlman's home: first Valentine, then Chadron, on to Lincoln, and finally Omaha. Their two daughters, Ruth and Dorothy, were Nebraskans born and raised.[13]

They moved to Chadron in 1886 where Jim and a partner, Hank Simmons, opened a small ranch (the Half-Circle X) and a meat market. Edward Rosewater visited Chadron the same year and sent a glowing report to his paper:[14]

> As to Chadron I can only say that it eclipsed my expectations in every particular. I had an idea that it was one of those mushroom frontier towns that thrive only by dance houses, gambling shops, and a mixed traffic of whiskey, six shooters, and cowboy supplies. But Chadron is the most substantial city in the new northwest. The location is decidedly romantic, with the dark fringed hills of Pine Ridge as a back ground, and several buttes standing out like pyramids in the western horison [sic]. . . .
> That Chadron is to be one of the principal cities in Nebraska I am fully convinced.

For about a decade Jim and Hank prospered, years during which Jim combined local politics with his business interests. But with the depression of the 1890s, ranching lost its allure--and profits--for Jim Dahlman. Business presently took a distant second place to Dahlman's interest in politics and his life as a professional politician began. He had entered Chadron's political life almost as quickly as he went into business. Well known in Nebraska's rugged northwest country by the time he and Harriet moved to Chadron, Dahlman benefited from his reputation of being trustworthy, courageous, and as an individual it was better not to have as an enemy. He made friends easily, usually emerging within a circle of comrades as the group's leader, maintaining those friendships for years. His background and personality soon won him votes as well as friends; in 1886 in Chadron's first city council election (Chadron was incorporated in December 1885), James C. Dahlman was elected a councilman for the third ward, the first of a seldom interrupted lifelong series of electoral victories.

Reelected for the 1887-89 and 1889-91 years, he chose not to run for the council in 1891 or 1893. Two terms as councilman and sheriff overlapped as he also ran successfully for sheriff of Dawes County in 1887 and 1889, then only for sheriff in 1891, his reputation as cowboy and marksman not hurting his campaigns. In the 1893 race for sheriff he lost one of the few political contests of his career. But success returned the next year when he ran for mayor of Chadron without opposition, and it stayed with him for reelection in 1895, again without opposition. In fact, in those two campaigns just about all the candidates for city office ran unopposed. Nominees for mayor, clerk, treasurer, police judge, and engineer were assured victory by securing the sole nominations made for the offices at a Peoples Caucus.[15]

For his services as councilman and mayor, Dahlman earned fifty dollars a year, payable in half year increments of twenty-five dollars. That amount was supplemented by warrants drawn on the city's poor fund to pay Dahlman for boarding prisoners, as evident in a city council motion in November 1888 to reimburse him for $106.25.[16] While serving Chadron as councilman and mayor, Dahlman took the lead in bringing to the frontier city a gravity waterworks, answering an urgent need for a complete and adequate system.[17] Chadron secured workers for city projects with an 1885 Ordinance which ordered male citizens to appear on two designated mornings, spade in hand, "for two days labor."

Upon payment of three dollars to the city treasurer commutation could be purchased, but if there was no payment, and no appearance at eight a.m. on Main and Second Streets on the dates indictated, a fine of one dollar per day for every day absent was levied.[18]

While Mayor in 1895, Dahlman became involved in the effort to bring a Trans-Mississippi exposition to Omaha, the prize crucial for the city given the government and private money an Exposition promised to attract. Other midwestern cities were also interested, lured by the prospect of encouraging economic recovery, all supporting the idea the entire region stood to benefit from an Exposition by drawing attention to its resources and opportunities. A meeting of the Trans-Mississippi Congress held in St. Joseph, Missouri, in 1894 approved the general concept and the question of site became the main topic of the next year's Congress, held in Omaha.

Governor Silas A. Holcomb appointed Dahlman, a fellow Democrat and strong supporter in his 1894 race for the state house, to be a delegate to the Omaha gathering, both men having ties to the powerful William Jennings Bryan. Representatives from twenty-four states and territories west of the Mississippi attended the Congress, and Dahlman was named to a committee of five Nebraskans (by presiding officer George Q. Cannon of Utah, who was favorable to the Omaha site), to prepare a resolution on Omaha's behalf. Bryan was selected by the committee, not without some difficulty given "gold" and "silver" splits, to introduce the resolution to the full Congress. It passed unanimously and to Omaha in 1898 came the Trans-Mississippi and International Exposition, spectacular in the grandeur and beauty of its buildings and exhibits.

But first there was money to be raised and Dahlman devoted himself to the task, lobbying among Nebraska state legislators in the western part of the state. A resolution signed by Mayor Dahlman of Chadron, passed by the city council, was sent to U.S. Senators and Representatives from Nebraska and other trans-Mississippi states expressing hearty approval of the Exposition and requesting passage of an appropriations bill. "The material interests of Omaha," read the lawmakers, "will be especially benefitted by such an exposition."[19] Dahlman's efforts and those of many others, prompted by the leadership and faith in the project of Omaha's ambitious Gurdon W. Wattles, raised the necessary funds, these coming from local contributors, Congressional and Nebraska legislature appropriations, donations from other states, and from Douglas County and Omaha. On June 1, 1898, President McKinley pressed a button in Washington which activated electricity at the Exposition in Omaha and it was underway amid pomp and pageantry.

On the north side of Omaha a wonderland was created, a score plus of buildings with Grecian style facades housing exhibits from eleven states and a dozen foreign countries. Gondolas glided (sometimes clumsily and dumping their passengers) along a half mile specially constructed lagoon, moving between the Palace of Liberal Arts, the Palace of Electricity, the Music Hall, and other grandiose structures facing one another across the lagoon. Every nightfall ushered in the marvel and beauty of the illuminated buildings and grounds. On a smaller tract on a bluff overlooking the Missouri River, visitors (there were 2,613,000 by closing day on October 31) walked among reproductions of Moorish, German, Japanese, and Chinese villages, or on the Streets of All Nations. On the adjacent midway, the star attraction was "Little Egypt," advertised as "the hottest hootchie-cootchie dancer outside the streets of Cairo."[20]

By the time the Exposition opened James Dahlman was a veteran of twelve years of politics, a Democrat like many fellow Texans who had come north. When Silas Holcomb was elected governor in 1894, Jim had been rewarded for his support with an appointment as an oil inspector, giving him an opportunity to travel widely in Nebraska, expanding even further his range of contacts. Reelected two years later, Holcomb recognized Jim's efforts for the Democratic party with a job as one of the secretaries on the State Board of Transportation. It was time for the Dahlmans to leave Chadron and they moved to Nebraska's capital city, Lincoln, placing Jim at a focal point of the state's political activity.

By now well known in his own right, he also had a powerful political ally in William Jennings Bryan. As a delegate to the Democratic National Convention in 1896, Dahlman worked fervently--and successfully--to secure the presidential nomination for his friend from Lincoln. He was one of two Nebraskans who convinced a Georgia delegate to nominate Bryan, thus getting his name entered earlier than waiting for his own state to be called. Chairing the State Democratic Committee that year, Dahlman had a strategic and leading role in delivering a strong victory for his party and its candidates in Nebraska, although Bryan was defeated nationally. On two more occasions the former cowboy helped capture his party's presidential nomination for Bryan. As a delegate to the Democratic National Convention in Kansas City in 1900, and in Denver eight years later (in between he was in St. Louis in 1904), he labored behind the scenes for Bryan. During those years from 1900 to 1908 he was also a member of the Democratic National Committee and served on its executive committee.

Pointing his index finger at his audience, Dahlman was a spirited public speaker, his enthusiasm balancing his party's usual lack of funds. It was public speaking that first brought Dahlman and Bryan into their long relationship, one that steered the Chadron resident into state and national politics and transported him from the western edge of the state to the eastern. A legal dispute involving construction of the Dawes County Courthouse brought Bryan, a Lincoln attorney, to Chadron in 1888 and he and Sheriff Dahlman met. A political rally was scheduled in neighboring Gordon and Dahlman invited the visitor to go along with a number of Chadron Democrats. Bryan accepted and learned with the others a chair's worst fears were realized when the scheduled speaker failed to appear.

Dahlman asked his Chadron companions if anyone was interested in substituting, and when no one responded the young attorney from Lincoln offered to help out. The chair with relief accepted Dahlman's recommendation, and speak Bryan did, for some two hours, captivating his audience, winning congratulations not only for himself but also for Dahlman who had suggested him. For both men the event was significant: for Bryan it signaled his first important political address in the state and "he was launched on his political career in Nebraska";[21] it would take Dahlman beyond local politics into the state and national domains.

When Bryan ran for Congress two years later Dahlman watched with keen interest, and by 1892, although he did not reside in Bryan's district, interest had evolved to active support. He helped raise two hundred dollars for his friend's campaign, and traveled to Lincoln to assist as he could. Henceforth Dahlman, with Bryan's warm assistance, emerged as a prominent Nebraska Democrat, holding a series of offices in his party, championing and promoting Bryan through many a political battle. Dahlman proved to be an excellent organizer, shrewd in his judgments, laboring largely out of public view.

Dahlman and Bryan were personal friends as well as political allies, and during the 1900 campaign Jim traveled with the "Great Commoner" on his private car *The Rambler.* After the miles were covered and the speeches delivered, Dahlman was with Bryan in his Lincoln home to share the unsuccessful election night. In preparation for another try, Dahlman served as a special pre-Convention emissary for Bryan, his message delivered from Wyoming through the central states to the eastern--Bryan must be nominated unanimously on the first ballot. When the delegates convened in Denver Dahlman carried on his work, quietly, persuasively, and very effectively.

A biographer of Jim tells us "Perhaps more than anyone realized at the time or since, Dahlman was W.J. Bryan's very close friend and confidant."[22] A Bryan biographer relates that "From the day he chanced to discover Bryan's oratorical prowess in Chadron, Dahlman had been a worshipped, trusted promoter of Bryan's fortunes, who, to put it mildly, deserved better than he was to receive at his leader's hand."[23] The reference here is to a split between the two men when Dahlman ran for governor in 1910. Nebraska's Democratic party that year was badly divided, with Bryan threatened by the growing strength of Ashton C. Shallenberger who had been elected governor two years before.

When the state Democratic platform convention was held in Grand Island, Bryan forces were defeated on the political issue of the day: liquor county option. Bryan had introduced a county option resolution but without success, the "wets" carrying the day. Then Dahlman, an opponent of county option and prohibition, arguing they were wrong both morally and constitutionally since they aimed to deny people the right to choose for themselves, became a candidate for governor. In Nebraska's then open primary, Dahlman won the nomination over Shallenberger, thanks in large measure to anti-Shallenberger Bryan Democrats, plus Republican "wets" who crossed over to defeat the "dry" Shallenberger. Just a year before the governor had signed into law a Sunday and eight p.m. on other days saloon closing statute, a measure particularly unpopular in thirsty Omaha.[24]

Bryan had succeeded in bringing down Shallenberger, but now his party had a "wet" as its nominee for governor. Bryan's dilemma was whether to support his friend and loyal supporter Jim Dahlman, despite his "wet" position, or deny support in the name of his own well known reputation as a "dry." In a speech delivered in Lincoln Bryan made his choice clear, attesting principles were more important than men. Therefore, announced the "Great Commoner," even though Dahlman had won enough votes to win the nomination for governor, he had no moral right to the office. Bryan the Democrat threw his support to the Republican candidate, and Chester A. Aldrich became the next governor of Nebraska.

Intimacy and trust between the "Great Commoner" and the Cowboy were shattered by the campaign, and although a cordial relationship was restructured they were never on the same terms as prior to the 1910 election. Bryan did not forsake his old champion completely, as demonstrated in a 1914 effort he made to secure Dahlman an appointment as Collector of Internal Revenue for Nebraska. However, the issue became embroiled in a patronage dispute between Secretary of State Bryan and Senator Gilbert Hitchcock as they bitterly competed for leadership of the Democratic party in Nebraska.

Bryan suggested Dahlman for the collector's post, with a Mr. Gruenther championed by Hitchcock. A compromise was suggested by the Senator, but a series of meetings and exchange of correspondence among Bryan, Hitchcock, Secretary of the Treasury W.G. McAdoo, and President Wilson failed to resolve the dispute, largely because of Bryan's evasiveness and procrastination. After months of delay, McAdoo tired of the controversy and he informed Hitchcock he was going to forward names for two vacant posts in Nebraska under his department, one being that of collector. He enjoined the Senator's cooperation, but pointed out he would perform his duty of making the recommendations with or without it. If his men were defeated, concluded the Secretary, Republicans would continue in the posts but he,

McAdoo, would no longer be responsible for the situation.[25] Dahlman's name was not one of the two and he failed to get a federal job. Shortly before Bryan's death, he wrote a letter to Mrs. Dahlman in which he summarized his years of working with her husband: "And he was a loyal friend in all my campaigns. It was always a delight to agree with him on public questions--which we nearly always did--and a great distress to differ with him on anything."[26]

Although Dahlman failed to secure appointment as Collector of Internal Revenue in 1915, he was reelected that year to his fourth consecutive term as mayor of Omaha, the city he had moved to in 1898. Although service as a secretary of the State Board of Transportation was politically advantageous, it offered little financial or tenure security. When an old Texan friend offered "Cowboy Jim" the opportunity to return to the cattle business he was ready to accept. He became secretary of the Flato Livestock Commission Company's Omaha office, and the Dahlmans moved from Lincoln to the city on the banks of the Missouri River. They moved into a house at 2901 Hickory, near Hanscom Park (not too far from the stockyards), and made it their home; it was the sole Omaha address they ever had.

Knowing the ranching industry from cowhand to rancher, bearing a broad range of friendships both within and without Nebraska, Dahlman prospered in the livestock commission business. By the end of 1905 he was president and general manager of the American Livestock Commission Company, becoming assistant manager of the National Livestock Commission Company of Chicago when the two consolidated on New Year's Day. His salary was a respectable $6,000 a year. During his first years in Omaha, Dahlman was politically active as a member of the Democratic National Committee and in the party's national conventions. Given his political experience, his contacts, his congeniality, and his way with words, it is little surprising Jim Dahlman's name emerged when Omaha Democrats began looking for a contender for the 1906 mayor's contest. Frank Moores, the incumbent, was nearing the end of his third term, but a serious illness foretold there would be no fourth. Confined to his home the last three months of his life (he died on March 23), Moores's condition had both parties searching for a successor by the end of 1905. Seeing an opportunity finally to win city hall, something they had not been able to do since James E. Boyd left the office in 1886, the Democrats scanned their ranks for a candidate.

A leading Democratic party organization, the Jacksonian Club, early on favored attorney Edward P. Smith, who was willing to make the race with law enforcement a major theme (thus Dennison a target). Stories vary somewhat as to Dahlman's emergence, but all agree he was sought out to make the race. Dahlman once explained he was in his commission office one morning and received a telephone call from a fellow downtown. His caller asked him to join him and a few others for lunch, during which they planned to discuss the political situation. Jim accepted the invitation and "The upshot of the whole thing was that I was talked into becoming a candidate on the democratic ticket."[27] Another description finds a group of businessmen coming to Dahlman, lamenting the long years since Omaha had a Democratic mayor and urging him to declare his candidacy. Succumbing to their pressure, he agreed, making his announcement to the Jacksonian's members by breaking into a secret meeting and declaring himself a candidate.[28] Pledges of support in hand from his business friends he proceeded to win the Jacksonians over.[29]

In a newspaper version, about thirty Democrats, representative of wards throughout the city, held a meeting in the Paxton Hotel's cafe, there passing a resolution calling for James Dahlman as nominee for mayor. A committee of three was appointed to request his acceptance, going to him directly from the Paxton, only to be told by their would-be standard bearer he did not care to discuss the matter since he had not given it much thought.[30] Dahlman did, however, agree to think their resolution over, promising to give his answer the following Saturday (it was Wednesday night) at a center of Democratic politics, George Roger's Cigar Store. True to his word, Dahlman appeared on time and gave the anxious men his response--he was in the race for mayor![31] Whatever the exact fashion of Dahlman's decision to run, in the face of Dahlman's support Smith withdrew his name from any further consideration and the Democrats had their candidate.

While the Democrats fairly easily settled on their champion, the Republicans fought an internecine primary war that divided the party and facilitated Dahlman's way into city hall. A three way race developed for the party's mayoral nomination, revealing not only party splits but placing Rosewater and Dennison behind different candidates. Erastus A. Benson was the early choice of the Fontenelle Club, an organization of elite Republicans who saw no distinction between loyalty to the Club and the Republican party. Indeed a candidate seeking its endorsement had to sign a pledge vowing loyalty and enthusiastic support of the organization and accept "reciprocal duties."[32] Outsiders who attempted to secure endorsements against insiders "lasted about as long as a chunk of angel food cake at a hobo reunion," charged a member of the Equal Rights League, a group created to combat the party's Fontenelle wing.[33] Organized during the fall of 1905, the League was financed by Rosewater and Gus Hennings and quickly attracted a large following.

Not surprisingly Rosewater's choice for nominee became fellow League organizer Hennings, but Moores and Dennison did not concur, thus splitting the Rosewater-Moores-Dennison machine for the primary. Something had happened to alienate Moores from Rosewater, and Dennison decided to stay with Moores. It was a political split not to be healed during the campaign and Dennison and Rosewater backed different slates in the city's run off elections. It proved to be Edward Rosewater's last city campaign, with firm Republican Victor and pragmatic Republican Dennison carrying forth the division initiated in Dahlman's first. Victor and Dennison did later cooperate on certain issues, but when it came to Dahlman they divided, Dennison always supporting "Cowboy Jim" and the *Bee* as consistently in opposition.

When the ailing Moores announced his support it went to William J. Broatch, throwing his weight behind an old enemy as the price of challenging Rosewater and Hennings. Shortly before his death the Mayor exclaimed there was one thing he wanted to do before he died--"to skin" Rosewater and Hennings. A means of skinning was to defeat Rosewater's choice for mayor. Dennison followed Moores's lead, although he was said to admit privately after Moores's death that Broatch had little chance of winning. In fact the machine was described as going to pieces even before Moores's demise. In such an environment, a "well posted" Republican observed Rosewater might think he could take the machine to Hennings, "but he didn't reckon with Tom Dennison, who has been his bosom friend for years, and with Frank E. Moores."[34] With the two men going over to Broatch, Rosewater lost the bulk of saloonkeepers and gamblers, important sources of campaign funding.

When primary day arrived Benson won the nomination with Broatch running third, the successful Republican nominees for city offices all Fontenelles. Broatch carried only three of the city's twelve wards, the first, third, and tenth, the last two dependable machine enclaves. Broatch's second best effort was in the tenth ward where he received 272 votes. His heaviest support came in the third ward, not surprisingly, his total there 431 votes to Benson's 126 and Henning's 110. In the core of Dennison's third ward domain, the second precinct, only nine votes were counted for Benson and nineteen for Hennings. Despite Broatch's lopsided majorities in the third ward precincts, he was unable to draw enough votes elsewhere in the city to secure the nomination.

The results demonstrated something about the extent and nature of Dennison's influence. His third ward delivered votes as he directed, but its overwhelming majorities were not sufficient in themselves to elect candidates or carry issues. In order for him to prevail, voters elsewhere in the city had to be at least moderately favorable at the polls to his choices. If they were not the machine might be defeated and sometimes was, as in the 1906 primary. Thus the necessity for alliances and compromises, and a reminder Dennison's power was shared not absolute. A reminder also the third ward's strength was decisive when the rest of the city was fairly evenly divided, or when lesser offices were at issue and little public attention focused on them except in the third.

Dahlman ran unopposed on his side of the primary, thus the contest for mayor was narrowed to the Fontenelle's man and the Democrat from Chadron. The split in the Republican ranks was not healed following the primary, indeed it worsened. Influential members of the Fontenelle Club had been able to nominate their man thanks to party divisions, but now they learned their nominee was probably going to be deserted rather than rallied to by other Omaha Republicans. Two important groups, certain businessmen and the "liberal element" (saloonkeepers and gamblers), saw in Benson a threat to their livelihood, fearing if he became mayor a prohibition campaign was likely to follow.[35]

A Benson victory was therefore interpreted as leading to a fight directed against saloons and related activities, resulting in restrictions or closings. The impact would go well beyond the "sporting" district, for breweries, real estate holders, and sundry other interests faced financial losses in a cleanup campaign. To safeguard their income, concerned businessmen became active on Dahlman's behalf, perceiving him as much more inclined to tolerate activities essential to their well being than his opponent. Prominent Republicans spread the word a Dahlman win was necessary to avoid a crusade against vice. Likewise, the saloonkeepers, madams, and gamblers who had supported Republican Moores now turned to Democrat Dahlman in the face of the Benson threat.

Unable to endure the switch to support a Democrat, Rosewater placed the *Bee* behind Benson, albeit in lukewarm fashion. An endorsing editorial predicted he would perform his duties with credit to the community, and with less than a sense of enthusiasm commented Benson was "fairly well informed on city subjects."[36] A week later the *Bee* carried a full page feature on Benson, with pictures of his family and home, with coverage of his campaign meetings on subsequent days. Dahlman was seldom mentioned in the *Bee*, and disparagingly when it did so. Not until late in the contest did the paper even indicate it knew he was running, finally printing a story about Dahlman being known out west as a gambler, the kind of man who played all night disapprovingly reported the *Bee*. A few days later a Dahlman gathering was labeled a three-ringed performance by Rosewater's paper, featuring a quartet, lots of funny stories and quips. An amusing evening said the *Bee*. Benson dismissed his opponent as a newcomer, comparing him to the boy in Sunday school who, when asked by the teacher who led the Israelites through the Red Sea, answered he didn't know because he just came into town last week. Two days before the election, a *Bee* editorial scored the Dahlman campaign as "in the order of a huge joke." Dahlman was posing as a courageous cowboy asserted the *Bee*, when in fact he was without business or property, and lacked any substantial backing.[37]

The last charge offended not only people at the *World-*

Herald, strongly behind Dahlman, but also Tom Dennison. The saloon and gambler elements with reasons to fear Benson were concentrated in the "Old Man's" third ward and their concerns were his. Party label mattered little to the political boss; what was important was protecting his clients' interests and thereby his own position. Large-scale defections by Republicans to the Democratic candidate were predicted, explained by one dissident as a case of having to do evil (vote Democratic) so that in the long term good would prevail. "That is the way it will have to be this time. We can stand the democrats for one term, but we can't afford to let this Benson bunch get such a grip that they couldn't be pried loose for a dozen years."[38] Little did he know that not one Dahlman term was in store but eight.

A deft campaigner issued from Dahlman's political experience. Plain spoken and humorous, his speeches were appropriately sprinkled with pledges of broad appeal: economy of administration, reduction of taxes, gas at a dollar or less, municipal ownership of public utilities, a crack down on crime and the "social evil," a fight against the corporations, and an end to Fontenelle machine rule. During one of Dahlman's addresses, a heckler shouted "What about the cowboy?" The question was made to order, giving Jim the opportunity to describe himself as a ranch hand who could ride harder and rope faster than any man he ever saw. And once in city hall he promised to be just as hard and fast. When he first met Teddy Roosevelt, Dahlman concluded, the future president was a cowboy. During another speech he returned to the theme as he again countered the "just a cowboy" comment. The man from Texas and western Nebraska said if a cowboy was acceptable in the White House, one was good enough to be mayor of Omaha.[39]

Dahlman detractors, pursuing the cowboy image, claimed if he was elected mayor he wouldn't even know how to write a veto message. Jim's retort was that if an ordinance came before him that was not in the peoples' interest his veto message would say everything necessary to be said. "I would write across it 'Nothing Doing' and sign my name. Do you believe the average man would have any difficulty in understanding that veto message?"[40] On election day voters responded they understood they wanted Jim Dahlman to be their mayor as Democrats swept the city offices, only one lone Republican able to win a seat in city hall. Dahlman's personal appeal, Dennison's backing, the rift in Republican ranks, entwined with fears of Benson, sent the first Democrat to sit as mayor in the fifteen year old city hall. Benson was able to carry half of the twelve wards, but the winner's large margins in the second, third, and tenth wards assured his victory. (Total votes were 7,388 for Benson to 10,182 for Dahlman.)

Dennison's efforts in the third ward resulted in the highest turnout in the city and gave Dahlman his highest ward total: 1,406 to 274 for Benson; the new mayor's second highest total came in the machine's reliable tenth, where Dahlman received 1,138 votes to Benson's 343. The second ward was third highest for Dahlman, with 1,177 votes cast for the winner, and 374 for his opponent. Within the third ward stronghold, the second precinct voted 420 for Dahlman, 22 for Benson, with its neighbor the third mustering 67 votes for Benson while turning out 373 for the winner.[41] Friend Bryan was on a worldwide tour at election time, and when word of Dahlman's victory reached him he sent a postcard with the lavish message: "All Asia rejoices."[42] Bryan returned from his tour in August, met by Dahlman and a delegation of Nebraskans on a tugboat in New York Harbor as his reception committee. From the tug's deck "Cowboy Jim" lassoed the voyager, a greeting which brought considerable publicity to Omaha's new mayor.

Dahlman demonstrated broad city support in becoming mayor, but votes in Dennison territory assured the victory and announced the "Old Man's" strong preference in the election. In other wards the vote was fairly close, but not in the second, third, and tenth wards. Returns in these wards clearly show Dennison was backing Dahlman in the election, moving from his customary Republican posture to help crown a Democrat mayor. Dennison's support of Dahlman is revealed in other than the voting returns. During a 1907 libel trial, a Dennison political opponent, Robert Smith, was on the stand attesting to his foe's bad reputation. Cross-examination by Dennison's attorney was carefully and artfully conducted to bring out the witness's prejudice against Dennison, arising from his support of Moores and Dahlman in their races for mayor. When Mayor Dahlman took the stand to testify on behalf of Dennison's reputation, he was asked whether Dennison was a supporter when he ran for his office. Replied the mayor, "Yes, he was."[43]

Finding in Dahlman an effective vote getter, a man not disposed to insist on too strict law enforcement in matters of morals, Dennison faithfully supported "Cowboy Jim" in the string of elections of future years. Popular among Omaha's wide variety of ethnic groups, Dahlman became affectionately known as "Jimmy the Dahl," honest, uncomplicated, and quite a showman. Usually the third ward's polling places were the busiest in the city, and resounding totals were turned in for the "Dahl."

The Republicans were still divided as the 1909 city election drew near, with Victor Rosewater now standing in his father's place against the Fontenelle Club. Rosewater backed Harry Zimman, a well known third ward politician for Republican nominee, the Fontenelles throwing their support to John Paul Breen. Dahlman had only one challenger on the Democratic side, Edward Berryman, and the mayor's renomination was little in doubt. In the primaries "the Dahl" garnered more votes than any other candidate in all but two wards, one of them the third where Zimman's second precinct showing gave him top place. Elsewhere Zimman did not fare as well and the nomination went to John P. ("P" for Prohibition his opponents now claimed) Breen. A lusterless campaign ensued, Rosewater supporting Breen to the extent of not supporting Dahlman. The Republican party's executive committee repaired somewhat the rift in the ranks by requesting Rosewater to write a platform capable of acceptance by the committee and the candidates. It was widely acknowledged Rosewater was skilled in such endeavors, although one skeptic remarked "He will probably get it so slick that the whole ticket will slip up on it when they try to stand on it."[44]

On election day not all the Republican candidates slipped since half of them were elected. But mayoral hopeful Breen went down to resounding defeat as Dahlman was rewarded with an even larger margin than he had amassed three years earlier. The challenger carried five of the twelve wards, but in none did he come close to matching Dahlman's numbers in the second and third wards. Breen's highest single ward total was 978; "Cowboy Jim's" supporters gave him 1,240 votes in the third (Breen accumulating 174, his lowest in the city), and 1,114 in the second (where Breen ended up with 360). The faithful second and third precincts of the third ward (there were five in all) were well delivered: 380 and 268 for Dahlman to 29 and 34 for Breen respectively.

As the 1912 elections approached, Omahans anticipated important changes because the city was going to elect its first government under the recently adopted commission form. Proponents of the change to nonpartisan elected commissioners, who in turn would select the mayor from their ranks, had advocated their new system as the means to weaken the "Old Man's" political machine. Voters had agreed to the new form of city government on September 2, 1911, by two to one; in only two wards did it fail to carry--the third and the tenth. However, the customary large voter turnouts failed to materialize in those wards to pass judgment on the commission form. The third ward's polling places, usually the busiest in the city, this time were third from the bottom, only 445 people bothering to vote (314 "no" to 131 "yes"). Apparently the machine had determined the *Bee* inspired change posed little threat to its dominance. The ability to get out the vote and have it properly cast was appreciated at the Budweiser as more significant than tinkering with the structure of government.

Over Victor Rosewater's signature, a petition containing 6,041 names (1,700 more than required) had been sent to Mayor Dahlman on July 27, 1911, requesting a special election on adopting the commission form of government in Omaha. The well educated Rosewater was a devoted structural reformer, anxious to have Omaha move in the same direction as other cities who were modernizing their city governments. A special election on the question was duly called by the mayor, the proposed change was adopted, and the voters went back to the polls the next spring to elect their first seven commissioners.

The machine easily demonstrated that change in structure was less important than getting out the vote. In the May 1912 runoff election, every voter could vote for seven of fourteen candidates, the top seven to be seated as city commissioners. The officially nonpartisan slate led by Dahlman, the Square Seven, consisting of four Democrats and three Republicans, was elected in its entirety. In Dennison's third ward Dahlman received the highest number of votes cast in any ward for any of the fourteen candidates, running second in city totals to fellow Square Seven candidate Charles Withnell. Not unexpectedly the Square Seven ran strongest collectively in the third ward, and there the Citizen's Union was expectedly least popular. The Dahlman led slate accumulated 9,065 votes in the third ward to a puny 1,197 for its opponents. Dahlman was duly selected by his commissioner colleagues to retain his title as mayor.

A dull campaign in 1915 was most notable for the widespread sentiment Dahlman was a sure bet to be reelected to the city commission and continue as mayor. All seven incumbents were renominated with strong third ward support, only one of them not placing among the city's top seven. Seventy-three names had confronted voters on the primary ballot and "Jimmy the Dahl" won more votes than any other candidate. Victor Rosewater, as three years before, generally shied away from the Square Seven, distancing himself in particular from Dahlman in the runoff. The mayor's position was so formidable that administration opponents satisfied themselves with a Big Six slate, conceding the seventh place to the popular mayor. And win he did along with four of his Square Seven colleagues, two of the Big Six succeeding in joining them on the new city commission. "Cowboy Jim" continued in his job as mayor. But three years later his long incumbency was broken, at least temporarily, when Omaha voters decided it was time for a change.

Primary day in 1918 reflected an atmosphere of electoral dullness, a light turnout ending apathetic campaigning by the seventy-five candidates who had filed for the city commission. Dahlman set the tone when he formally launched his effort to hold his job by announcing politics was secondary to the war effort, adding he regretted a political campaign at such a time but owed it to himself and his associates to run again.[45] Omaha's newspapers reflected the nation's attention to the war, and little was said in their pages about the forthcoming primary. When it took place in early April, five of the six commissioners seeking another term were renominated. Dahlman easily ran well ahead of his announced rival for mayor, Edward P. "Ed" Smith.

However, within the next month the "outs" mounted a strong effort to discredit the "ins." The campaign's tone was sounded in a speech by candidate J. Dean Ringer. It was his intention, he declared, to become head of the police department and then to clean up the "bunch of crooks" in a "certain well known ward" who had been disgracing the city for years.[46] Omaha church leaders and groups joined the fray, anxious to help cleanse the "cesspool of iniquity." Administration opponents closed ranks as an Allied candidate slate promised an end to bossism and machine rule. "Demon rum" was a familiar target, for despite prohibition (Nebraska had gone "dry" in 1917) the opposition lamented Omaha remained awash in liquor. Other infractions of the law abounded, charged the challengers, because of the corrupt police department.

Realizing the strength of Dennison and his associates resided in their ability to get out the vote, the Allied candidates devoted themselves to a similar goal. A bitter dispute broke out when certain churches sent members to stand near public school grounds, handing campaign information to children for delivery home. When critics charged the material was unfit for children's eyes (a mention of prostitution), the now dubbed "Church" slate's defenders piously replied the smaller children were unable to read it.[47]

A longtime city editor of the *World-Herald* recalled a statement alleged to Dennison early in the campaign: "I think we better let the bastards have it their way for awhile; let's lie low this next election--they'll be glad to see us back." When the votes were counted only Daniel B. "Dan" Butler of the incumbents survived. Dahlman was beaten, with Thomas Falconer the only individual besides Butler recommended to the voters by Dahlman successful--and Butler had said his name was on the slate without his consent, while Falconer disclaimed any association with Dahlman.[48] Five of the Allied took their places on the city commission, including Ed Smith, duly elected mayor. Although the third ward came out strong for Dahlman as usual, even there he ran second to Butler; overall in the city "Cowboy Jim" ran tenth. And instead of the Allied candidates running poorly in the third, as was usually the opposition's fate, Smith, Roy Towl, and Harry Zimman all did very well.[49]

The reformers' success may in part be attributed to the machine's lying low, permitting a rare vote getting opening. Opponents of the Dennison-Dahlman combination seized the opportunity, and men dedicated to its defeat argued strongly and persuasively about the need for cleansing and change. They were staunchly supported by the churches, and long-time allies of Dennison, the liquor and associated interests, were unsure of themselves in their new prohibition environment. Finally, a war waging in Europe relegated local politics to the shadows so far as news coverage was concerned, and produced an atmosphere conducive to electoral change. The nation's troops were abroad fighting for democracy while charges were hurled about at home condemning a political machine for too long exercising dictatorial power. Best to win and secure freedom on both fronts.

The new commissioners entered office lacking internal unity despite having campaigned on the same slate. Two factions had allied to enter city hall, but their divisions prevented them from constructing a coherent city administration. Having succeeded in gaining power together, they discovered governing strained and pulled them asunder to the point of ineffectiveness. Mayor Smith led a group in the city devoted to structural change, promising resolution of Omaha's problems and upgrading its image in terms of governmental efficiency, economy, and successful application of the commission form of government. In a February 1919 address to ministers, the mayor confessed he had no desire to be identified as head of a moral reform administration--of a clean administration, a business administration, yes.[50]

A different interpretation of reformism was typified by Police Commissioner Ringer, who was dedicated to a crusade against immorality. No haven in Omaha for vice and immorality he promised, and with zealous energy attempted to institute strict law enforcement of gambling, prostitution, and prohibition legislation. The two factions struggled with one another, each committed to its vision of proper policy and the city seemed less and less governed. During the summer of 1919 a recall petition against Smith, Ure, Towl, and Ringer secured over 5,000 signatures, and although dismissed on a technicality it signaled rising discontent.

In addition, Omahans long accustomed to controlled crime under Dennison's firm hand became disillusioned with

114

law enforcement under "Lily White" Ringer. The police department's stature declined as Ringer's detractors charged his morally inspired pursuit of prostitutes, bootleggers, and gamblers was diverting police efforts, and decent citizens were confronting an outbreak of major crime. A growing conviction the city was out of hand, that law and order had been undermined, was solidified with the September 28, 1919, race riot at the Douglas County Court House. Dennison had purportedly said three years earlier, "They'll be glad to see us back." And back they came in 1921, voters aroused by the riot and "the inept actions and the inconsistent objectives of the reformers themselves."[51] Dahlman, who held positions during the intervening years as an inspector of the secret service and police section of the railway administration of Nebraska, as a federal inspector of income tax returns on estates and inheritances, and as a U.S. Marshal, in February 1921 was presented petitions with 10,000 signatures urging him to run for city commissioner. Backed by names ranging from high to low in Omaha's hierarchy, "Cowboy Jim" filed.

His soon formed United Seven ticket challenged the Progressive Seven slate headed by A.L. Sutton (Ed Smith did not seek reelection). Sutton's group advertised itself as the clean slate, and asked voters whether they wanted Ringer or Dennison, morality or immorality. The United Seven stressed disarray in city hall and the need for law and order. John D. Creighton, of a pioneering family and pillar of the Omaha establishment, joined other prominent Omahans in endorsing Dahlman: "I know what Dahlman did in the office of mayor. The old council with less than 100 policemen did more effective work in behalf of law and order than the present commission has done with 300 policemen."[52] The entire United Seven ticket was elected by large margins in the highest voter turnout in the city's history, the first in which women cast a ballot. The third and fifth wards were United Seven bastions, producing comfortable margins to reinforce strength elsewhere in the city. Three thousand votes separated the lowest man among the victors from the highest of the vanguished.

"Cowboy Jim" returned to his office in city hall, leading his slate again three years later, now the Square Six since Dan Butler was dropped following a rift between himself and other commissioners. Dahlman told voters Butler had become arrogant and unappreciative, a man who had grown "fat and sleek" in public service. Nonetheless, Butler was reelected along with the other six incumbents. However, he ran seventh and last, almost 3,000 votes behind the lowest of the Square Six, his support taking a sharp drop from the third ward's endorsing vote of 4,100 three years before to 1,771, and from 4,145 in the fifth ward to 1,668.

Butler was on the opposition Civic Alliance slate at the next election, but to no avail this time as the voters retired him, temporarily, from twenty-one years of holding a county or city office. During the campaign Butler railed against his commissioner colleagues, stating Dahlman was a member out of sheer luck and Joseph Hummel was "a doddering old man who is only a rubber stamp at council meetings." The Square Seven according to Butler was more properly called the "Smelly Seven."[53] Omaha had an "Invisible Government" warned the Civic Alliance, its campaign literature carrying a cartoon showing the commissioners seated around a table in the shadows of men standing behind them--identified as Frank Johnson, Dennison, Nesselhous, and three gang lieutenants.[54] Nonetheless, city hall's string of victories continued in 1927 as the six incumbent Square Seven were reelected (the seventh candidate, John T. Marcell, did not make it), with only A.A. Westergard of the opposition able to break the ranks.

For the first time in twenty-four years, Omaha voters in the 1930 spring city election were unable to cast a vote for "Cowboy Jim." He had died in January, but of course the elections went on as scheduled. Politicians perish but politics and campaigns endure. A Square Seven slate formed and again it was victorious, six of its seven members elected (Westergard was now one of the Square Seven). Roy Towl was the exception, a survivor of the ill-fated 1918-21 city commission, destined to play a key role in the machine's final defeat in 1933. But in May 1930 Dennison's entourage toasted (illegally of course) and reflected upon three decades of electoral successes and attendant influence in political circles.

Jim Dahlman, however, was gone and his passing presaged the passing of an era. Omahans had taken pride in their cowboy mayor, a living symbol of the frontier world that had produced their boisterous community. But as it expanded and matured, as its buildings went higher and the streets filled with automobiles, a new image was groping for recognition. The cow town, wide-open reputation seemed unbefitting a major railway crossroads and leading stockyards center. New businesses were appearing, increasingly regional and national, changing perspectives in commercial circles. A new generation was replacing the one of Dahlman's prime years, its city not the same as Jim's or the "Old Man's," its perceptions different and without memories of the glory days. The machine Dahlman was so long a part of survived him by three years, then its demise confirmed what his death had suggested--an era had ended. Few, however, would have had the temerity to predict on the morrow of the decisive victory greeting the 1930s that it was the machine's last.

Dahlman was not present to inaugurate the last winning campaign in the spring of 1930 with a parade in South Omaha, nor to celebrate another conquest of city hall. He and his wife had gone to Excelsior Springs, Missouri, on January 12 to rest before the forthcoming election. Although recently bothered by a cold, Jim was thought generally to be in good health. But on Sunday the eighteenth he suffered a stroke, remaining conscious until Tuesday evening; at a half-hour before midnight, with Harriet at his side, "Jimmy the Dahl," Texan, cowboy, sheriff, politician, Omahan, drew his last breath. Under a flag draped casket he was lain in state in the council chambers of Omaha's city hall. An estimated 25,000 persons came to pay last respects to their celebrated and ofttimes celebrating mayor, passing through in seemingly endless lines. Public services were held there in the chambers, with private ones following at All Saints Episcopal Church; he was buried at Elk's Rest in Forest Lawn Cemetery. Words from a poem written about "Cowboy Jim," one he much enjoyed, provide a fitting epitaph:[55]

> Life's ways are none too pleasant--but--
> I'm gentled with her groomin',
> And if I wink when she don't see, it's
> nothin' more than human.
> I'm roped, corralled and branded too,
> but I am now confessin'
> That if the rodeo come round again, I'll
> teach some bronk a lesson.

A week after the services, members of the city commission called on Harriet Dahlman and offered her the position of mayor of Omaha. She declined, saying, "No, I am a homemaker," adding there were a number of women in Omaha qualified for the job but she was not one of them.[56] The commissioners proceeded to elect Richard L. Metcalfe to join them for the months remaining of Dahlman's term as commissioner and mayor.

Unless they recalled the 1918-1921 hiatus, most middle aged or younger Omahans had little or no recollection of any other mayor than James Dahlman. Those whose adult years spanned "Cowboy Jim's" era carried many memories as they passed his casket, the city hall evoking them, the chambers yet filled with his presence. They remembered a quiet but forceful man who seldom raised his voice, skillful in remembering names. His office was always open to all callers, with a special welcome in store for cattlemen in town for a few days. Usually they stayed at the Paxton Hotel, a short walk from there to city hall for a chat with Jim.[57]

When the mayor needed transportation, he took a taxi or rode the streetcar. He neither owned an automobile nor accepted an official one (he said the city charter made no provision for it). He was a light eater and it was well known his stand against prohibition reflected not only his frontier background and the nature of the city he presided over but his own habits as well. Before prohibition closed the saloons, Dahlman had appreciated not only their wares, but also their political value as gathering places for political discussion. When word spread he was making the rounds, policemen stayed clear of his path, aware the mayor was fond of taking them with him.[58]

He was seldom at city hall past five or six o'clock, and home was reserved for family life, free of discussions of political or city affairs. His son-in-law, Austin Collett, served an appointive post as commissioner of public works in the Dominican Republic in 1914 upon recommendation of then Secretary of State Bryan, another mark of Bryan's and Dahlman's ongoing relationship despite the 1910 troubles.[59] The mayor's daughter, the appointee's wife, had long been a close friend of Bryan's daughter. Dahlman took grandfatherly pride in his two grandsons, both of whom became Naval Academy graduates, entering the service of their mother's second husband, Commander (at time of Dahlman's death) C.C. Baughman. "Cowboy Jim" had been gone for

118

over a decade when the eldest of his grandsons, John, was shot down over the Pacific during the second world war. Stationed aboard the aircraft carrier *Enterprise* as commander of a torpedo plane squadron, Jim Dahlman's grandson was killed in action the morning of October 26, 1942, during the Battle of the Santa Cruz Islands. After a dozen Japanese Zero fighters had attacked the formation, a fellow pilot saw that "The TBF piloted by Lieutenant Commander John. A. Collett, the CO of Torpedo Ten, was spinning, with flame and smoke pouring from the engine and back over the cockpit."[60] In commemoration, a destroyer, the *U.S.S. Collett*, was launched in John's honor on March 5, 1944, with his brother as its commanding officer. The *U.S.S. Collett* sailed under James Collett's command until a month beyond the Japanese surrender.

Omaha's children during "Cowboy Jim's" years as chief executive were treated to an annual Christmas Party, and every summer the Krug amusement park was free for a day to the city's youngsters, thanks to him. Young and old alike took delight in hearing tales from their mayor about his exploits when he was sheriff of Dawes County, such as the time he prevented a lynching by distracting a crowd bent on taking one of his prisoners. Knowing his fellow citizens' zest for baseball, he instructed a deputy to get up a game on Chadron's outskirts. As Jim had foreseen, the crowd was drawn to the ball game and he slipped his prisoner to another community and safety. An old-timer from early days together in Nebraska's northwest recalled Jim breaking up another lynch mob in a more direct fashion. Standing in front of his jail, Dahlman surveyed with his "cool gray eyes" the crowd gathering in front of his jail, then calmly announced he was going to shoot anyone who attempted to cross the steps. The aspirant lynchers reconsidered their ambitions and drifted away, their intended victim later tried and sent to prison.[61]

Facing mobs and using guile or force to thwart them were far less enjoyable pastimes for the sheriff than were the horse races and betting that flourished in and around Dawes County. Among Dahlman's most talked about races, and there were many, was one pitting his "Fiddler" against a horse owned by Joe Larvie. Dahlman had brought "Fiddler" back with him from a Texas cattle buying trip, leaving a trail of horse race victories all the way north. As word of the race between "Fiddler" and Larvie's gray spread, interest heightened and spectators began showing up a week early at the race site, White Clay, Nebraska. On the day of the race, hordes of Indians, soldiers, ranchers, and cowhands gathered on the bustling two acre betting ground. That day "Fiddler" lost his first race, the defeat credited to an Indian who, just before the contest, made good medicine on the track on behalf of Larvie's entry.[62]

Dahlman did better in a 100 mile race he helped organize, the horses running the distance in a five mile route around Chadron. The mayor gave careful instructions to the rider of his "Baldy" on pacing the horse, and it was the only one even to finish the race. When humane society officials showed up, somebody rapidly organized a foot race down main street and in the resulting commotion no action was taken against the horse race participants. Dahlman was also involved in a 1,000 mile race, which started in Chadron and ended at Chicago's World's Fair. He appears in a picture taken before the race started, dapper in derby hat, bow tie, and white shirt, standing beside one of the riders, the once infamous horse thief Doc Middleton. Much publicity surrounded the race, but it ended inconclusively amid disqualifications.[63] In another race Dahlman lost the $1,000 he wagered on a horse he had brought in from Chicago. An attempt to recoup by playing faro from sunset to midnight resulted not in balancing his books, but in the loss of an additional $1,600.[64]

In later years, Dahlman liked to tell the story about a robber who ordered a prominent citizen to "put em up," but who put up a fight instead of his arms. When the robber finally had him down he gained only a $1.75. Why, the robber asked the victim, had he fought so hard against a man with a gun when he carried so little to be stolen? "'Well, I'll tell you,' came the reply, 'I didn't care to expose my financial condition.'"[65] He also liked to relate how an educator critical of current teaching methods visited an Omaha school, bent on demonstrating students had lost their powers of observation. Placing himself in front of the board, chalk in hand, he invited the class of fifth graders to give a number of two figures. "Seventy-two" called out one student and 27 was placed on the board; in response to 39 the visitor wrote 93. When a third number was called for by the learned guest, a not so unobservant member of the class called out "66," adding "Now let's see the son-of-a-gun get out of that."

Omaha's popular mayor was frequently called upon to deliver, and to listen, to speeches. He liked to tell about the evening a dance was scheduled once speech making was over. As principal speaker he came on after several other worthies had been heard, and proceeded to speak at some length on a topic of interest to him. By the time he finished it was too late for any dancing. A friend offered him a ride home and he gratefully took a place in the front seat next to the driver; in the back seat were two daughters of his driver and a friend of theirs. Dahlman asked them how they enjoyed the program. Not recognizing him, one of the girls complained if that last baldheaded speaker had not talked so long they could have danced. From that evening the mayor promised himself to keep his speeches brief. "Whenever I find myself inclined to talk at length I think of the bald-headed speaker who deprived the young people of their dance and I stop short,' he would say."

Although the mayor put limits on his addresses, in one field he remained bountiful. An estimate of 8,000 has been placed on the number of times he pardoned Omahans for minor offenses. Better for a husband to be working and providing for his family, he said, than for him to be spending time in jail. There was no reason, as he saw it, for wife and children to suffer because the father was arrested for drinking too much. Critics assailed him for his judicial generosity, but Jim disarmed them by commenting, "When I give a pardon to a boy or girl for a father I look up to my maker and give thanks for having been given a generous heart."[66] There were reasons other than generosity for granting pardons, such as the one he granted Sam Joe, proprietor of a chop suey cafe. On a second offense disorderly house charge (violation of the eight o'clock closing law), Sam was given thirty days in jail for allowing guests in his place to drink beer after hours (from tea pots and coffee cups). Two days after the sentencing the mayor pardoned Mr. Joe, declaring the proprietor was not to blame for the men drinking in his cafe. It was their fault and two of them had told him so.[67]

There is evidence, however, that pardons from the mayor's office may sometimes have been inspired by less than lofty inspiration and in response to attorney requests rather than appeals of children. One of Metcalfe's first departures from the Dahlman years was his announcement that the practice of lawyers coming to city hall to request a pardon and then collecting a fee from his client for the service was no longer acceptable.[68] The "pardon racket" did not really stop until May of 1933, following the defeat of the machine in the city elections, when Roy Towl, the new mayor, put an end to the practice of attorneys coming to the mayor's office seeking pardons.[69]

When Dahlman died, an old friend, C.L. West, suggested that instead of people sending flowers they should send money to Mrs. Dahlman. She needs the funds, said West, to buy a burial place and headstone for her husband. Mayor Dahlman never made a penny, was the message, serving Omaha honestly and without personal gain for twenty-one years.[70] Among Jim Dahlman's qualities, the one most often mentioned by his contemporaries, was his honesty. Those who worked with him and those who worked against him rally on the point of "Cowboy Jim's" honesty. He died broke (Harriet went to work for the city shortly after Jim's death, making eighty dollars a month in the Welfare Department some three years later), more interested in friends than wealth according to a long-time family friend.[71] Although Dahlman cooperated with Dennison, the word was he did not directly share in the profits of the gang's activities. He was the machine's public figure, benefitting from it politically, but not present when the financial spoils were divided. A gang opponent observed Dahlman was paid off by being reelected mayor, a job he relished.

However, there were more than political dividends concluded a special investigator brought into Omaha by Joe Polcar in 1913. Dahlman's "extravagant expenditures" in the face of known insolvency indicated income other than his city paycheck, reported the detective. More money was spent by the mayor than his salary allowed, Polcar was told, with additional funds flowing from brewers and the Dahlman Democracy, a political club organized on his behalf.[72] There is no mention in the report, however, of Dahlman receiving money from illicit machine activities. By and large, "Jimmy the Dahl" appears worthy of his reputation for honesty.

An assessment of the Dennison/Dahlman relationship by

one who observed it from a city editor's position for many years, was that Dahlman was a beneficiary of the "Old Man's" activities but not a conscious agent. An attorney who was part of the movement that helped bring down the machine in 1933 (the Independent Voter's League) felt Dahlman garnered the machine's support because he was not inimical to it. And he was not inimical to it because gambling, drinking, and prostitution were not unfamiliar to a frontier cowboy. Dahlman did not stand alone in his willingness to forsake strict enforcement of the laws against vice in Omaha. His attitude was shared from working class to upper class members who relied upon the third ward for diversion and profit.

The fact that saloons and brothels were concentrated in Dennison's ward made them more palatable, because vice was far removed from the greater part of the city. Moral reformers deplored sinful conditions and lax law enforcement, but in general the public's attitude and the mayor's coincided. Furthermore, the Dennison organization, with Mayor Dahlman in the limelight, was credited with running an orderly city, one where the "lid was kept on." Of course there was the gambling and drinking, but these vices were controlled by Dennison, ran a familiar refrain, and controlled vice brought the decent citizen security. While the mayor did not interfere with the organization's illegitimate businesses, neither did he participate in nor grow wealthy from them. Dahlman was valuable to Dennison as a man who was successful at the polls but did not intrude into actually running the city. When decisions were made, Frank Johnson and Tom Dennison were in charge, their wishes acted upon by mayor and city commissioners when word reached them from the offices of the Omaha Printing Company or Tom Dennison.

Dahlman was a popular and amenable front man for Dennison's organization, attracting votes particularly in the ethnic southside, helping to pull other Dennison choices to city office. He was an important political resource who demanded little in return. "Cowboy Jim" tended well to his ceremonial duties as mayor and he spoke out on the popular issues of his day. Immersion in city administration was neither his style nor desire, thus Dahlman and Dennison were able to forge a long lasting political relationship beneficial to both. The result was a common one in machine run cities: a mayor in the spotlight with a boss controlling the switches. An effective speaker and experienced negotiator, Dahlman championed many causes and brought his substantial public influence to bear on numerous city issues.

His personal opinions and machine interests may not always have been congruent, but generally they seem to have coincided. Or at least they were not significantly divergent or of a nature that Dahlman's position might pose a threat to the organization's activities. Some issues were of little interest to Dennison, and Dahlman then became somewhat of a free agent. For example, the establishment of a municipal airport seems to have attracted little attention from the "Old Man," yet Dahlman was among the supporters. He championed home rule (certainly in Dennison's interest), appearing several times before legislative committees in 1911 on behalf of a constitutional amendment to provide it. When Omaha gained home rule the following year, thanks to adoption of the amendment, Dahlman took a strong stand neither for or against the proposed commission form (the organization felt little threat from the change), but was instrumental in having initiative, referendum, and recall provisions included in the city charter.

As mayor, he advocated reduction of electric light rates, dollar gas, and endorsed ordinances levying occupation taxes on the street and railway, telephone, gas, telegraph, and waterworks companies. On the women's suffrage issue he felt women were as qualified as men to vote, but his position in an unsuccessful 1914 effort to amend the state constitution to that end was equivocal at best. At one point he predicted failure because many people feared if women secured the right to vote prohibition soon would follow. In fact, he said, if he voted against the amendment it would be for that reason, because if it passed he estimated that within four years Omaha would have prohibition, setting the city back a decade. On the other hand, he said if he voted for the measure it was because "laboring" women should have the right to help make the laws they worked under. In any case the mayor felt women's suffrage promised little difference other than doubling the vote, because husband and wife would most likely vote the same according to their shared interests. He believed there were as many women eligible for public office as men, and predicted

124

women voters within ten years, his only reservation being the prohibition question. "The women will never give up," he acknowledged, "till they get it."[73]

Nebraska's women did appear to secure partial suffrage with the passage of a bill in 1917 granting them the right to vote for state, county, and municipal officers (federal offices being the province of the national constitution). Nonetheless, women were unable to vote the next year because of legal delays created by anti-suffragists' efforts to rescind the law through a referendum. A lawsuit by pro-suffragists enjoined the secretary of state from putting the issue on the ballot. Large-scale fraud in securing the requisite referendum request signatures, especially in Douglas County, was charged in the pro-suffragists' suit. In June 1919 the fraud contentions were sustained and the law went into effect. Not long after, the 19th Amendment to the U.S. Constitution settled the issue of voting rights for women.[74]

When Dahlman first became mayor of Omaha, horses and wagons dominated the city streets and automobiles were just making their appearance. By the time he died, cars filled the streets and horses and wagons were long gone. When he first became mayor, a walk a few blocks west of city hall placed him among large grassy and treed lots, hosting frame houses. A similar walk during his last years and he was surrounded by concrete and steel. His city had grown from a mere 9.6 square miles in 1887 to the 39 square miles he presided over in his last year; he had watched the population double between 1900 and 1930 to 214,006.[75] While he occupied city hall, streets were widened, viaducts were built, a major thoroughfare--Dodge Street--was lowered, and Omaha's skyline was raised. Growing steadily but cautiously during Dahlman's years as mayor, Omaha seemed content with political and business leadership emphasizing stability rather than the challenges of ambitious change. One change underway, however, by the time of James Charles Dahlman's death was the transformation in the city's self image from a wide-open turn of the century frontier town to a conservative community of the plains.

"Cowboy Jim" was an embodiment of the frontier spirit, flamboyant, liberal, and free spirited, willing to wink at humankind's weaknesses, willing to assist when necessary.

There is little profit in attempting to assess his years as mayor, for neither Omaha's successes nor its failures can be attributed to him. His place in the political machine renders the effort pointless, for his lot was to follow not to guide. James Dahlman was well prepared for the role he played, and the city was a proper stage for his performance. His death was timely in that the city spirit he typified was passing, and in the one being born "Cowboy Jim" was going to be out of place.

For thirty some years Jim Dahlman was at the center of Omaha's political life, the key public figure of a machine owing its long tenure to ballot box successes. "Jimmy the Dahl," the compliant "perpetual mayor," was a popular vote getter and his popularity helped to ensure that ballots were properly cast. No better service could have been tendered Tom Dennison.

NOTES

Chapter IV

[1]Fred Carey, *Mayor Jim: An Epic of the West* (Omaha Printing Co., 1930), p. 9. Carey's book is a friendly reminiscence; Tom Dennison is not mentioned even once.

[2]MOW-H, January 22, 1930.

[3]*Ibid.*

[4]MOW-H, January 23, 1930.

[5]Maria Sandoz, *The Cattlemen* (Lincoln: University of Nebraska Press, 1978), p. 408; and interview with W.B. Quigley conducted by Orville D. Menard, June 4, 1979, Valentine, Nebraska. Quigley's father was a friend and fellow cowboy with Dahlman.

[6]Sandoz, *The Cattlemen*, p. 428. See also W.D. Aeschbacher, "Development of the Sandhill Lake Country," *Nebraska History*, 27 (July-September, 1946), p. 211; Robert Burns, "The Newman Ranches: Pioneer Cattle Ranches of the West," *Nebraska History*, 34 (March, 1953), p. 29.

[7]Carey, *Mayor Jim*, p. 35. Dahlman's version of the events may be found in James Dahlman, "Recollections of Cowboy Life in Western Nebraska," *Nebraska History*, 10 (October-December, 1927), pp. 335-343, first presented as a speeech of the same title at the Annual Meeting of the Nebraska State Historical Society, January 10, 1922. Dahlman papers, A/MSS, Nebraska State Historical Society.

[8]Carey, *Cowboy Jim*, p. 39; Bee, January 22, 1930.

[9]*Ibid.*, pp. 46-47.

[10]*Chadron Chronicle*, January 23, 1930.

[11]Two dates are given for the marriage; Sheldon's *Nebraska* cites December 20, the MOW-H, January 22, 1930, says the 18th.

[12]Nellie Snyder Yost, ed., *Boss Cowman: The Recollections of Ed Lemmon 1857-1946* (Lincoln: University of Nebraska Press, 1969), pp. 141-142.

[13]Ruth was born September 18, 1885, Dorothy on June 1, 1898. Ruth first married Austin J. Collett, an engineer whom she divorced, remarrying C.C. Baughman, a naval officer. Dorothy pursued a government career in Washington, D.C., and never married.

[14]*Chadron Record, Historical Edition, 1979.*

[15]For mayoral results, see Minutes of Chadron City Council, Record, City of Chadron, November 2, 1888/November 3, 1894 and *Ibid.*, December 5, 1894/May 4, 1903. Sheriff race results are in Abstracts of Votes Cast, Dawes County Elections, Vol I, p. 6 (1887), p. 20 (1889), p. 47 (1891), p. 86 (1893) with Dahlman in this last year running second in a field of three.

[16]Minutes of Chadron City Council, December 24, 1885/November 9, 1888, p. 189.

[17]*Dawes County Journal*, Vol IV, January 1888; Minutes of Chadron City Council, December 24, 1885/November 9, 1888, p. 177; Carey, *Cowboy Jim*, pp. 67-68.

[18]For copies of notifications sent to Chadron men see Chadron City Hall, Box 1895-1896; see also Minutes of Chadron City Council, December 5, 1894/May 4, 1903, meeting of August 21, 1895, p. 60.

[19]Minutes of Chadron City Council, December 5, 1894/May 4, 1903, resolution dated April 1, 1896, pp. 110-111.

[20]Mark Frisbie, "The Fair That Put Omaha On the Map," *Sunday World-Herald Magazine of the Midlands*, May 30, 1976, p. 19. See also "Mind-Numbing Show of Shows," *Ibid.*, September 21, 1980, pp. 24-27.

[21]Carey, *Cowboy Jim*, p. 66.

[22]*Ibid.*, p. 115.

[23]Louis W. Koenig, *Bryan: A Political Biography of William Jennings Bryan* (New York: G.P. Putnam's Sons, 1971), p. 469. On the 1910 election see Paolo E. Coletta, "The Nebraska Democratic Campaign of 1910," *Nebraska History*, 52 (Winter, 1971), pp. 359-382.

[24]"Liquors--Eight O'Clock Closing," *Laws of Nebraska--1909*, Chapter 22, Senate File No. 283, p. 345.

[25]Letter, W.G. McAdoo to Gilbert M. Hitchcock, July 1, 1915, Gilbert M. Hitchcock Papers, Nebraska State Historical Society, MS 3640, Box 2, Folder, Political Correspondence, 1904-1924. The file contains memos and letters pertaining to the patronage dispute. See also Paolo E. Colotta, "The Patronage Battle Between Bryan and Hitchcock," *Nebraska History*, 49 (Winter, 1968), pp. 121-137; Dahlman Scrapbooks, Omaha Public Library, Vol. 11, pp. 44, 52, 55, 56, with clippings from the Bee, August 25, 1914; OW-H, September 24, 1914; Bee, October 13, 1914; OW-H, October 26, 1914. Cited hereafter as DS.

[26]Carey, *Cowboy Jim*, p. 117.

[27]Bee, January 22, 1930.

[28]EOW-H, April 26, 1924.

[29]MOW-H, January 22, 1930.

[30]EOW-H, January 18, 1906.

[31]Carey also discusses the Paxton Hotel meeting; see *Mayor Jim*, pp. 95-96.

[32]EOW-H, January 29, 1906.

[33]*Ibid.*, April 18, 1906.

[34]*Ibid.*, February 22, 1906.

[35]*Ibid.*, April 7, 1906.

[36]Sunday Bee, April 15, 1906.

[37]See the Bee, April 24, 25, 27, and 29, 1906.

[38]EOW-H, April 18, 1906.

[39]*Ibid.*, April 24, 1906; Carey, *Cowboy Jim*, p. 98.

[40]Carey, *Cowboy Jim*, p. 98.

[41]Election results unless otherwise cited are taken from appropriate years, City of Omaha Elections, Election Commissioner's Office, State of Nebraska, County of Douglas, City of Omaha.

[42]Carey, *Cowboy Jim*, p. 101.

[43]ODN, April 23, 30, 1907.

[44]EOW-H, April 9, 1909.

[45]*Ibid.*, March 18, 1918.

[46]*Ibid.*, April 27, 1918.

[47]*Sunday World-Herald*, May 5, 1918.

[48]ODN, April 22, 23, 1918.

[49]Dahlman in the third ward polled 1,430; Butler 1,469; Smith 1,161; Towl 1,009; Zimman 1,224. Other Allied candidates did not fare as well: William Ure 999 and J.D. Ringer 873. EOW-H, May 8, 1918.

[50]See Rickard, "The Politics of Reform in Omaha," p. 434.

[51]*Ibid.*, p. 420.

[52]EOW-H, April 21, 1921.

[53]*Ibid.*, April 20, 1927.

[54]*Ibid.*, April 29, 1927.

[55]Jean Palmer Nye, unpublished poem, "The Cowboy Mayor." In a letter to Mrs. Nye who lived in Shenandoah, Iowa, and was a member of the League of American Penwomen, Dahlman wrote his thanks and told her "You certainly had your ear to the ground when you caught that 'song of the wild' and you certainly had a tight hold on the hand of the muse when you put it into that seducive [sic] little verse." Letter, Dahlman to Mrs. Jean Palmer Nye, dated May 10, 1926, Dahlman papers, A/MSS, Nebraska State Historical Society.

[56]Bee, January 19, 1930.

[57]Quigley interview.

[58]Interview with Herman J. Creal conducted by Orville D. Menard, August 9, 1979, Omaha, Nebraska. Mr. Creal was a policeman during a few of the Dahlman years and spoke from personal experience.

[59]DS, Vol. 10, pp. 115, 124, clippings from *The Mediator*, December 6, 1913; OW-H, January 10, 1914.

[60]Edward P. Stafford, "Action off Santa Cruz," in S.E. Smith, ed., *The United States Navy in World War II*, copyright S.E. Smith, n.p., 1967, p. 367. See also Samuel Eliot Morison, *The Struggle for Guadacanal, August 1942-February 1943* (Boston: Lttle Brown and Company, 1950), p. 104. Morison provides the composition of forces for the October 26 battle, listing Collett on the *Enterprise* as commandeer of VT-10, consisting of twelve torpedo planes. Morison notes that Lt. Cmdr. Collett was "sunk in this action." Also telephone conversation between James Collett, James Dahlman's grandson, and Orville D. Menard, November 5, 1984, Omaha to Annapolis, Maryland, and correspondence from Collett to Menard, March 29, 1985. Also interview with Dorothy M. Cathers conducted by Orville D. Menard, July 16, 1979, Omaha, Nebraska.

[61]EOW-H, April 18, 1921; see also Carey, *Cowboy Jim*, pp. 69-70.

[62]Sandoz, *The Cattlemen*, p. 408.

[63]*Ibid.*, pp. 414-418; Yost, *Boss Cowman*, pp. 191-194. The Chadron Record Historical Edition, 1979.

[64]Sandoz, *The Cattlemen*, p. 416.

[65]This story and the two following are taken from Carey, *Cowboy Jim*, pp. 133-137.

[66]Bee, April 26, 1915.

[67]DS, Vol. 10, pp. 133-134, clippings from OW-H, March 14, 1914; ODN, March 16, 1914.

[68]EOW-H, February 7, 1930.

[69]Memorandum, n.d., Towl papers, Box 2, Folder 1933, June-July, Mayor.

[70]MOW-H, January 23, 1930.

[71]Quigley interview.

[72]Special Report, Kansas City Investigator #B-91, December 20, 1913, and January 14, 1914, Rosewater Collection, Box 1927.

[73]DS, Vol. 11, pp. 44-45, clippings from OW-H, August 26, 29, 1914. The vote on the amendment statewide was 100,892 against, 90,782 for; in Douglas County the vote was 10,654 against, 9,486 for. EOW-H, November 19, 1914.

[74]See Ann L. Wiegman Wilhite, "Sixty-Five Years Till Victory: A History of Women's Suffrage in Nebraska," *Nebraska History*, 49 (Summer, 1968), pp. 149-163; Elizabeth J. Lindsey, "A History of Woman Suffrage in Douglas County Nebraska," unpublished manuscript, Omaha Public Library; Chapter 30, House Roll No. 282, "An Act Relating to Elections," *Laws, Resolutions, and Memorials Passed by the Legislature of the State of Nebraska, Thirty-Fifth Session, 1917*, pp. 95-96.

[75]On Omaha between 1900 and 1930 see Larsen and Cottrell, *The Gate City*, pp. 127-189; also Dustin, *Omaha and Douglas County*, pp. 85-109.

Thomas Dennison, the man with "the steely blue eyes and the narrow whimsical smile."

"Cowboy Jim" Dahlman, Omaha's "perpetual mayor."
Bostwick-Frohardt Collection, The Durham Museum.

William "Billy" Nesselhous.

133

Tom Dennison (on the left) and "Billy" Nesselhous.
Reprinted with permission from the Omaha World-Herald.

Circus Parade, corner of 16th and Farnam Streets, 1910.

Tom "The Old Man" Dennison, 1931. Reprinted with permission from the Omaha World-Herald.

135

CHAPTER V

Operations: Elections

Ballots boxes are never stuffed,
unless its absolutely necessary.
--Martin Lomasney

One factor was essential for a political boss to serve his varied constituencies by delivering services and assuring protection: his organization had to be successful at the polls. To the degree the machine provided properly marked ballots for city and county commissioners, sheriffs, judges, city prosecutors, county attorneys, and sundry other offices, its broker role was enhanced. Securing votes was a machine imperative because all others depended upon its fulfillment.

Preparing for an election was not a sometime thing, confined to the few weeks prior to actual balloting. It was a constant preoccupation and carefully calculated everyday machine activities were carried on with an eye to victories for its candidates, the larger the majorities the better. Strong organization complemented by famed welfare and patronage endeavors were machine reliables in these year round efforts. Then as election day approached and finally arrived, an armory of political weapons was drawn upon to boost returns. An early twentieth-century Philadelphia political ring member one year reminded his listeners Independence Hall was in his ward, proceeding to name men who had signed the Declaration of Independence. Those fathers of American liberty had voted in his ward he proudly concluded. "'And,' he added with a catching grin, 'they vote here yet.'"[1]

Political machines were marvels of ingenuity as they sought electoral dominance, their leaders intent on prevailing in a highly competitive business, seeking advantage as opportunity presented itself or was created. Loyalty earned through services rendered was a mainstay in the delivery wards, the working class immigrant neighborhoods, and on election day a "thank you" was registered with a vote. Fraudulent registrations and voting practices were resorted to on a large-scale, and even the name on a bronze statue in front of a library in Pittsburgh made its way onto a list of registered voters.[2]

Methods varied but purpose--winning--was universal. Few bosses exhibited the flair of Boston's Boss, James Michael Curley, but they shared his sense of what pressure was able to accomplish when properly applied. For example, Curley in 1914 informed John Francis "Honey Fitz" Fitzgerald (John Kennedy's grandfather, seeking his third term as Boston's mayor), that unless he withdrew his name from contention, his love life and purported relationship with "Toodles" Ryan would be exposed. "Honey Fitz" determined to stay in the race despite the threat, but reconsidered when Boston newspapers carried a story of Curley's intention to deliver three addresses in the fall: one on "Graft, Ancient and Modern," a second on "Great Lovers: From Cleopatra to 'Toodles'," and the third on "Libertines: From Henry VIII to the Present Day."[3]

Whatever schemes, frauds, and tricks a machine resorted to, organization and personal contacts comprised the vital substructure of machine power. Enrolling people on registration lists, canvassing, and getting out the vote were primary tasks of a machine's ward and precinct workers, their other responsibilities tightly bound to these ends. From the lowest levels of the organization to the highest, the "gang" labored to fashion a network of loyalty and obligation. Creating such a reliable system, called in on election day, took time as the evolution of voting in Omaha's third ward demonstrates. A year after Dennison's arrival in Omaha the third had the lowest turnout of the city's then nine wards in the mayoral election. Its sympathies were electorally on the side of the winner, but only by a very narrow margin. Two years later the future machine bastion increased its turnout, but went for the Democratic candidate for mayor, who nonetheless lost the election. The third was not yet a ward to be taken seriously.

In 1897, the year Dennison's name was first publicly associated with a city campaign, the third was fourth in voter turnout among the wards, short of third place by only twelve votes (the margin two years earlier was 111 when the third was also fourth). A close race was reflected in the ward as it went 48 per cent for Dennison's ally Frank E. Moores, who won the election, to 52 per cent for his opponent. Three years later the reelected Moores gained 65 per cent support in the third ward (53 per cent city wide), now the second highest ward in voter turnout and providing the mayor his highest ward total. The returns mark Dennison's consolidation of power.

In a four way race in 1903 the third ward gave almost half of its support to winner Moores (48 per cent) while his main opponent came in a distant third (13 per cent), although he ran second to Moores in total votes cast in the city. "Cowboy Jim's" election in 1906 vividly highlights the machine's now smoothly functioning ability to get out the vote in Dennison territory. The third ward registered not only Omaha's highest turnout but delivered 84 per cent of its votes to Dahlman, with the second precinct over-whelmingly in his favor (420 votes to 22). Dahlman carried half of Omaha's now twelve wards by sizeable margins but was strongest in the Dennison controlled ward. The returns show Dahlman's widespread popularity, but the unusually large majorities in the third ward, especially in its second precinct, disclose more than his charm was delivering--and counting--votes. Dahlman became mayor with a margin of 1,132 votes in the third ward alone, more than enough to counter his opponent's cumulative 738 edge in the six wards he carried.

Three years later Dahlman was reelected, again thanks to the machine's concerted efforts. Improving upon its 1906 performance by 4 points, the organization brought in 88 per cent of the third's votes for "Cowboy Jim," with the second precinct giving Dahlman 380 votes to his opponent's twenty-nine. In no other ward did Dahlman receive more votes nor his opponent less. In the five wards he carried, John Paul Breen had a total margin of 582 votes--Dahlman in the third alone led by 1,414.

The coming of the commission form in 1912 failed to stem the machine's third ward dominance and consequent influence in city hall. In election after election, except for 1918, large majorities were delivered in the third ward to Dennison backed candidates. A glance at third ward returns quickly reveals which seekers of a public office the "Old Man" was backing. Men going to the polls in the first commissioner's race voted for seven of fourteen candidates. The opposition Citizen's Union attracted a grand total of 1,172 votes in Dennison's base territory (196 was the highest total therein for an individual Citizen's Union hopeful). The Dennison/Dahlman slate accumulated 8,962 votes in the third ward, with the mayor's name marked 1,363 times by voters there, his highest total in the city. The candidate coming in lowest on Dennison's slate in the third was a satisfying 1,021 ahead of the nearest Citizen's Union man.[4] Dennison and his lieutenants at Headquarters had ample reason to take pride in the efficacy of their loyal workers.

Only in the third ward did individual Union slate candidates all fall beneath 200 votes each; despite favorable returns elsewhere in the city, the gap created in the third was too great and not a single one of them was elected to the new city commission. In the second election under the commission form, two Big Six opponents of the Square Seven did succeed in being elected. While machine preferences are clear in the returns, they were not as decisive as the previous time out and three of the Big Six even tallied more than 200 votes in the third ward (251, 233, 201 to Dahlman's 977), and two of the trio were elected.[5] The ratio was reversed in 1918 as the reform minded--although divided--Allied ticket became the city commission's majority. Only two of the Square Seven survived the voters' determination for change. Dahlman ran strongly in the third ward as usual, also in the fifth and seventh, but ballots marked for him and most of his colleagues were outdistanced by Allied returns throughout the city. Even within the third ward the opposition was credible, well exceeding the 200 plus performance of opponents in the previous elections.[6]

Weary of the reformers' squabbles and their seeming inability to maintain order in the city, Omahans in 1921 returned a Dahlman slate to power by secure city wide majorities. In the third ward alone Dahlman's name was marked 4,049 times; counting all wards the returning mayor's slate won 59 per cent of the vote--achieving 77 per cent in Dennison's stronghold.[7] Over the next three city commissioner elections the third ward faithfully delivered for the favored ticket, consistently on the side of the winners, and attending to electoral work in other wards to see that they too voted properly. Dennison's efforts to get out the vote were not confined to the third ward; here was merely his home and assured base. His lieutenants were busy elsewhere in the city, especially in South Omaha after the 1915 annexation in the redrawn fifth, sixth, and seventh wards. Ethnic and blue-collar Omahans lived in these wards, as in the second immediately north of the third. All became dependable Dennison territory. From its third ward base and colonies, Omaha's political machine gathered the votes to earn it a significant, often determining role in the electoral process of transforming candidates into city and county officials. Tom Dennison and Frank Johnson then counted on the loyalty of those they helped place in office. Because of the organization's ability to reward with election or punish with defeat, incumbents were not accountable to the people as democratic theory suggests, but to the machine. However, while the "Old Man" recorded an impressive series of successes in city commissioner elections, he was less successful in other electoral endeavors.

Decisions favored for Omaha from offices in the Budweiser or the Karbach Building were not always realized, despite overwhelming majorities piled up in the third ward. Dennison controlled the third but that did not always bring victory. His strength in his own precincts on these occasions is obvious, but to no avail given electoral weakness combined with concerted opposition elsewhere in the city. He could deliver some of the people almost all the time, but was unable to deliver all of the people at any time. There had to be a certain congruence between his wards and the rest of the city for him to prevail, and his power even then was limited to local affairs.

The "Old Man's" ability to deliver the third by astounding majorities yet lose was demonstrated in a race for the United States House of Representatives in 1912. A month before the election Dennison was berating U.S. Representative aspirant Howard J. Baldrige for having convinced him to support Charles Foster's election as a police judge. Once on the bench, thanks to third ward support, Foster had proceeded to dispense justice in a manner unanticipated by Dennison and his colleagues. Both Baldrige and Foster therefore went down in Dennison's mental book as double-crossers. During the last thirty days of the Congressional campaign, however, Baldrige worked out an alliance with the pragmatic Dennison, the way smoothed by large amounts of money the candidate had at his disposal for the race.[8] Throughout the city--almost--the election turned out to be a cliff-hanger. Then there was the third ward. Dennison's preferences were soundly registered in its second and third precincts where his favorite won 341 to 72 and 347 to 40. Nonetheless, incumbent Charles Lobeck's rural area returns, plus a surprising defection in Dennison's neighboring second ward, sent him back to Congress.

A word on the fate of Police Magistrate Foster, the gentleman who disappointed Dennison in his too fervid application of the law. The "Old Man" had agreed to support Foster in the 1911 election and the third put 682 votes in his column, with his three opponents receiving there 52, 28, and 20 votes. In the solid second precinct, Fosterites turned out to grant him 284 votes, his rivals gaining 5, 3, and none; similar returns emerged from the ballot boxes in the third precinct: 210 for Foster, 10, 9, and 2 for the others. Following its downtown lead, the tenth ward was generous with Foster and he won election to office in an unhot contest. If only Foster's third ward votes had been counted he would have run a close second in the race to the city wide total of 732 for the closest challenger.

By the next election Dennison had learned to his dismay that Foster's concepts of justice were unacceptable. Three years before, third ward manipulation had almost single-handedly put him in office. This time, in a convincing display of the capacity to alter voting behaviors, the Budweiser saw to it in the primary that the share of ballots marked for Foster in the third ward dropped to fifty-one, 313 behind Dennison's new choice. Foster managed to eke out a mere fifteen votes between the second and third precincts. Nonetheless, voters elsewhere in the city cared enough to grant him nomination. In the general election Foster's lowest number of votes were counted in the third ward, but elsewhere in the city he was better perceived and he struggled on to reelection by a 202 vote margin.

Other elections demonstrate similar consequences when Dennison and the third ward entered the fray, only to be reminded their strength diminished as it moved from its geographic base. And they were not always infallible within the third ward, as the results of the 1908 Ashton Shallenberger/George Sheldon race for governor demonstrate. In the campaign's waning days, Governor Sheldon made a trip to Omaha to shore up his Republican support, visiting Dennison at the Budweiser. They met in the "Old Man's" back office and reached an agreement. Nonetheless, on election day Sheldon lost his job as governor; he carried half of Omaha's wards but the third was not among them, losing there by thirty votes. Of the ward's five precincts only the second went for the incumbent but by an uncharacteristically small margin for a Dennison candidate (62 votes), not enough to carry the ward. Sheldon was unpopular in the third given his support of county option on prohibition. The memory of Sheldon's attempt to have a county option law passed in the legislature, reinforced by his carrying the issue into the campaign, was more than even Dennison was able to overcome.[9]

Omaha's mayor entered the race for governor of Nebraska two years later against Shallenberger, sweeping the Democratic primary in Omaha with large majorities in every ward, the third rewarding Dahlman with 401 votes to Shallenberger's 29. "Cowboy Jim" won the nomination state wide by a narrow 200 margin following a recount, but he lost in the general election by some 17,000 votes. He carried all but the twelfth ward in Omaha, the third coming in at 93 per cent for him. But the "dry"/"wet" dispute, and Bryan's disavowal of his old friend, proved too much for the challenger in the rest of the state and too much for his third ward champion, Thomas Dennison. Once again the "Old Man" learned of the limits to his power as he convincingly delivered his ward to Dahlman, but to no avail since the rest of the state was unimpressed.

When Omahans went to the polls not to choose among candidates for office but to register approval or disapproval of public issues, the machine's role varied according to the level and type of community support. Dennison's business allies and their perception of a measure's effect on their interests translated into organization action or indifference depending upon foreseen benefit or harm. General public sentiment was also a factor. If the public was uninterested the machine's workers ensured its allies, if interested, prevailed. But if a strong voter predilection was assessed, as sometimes mobilized by reformist or temporarily politicized groups, no marching orders were issued by Headquarters. Pragmatism prevailed and accommodation to a new situation followed the returns.

Referendums on water works bonds, and Omaha's adopting a commission form of government are cases in point. For many years the city carried on a dispute between advocates of municipal ownership of the water works, and continued private ownership operating under a city franchise. A long legal struggle was engaged in 1903, the issue revolving round the appraised value of the plant thus cost to the city to buy the water works from a New York based syndicate. The case made its way to the U.S. Supreme Court, which handed down its decision in April 1910, upholding a lower court decision ordering Omaha to pay a full appraisal made four years earlier. Controversy over accumulated interest followed the high court's determination, with a return to the courts in the fall of 1911 resulting in Omaha's being relieved of any obligation to pay interest. Next, a report filed by a district court appointed officer to determine the value of plant property called for nearly $222,000 more than the 1906 agreement. The city considered the difference tolerable, but the district court ruled Omaha had to pay only the original evaluation, therefore the Water Company took preliminary steps to appeal.

A compromise was finally worked out (centering on mutual agreement to settle obligations of unpaid hydrant rentals by the city to the company, and unpaid occupation taxes by the Water Company to Omaha), obviating a return to the courts and the city became owner of the water works on July 1, 1912. Meanwhile, as the courts dealt with the legal issues involved during these years from appraisal to possession, citizens in Omaha were called to the polls to say "yes" or "no" to a bond issue for purchase of the Water Company. Ballots in 1909 first carried the proposal, and Dahlman, seeking his second term as mayor and in favor of municipal ownership of utilities, called for an affirmative vote. He was reelected and the bond issue was approved. Although the "Dahl" won handily in the third ward, only there, in a very close vote, was a "no" majority registered on the bond issue (535 "yes," 549 "no"). Apparently Dennison and his colleagues were far less interested in the bonds than in Dahlman's reelection, registering too the futility of opposing a popular measure.

Two years later the City Water Board (created by state law eight years previously to take over eventual management of the water works) called a special election for a new issue, foreseeing a need for more money to finance litigation expenses and plant improvement once ownership of the water works was realized. Assuming the bonds would pass, the Water Board did little campaigning and the newspapers were silent on the question until the day before the election. Public indifference characterized the pre-election atmosphere. Then there was a quick exchange between the *World-Herald,* the *Daily News,* and the *Bee,* with Victor Rosewater accused of working for defeat of the bonds because of a potential loss of revenue if the Water Works Company abandoned rented space in his building. He responded his opposition was based on the election's prematurity since the matter was still in litigation.[10]

On election day voters cast a majority of their votes in favor of the bond issue, but it failed to secure the two-thirds necessary for adoption. The margin of victory was largely denied by the third ward, with some assistance from the tenth, the only two wards where there was a majority of negative votes. Turnout was generally light except in the third ward, where more voters turned out than in any other ward, registering Dennison's and Rosewater's preference. In the Budweiser's neighborhood there was a remarkable shift of sentiment since the close result of two years before. Now 746 third ward citizens were against the bonds and only 94 for. More negative votes were counted in the second precinct than the combined total vote in the first, fourth, and eighth wards. A record of sorts was achieved in the precinct as 349 "no's" were marked, and "yes" only five times. Dennison and Rosewater prevailed, the former displaying his usual "fatherly interest" in a pool hall polling place.[11] Elsewhere in the city, the electorate paid little attention to their polling places, giving the third ward its opportunity and it took it.

Thirty-six days later a repeat water bond special election was held, the voters coming out in twice the numbers they had in June, displaying their awakened interest in the issue. This time the measure passed overwhelmingly (7,320 for, 658 against), even the third and tenth wards approving, these two, significantly, the only ones declining from the June election turnout. While in several other wards voters doubled in number, in the third they fell off by almost two-thirds (voting 216 for, 111 against), and the second precinct, producer of 354 voters a month before, now mustered a mere 45 (42 voting "no"). Ten minutes after the polls closed, Dennison's second precinct reported its returns, the first in the city to act with such alacrity.[12] Only one other precinct in the city, the fifth in the third ward, recorded a "no" majority. Obviously the third ward laid low in the special election, honoring a popular swing toward the bonds. Dennison was also aware important business interests in the city approved the measure. The Commercial Club was supportive and its large membership included influential business leaders, a point not lost on Dennison given his contacts and upperworld responsibilities.[13]

Omaha's changing its governmental structure likewise demonstrated the Dennison machine in inaction when faced with a popular measure. In tune with developments in other parts of the country, Omahans in 1911 began pressing for a commission form of government.[14] A primary sponsor of the movement was the Ad Club, another influential Omaha business organization. Soon after the state legislature provided its permission for a change from the mayor-council system, the *Bee* circulated a petition requesting a special election on adopting the commission form. Seventeen-hundred more signatures than required were gathered and voters were called to the polls to settle the question of commission government for Omaha.

Dahlman at first opposed the legislative bill, but dropped his opposition when his criticisms that it contained no provisions for recall, initiative, and referendum resulted in amendments adding these direct democracy features. Urging "yes" votes on their readers, all three of Omaha's major dailies advocated the change. On election day inactivity at Dennison headquarters reflected intensity of interest elsewhere. Moreover, he and his associates made the assessment, proven correct, that tinkering with the machinery portended little effect on their influence in city elections. A light vote characterized the lower wards, the third casting the city's second lowest total and recording the only vote against adopting the commission form (131 "yes" to 314 "no"). Support elsewhere by comfortable margins ended Omaha's mayor-council system, the third ward's leaders showing little interest in the outcome, foreseeing commissioners as accountable to them as councilmen despite the popular change.[15]

Dennison's electoral efforts display three patterns: win, lose, and withdraw. Candidates he backed for local office accumulated a record of successes, especially to city hall. In every election but one under the commission form, Dennison men were in the majority or held all the seats until 1933. These were the elections most important to him and here he exerted his greatest efforts, for his role in the city depended upon success for his slates. When he attempted to influence races for office whose responsibilities went beyond the city's borders, he often discovered delivering the third was insufficient to influence outcomes. His power base, like that of most bosses, was within his city and it is no accident city bosses are known to us rather than state bosses. While his votes were helpful to Congressional and gubernatorial candidates over the years, he was not in the same league when he stepped into state or national contests, and lesser influence or defeats came his way.

The third category, withdrawal, discloses a pragmatic political boss willing to accept the inevitable when confronting an issue enjoying popular support and significant backing in the general business community. Dennison, unburdened by ideological blinders or binding partisanship, was able to adapt and avoid useless expenditure of time and energy needed for other battles of greater significance to him and promising victory--like a city commissioner election. It was winning elections to local office that was the measure of a political boss's effectiveness: no victories no power, no power no capacity to play the role of broker in the city game of *quid pro quo*. Throughout the machine hierarchy it was well understood that positions and privileges depended upon delivering the vote, and the organization was an entity dedicated to that task, every member committed to doing his part in getting people registered and voting them on election day. Anyone faltering in dedication or achievement was unlikely to remain long in the organization, and anyone who dared "cross" the "Old Man" by lending support to a nonauthorized candidate suffered the consequences.

The danger of "crossing" the "Old Man" is seen in the fate of Morris Milder, a long-time worker in the organization. An expert bookkeeper, Morris moved from collector (picking up protection payments) to recorder of collections for Dennison. A shrewd and capable man, Milder, noted for his impeccable manners and immaculate dress, also went into the oil business. First he owned the Northwest Petroleum Works, then opened the U.S. Oil Works when the middleman role of his Northwest company was squeezed out by refineries who decided to sell direct to filling stations.[16] He did very well with his oil firm, his products fueling and lubricating city and county vehicles (the market of police and sheriff autos, fire trucks, and official cars), as well as many business vehicles in the city thanks to Dennison's influence. Meanwhile he continued working for Dennison, including election time responsibilities.

It was customary for the backers of slates to have small cards printed listing the names of their candidates, these then handed out by workers at the polling places. As the 1928 election approached, Dennison left town but not before reaching an agreed upon slate for the organization, a slate not containing the name of R.B. Howell for U.S. Senator. While Dennison rested in California, Milder one night entered the Karbach Building Headquarters with several thousand printed slate cards to be given to organization poll workers for distribution to voters. Howell's name led the list. Milder had added it to Dennison's slate, relying on voters accustomed to voting the machine's suggestions to mark their ballots for Howell as well as the rest of the approved slate.

Two of the "Old Man's" lieutenants noticed the change, and after Milder left the office, George Yeager and William "Billy" Maher destroyed all but a few of the phony cards. Surviving samples were saved for Dennison, who was called immediately about the incident. He returned from California a few days later and Milder's ruination began as Dennison put out the word to "rap" Morris Milder and the U.S. Oil Works. Suddenly his Omaha customers, public and private, turned to other distributors for gasoline and petroleum supplies, and garage owners and taxi companies were instructed to stop buying from Milder's company. Dennison issued orders to one associate to have an oil burner installed in his home by the U.S. Oil Works and then refuse to pay the bill. Dennison's wrath reached out to another Milder, and he had stink bombs smuggled into a hotel Morris's brother Hymie had a partnership in. Morris "went busted over that election" was one loyal machine worker's summation of the campaign against the "crosser."[17] Milder a few years later decided to leave Omaha.

In order to exercise the power that crushed Milder, Dennison called upon contacts both in public and private offices. To secure the former (and as a lure to the latter) elections had to be won, meaning sufficient money had to be raised to finance campaigns. Although collections and sundry payoffs provided a steady source of income, election time meant extraordinary expenses to be met and therefore additional fund raising. Illegitimate businesses, whose payments were adequate during the year to secure freedom from police harassment, were subjected to special assessments at election time. Unless payment was forthcoming, law enforcement officials suddenly became rigid in their interpretation of vice statutes.

The legitimate business community was also expected to help with expenses, its assistance coming forth as "campaign contributions," the size of the donation commensurate with the size of the business. Reminders of favors both granted or potential were the essence of solicitations, circulated by and among those who understood privilege was a commodity to be purchased. "Boodle" (bribery for specific projects) was not at issue or in mind; the consideration was a campaign contribution to an organization long and well placed to advance--or injure--a firm's well being. Reluctance to contribute the anticipated amount invited messengers and messages from Headquarters. Before his fall, the dapper Morris Milder embarked upon many a mission, bearer of reminders of the vast assortment of ordinances at the behest of city hall, ranging from nuisance level to depredation. If his entreaties failed to lighten wallets, city inspectors became assiduous in fulfilling their duties, rights of way or easements vanished, and licenses were suddenly revoked.

City workers were also called upon to help bear campaign costs, their entitlement to a job contingent upon willingness to pay for it. Their support was not referred

to as a campaign contribution, as in the case of the legitimate business community, nor was it the protection money
of the illicit partners; for the city workers the term was
"macing." Macing was a familiar fund raising tactic in
American cities, and public employees from custodian to
heads of departments were expected to help meet election
expenses with contributions depending upon position held.
The machine made its special assessments at election time,
differences in terminology a measure of the stature of the
donator in the community.

Throughout the year, regular payments were due to
Headquarters in order to help finance its welfare activities. The image of the political boss as Robin Hood, taking
from the rich to give to the poor is romantic but misguid-
ed. The bosses did not run charitable organizations solely-
-or even mainly--for the sake of benevolence. Nor did they
take from the rich without giving something in return.
Their motives and means were more complex, tied to their
electoral goals and the prizes stemming from victory. It is
true the boss took from the rich, both from those whose
wealth was acquired under legal constraints and those whose
money was made despite the law. But it was not a highway-
man's theft that secured their purses, but payments made in
anticipation of benefits. To provide those benefits it was
necessary to exert influence in city hall, and the boss
expended the raised monies in a manner to provide votes for
his slate on election day. Enter the machine function of
providing welfare. Money expended for welfare provided the
foundations for election day turnouts, the voters coming
forth to repay with their ballot favors received during the
year, reminded of them by the ward and precinct workers.

Machine welfare activities were concentrated in the
downtown and South Omaha wards, the "down-and-outer," man-
ual worker, immigrant wards. Here were the people who needed help in finding a job and shelter, meeting their clothing and food needs, securing assistance when in trouble
with authorities. Dennison helped the big people, yes, and
they paid for his help, making possible his assistance to
the little people, earning their gratitude and loyalty.
With a simple "Jimmy the Dahl" vote the ledger was balanced. Realizing that "If a will to help the poor and the
needy was no adequate program to govern a nation, it was
more than enough to capture a city ward," Dennison early in

his Omaha years organized saloonkeepers and gamblers into a welfare league.[18] From these beginnings charitable activities grew into a mainstay function of the political machine Dennison constructed, his hierarchy of precinct and ward workers identifying who needed what. He worked mostly indirectly, referring someone who came to him for assistance to the appropriate neighborhood lieutenant, mindful personal contact on a local basis bore better electoral fruit than one further removed. A Dennison opponent and former state appointee in the Douglas County Election Commissioner's Office graded the welfare activities of the machine "A plus." "What was wrong," he asked, "with giving a voter a ticket on election day along with a reminder of past favors?" Dennison's men would say, "'all we're asking you to do is, you vote for these men. Take that into the polling place with you.' There's nothing illegal about that."

"He gave away a ton of money, a ton a week," captures the spirit and image of the operation if not its actual expenditures, and the "Old Man" remains in memory as the man who "did more for poor people than anyone for years to come."[19] These broad comments were based upon the fact of food distributed, coal supplied, pastors and flowers for funerals otherwise not affordable, and assistance in bureaucratic or legal tangles. A typical example is Dennison one day giving a young man working for him the address of a woman who had just lost two children to diphtheria. Following instructions, he went to the home and informed the grieving mother he had just arranged six months credit for her at the corner grocery store, then inquired about her coal supply. It was near gone she replied, and she was then informed her coal bin would be filled the next day. When she asked who the good Samaritan was the boy replied, as he had been instructed, he was not to reveal the name. "That's the kind of man he was," the messenger fondly recalled.

Other accounts of Dennison's assistance likewise savor memories of his desire for secrecy. However, being a calculating boss, Dennison knew his kindnesses would soon be public knowledge as word quickly spread of his generosity. While the "Old Man" remained properly modest, the grocer told customers about the credit granted, and the coal dealer passed on the story of his delivery; in short order stories of the gifts bestowed on the grieving mother were widespread. Thus circulated, welfare did not have to be visited upon every household on the block to have an effect on all of them; Dennison was shrewd about where he delivered his coal and groceries and counted on a ripple effect of gratitude.

When the machine was defeated in 1933, the victors discovered upon taking office that their predecessors had cleverly used city facilities to assist in the machine's charities. A city farm north of town along the river produced turkeys, ducks, and geese. Keeping track of one or another group's preferences for various holidays, the organization prepared as appropriate for an ethnic group its favorite, then made delivery with the compliments of Dennison man Joseph Hummel, city commissioner in charge of parks. Hanscom Park also engaged in a charity of sorts thanks to its greenhouse. Many bulbs were imported by the city, and flower lovers, especially flower club leaders, were recipients of free bulbs with compliments of the park commissioner. A sense of gratitude was earned by the gift of the bulbs, a minor outlay in search for an important vote.[20] Through means subtle and not so subtle the organization sought loyalty to be displayed on election day.

Hummel was one of the most popular of Omaha's city commissioners, consistently a high vote getter, particularly from Omaha's sizeable German population. He labored long days for his department, his efforts producing beautiful parks linked by a graceful boulevard system. Friends said "he lived and breathed his parks," and he remained active in city politics long after the Dennison machine had faded from the scene. Joe had an interesting way with words, once telling his fellow commissioners after a heavy rain that "The water came off the pidium, coagulated in the intersection, and inudiated the city. All inudiated." On another occasion he entered the city attorney's office after the commission had just demoted a controversial police chief to patrolman. Hat on, cigar in mouth, he announced "Well, we done a good thing; we got rid of that damn Kahsar--he just unsurped the powers of this council." A dispute over the location of the municipal university led Joe to confide to a friend after an annexation struggle: "We made a mistake; we didn't get together and formiliate a procediture before we went down there." Hummel's way with the voters and Dennison's lack of concern with the parks made for a comfortable working relationship, for Joe was a faithful ally.

In the precincts and wards Dennison's workers labored for cooperative and reliable city commissioners like Joe Hummel. Ward and precinct representatives had the responsibilities of knowing everyone, to be known, and to care for their charges when appropriate. They welcomed future constituents by attending their christenings, honored them by attending their weddings, helped them pay fines--or get out of them--and bid them farewell at their funerals.[21] And between their earthly arrival and departure, they helped find them jobs in either the public or private sector. Well before the era of Tom Dennison, King George III summarized the essence of what became known in the United States as the spoils system, the vehicle of machine patronage: "Every man is good enough for any place he can get."[22] And getting a place frequently meant going to the local machine worker who provided the words of recommendation which meant employment for the seeker and another vote for the machine. A Chicago alderman well understood the inducements that nurtured the patronage system: "To participants, the machine offers income, careers, preferements, recognition, prestige, wealth and protection . . . . The machine offers him an opportunity to realize his ambitions, and exacts only regularity, unwavering loyalty, work, devotion, contributions, and delivery of the vote."[23]

One did not have to be a part, however, of Omaha's third ward hierarchy to solicit votes for the organization's candidates, do it favors, and otherwise earn the gratitude of Headquarters. On behalf of anyone willing to lend assistance, Dennison exerted his influence. Throughout the city men and women labored, professional and nonprofessional, who were beholden to the machine although not a member of it, for their jobs, prosperity, and careers. There were recommended attorneys, judges on the bench, preferred firms, as well as policemen on their beat, or laborers in the packing houses and elsewhere because of a nod from Dennison in return for support. Not everyone the machine assisted gained a career or wealth; these were largely enjoyed by those already well placed, persons fostered by the machine but not created. The mass of individuals who secured employment through Dennison were granted menial jobs which promised little as paths to fame and fortune. But they were jobs, gained at Dennison's employment agency, and for his downtown and South Omaha clientele, often uneducated or immigrant, that was sufficient to earn their gratitude.

Men who worked in the machine as precinct or ward leaders, most sharing with Dennison little formal education and without access to the professions or homes of the "silk stocking" wards (at least through the front door), failed to gain prestige among the city elite, but they did win the recognition and admiration of their neighbors. Because they represented Mr. Dennison, they mirrored his authority and importance; the status and rewards of a precinct or ward worker became vicariously those of their group, and proved that the land of opportunity had smiled upon one of their kind.

A boss's job pool, it is important to note, was not limited to the public sector. "Not only does he procure for his supporters positions in the service of state or city . . ." Teddy Roosevelt recognized, "but he is also able to procure positions for many on horse railways, the elevated roads, quarry works etc."[24] In Omaha scores of people worked for private firms because Dennison had access to their top officers, multiplying his organization's capacity to win loyalty by transforming the unemployed into the employed. Receiving word from a lieutenant that a promising applicant (a potential vote) was on hand, Dennison responded by referring him to Tom Quinlan at Brandeis Department Store, or to Jim Davidson at the power company when it was privately owned. Joe Hayden, a gentleman very close to Dennison and owner of a large retail firm bearing his family name, was another job source, as was Pete Jolly of Cudahy packing who sat with Dennison at prize fights. Stockyards officer Everett Buckingham helped provide jobs, as did Paul Gallagher at Paxton and Gallagher wholesale grocers, who put to work men Dennsion sent him. Employment at Paxton-Vierling Steel Works was a matter of Dennison sending an aspirant to Bill Russell, who spent many an hour at Headquarters. Anyone seeking a job with a lumber and coal company was sent to Gould Dietz who owned one; Bert Murphy provided work in the automobile and trucking industry. Jimmy Lee was the man contacted at the Omaha National Bank, and Tom Murphy at the U.S. National for positions at their disposal.[25]

Through these men and many others the "Old Man" manipulated a large pool of private sector jobs, important not only for their numbers but also because they were not directly dependent upon success at the polls. A reversal of fortunes, as in 1918, meant many faithful Dennison people remained employed, since those now unwelcome in public posts by the interim government went to work with the "Old Man's" friends in private industry. For example, one Dennison associate spent twenty-two years on the police force with but one break during his career. That came when reformer Ringer was police commissioner; officer Bert Thorpe resigned (or was resigned) and was off the force for eighteen months. Thanks to Dennison he became a guard at the U.S. National Bank, boasting to a friend in the bank's basement that Tom had taken care of him with a referral.[26] Following Dahlman's triumphant return as mayor, Thorpe was reappointed as a police officer.

The power to grant a job carried with it of course the power to say "no." A young man once asked Sheriff Michael Clark, a Dennison man, a week before an election if he could be appointed a deputy if Mike won reelection. Clark promised if Tom Dennison gave his O.K. then "he would put him on." But the "Old Man" did not go along, bluntly telling the applicant he might want to give the job to somebody else.[27] Holding a job in reserve so as to reward a faithful supporter was one method to use the patronage power. Another was to use it for punishment, removing from a patronage position anyone who failed properly to use the job to advance Dennison's and the machine's interests. Early on in the "Old Man's" boss career, he signaled the fate of those who fell into disfavor. A policeman involved in a raid on a Dennison policy house was told by Dennison in police court the next morning, "I'll get you." And get him he did, the ex-officer testified several years later.[28]

Jobs for the faithful in public posts sometimes drew criticism, as happened in a grand jury report the year Dahlman and his ticket were voted out. The court house was a "deplorable political pie" bemoaned the jurors, with its charwomen and janitors costing almost $10,000 a year more than the cost for similar services for similar floor space at either the City National Bank Building or the Omaha National.[29] Patronage in the form of nepotism was also not unknown, and two of Tom's brothers, John and Pat, shared many years in the service of Omaha caring for its streets and sidewalks. Welfare, favors, patronage, all existed for one purpose--to bring forth voters to mark their ballots for machine candidates. But to ensure the final tallies placed Dennison men in office, a host of subsidiary tactics were adopted ranging from the legally clever, to flagrant violations of the law. The latter were more characteristic of the machine's earlier days, but old habits died hard, despite electoral reforms to curtail illegal electoral practices.

In the early 1920s the organization was still in the business of importing voters, one year taking advantage of migratory road builders across the river in Iowa. The men were rounded up in Council Bluffs, then escorted to Omaha to register to vote, where all recorded their residence as being in third ward hotels. When an election official checked the suspicious looking registration lists, not to his great surprise he discovered many a newly registered voter was not really staying at any of the hotels. In an election some years earlier, in 1911, eight men were reported to have traveled about the third ward in a big touring car. As they made their way from precinct to precinct, the gentlemen proceeded to register to vote in each one. Several days later a check of third ward registrations revealed addresses where in fact vacant lots existed. In other instances, empty houses were occupied according to addresses given by voter registrants. When occupants of houses that were lived in were questioned, they were unable to identify the names of men who, according to their voter registration, also lived there.[30]

One Dennison worker recalled casting his first vote at age nineteen, informed by the "Old Man" he suddenly reached twenty-one on election day. When not casting premature ballots, the young man had the task of reading the obituaries of local newspapers, taking down names and addresses of individuals to be resurrected on election day. As he said of men whose names were drawn from the death notices, "He was dead, but he voted." For one pre-World War I election Dennison directed his youthful aide to a fire station polling place in the third ward. "I want you to be in charge there," said Dennison, "Its all taken care of." About one o'clock in the afternoon a well dressed gentleman appeared and ordered the ballot box to be carried upstairs. There the guest proceeded to open the urn and began building two piles: one of ballots properly marked for organization candidates, the other for necessary corrections. Ballots in the former pile were redeposited, as were the latter, after additional pencil marks were added to spoil, amend, or fill in the ballots as they should have been in the first place. "They couldn't lose boy," said the reminiscing poll worker.

One way to add to the proper stack was to have ballots properly marked from the start, and here an early bribe technique called the "ignorant voter" came into play. Slate tickets in hand, Dennison workers positioned themselves outside polling places, stopping voters on their way to perform their civic duty. They were offered money in return for a straight slate vote, and to ensure the voter cast a proper ballot talked him into playing the ignorant voter. Agreement reached, the bought voter entered the polling place, Dennison slate card in hand, and took an oath to the election judge swearing inability to read or write, thus empowering the official to mark the ballot as the "illiterate" instructed. That is, the slate vote. The judge, also fixed and part of the scheme, wrote the voter's name on the slate card as evidence of fulfillment of his obligation, and the ignorant voter was paid by a Dennison worker upon presentation of his receipt. Not confined to the third ward, the scheme was employed in other wards by machine workers for several years.[31]

A means in the machine's earlier days to neutralize persons who made a nuisance of themselves on election day by challenging voters, snooping around polling places, or otherwise being uncooperative was to have them arrested. Placed in jail until the polls closed, they were out of harmful way, and experienced the ploy known as "burying prisoners."[32] Influence in the police department made the maneuver possible, and friends there also helped harass saloonkeepers or madams who were less than enthusiastic about the machine's preferences. Reminders and threats of arrests and prosecutions were common as election day approached, and pressure was exerted on owners, employees, and customers on behalf of favored candidates. A leaflet circulating in the third ward one year carried the information that John Simpson, President of the Afro-American League, was going to preside over a meeting called in support of a candidate challenging the Budweiser favorite.

Simpson's employer, saloon owner Richard Donnelly, was notified by city authorities that if Simpson held his meeting the saloon would be closed at midnight; and if Simpson so much as worked in the primaries for the opposition, Donnelly was going to be locked up. Simpson lost his job and the saloon remained open.[33] Donnelly's experience was not an isolated one and other saloon owners felt similar weight pressing from city hall. One of them, who had the temerity to have his name associated with anti-Moores's literature, was ordered to get out and work for Moores in the campaign or be forced out of business. Indeed, some anti-Moores saloons were forced to close.[34]

Pressures from city hall were not reserved for saloons since anyone, whether legitimate or illegitimate, was subject to coercion in one form or another and not only in the machine's adolescent years. In the later 1920s, for example, a plumbing contractor placed big signs in his firm's windows supporting the candidacy of a good friend for the city commission, but not a friend of Dennison's. Efficient, law-abiding, and stringent in meeting city requirements, the company was prosperous and acquired an abundance of contracts. Nonetheless, a few days after the signs went up notice was received its plumbing license was revoked. Going to city hall to seek redress, the owner brothers were instructed to go see Tom Dennison. He kept them waiting for several days before he received them, letting the effects of the revocation sink in. Then he informed them they had better remove the offensive signs from their windows and prominently display proper ones in their place. Furthermore, a $500 contribution to the campaign fund was in order. The signs went down, the contribution was delivered, and the windows were "plastered top to bottom" with the preferred slate, and the license was restored.[35]

A turning point of sorts came with the 1912 elections, a year of flagrant electoral transgressions resulting in a state investigation and thence to legislative remedy. The usual charges of registration frauds and false ballots accompanied the spring city primary (the third ward's third precinct added more votes to its tally than there were ballots issued by the city clerk.)[36] These were simply warm ups for the May election when machine workers were all given annotated registration lists for their precincts. False names or those of deceased registrants were identified for the workers, who in turn supplied these names and addresses to floating voters when they hit their precinct.

False registrations were abundant and nonexistent dwellings on vacant lots sent forth voters. The opposition Citizen's Union hired four Burns detectives from out of town to investigate electoral conditions in Omaha, men identified as specialists in electoral fraud all over the nation. Their three week examination, which went through the May election, led the Burns chief detective on the job to exclaim he uncovered "in Omaha the most effective and the most daring organization for carrying on elections frauds that he has ever seen."[37] The investigators reported the ignorant voter scheme was widespread in the lower wards. One voter in the April primary when asked if he could read or write had answered "yes," stated the detectives; nonetheless, the election judge in this second precinct, third ward polling place disagreed and obligingly marked his ballot for him. Also in use was the "short pencil," a matter of a "gang" election judge holding a pencil stub between his last two fingers, then when counting, surreptitiously putting extra marks on opposition ballots thus invalidating them.

They disclosed the "endless chain system" was prevalent in the third ward. To initiate the chain a machine precinct worker neglected to deposit his ballot after receiving it. Instead, he took it with him when he left the polling place to mark elsewhere. Then he passed it on to a "gang" or bribed voter on his way to the polls with instructions to deposit the marked ballot after going through the motions of voting, and to bring his issued unmarked one back to the worker. Thereby the machine had another vote to cast, in an endless chain, secure in the knowledge every voter was doing his job since a blank ballot had to be delivered before he was paid off.[38] Finding people to participate extended to city jail. Among the most grateful Omahans on election day was the prisoner in city jail on a vagrancy charge who was let out of his cell to clean the chief's office. When the turnkey asked him if he was registered to vote, he said "yes." In that case, the turnkey advised, you had better go vote and he was released. As a matter of fact, he was one of several prisoners freed that day to go to the polls, including several who had not bothered to register.[39]

State action on voting conditions in Omaha was finally prompted by scenes of wild disorder in the November 1912 general election. It was not the third ward that inspired the initial attention, but the first's second precinct. Three election officials there spent the day getting drunk, and Morris Milder wandered over from the third ward to help them in their electoral duties. When one sober election judge called the district court for help, a clerk in a county judge's office who lived in the precinct was sent to investigate. He entered pandemonium. Milder was helping the drunk officials by counting Congressional ballots, and many of these by now were strewn about on the floor, torn in half. Furniture was upset, and so were the few people now gathering there to observe democracy in action. His count finished, Milder presented the returns: 203 for Baldrige, 81 for Lobeck, totaling ten more votes than names on the poll book.[40] Events in the precinct and indications of gross election irregularities in neighboring wards resulted in a state level investigation of conditions in Omaha.

A special committee on contested elections was appointed by the Nebraska Senate's president to probe election day activities in the second precincts of Omaha's first and third wards. The committee heard witnesses, took depositions, and reviewed the ballots cast in the two precincts. On the basis of their investigation, committee members were convinced in these two precincts the elections boards "were composed of men who were grossly ignorant, incompetent, and totally indifferent to the duties and to the rights of candidates."[41] The committee concluded that "It has been well known for many years that the voters in certain voting precincts in the city of Omaha have been practically owned and controlled by certain representatives of vice and that an absolutely honest election has not taken place in such precincts within the memory of man."[42] Their judgment was fueled by finding, for example, that according to the poll book of one precinct, men listed on the registration rolls voted in exactly the same order as they had registered. And all the registrations and poll book signatures were in P.J. "Pete" Rooney's handwriting, a close Dennison associate. Pete had opened a rooming house just prior to the November election (closed right after), and on the last day of registration twenty-two potential voters registered from its address. Twenty of them were listed in the poll book as having voted, all casting their ballots in the same order as they had registered.

In the last half hour of voting, 173 ballots were cast in one of the precincts, which meant close to six voters per minute performed their civic duty, on a ballot calling for so many decisions it was eight feet long. Witnesses whose names were listed as having voted testified they had not, multiple voting took place, and miscounting of returns was obvious:[43]

> All the way through we find arbitrary figures put down in this unofficial and makeshift poll book, with exquisite neatness of tally marks. The compiler began with the figure 6, which was awarded to Dodge, and followed with 7 for Lee, 8 for Howard and on up in more or less consecutive numerical order to 47, which was given to Senator Norris.

The report energized legislators who had been seeking the appropriate time for introduction of election reform aimed at Omaha. One of the leaders in the effort to have the investigation conducted, N.P. Dodge, later wrote:[44]

> Thus, after years of mystery and indignant condemnation of us who had even dared question the regularity of elections, the people were dramatically informed that in many precincts, in the lower wards at least, no ballots were ever counted, but returns were certified to by the election officials in accordance with the instructions of the 'boss' who was told by 'higher ups' whom they wished to defeat.

Dodge's proposal, "An Act Creating the Office of Election Commissioner," became law in the spring of 1913, and henceforth elections in Omaha and Douglas County came under the jurisdiction of an official appointed by the governor. The first Election Commissioner, Harley G. Moorehead, an attorney who had never held public office, dedicated himself and his office to enforcement of what came to be known as the Honest Election Law. Dodge and his followers were intent on stopping false registrations, dishonest voting, and fraudulent returns. To those ends Morehead, with a two year term but reappointed by a series of Republican and Democratic governors, appointed as required by the law members of both major parties to serve as election judges and clerks (candidates, public employees, or sellers or workers for a seller of intoxicating beverages were ineligible) to supervise polling places. Unlike the old law, the new one did not require residence in a precinct for service

161

on election day, enabling the Election Commissioner to draft judges from other parts of the city to serve in the third ward or elsewhere. Any person appointed by the Election Commissioner was subject to immediate removal for misconduct or neglect of duties.

A personal representative of the commissioner, an inspector, was appointed for every voting place to oversee the law's implementation, empowered to challenge any voter whose name was not on registration lists, or who appeared in any way to be voting illegally. Supervision of the conduct and fulfillment of the responsibilities of judges and clerks was also an inspector's job. An initial task was to undertake a canvass of the city to establish a valid list of qualified voters and their residences, "which lists shall be used for checking, revising and correcting registration."[45] Within ten days of an election, or other times if deemed necessary, the commissioner, through his inspectors, was empowered to challenge any registrant. Challenged voters had to secure an affidavit affirming their legal right to vote or be denied the right. On election day no voter henceforth was given a ballot until name and residence were verified as being on the lists, their name then consecutively entered in the poll book by the clerks, and the voter signed the book himself or later herself.

In large measure the Honest Election Law accomplished its purpose, and reports of election scandal so common in the early years become more rare after its passage. But fraud and other malpractices, while reduced, did not disappear from the lower wards. Again displaying its adaptability, the machine learned to live with the Honest Election Law, becoming less obvious in its electoral legal transgressions, and finding more devious--but not illegal--techniques to assure victories. Seventeen years after the Honest Election Law was passed, the Dennison machine waged its last successful city election, employing a variety of tricks to assist the Square Seven. A minister, using his pulpit to denounce Dennison and the Square Seven as election day approached, one Sunday was surprised to uncover a fifty dollar bill in his collection plate. He received a telephone call the next day and was told by his unidentified caller more of the same was likely for his Sunday services if he got on the right side of the fence. Attacks in the church on Dennison ceased and the Reverend soon was speaking on behalf of the Square Seven, sharing the same platforms as other Dennison agents.[46]

The church vote was also in mind as the machine schemed to defame opponents of its incumbent commissioners. One afternoon Dennison called Tom Crawford to his office and showed him a small card which carried an indecent poem about priests and nuns. The "Old Man" had been handed the item a few minutes before as he stood in front of the cigar store, and now he told Crawford he had an idea. He wanted copies of the poem reprinted, and on the reverse side of the card was to be listed the names of Towl, Butler, and the rest of the opposition slate. With instructions to be careful in carrying out the maneuver, Crawford was sent to the Omaha Printing Company to have about 5,000 of the cards printed. Clint Miller, Johnson's right-hand man, protested it was a terrible thing to do, but agreed when Crawford pressed upon him it was Dennison's order. Arrangements were made to have the cards prepared after hours by a particularly trusted employee, and delivery was promised over the next day or two. Johnny Marcell and his assistant, Roscoe "The Toad" Rawley, the "Old Man's" South Omaha representatives, were given responsibility for distributing the cards in their predominately Catholic neighborhoods. "There won't be a Catholic in the town vote for those fellows," chortled Dennison, "that card will beat them out of every Catholic vote in town."[47]

The Ku Klux Klan was also drafted, unknowingly, to advance the Square Seven's cause. Catholics and blacks being targets of the KKK, Dennison and his men arranged to have crosses burned at a major intersection in Catholic South Omaha at 36th and Q Streets, and in the front yard of prominent black Square Seven supporter, Dr. John A. Singleton, in the predominantly black near north side. While the crosses burned, Dennison men circulated in the neighborhoods charging that Towl and his ticket were Klan members. Dennison men charged Dan Butler, a Catholic, was really a Klanner at heart and had come to terms with them in return for electoral support. Safety from the Klan was possible only by voting for the Square Seven.[48]

Through two of his men he had infiltrate the Omaha Klan, Dennison was kept informed of its membership and meeting proceedings. To embarrass and injure political opponents, Dennison had their names inserted into a Klan membership list and then circulated the now bogus roster. When not using the Klan to hamper the enemy slate, Dennison used his widespread business allies to assist him in the task. For instance, the wife of a railroad agent became deeply involved in the 1930 Towl campaign, and was doing an effective job in advancing his candidacy. To quash the woman's enthusiasm, Dennison summoned Tom Murphy to his office for a conference. The banker pointed out that Bert Murphy of Andrew Murphy and Sons Auto Company was bringing his cars into Omaha via the railroad in question, the Chicago Great Western. Bert was now called and he soon joined Dennison and the others.

They decided a call from the auto dealer was in order, with Murphy to complain to the agent that his wife's political activities were attacks on his friends. If she continued in her endeavors on behalf of Towl, the Chicago Great Western could expect to lose the car shipments of Andrew Murphy and Sons. Next a letter was sent by Crawford to the railroad's headquarters, containing a litany of complaints on behalf of Omahans, writing that they too were being injured by the agent and his wife because of her political work. All of them, warned the letter, would be looking for new transportation if the woman did not find new interests. "I recall distinctly," wrote Crawford, "that the wife of this agent ceased her activities very shortly thereafter the complaint of Bert Murphy and this signed letter, but anonymous, which was sent to Chicago."[49]

In an earlier election a gentleman who ran a cigar store in the Brandeis Theatre Building decided to run for city commissioner. Dennison's slate was already set and included the name of Harry Zimman, who was expected to draw the Jewish vote. Fearing a divided result because the challenger was also Jewish, Dennison sent word to Brandeis contact Tom Quinlan to get the fellow to withdraw. Quinlan tried to satisfy Dennison's request, but was unsuccessful. The "Old Man" then passed word that unless the fellow was removed from the race, Brandeis's taxes would not only increase, but some new ones would be assessed. In a couple of days, the candidates for city commissioner were one person less.[50]

The slate ticket cards candidates had printed for

distribution opened up to the machine additional opportunities to be duplicitous without breaking the law. Roy Towl and John A. Bruce discovered one day their slate card was being circulated but without the name of machine defector Dan Butler. He had joined forces with them and his name was included on cards Towl and Bruce had printed. An "eleventh hour dodger" was abroad in the city, phony cards printed by the Dennison forces leaving Butler's name off to nurture the rumor Towl's slate had split and Dan Butler was disavowed. Headquarters' purpose was twofold: when the dodger was distributed either Butler's friends would resent the eleventh hour dismissal of the long-time politician and vote against the traitors, Towl and Bruce; or, second, followers of the two men would notice Butler had been dropped and vote against him. Either way the organization stood to benefit.[51]

Slate tickets were used by Dennison not only to confuse voters but to pacify candidates. Feeling the county treasurer had not been solicitous enough about patronage despite machine backing, Dennison shifted his support one election from incumbent Otto Bauman to Ira Jones, and ordered tickets printed with Jones included. However, he also ordered several hundred with Bauman's name in place of Jones's. These were kept at Headquarters and when Bauman appeared, irate because he had heard Dennison was backing Jones, he was shown a stack of the cards bearing his name, proof Dennison had not switched sides. Bauman was invited to take the tickets along, and before he left heard the "Old Man" instruct Crawford to tell the boys to be on the look out for the ones without Bauman's name. Probably the work of somebody who duplicated our slate to cause trouble, the Boss consoled the appeased candidate.[52]

After the 1930 fall election, Dennison and Nesselhous sought to sow confusion and mistrust at the gubernatorial level by having 500 tickets printed exactly like those Harry Lapidus, a prominent Omaha businessman and Dennison foe, had requested in support of his champion, Arthur Weaver, for governor. Another 500 followed, similar to the first batch except Charles Bryan's name was substituted for Weaver's. A personal friend of Dennison's who was also a friend of Weaver's was given about 100 of the false tickets and requested to pass them on to Weaver, who had lost the election. The scheme was designed to suggest to Weaver that

Lapidus had double-crossed him by supporting Bryan; accurate cards were sent to Bryan to bolster the case against Lapidus, and thereby prevent any favors from Lincoln going his way.[53]

Dan Butler was a particular target in the 1930 city election, considered a turncoat at Dennison Headquarters for joining the opposition after years of organization support. Using highly placed friends in the business community as transmitters to the Bishop of the Catholic Diocese of Omaha, Dennison invented the story that Butler had denounced his Catholic religion and signed an article of agreement with the KKK in return for promises of electoral support. Dennison's intention was suppression of any church hierarchy backing for Butler. To injure further Butler's reputation among the laity, Dennison lieutenants distributed flyers attesting to the apostate's clinging to the Klan.[54] Not content with the rumors spread, the organization decided to recruit campaign workers for the targeted Butler. Derelicts were rounded up, the dirtier and more stained the better, warmed with liquor and scattered around town to ring doorbells. When doors opened the haggard and inebriated campaign workers presented cards to the occupants bearing Butler's picture, mumbled a word in his favor, then wobbled on to the next house to promote Butler's cause.[55]

Even nuns working at St. Joseph's Hospital were not beyond Dennison's concern and reach at election time. Hospitalized shortly before voters were to go the polls, the "Old Man" learned one of the nuns was related to Butler and he anticipated many of the sisters would vote for him because of the personal relationship. He therefore talked with many of them, warning if Butler won election as a city commissioner St. Joseph's stood to lose its city business, and word would be passed among his well placed friends to seek health care elsewhere. According to Tom Crawford, Dennison laughed heartily when he told the story, summing it up with "Well, we will have no more trouble with Butler getting votes from St. Joe . . . ."[56]

By 1930 Moorehead and his successor as Election Commissioner, William McHugh, had managed to trim greatly the machine's most egregious election activities. But not completely as seen in the method devised for voting the ill and hospitalized. The law provided ballots could be picked up and signed for at the Election Commissioner's office by representatives of persons unable to go to a polling place. Organization workers dutifully took these steps, machine intelligence providing names of the hospitalized and infirm. Then they proceeded to the proper addresses and presented a ballot, along with a soft lead pencil. Bedridden but now voting, the infirm marked the ballot and returned it to the agent, who now departed from the law by putting the ballot in his pocket unsealed. Before being returned to the Election Commissioner, the ballots were taken to Headquarters for review and necessary erasures and additions. Some 120 ballots were thus corrected in one primary.[57]

Floating voters, stuffed ballot boxes, false registrations, endless chains and short pencil ploys, eleventh hour dodgers, derelicts for canvassers, misleading electoral cards, all were brought into service by the Dennison machine over the years. Underlying them was the most important and elemental electoral consideration--organization. Voters had to be registered, with an eye to legality after the Honest Election Law, and voted on election day. Elections were the life nurturing substance of the organism we have called a machine, and organization was the fundamental element of its existence. An early member of the Independent Voters League mused, long after Dennison was gone from the scene, that the Honest Election Law kept voting fraud to a minimum in Omaha, but the machine retained power because it got out the vote, a testimonial to its organizational vitality. In a story about the "Old Man" written just after his death, Omahans read that:[58]

> From the start Dennison built up a political machine that extended over the entire city. His genius along these lines created a system that was the wonder of friends and enemies alike, one which political leaders in other cities came to see and study.
>
> His file contained the name, political affiliation, character and weaknesses of almost every voter in the city. On election day his ward chief, precinct lieutenants, and block workers saw to it that every favorable vote was cast early.

One of the workers who was out there bringing in votes recalls that Dennison's index file included every registered voter in Omaha, indicating affiliations and background. Always up to date the file "was guarded like gold."[59] The secret of Dennison's success was his precinct workers who labored in the second through the seventh wards, with some efforts in the eighth. The others were "tough" for the machine and efforts were accordingly concentrated in lower downtown and South Omaha: "those were our wards."[60]

Machine workers at the grassroots level were carefully selected, and a primary consideration was ensuring the spokesman was of the prevailing ethnic background as those he was responsible for on election day: an Italian for Little Italy; a Czech in Little Liberty; an Irishman on Irish Hill; a black for the north side. Representative organization figures included Nick Pappas who delivered a solid Greek vote; Leo Cantoni was one of several contacts with the Italian community, others being Louis Piatti in the old days, later Joe Salerno. The Dahir brothers, Tommy, Nick, and Louis were responsible for the Lebanese and Syrian vote, with Dick Fitzgerald and Paul Trainor taking care of a precinct in central Omaha with an Irish contingent, the latter rewarded for his services with an appointment to the fire department.[61] Over the years, four names are associated with the black community: Victor Walker, William "Billy" Crutchfield, John H. "Jack" Broomfield, and Harry Buford.

South Omaha was delegated in general to John Marcell, an attorney and south side city prosecutor. "Toad" Rawley, proprietor of an appliance store near Marcell's office, was second in command. Under them were many machine workers, and we find, for example, Frank Kawa who was faithful in delivering the Brown Park area, and Joe Teshnohlidek, both later becoming restaurant owners. These men and scores like them were busy before elections getting people registered to vote, then on election day seeing that ballots were cast the right way. To assist them, Headquarters made available to precinct workers copies of registration lists, indicating any changes because of deaths or moves since the last election. Polling books were scanned to see who had voted, and a vehicle dispatched to bring in those who had not yet appeared.[62] Lining up transportation on election day was a major organizational task. Dennison men made the rounds of automobile dealers for courtesy cars, and every cab company was expected to help out with donated taxis. Members of the organization who owned autos were expected to place them at the machine's disposal for the day, and rental agencies had a guaranteed customer for their fleets. An owner of an early car rental business in Omaha recalled that all his vehicles were hired by the machine on election days, with special insurance taken out. Driver availability was no problem because organization workers were happy to serve as chauffeurs.[63] Car rental firms were like the bars on election day; they were in effect closed to the public since the machine monopolized them and no automobiles were available for rental to anyone else.

To guarantee working people cast their ballots, Dennison made arrangements with cooperative Omaha firms for blocks of employees to be permitted to leave work at specified times to go vote. On election day workers received from their superiors a machine slate, bearing the address of their polling place on the back along with departure time for machine provided transportation. Voters were advised if Dennison's opponents won, business likely was going to suffer and lay offs follow. At prescribed times a car pulled up to take a waiting group to polling places and then bring them back.[64]

Considering the volume of manpower needed at election time to attend to machine responsibilities, it was necessary to recruit additional help. On such occasions, police department and city hall employees, while on public time and payroll, were called upon to serve Tom Dennison and his organization. Securing a list of selected policemen's names from an assistant, the "Old Man" telephoned the chief of police to tell him he wanted the men on the list for the campaign. Accordingly, these officers were placed on special duty for perhaps three weeks. Individuals from city hall worked along with them as a consequence of a similar call from Dennison to the mayor or a city commissioner who in self-interest honored Tom's request for personnel to help win the forthcoming election.[65] Using the police department for electoral purposes was a long-lived machine technique, going back at least to the turn of the century. "Policemen became full-fledged ward heelers yesterday" announced a newspaper in 1900, reporting that in "civies" and in uniform officers were working for the machine ticket. At midnight the day before the election, half the night shift was instructed to appear on election day in civilian clothes, then were detailed to downtown wards to get out the vote.[66]

Given the scope of operations, it was impossible for Tom Dennison to supervise everyone working for him at the ward, precinct, and block levels. Intermediaries were necessary, lieutenants in the machine's service. Faithful and loyal service was demanded by the "Old Man," and those who delivered were rewarded with money, position, plus the psychic recompense of feeling important because admitted to the sanctum of power at Headquarters. Tenure within the circle was indefinite, for any straying from loyalty or laggardness in performance resulted in demotion. Morris Milder's fate is witness to the consequences of "crossing" the "Old Man," his experience not an isolated one but typical.

Some years before Milder fell from grace, John Lynch, a man schooled and promoted by Dennison to county commissioner, was broken by Dennison for violating the code of loyalty. Dennison brought Lynch up through the organization, granting him title, access to power, and the wealth to be gained from sharing in Dennison's gambling activities. From 1914 to 1917 they were two of four partners in the Riverside Inn, located three miles north of Omaha on the Missouri's west bank. A drinking and gambling establishment, the Riverside was financed by Dennison and Nesselhous, with County Commissioner Lynch the partner responsible for providing protection from county legal authorities. Jack Haskell, the fourth partner, a former Western League umpire known as the Beau Brummel of the third ward, was club manager, called in from Denver by Nesselhous to take the job. Proceeds were cut four ways, 25 per cent each, with envelopes available at the Budweiser's bar about the fifth of every month for the partners.[67]

In the earlier days of their relationship, Lynch headed for the Budweiser to discuss affairs, Tom seated at his roll-top desk, Lynch comfortable in an easy chair. As American entry into World War I approached, Lynch's ambition surpassed his judgment. Gossip began to circulate that a struggle for machine leadership was going on in the third ward. People asked one another in the streets around the Budweiser, "are you a Dennison or a Lynch man?"[68] The challenger ceased going to the Budweiser and the "Old Man" went to the courthouse, to a gym that Lynch had installed, to see the commissioner. In February 1918 the gym figured prominently in Johnny Lynch's downfall.

He was now an enemy, a threat to Dennison's power and he had to be destroyed. Court action to remove the disloyal Lynch was initiated by Dennison's sheriff, Mike Clark, on grounds he was monopolizing public property with his gym, and for defacing and damaging the room with athletic equipment. Official misconduct for bringing alcohol and women to the gym was also charged. At Lynch's trial, Dennison loyalist Pete Rooney and others testified of all night parties with women and booze brought to the courthouse and Lynch's gym. Taking the witness stand, Dennison uttered words that marked the end of the forty-two year old Lynch's political career. "He was my business partner," Dennison related, "and he double-crossed me and my friends."[69] Asked why he gave testimony against a man who had been his friend, Dennison criticized his former protege for having tried to run him out of town and for "jamming" his friends, men who had been with him for many an Omaha political fight. Lynch had to be stopped, Omaha's political boss announced. Throughout the trial, Dennison was a conspicuous spectator.

Declared guilty on five charges, Johnny Lynch's near eight year career as a county commissioner ended on February 21, 1918, the actual ouster coming a week later when a motion for a retrial was denied. Four months later the deposed commissioner was again in the news, indicted by a grand jury for violation of the Mann Act. A former switchboard operator employed by Lynch at the courthouse was named as the individual he transported to Kansas City in violation of the statute. The indictment was dismissed because of faulty wording, but a new one in November sent Lynch to jail for Christmas and a three month term.[70] Lynch went to Kansas City after his release, his political career, private life, and financial condition all a shambles. When the "Old Man" said he was through with Johnny Lynch, recalled Billy Maher, his fate was sealed; old debts were settled as everybody took "ace-deuce at him."[71]

Lieutenants like Milder and Lynch suffered harsh reprisal when they challenged the "Old Man." But for the most part his inner circle was devoted, fealty and reward keeping the kingdom fast for three decades. More typical than the two ill-fated "crossers" was a man like Pete Rooney, an illiterate ex-wrestler who, under Dennison's auspices, became owner of the Underworld. Another "Pete," Peter Loch, was a Headquarters regular, like Rooney an ex-wrestler become saloonkeeper. Coming to Omaha in the mid-1880s, he opened a gymnasium and went into politics at the same time, the gym soon replaced by a saloon. His role and that of others in the pre-World War I machine was commented upon by Joe Polcar's special investigators. Dennison was the head of the machine and graft; his chief lieutenant at the time was identified as Johnny Lynch, with Pete Loch next, with Morris Milder mentioned as working his way into the inner circle. Dennison, said one report, met monthly with Lynch at Loch's home, "there to assign the spoils for further distribution among the faithful." Rooney was noted as moving up, and Jack Broomfield was understood to be the black lieutenant in the machine.[72]

Of Dennison's black lieutenants, Walker at one time was known as the sub-boss of the third ward, his power alleged to have been second only to Dennison's. He came to Omaha in 1888 and became a policeman, leaving the force six years later to become a lawyer. After a few years of law practice he bought the Midway Saloon at 12th and Capitol Avenue, prompted by Dennison who said he could not trust the man who had the place, Oscar Picketts. Walker ran the Midway for about two years, then Dennison deposed him for reasons unknown. Years later Walker related he was grabbed one day from behind by a policeman and wrestled to the ground. Dennison appeared and began kicking him; Walker from that point was through at the Midway and in Omaha politics. He returned to his law practice for about four years, but then left the field to become a waiter on the Union Pacific Railroad.[73]

His place at the Midway and in the organization was taken by Jack Broomfield, a native of Savannah, Missouri, a pullman porter until he lost a leg in a train wreck. Arriving in Omaha in 1887, he labored at various jobs then with Crutchfield took over the Midway. Known from coast to coast, the Midway catered primarily to blacks, serving drinks, offering faro, roulette, dice, and cards--under a sign that read "If you have a family that needs your money, don't gamble here."[74] Both Crutchfield and Broomfield became familiar figures in the third ward's night life and politics, the former opening his own place by 1914. Broomfield kept the Midway until state prohibition forced its closing in 1917, but by then he was a wealthy man. He continued as a leader in the black community up to his death ten years later, much of his wealth expended by helping fellow blacks. When told of his long-time lieutenant's death, Dennison extolled Jack Broomfield as "one of the old school of political workers and he could always be depended upon to take care of the colored vote and he never failed." An epitaph of sorts was then added by the Boss, who was a pallbearer at the funeral, "He was true blue and always loyal."[75] Words of no higher praise could pass from Dennison's lips.

During the machine's later years, Dennison's valued lieutenant in Omaha's black community was Harry Buford, a police officer, Dennison's chauffeur, and his eyes, ears, and mouth on the north side. Harry S. Buford was the son of Henry J. and Elizabeth "Lizzie" Buford, born in Kentucky on July 10, 1887, and came to Omaha with his parents the year before Dennison's arrival. His father became a waiter at the Millard Hotel, and Harry joined the police force in 1912, a compact and fast man who looked like a middleweight boxer.[76] He started on the force when police vehicles were horse drawn, but as automobiles replaced them he became an excellent driver. Buford was widely known as a fearless but courteous man who became the pipeline for the police and the machine to the increasingly black near north side.[77] At some undetermined point, Buford came to Dennison's attention and he rose in the ranks, both police and machine, to become the "Old Man's" faithful messenger, indispensable lieutenant, and vote getter for his part of the city.

When Dennison was being tried for conspiracy to violate the prohibition act, Buford, during a recess, himself a suspended police lieutenant and also under indictment, wept as he spoke of the "Old Man." "I love him," said Buford. "The things they say about him are not true. I was glad to be with him, but only when I was off duty. I don't care if the whole world knows it."[78] Although the trial signaled the end of boss rule in Omaha, Harry Buford remained on the force until his death nearly twenty years later. When the victorious reform administration took over in 1933, he was broken to patrolman on order from the new police commissioner, who added that Buford's chauffeuring days were also over. His subsequent career was a checkered one as he accumulated both commendations and reprimands, promotions, and demotions. Three times he held the rank of lieutenant, the highest ever gained by a black man on the Omaha Police Department during those years, the rank held when he announced the end of his career as a policeman. His retirement statement came in the midst of yet another controversy, following charges of his intimidating and interfering with officials of an American Legion Post. As an investigation was put in process to probe misconduct allegations, Buford decided to resign; the hearings were called off and the case was closed.

Often Buford had been heard to say he loved his job and would die in a few weeks if he left it. On January 8, 1951, just a little less than two weeks after announcing his forthcoming retirement, Harry Buford suffered a stroke. He died at his large and beautiful brick home on north 30th Street. When the Bufords had moved there years before, it was amid speculation that Dennison was in some way involved in providing the residence, one well beyond the salary of a police officer, but who well deserved gratitude for his work and loyalty to the "Old Man."[79]

While Walker, Crutchfield, Broomfield, and Buford tended to the near north side, in South Omaha Dennison relied upon John Marcell and Roscoe Rawley, the latter short and about as round as he was tall, hence his nickname, "Toad." In addition to election responsibilities, they oversaw gambling and later bootlegging in South Omaha. Marcell served for several years as a city prosecutor, previously serving, prior to annexation, as South Omaha's deputy city clerk, studying law at night at Creighton University. Following South Omaha's annexation, Marcell was appointed clerk of the central police court, a post he held until the reform ticket took over in 1918. For three years he was in private practice, then with the Square Seven's return to office he was appointed deputy city prosecutor, then south side prosecutor.[80] More importantly, Marcell was the man to see in South Omaha by anyone seeking a favor from the organization.

Roscoe Rawley tersely explained his own role in the machine, and that of men like him, one evening at a political rally. He was asked why a candidate for sheriff was not on the slate he was touting, since Rawley and the man in question were both Democrats. "I do as I am told," replied

Rawley. "Dennison and Nesselhous told me what to do. You know I've got to take orders and you shouldn't be agitated about it."[81] The "Toad's" comment summarized the world of the lieutenants, the ward heelers, the precinct captains, and others who worked for the machine. Their lot in life was to serve their patron.

There were others in the city working on other terms and at another level with Tom Dennison, similarly seeking benefits from their association with him, but much different from him and his faithful machine workers. Unlike the political boss and his lower ward followers in status and propriety, they nonetheless were component parts of Omaha machine politics. Broad in scope and far-reaching in significance, a close relationship long existed between the "Old Man" and the legitimate business community.

NOTES

Chapter V

[1]Steffens, *The Shame of the Cities*, p. 139.

[2]Stave, *The New Deal and the Last Hurrah*, pp. 62-65; see also Dorsett, *The Pendergast Machine*, p. 41; Banfield and Wilson, *City Politics*, p. 118; Orth, *The Boss and the Machine*, pp. 96-97; Gosnell, *Machine Politics Chicago Model*, pp. 86-89.

[3]Alfred Steinberg, *The Bosses* (New York: Mentor, 1972), pp. 147-148.

[4]EOW-H, May 8, 1912.

[5]*Ibid.*, May 5, 1912.

[6]*Ibid.*, May 8, 1918.

[7]*Ibid.*, May 4, 1921.

[8]MOW-H, November 8, 1912; EOW-H, November 9, 1912.

[9]MOW-H, November 2, 1908.

[10]EOW-H, June 26, 1911; ODN, June 26, 1911; Bee, June 27, 1911. On the Water Works struggle see William F. Schmidt, "Municipal Reform in Omaha from 1906 to 1914 as Seen Through the Eyes of the Omaha Press," masters thesis, University of Omaha, 1963.

[11]EOW-H, June 28, 1911.

[12]*Ibid.*, August 3, 1911.

[13]*Ibid.* Two years later the third and tenth wards voted in the majority for granting a twenty-five year extension to the Omaha Gas Company. The measure failed and Omaha was on the way to municipal ownership of the gas works. See Schmidt, "Municipal Reform," pp. 60-83.

[14]Hays, "The Politics of Reform in the Progressive Era," pp. 434-435. See also James Weinstein, "Organized Business and the City Commission and City Manager Movements," *Journal of Southern History*, XXVIII (May, 1962), pp. 166-182.

[15]EOW-H, September 3, 1911; Bee, September 3, 1911; Schmidt, "Municipal Reform," pp. 47-50.

[16]Gordon interview, June 20, 1979; Zerbe interview, August 18, 1979; letter, Murphy to Towl, April 2, 1932, Towl papers, Box 1, Folder 1932, April, City Hall; letter, Murphy to Towl, March 23, 1932, Towl papers, Box 1, Folder 1932, March, City Hall; Special Investigator report, 1913, Rosewater Collection, Reel 3, Box 1927.

[17]Maher interview, October 30, 1979; EOW-H, November 11, 1932; letter, Crawford to Robert Smith, May 9, 1932, Sorensen papers, Box 35, Folder 35; letter, Murphy to "Gene," June 21, 1932, Sorensen papers, Box 35, Folder 35; letter, Crawford to Irvin Stalmaster, September 12, 1932, Sorensen papers, Box 39, Folder 191; letter Crawford to Stalmaster, September 12, 1932, Box 35, Folder 66; letter, Crawford to Stalmaster, September 13, 1932, Sorensen papers, Box 35, Folder 66. In April 1933 Milder's $110,000 home in exclusive Fairacres was destroyed by fire.

The blaze was a case of arson; no suspects were mentioned. EOW-H, April 17, 1933.

[18]Quotation is from Boorstin, *The Americans*, p. 261. On the welfare league see MOW-H, February 15, 1934.

[19]Maher interview, October 23, 1979; Creal interview, August 9, 1979.

[20]Frost interview, October 30, 1979.

[21]On the political role of funerals see Edwin O'Connor, *The Last Hurrah* (Boston: Little, Brown and Company, 1956), chapter eight where O'Connor describes Knocko Finnigan's wake.

[22]Bryce, *The American Commonwealth*, II, p. 128; see also p. 102 where Bryce explains patronage as the source of power and cohesion for city machines.

[23]Gosnell, *Machine Politics*, p. 233.

[24]Roosevelt, "Machine Politics in New York City," p. 81.

[25]Maher interviews, October 6, 23, 30, 1979. Letter, Towl to Harold Wilson, Deputy Prohibition Administration, Omaha, February 3, 1932, Towl papers, Box 1, Folder 1932, February, City Hall.

[26]Thorpe later denied making the statement, but not very convincingly. Deposition of Witness, Bert A. Thorpe, taken before John S. Taggart at #6703 Florence Boulevard, Omaha, Nebraska, November 18, 1932, p. 12 in U.S. Department of Justice, U.S. District Court, Eighth Circuit, District of Nebraska, Omaha Division. *Document No. 7025--Criminal, the U.S. of America vs. Thomas Dennison, et al. Indictment: Conspiracy to Violate National Prohibition Act. Signed: Earl D. Mallery, Foreman. Filed August 5, 1932, signed R.C. Hoyt, Clerk of the Federal District Court.* Hereafter cited as Document No. 7025.

[27]ODN, February 19, 1918.

[28]EOW-H, April 23, 1907.

[29]Bee, April 19, 1918.

[30]EOW-H, July 28, 31, 1911.

[31]*Ibid.*, November 6, 1900; ODN, November 4, 1911.

[32]EOW-H, March 6, 1900; *Ibid.*, November 2, 1909.

[33]*Ibid.*, September 7, 1900.

[34]*Ibid.*, February 17, 1900.

[35]Frost interview, October 30, 1979.

[36]Bee, April 11, 1912.

[37]EOW-H, May 6, 1912.

[38]*Ibid.*

[39]*Ibid.*, May 7, 1912.

[40]*Ibid.*, November 9, 1912.

[41]"Report of the Special Committee on Contested Elections," *Nebraska, Senate Journal of the Legislature of the State of Nebraska, Thirty-Second Session*, p. 422.

[42]*Ibid.*, p. 423.

[43]*Ibid.*, p. 426.

[44]N.P. Dodge, "Dodge Honest Election Law," n.d., p. 5.

[45]*Laws of Nebraska 1913*, Senate File #126, Introduced by Mr. Dodge, "An Act Creating the Office of Election Commissioner . . . ." Section 9, p. 122.

[46]Letter, Murphy to Towl, May 18, 1932, Sorensen papers, Box 35,

Folder 65.
[47]Letter, Crawford to Dennis E. O'Brien, April 15, 1932, Sorensen papers, Box 36, Folder 66; letter Crawford to O'Sullivan, July 6, 1932, Sorensen papers, Box 35, Folder 65; letter, Crawford to Towl, March 29, 1932, Towl papers, Box 1, Folder 1932, March, City Hall.
[48]Letter, Crawford to Towl, April 18, 1932, Sorensen papers, Box 35, Folder 65; letter, Murphy to "Dear Friend Gene" [O'Sullivan], June 11, 1932, Ibid.
[49]Letter, Crawford to Towl, September 8, 1932, Sorensen papers, Box 39, Folder 191.
[50]Maher interview, October 23, 1979.
[51]Letter, Crawford to Towl, April 18, 1932, Sorensen papers, Box 35, Folder 65.
[52]Letter, Crawford to E.D. O'Sullivan, July 6, 1932, Ibid.
[53]Letter, Crawford to Towl, March 17, 1932, Towl papers, Box 1, Folder 1932, March, City Hall.
[54]Letter, Crawford to Dan B. Butler, May 2, 1932, Sorensen papers, Box 35, Folder 65; letter, Murphy to O'Sullivan, May 2, 1932, Ibid. In this letter Murphy [Crawford] writes that Bishop Rummel told Dennison's emissary "he would instruct every priest of the diocese that they shall not speak in Butler's behalf at anytime."
[55]Frost interview, October 30, 1979.
[56]Letter, Crawford to Butler, May 2, 1932, Sorensen papers, Box 35, Folder 65; letter, Crawford to Towl, April 19, 1932, Ibid.
[57]Letter, Crawford to Towl, April 11, 1932, Ibid.
[58]MOW-H, February 15, 1934.
[59]Maher interview, October 30, 1979.
[60]Ibid.
[61]Maher interview, November 6, 1979; Zerbe interview, July 18, 1979.
[62]Letter, Murphy to Mrs. Cora Marling [Towl's secretary], April 18, 1932, Sorensen papers, Box 35, Folder 66.
[63]Zerbe interview, July 16, 1979; Maher interview, October 30, 1979.
[64]Maher interview, November 6, 1979; letter, Murphy to Towl, May 11, 1932, Sorensen papers, Box 35, Folder 65.
[65]Letter, Crawford to Towl, April 13, 1932, Towl papers, Box 1, Folder 1932, April, City Hall; see also EOW-H, March 7, 1900.
[66]Ibid.
[67]ODN, February 16, 17, 1918.
[68]EOW-H, March 10, 1917.
[69]Ibid., February 16, 1918; see also February 12, 13, 14, 18, 21, 22, 1918; Bee, February 14, 16, 20, 23, 1918.
[70] Bee, June 2, 1918; EOW-H, November 20, 1918; December 2, 1918.
[71]Maher interview, October 23, 1979.
[72]Special Report, K.C. Investigator, C.F.M.P., December 20, 1913, Rosewater Collection, Reel 3, Box 1927.
[73]ODN, April 24, 1907.
[74]EOW-H, September 8, 1927.
[75]Bee, September 8, 1927.
[76]The United States 1900 census lists Harry's birthdate as 1887; an

undated newspaper clipping (source unidentified) in the possession of Mrs. Bertha Calloway, proprietor of Omaha's Great Plains Black Museum, gives his year of birth as 1888.

[77]Zerbe interview, October 23, 1979; interview with Wray Scott, conducted by Orville D. Menard, July 22, 1980, Omaha, Nebraska.

[78]EOW-H, November 3, 1932.

[79]See *Ibid.*, December 27, 28, 1950, and January 8, 1951.

[80]Biographical information on Marcell is from the *Omaha Metropolitan Police Relief and Pension Fund Association Annual, 1926* (Omaha: The Beacon Press, 1926), p. 197. Note: the Beacon Press was another press favored by the Dennison organization.

[81]EOW-H, October 27, 1932.

179

CHAPTER VI

Operations: The Business Communities

A boss was not necessarily a public enemy.
--George B. Cox

Legitimate Business

When Tom Dennison was in his prime the orientation and foundations of the business community were largely local, except for the railroads and packing houses. Firms locally owned and locally market reliant were particularly susceptible to involvement with the political boss, given their dependence upon city officials and authorizations. Certainly the major interstate enterprises were also concerned with who wielded power in city hall and on whose behalf, but the prosperity of local bankers, contractors, department stores, wholesalers, and various retailers was an immediate imperative leading to the door of the political power broker, the Boss.

His favorable intervention eased access to contracts, licenses, preferential tax treatment, and numerous additional favors and immunities flowing from city hall to those willing to cooperate. Building codes not too stringently enforced, inspectors disposed to less than fervent inspections were boons the "Old Man" was able to arrange for contractors, and banks appreciated public fund deposits. These were all subject, of course, to either reversal or denial. In addition, the law's majesty was brought to bear upon the disfavored, who were subject to additional punishments inflicted through the private sector in the form of boycotts as suggested by the boss to his more cooperative business associates. Dennison's broker role in these matters was encapsulated by George Leighton in his study of the young Omaha: "It was the function of this man to act as the business agent of the great absentees and the dominant local business interests: to run the machinery, turn in the requisite majorities, and collect the tolls

181

from gamblers, saloonkeepers, and whores--tolls that helped swell the bank accounts of those same local interests."[1] Roy Towl, fervent opponent of the "Old Man," informed the deputy prohibition administrator in Omaha of Dennison's lining up big business in the city, naming, among others, Frank Johnson, George Brandeis of the department store business, and hotel magnate Gene Eppley.[2]

A Dennison partisan who revered him explained machine financing:[3]

> That's where the money came from in Dennison's campaign funds, from the businessmen, really. He put in some money, sure; I put in money, yeah, because I was entitled to put in money--I was getting favors. But the big bulk of the money that was put in and spent to elect the city commissioners was put in by the big businessmen.

A revealing perspective is mentioned here, an entitlement not an obligation to contribute money to the machine.

Clearly interrelated, the political machine, based in the third ward, and the highest levels of the city's elite gave structure and direction to Omaha for over three decades. Dennison had subservient lieutenants and lesser figures within his hierarchical machine organization, but he neither reigned nor presided over higher echelons of the upperworld. Themselves men of power, members of the business elite cooperated with the political boss because of influence at his disposal, forging a mutually beneficial compact to conduct theirs and the city's business. These were equals not lackeys.

Frank Johnson played a key and powerful role as a spokesman, but Dennison had his own personal affiliations with many business leaders, and discussions and conferences with them were common. They took place neither in board rooms nor over lunch at the prestigious Omaha Club, but more discreetly in private offices, weekend gatherings, or in the intimacy of a luxurious home. Sometimes men of high station came to Dennison's office, including Frank Johnson (on occasion the role of visitor and visited reversed) and Tom Murphy, a vice president of the U.S. National Bank who was close to the "Old Man."[4]

Informal meetings were frequently held on Sunday morning in a livery stable barn, Dennison conferring with Otis M. Smith who headed a grain company, attorneys Frank Lincoln McCoy and Arthur Mullen, and a bank president.[5] From her store of memories, a descendant of leading architect John Latenser summons Tom to the magnificent Italian Renaissance Latenser mansion in the hilly woods northeast of Omaha. In the drawing room where luminaries visiting Omaha were hosted, Enrico Caruso among them, architect Latenser and Boss Dennison discussed the many buildings going up in downtown Omaha. A coterie of contractors and subcontractors were around Latenser, and public work projects in particular were understood to funnel through Dennison and Johnson to his circle.[6]

A listing of the men affiliated with Dennison reads like a Who's Who of the city: Tom Quinlan who worked for George Brandeis; retailer Joseph Hayden was a good friend of Dennison's; Paul Gallagher (whose daughter married Tom Dennison's grandson, Dr. John Ragan); the power company's James Davidson; Peter Jolly at Cudahy packing, who sat with Dennison at prize fights; stock yards officer Everett Buckingham; Gould Dietz in the lumber and coal business; Bert Murphy, whose firm sold the La France fire trucks favored by the Omaha fire department; Jimmy Lee at the Omaha National Bank, generally was treasurer for money contributed to Square Seven campaigns; and banker Tom Murphy, Lee and Murphy both "fine, handshaking Irish politicians."[7]

Having a banker friend proved advantageous in the mid-1920s when the U.S. government was conducting a tax inquiry on Dennison. As federal officers became more and more bothersome, the contents of Dennison's safe deposit box were removed by a bank official and secured in a box listed as not rented. Explaining a similar favor bestowed on a Dennison friend, an estranged wife testified that when her lawyer opened her husband's safe deposit box the same bank officer had a key and emptied it. In answer to the question whether Tom Murphy had helped Dennison in similar fashion, Grace Housky replied "Frank [her husband] said that is what Tom Murphy had done for Tom Dennison, he changed the box and covered it up some way, he did, absolutely."[8]

A preeminent place among Omaha's early leading businessmen belongs to Gurdon W. Wattles. He arrived in Omaha the same year as Tom Dennison but in different circumstances, summoned to the position of vice president of the Union National Bank. A native of New York, Wattles came to Omaha after many years as an educator in Iowa. He swiftly moved to prominence, his appointment as president of the Trans-Mississippi Exposition testimony to his quickly recognized abilities. A man of prodigious energy, he advanced to president of the Union National, then again was a vice president when his bank merged with the U.S. National; soon he moved up to chair the board of directors.

Overlapping interests led him to organize the Omaha Grain Exchange in 1903, where he served as president for six years, raising the city to the country's fourth largest grain market by the time he stepped down. He attended the National Republican Convention in 1904, was the western director of a railroad, and became involved in the building of a leading Omaha hotel, the Fontenelle. He found time in 1908 to become president of the Omaha and Council Bluffs Street Railway Company, eight years later joining its board of directors. "He had all the right credentials to direct Omaha's fortunes in the post-frontier era," record two historians of Omaha, "humble beginnings, outstanding ability, a fine intellect, impeccable manners, driving ambition, and a ruthless streak."[9]

That streak was prominently displayed in 1909 when Wattles defeated an attempt by the Amalgamated Association of Street and Electric Railway Employees to organize his workers. He ruthlessly broke their strike by importing strikebreakers and flinched not a moment in using them, taking pride in the rough and ready bunch he had been sent by the New York strikebreaking company he had engaged. Unqualified success resulted from his and his hired men's efforts, and the union forming effort was destroyed. "A concealed but well defined connection between the Traction Co. and Dennison" was reported to exist, suggesting here, as with other firms, an important machine function in relation to the business community: protecting it from labor unrest and forestalling unionization.[10] While the machine with one hand assisted its lower class clientele with welfare and jobs, with the other it simultaneously contributed to its subservience to employers. Since the machine attended to basic worker needs it created a sense of gratitude and complaisance, disarming widespread worker unrest to the benefit of employers.

Another method of assuaging labor problems was accomplished through the subtle role of machines in abetting assimilation of immigrants into the American flow of life and middle class values: maintenance of order, quest for prosperity, and being good citizens. Without conscious design "the selfish quest by the politician for electoral support and power was transmuted by the 'invisible hand' into the major force integrating the immigrant into the community."[11] What was true for the immigrants was true also of their native born co-workers, both finding in the political machine an important agent of their political socialization. Through it they imbibed an obligation to participate as voters, and learned opportunity and success were realities in the United States as they watched their comrades use politics for upward mobility. They also came to appreciate politics as business, wherein ideological definition of issues had really scant relevance in the practical world of advancing one's own interests. Political parties and practices bent to pragmatism rather than missionary efforts in the name of principle became their norm.

It was obvious to workers that the "Old Man" and his organization were involved in tending to basic human needs, and that receiving assistance was proportionate to participation and loyalty defined as obedience. Adapting to those prerequisites, the Boss's new followers experienced personalized government through close to home precinct captains and ward representatives. Thanks to the machine, government became perceived not as an enemy, but a helpmate to those in distress, presaging public welfare soon to arrive. Meanwhile, a people's lobbyist presided at the Budweiser or Karbach Building, a spokesman to advance or defend their interests, albeit individually and not class, or group, or ideologically motivated. The titled and privileged had long been heard in the councils of government to their own benefit. Now the "Old Man," spurred by an eye on electoral returns, gave the common people and the "down and outers" a channel of communication with their grievances and needs.[12]

The political machine's assimilation and socialization functions help explain a practical, largely nonideological electorate, one not driven by class consciousness and revolutionary romanticism. Thanks in part to bossism, the American liberal tradition of equality of opportunity combined with a conservative ethos of civic obedience. Obviously not all workers or spokesmen for them became dutiful compatriots in the political and economic systems. Sometimes workers did challenge their employers, as seen in the traction strike, and others that preceded and followed it. But even then, unionization was seen as necessary from a practical American economic point of view instead of one inspired by foreign notions of politicized class conflict.

Mindful that organization is the means to transform individual powerlessness into collective power, business leaders, who opposed unionization when it threatened their authority, allied to wage the battle. In 1903 Wattles and some friends formed the Omaha Business Men's Association (BMA), coming together with an uncompromising determination to render the workers' movement impotent. Announcing that 800 of the city's principal firms had rallied (individual memberships were confidential), the BMA defined its purpose as defensive, necessitated by labor unions threatening to control or ruin businesses.

The BMA would protect its members' rights, asserted the founding statement, and so long as those rights were not infringed the organization sought no fight with organized labor. Formation of unions by workers was accepted "for lawful purpose," but threats, personal violence, picketing, and boycotting in such a manner as to be unlawful would be met by force.[13] An attack in a labor periodical thirty-two years after the BMA was formed communicates an acknowledgment of its success:[14]

> For a third of a century Omaha business had been cursed with the machinations of a gang of industrial cut-throats styling themselves as the "Omaha Business Men's Association."

> In keeping with the methods pursued by this gang, secrecy has always been the watchword. During its entire existence not half a dozen men have been brazen enough to confess membership in its ranks.

> Organized for the sole purpose of exterminating trade unionism in Omaha, the methods of warfare have been typical of the savagery of its dictators.

It is safe to assume the BMA's membership roster included many men who had working relationships with Tom Dennison, one of them being Frank Johnson's, who once served as a member of the group's executive committee. The BMA was not the only business organization in the city. A much larger and more public group with diversified interests appeared with the Commercial Club. A listing of the organization's 1906 standing committees displays the Club's wide range, its members assigned to responsibilities for finance, grain market, insurance, irrigation, lifestock and poultry, wholesale trade, location of industries, manufacturing, retail trade, transportation, and public affairs. The last named was by far the largest with thirty-nine members, the others varying from three to nine.[15]

Names associated with the BMA also appear on the Commercial Club's membership rolls, as business leaders overlapped their affiliations and frequently were officers in both. In each club, therefore, were men familiar with the particular talents and services of Tom Dennison: Brandeis, Hayden, Edward Rosewater, and Wattles to name a few. A third organization, the Knights of Ak-Sar-Ben, an educational and charitable organization, was the third tier of an interlocking network of leading businessmen. Among the Kings of Ak-Sar-Ben, the royal designation for the city's most distinguished citizens, crowned annually amid the great pomp and splendor of the mythical Kingdom of Quivera, are the names of Gurdon Wattles, Gould Dietz, Everett Buckingham, James E. Davidson, George Brandeis, Eugene Eppley, and Bert Murphy.[16]

Thomas Dennison belonged to none of these organizations, and his social life was far removed from Quivera. But his political profession, broker in the politically decentralized city, brought him into close contact with their members. The result was an unofficial center of political power only a few blocks east of city hall and the courthouse. From machine Headquarters behind a bar or above a cigar store, the Boss arranged for requested services to flow from the offices of public officials. Cooperating with his high placed business allies, he rationalized the political system by bringing it centralization and a sense of order. And he was the man at the center, therefore instrumental in securing the desired privileges.

Whether large or small, firms were needful of favors from local government to pursue their profit making ends. The "Old Man," with his special access to diverse and fragmented agencies, was able--for a price--to assist with a lucrative contract or a license to sell apples. A case in point was the World Theatre which desired to erect a canopy, but discovered a city ordinance prohibited such a structure over the sidewalk. Contacts were made and the district manager received a message that upon payment to Dennison of $5,000, city authorization to erect the canopy would be forthcoming. Several letters passed between Omaha and the theatre's New York headquarters before they decided not to be "shook down."[17]

Many others, however, went along with the system, not out of approval of machine politics or taken in by Dennison's Irish charm, but because he was a skilled boss. Businessmen who collaborated with him accepted a practical course of action given the situation, the prevalent one in city after city. "To get along go along" was the operative code, one the "Old Man" understood well. Men who dealt with and befriended Dennison neither suffered from defects in their character nor deserve post-mortem accusation. Association with the "Old Man" was for them a *modus vivendi*. Once or twice a year an extravagant party was hosted by the business establishment for Dennison's third ward machine workers. At the fashionable Blackstone Hotel, the "blowout" was a sort of recognition and appreciation affair by the high placed for the "gang's" contributions to the city's well being, that is, theirs.[18]

A gathering of another sort in 1921 offers further evidence that a Dahlman/Dennison administration was much preferred by a large sector of Omaha's key businessmen to any alternative, especially the one in power the previous three years. After filing on deadline day, "Cowboy Jim" launched his campaign to regain city hall with a rally at the Paxton Hotel, brandishing petitions bearing the signatures of thousands of Omahans and on behalf of a sizeable majority of Omaha's firms, including Brandeis Department Store, Hayden Brothers, the Nebraska Clothing Company (a leading quality clothing store), and Eppley's Hotel Fontenelle. Among other prominent men attending were Ben Gallagher, and Henry Barlow of Hayden's. Everyone there, from worker to executive, welcomed Dahlman's promise to oust discord from city government and restore order to Omaha.[19]

Throughout the Dennison years, certain firms were favored by the organization and its allies, while others

188

were blacklisted for one reason or another. The former enjoyed the trade, both public and private, sent to them by a word from Dennison on their behalf. Three hotels were boosted by the machine, the Fontenelle, the Paxton, and the Hill; two garages, the Relay and the Davenport, had assured workloads because of the "Old Man's" favor. A particular plumber, a music company, laundries, jewelers, beverage firms, a favored grocer (a moment's reflection reminds one of the possibilities here, for example the fire department and its stations), funeral parlors, and insurance agents owed part of their prosperity to ties with the organization.

Similarly, friendly and cooperative paving contractors took care of city streets, and a favored electric company did considerable work for the city and county (perhaps not coincidentally a firm official was a son-in-law of machine old-timer Tony Hoffman). A loyal dairy monitored the voter registration of its employees and promised 100 per cent support of the organization's ticket. A rival dairy to the sanctioned Alamito failed to respond enthusiastically, and from Headquarters came the word to shut Robert's dairy off wherever possible. When a firm antagonized Dennison in some way, as did Robert's, word soon circulated in organization circles to cut it off. The Omaha Fixture and Supply Company of Harry Lapidus was denounced because Dennison thought he was a troublemaker, and customers received word to buy from out of town dealers instead of going to Lapidus. A battery company lost city and private customers when its owner filed for city commission and refused to listen to Dennison, a similar fate vested upon others with similar temerity. The Metz Cigar Store and the Orpheum Cigar Store were placed off limits by Dennison when their proprietors refused to submit to his dictates.

Neither ideological, nor racial, nor religious factors appear relevant to drawing the gang's antipathy: only the zeal for identifying political rivals applied. Retaliation was not confined to principal actors, for their friends and associates also suffered. When Dan Butler turned his back on Dennison, a coal company, a funeral home, and a testing lab lost business because they supported the apostate. Trade previously theirs was diverted to other coal dealers, mortuaries, and labs. A shoe shiner was discharged from a shop in the Paxton Hotel on word from Dennison he was pro-

Butler. A baseball club and its park were ostracized because its proprietor, according to Dennison, had heeded the advice of the anti-Dennison state attorney general and gone to Lincoln to assail Omaha's horse race track (owned and operated by Ak-Sar-Ben). Potentially significant losses were certainly grave concerns for anyone considering actions adverse to Dennison's interests.[20] The capacity to reward allies with dollars funneled in their direction, and punish foes with loss of trade was real and exercised.

Not only battery companies, funeral homes, dairies, shoe shine boys, and ball parks were subject to Dennison's extensive network. Professional people were not exempt from Tom Dennison's ability to advance or hinder a career and income. Attorneys and physicians were wooed and rewarded if won, but turned upon when rejected or later turned disloyal. A list of acceptable and unacceptable attorneys was kept at Headquarters, the former receiving law suits and other legal cases upon referral from Dennison, the latter of course having potential clients warned away. Election campaigns brought polite requests from Dennison, asking attorneys to write letters to colleagues and friends on behalf of the organization's slate, taking advantage of their customary status in the community.[21]

Dennison's recruitment tactics were appropriate to the task at hand. A new attorney in Omaha had occasion to meet Dennison briefly one morning, and was somewhat surprised when two or three days later a fellow came to his yet not very busy office with legal problems. He was there on the "Old Man's" recommendation he volunteered; the wooing had begun. Another fledgling attorney in the late 1920s (recruitment was ongoing) was informed one day the "Old Man" wanted to see him at his Karbach office to enlist him on his Speakers Bureau, a Dennison sponsored group for the public affairs minded. Raised in an anti-Dennison family, the future early member and force in the Independent Voters League (IVL) ignored the invitation and no clients ever came his way from the "Old Man."

Dennison did succeed in recruiting other attorneys however, men willing to accept his assistance for advantages gained. A select few were depended upon by Dennison for cases involving himself or others he was particularly close to: in this group before World War I were W.J. Connell,

Dennison's attorney in early libel suits and at the Red Oak trial, and A.S. Ritchie, "the gang's lawyer in police and criminal cases."[22] Dan Gross and former Congressman Albert W. Jefferis were favored attorneys in later years, with "Judge" Benjamin Baker spanning both the pre and post-War periods. Baker was a tall robust man who served during his long career as a U.S. District Attorney, and as a federal judge in the Southwest. In Omaha "Judge" Baker earned a reputation as a fine trial lawyer and began a long association with the "Old Man," serving as his attorney in the 1932 conspiracy trial.[23]

Members of the medical profession were also on most favored or least favored lists, and health positions within city and county government were subject to influence from Headquarters. Dr. Richard Lucke's brief tenure as a police surgeon ended upon a request from Dennison to Mayor Metcalfe. A nephew to Dennison through marriage, Dr. Thomas Bolar, served as head surgeon of the City Hospital, an institution whence came individuals with diseases necessitating isolation for treatment. Dr. Bolar was also responsible for weekly medical examinations of the city's prostitutes. Their south side contingent once protested to Joe Potach, a Dennison police officer, the weekly cost was unfair. Given their profession they were unwelcome on public transportation and had to take a taxi downtown, which cost three dollars, then they were charged another three for the exam. Potach dismissed their complaints with the advice to do as told or get out of town.[24]

Another medical doctor, Lee Van Camp, spent several years as county physician, and was identified by federal treasury department investigators as a member of a "political clique controlling politics in Omaha . . . ."[25] Van Camp was indicted in late 1925 on five counts of dealing in morphine in violation of the Harrison Act, but the case never made its way to a courtroom. On grounds the grand jury was not lawfully constituted, the indictment was dismissed, but the U.S. Attorney, James C. Kinsler, succeeded in securing new indictments in March on similar charges. Subsequently, three years of maneuvers prevented the case from coming to trial, proving their worth when the government's witness against the Doctor died in March 1928 of pneumonia. Absent the prosecution's key figure, an informer named Robert Stroud, all charges against Van Camp were dismissed, a man "affiliated or aligned with the Dennison, Nesselhouse [sic] gang" according to Kinsler.[26]

Troubles for Mr. Stroud started when Dennison forces took an interest in Van Camp's case. Police arrived at Stroud's home one morning, roused him from bed and took him to the police station under arrest, threatening to charge him with nine holdups. He was held for two days before he was booked for vagrancy. During his court appearance, Stroud explained he had been subpoenaed to come to Omaha for a case. He offered to produce his subpoena, and told the judge he was making two to three hundred dollars a month working with the Narcotics Department. Two narcotics agents supported his explanation, but Municipal Court Judge Sophus Neble Jr., declared Stroud guilty of vagrancy and sentenced him to sixty days in jail. Being an informer, ruled the judge, was not a legitimate occupation.

Stroud's sentence was suspended on condition he immediately leave town, and stay out, until actually needed in court as a federal witness. Then he was to leave Omaha forever, ordered Neble, because his kind was not wanted in the city.[27] Appeal of the Judge's decision was considered but decided against by Stroud's wife after she talked with Mr. Kinsler. A conference between Kinsler and A.F. Brungardt, the city prosecutor, had convinced Kinsler it was better not to pursue the issue. According to Brungardt, Nebraska Law required the defendant to appear personally in Omaha to sign an appeal bond of about $250, an amount Kinsler doubted the Strouds could raise. The city prosecutor then made it quite clear Stroud was definitely *personna non grata* by telling Kinsler if the informer did appear in Omaha there would be three more charges filed against him for "shortchanging" people in the city.[28]

The link between Dr. Van Camp and Dennison, and the "Old Man's" mediating role in the Doctor's legal problems were undeniable in the U.S. Attorney's summation to the Attorney General's Office in Washington D.C.:[29]

> While there can be absolutely no question of doubt that Robert R. Stroud was framed, ganged, arrested, tried and sentenced as the result of a gang conspiracy to obstruct justice, it is to my judgment that we are not in a position at the present time to sustain a charge of conspiracy against any of the parties concerned; and all things considered, it would not be good strategy

to attempt to do so at the present time.

A memorandum prepared for the U.S. Solicitor General by an assistant attorney general informed him the U.S. Attorney in Omaha and the Narcotics Bureau were convinced the Stroud situation demonstrated a strong effort by the "gang" to hinder and prevent narcotics violation prosecutions.[30] The county physician remained on the job. Dennison was prepared to assist De Camp and his other friends with the many means at his disposal. Boodling, an organized system of officials proffering their services for a price, goes unmentioned in interviews, correspondence, and newspapers because it was unnecessary in Omaha thanks to Dennison.[31] With him serving as a go-between, favor seekers prepared to pay were spared the spectacle of directly dealing with public officials. Omaha was not free of kickback rumors, and stories long circulated about the poker games played the nights before the city or county bought goods and services. At these tables, an organization representative was expected to win big over a designated loser who the next day received the contract. Other evidence of less than strictly ethical conduct surfaced when the IVL backed new city commission took over in 1933. An incoming commissioner read bills waiting on his desk from a grocer for meat, charged as food for animals at the city zoo in Riverview Park. He learned the animals were eating exceedingly well at considerable cost, given the T-bones, porterhouse, and other expensive cuts purportedly delivered to them.[32]

Business was sometimes funneled in desirable directions by establishing specifications for public work impossible for an undesirable contractor to meet. Once again we find Morris Milder a case in point when the city commission voted in 1931, during Milder's time of travails, to change the "specs" for garbage collection. Milder and a partner with their Nebraska Live Stock Company possessed the current contract, but announced they were not in a position to bid for renewal under the new specifications. Small vehicles and trucks were previously permissible, these transferring their loads to larger trucks for the final haul to a disposal site. Henceforth, only large trucks were authorized to make pick ups and transfers were no longer permissible. Buying a fleet of large trucks was too much for Milder.[33]

Success in this instance, as in so many others, depended upon the "Old Man's" influence in city hall and the county courthouse, where he rarely if ever appeared. He was a key figure in Omaha's shadow government, one he fashioned and developed with skill and tenacity. His web of connections between himself and licit businessmen sustained a system of privileges passing through his political machine in return for favors and financial support. Controlled corruption was the result, managed by Thomas Dennison, the gentleman responsible for making arrangements otherwise embarrassing or legally compromising for both businessman and elected official. Payments were made, instructions were accordingly issued and subsequently followed, all coordinated by the man who controlled corruption far from public view.

The Illegitimate Business Community

There were many men like Thomas Dennison in the United States during his years of power. They were businessmen whose industry was politics, providing goods and services in return for profits. Similar to their more conventional business counterparts, they maintained contacts with men in their field in other cities. Just as one businessman might telephone or visit a colleague miles distant for information or assistance, so did the bosses. Connections were maintained among the bosses of different cities, and they were a particularly important aspect of the boss business in serving their clients of the illegitimate business community. Dennison had his old friend Vaso Chucovich in Denver, and he maintained links with his counterparts in Minneapolis, St. Paul, Chicago, New Jersey, and Kansas City. Their common concerns included travels of underworld figures, which were monitored by the bosses. Arrangements were made between city bosses to offer protection for fugitive clients. Criminals from Chicago or Kansas City went unmolested in Omaha so long as the terms of their arranged "visa" were honored, that is, stay out of trouble while here.[34]

Within the fraternity of bosses, Dennison had a wide range of acquaintances and friends, especially in the West dating from his roving and gambling days. Thus a telephone call to Butte, Los Angeles, or San Francisco, as well as points in between, summoned requested assistance or information. His talents as a political organizer and success in his chosen field brought those similarly involved to his office to discuss his system, "one which was the wonder of friends and enemies alike, one which political leaders in other cities came to see and study."[35] Several of the bosses were personal friends of the "Old Man's," including Kansas City's Pendergast brothers, Jim and Tom. A Dennison grandson remembered the latter being accorded a privilege reserved for a select few--being a guest at the Dennison home.[36] Nesselhous also was familiar with Tom Pendergast and sold or gave to him a famous horse, named Color Sergeant, from his stable.[37]

As businessmen, the bosses helped one another supply the basic commodity of their enterprise, votes, making electoral loans to one another. A gentleman who spent his career in the Douglas County Courthouse, spoke confidentally about the reiprocal arrangement between Dennison and Tom Pendergast when additional "ghost" voters were needed. Omaha's boss sent fraudulent voters to his counterpart down river when requested, and Pendergast repaid the loan in kind when called in by Dennison. Favors and services were stock in trade for the bosses and an intercity tie is seen in the experience of a young man who arrived in Omaha from Louisiana with the ambition of becoming a bail bondsman, a field jealously guarded and adverse to competition. As a warning, two times the newcomer was shot at, the bullets breaking the glass in his auto's back seat. Despite the danger, the aspirant bondsman persisted and one day learned two men he had supplied sizeable bonds skipped on him and left town. Shortly thereafter he came upon Dennison who was in front of the Henshaw Hotel, wearing a derby and leaning against the building. Dennison stopped the out-of-pocket bondsman and said he understood a couple of men had jumped on him. He advised the young man to pay a visit to Kansas City and see Jim Pendergast. "Tell him I sent you. I think you'll find the people."

After the train ride to Kansas City, the bondsman first entered Pendergast's outer office where a number of people were milling about. He was then ushered through a middle, smaller office where several men were seated, including the two he had bonded. Finally in an inner office he was presented to Pendergast, and he explained why Tom

Dennison had sent him. "I understand that," replied Kansas City's Boss, then he asked whether the two fellows who had jumped on him were next door. A "yes" reply, and Pendergast had the two brought into his office then proceeded to berate them for causing the visitor a great deal of trouble and expense. Therefore, said the Boss, amends were in order and he directed the pair to pay back not only the bond money (around $1,500) but also, taking into consideration the Omahan's time, the train fare, and inconvenience suffered, an additional thousand.

The next day, back in Omaha, the repaid plus bondsman approached Dennison in front of the Henshaw and thanked him for his assistance. "Get out of here you son-of-a-bitch," Dennison muttered, "I don't want to see you anymore." What had happened, mused the rebuffed young man, was that Dennison felt he had evened the score for the two warning shots. The newly approved bondsman had earned the right to work in Omaha, and went on to a long career in the city.

Tom, the younger Pendergast, came to Dennison's assistance some years later to help settle accounts with a furrier who lost two valuable mink coats in a robbery. Just getting started in the trade, the store was going to take a sizeable and painful loss, even taking insurance into account. An attorney representing the insurance company investigating the robbery asked the despondent victim whether he had not at one time worked for the *World-Herald.* "Yes" was the response, for several years in fact. When asked whether he knew Tom Dennison, the gentleman said he knew him well and also Frank Johnson; he had done them lots of favors in years past. The attorney quickly suggested the former newsman pay a visit to Dennison and explain his predicament--the very expensive stolen coats and the inability to absorb the loss. As suggested, a visit was made to the "Old Man," who listened and then said, "You did a lot of things for me when you were with the *World-Herald.* I'll see what I can do for you." Twenty-four hours later the coats were back in the Omaha store, shipped from Kansas City by express. A beaming furrier asked the insurance lawyer what he should do next, and was told to go back to Dennison, thank him and then ask what the bill was. Again instructions were followed, and when the "Old Man" was asked the price he answered there was no charge because of the favors done earlier for him.

Dennison's clients ranged from the highest ranks of Omaha society to its lowest. Like licit businesses, the illicit also needed the assistance and favors available from city and county government. In particular, protection from too energetic enforcement of the laws against gambling, prostitution, and later bootlegging was important to their well being. The Boss did for the underworld what he did for the upper: he brought a sense of order to their business environment, easing the way to higher profits. As the underworld's centralizing agent, he was the man who controlled crime. A common recollection of the Dennison era, from executive or bootlegger, is the city as a safe one, its citizens walking the streets without fear of molestation. Omaha's reputation as a wide-open town remained vivid and deserved, but gambling and prostitution flourished only in those areas of the city reserved for vice. And there conditions were under control, regulated by Dennison's organization, assisted by the police department.[38]

When the report of a special investigator sent into Omaha in 1931 by State Attorney General Christian Sorensen was given to Roy Towl, the commissioner's consternation over the vice described made its way into the newspapers. Towl lamented that the Harding Report (named after Dan W. Harding of Minneapolis), produced after a month's probing of the city's seamier side, described disgraceful conditions. Detective Paul Sutton retorted Omaha was the cleanest city of its size in America, and dismissed Harding's report with "These people weren't on the streets, we keep them off the streets."[39]

Sutton's view of Omaha was the generally accepted one, a city where Dennison "kept the lid on" and he ran an orderly town (a reason many businessmen in good conscience supported him). Activities ranked as sinful were avoidable by avoiding those city blocks where they thrived under Dennison's watchful eye. His system permitted those who purchased the privilege to run their brothel or games of chance without police interference, securing a license of sorts. Aspirant independent operators who challenged the "Old Man's" guild provided opportunity to demonstrate to the morally offended that righteous laws were indeed being enforced. Criminal and assorted other underworld elements occasionally came to Omaha to ply their trades, adding themselves to the indigenous illegitimate business population. However, they had to report to Dennison for permission to operate in return for a percentage of their profits. Agreements were worked out and the now protected thief, gambler, or whatever went about his or her business. Josiah Flynt Willard had marvelled at the turn of the century that Dennison "controlled the guns," authorizing which ones were permitted to enter the city and for how long.[40]

One night a burglar made his errant way into the Paul Gallagher home and jewels were taken, obviously an out-of-town thief or he would not dared have touched the Gallaghers, a family well within Dennison's circle of elite compatriots. Gallagher's wife Rachel called brother-in-law Ben, who was closest to Dennison, and irately reported the loss of her jewels. He told her not to worry, that he would take care of the situation. All the stolen jewelry was returned to the Gallagher home in a package delivered the next day.[41]

Dennison men and police officers (frequently the same thing) kept a lookout at the train stations for known underworld figures, escorting them to Headquarters for Dennison's benediction. A private detective reported in 1914 that several crooks of international reputation were in Omaha, the machine protecting and profiting from them.[42] Seventeen years later a police officer friendly to Roy Towl related he had talked with "Gorilla Bob" a couple days previously, who had just left Dennison and Nesselhous. "Gorilla Bob," the officer went on, was a nationally known pickpocket.[43] Anyone who came to town and attempted to ply their trade without Dennison's approval was picked up by the police and given a choice: immediately leave the city or go to jail.

Omaha under Dennison provided a safe harbor for fugitives from other cities who purchased sanctuary in the back of the Budweiser or later in the Karbach Building. For the notorious, terms of their stay often included abstaining from any illegal activity while in Omaha, and any violation hustled them swiftly from town. A professional thief named George Burrier appeared in Omaha in 1907, and was promptly informed by the "Old Man" he could stay in Omaha and be protected so long as he committed no crimes during his stay. "I was told," said Burrier, "as long as I left Omaha alone I could live there and be protected."[44] Most often these special cases from Chicago or Kansas City were either being sought by the police in their own cities or eluding a summons to testify in court.[45] They went unmolested in Omaha so long as the terms of their visa was honored.

Those who were more permanent, not merely passing through or in hiding, also had to pay tribute to organization collectors in exchange for the privilege of operating without police interference. Payments were made in various forms, basically monthly pay offs to the campaign fund for campaigns which never seemed to cease. When elections did come around supplemental contributions were required, plus manpower was demanded to swell the ranks of the machine's workers and voters. Failure to pay or show up resulted in loss of protection, although the force of the law was often not applied until public pressure made it convenient for those on the nonprotected list now to be raided.[46] Thereby the police and city officials proved their commitment to law enforcement and attempts to clean up the city.

Another means of collecting was the organization's insistence its Club be patronized, a reference to Dennison's and Nesselhous's gambling establishment in the 1920s, the Friar's Club. Making their monthly payments to a collector, people sometimes heard as money was being handed over, "We haven't seen you around the Club lately. What's wrong? Why don't you drop around and pay your respects?" When they did their losses became additional insurance against the hazards of operating their illegal business.[47]

The deposed proprietor of the Midway, Victor Walker, once commented that when he operated the famous resort he regularly turned over a percentage of his receipts to a police captain for a campaign fund. Despite the payments police began annoying his customers, and Walker asked Dennison what he should do about it. Dennison told him salaries in the police department were inadequate and left the men dissatisfied, thus something additional was necessary. Walker complained he was already paying enough. The only remedy, he was informed, was an additional fifty dollars a month, paid to Dennison with the understanding the money would be passed on to police officers. The purpose of these payments, Walker explained, was "To protect my business at 1124 Capitol Avenue" by increasing police income.[48]

An anonymous letter to then commissioner Towl spoke to the plight of the bootlegger: "You know that all buttleggers are paying protection. I paye myself and was rested too. And was thretened with death. I payed Joe Potach plenty. And still do."[49] Officer Joe Potach was a Dennison man, a close one, a career policeman with many years service on the morals squad. Renowned as a "tough copper," Potach was courageous and devoutly loyal to the "Old Man." In addition to his police department duties, Potach was a collector and a relayer of messages for Dennison, some not pleasant for the recipient, earning Potach the title of "The Enforcer."

A memorandum to Towl offers a glimpse of Potach's extracurricular functions as it listed: speakeasy, 14th and Williams, "Pays Potach"; Greek joint, Oasis of Q Street, "Potach protects. They boast about it"; 24th and N, southwest corner, "Favorite of Potach and pays him"; Smith's lunch, "Pays Potach. Liquors in ice box in cellar, also in rear and upstairs"; The Belgian, "Potach protects"; Corner 24th and Q, "Potach protects"; 4821 South 24th Street, "Out on parole entire basement fitted out for barroom. Pays Potach."[50]

Allegations of Potach taking protection money led to a criminal libel case brought by the officer against two well known bootleggers, Gene Livingston and George "Dutch" Volker. Following an incident in a billiard parlor between Potach and Livingston, the later began making oral comments later put into a written statement about his paying the policeman monthly protection money for several years. Potach brought the libel charge in denial of Livingston's accusations. In court, Livingston testified that for over four years, beginning in February 1924, $100 a month had been handed over on Potach's demand, the amount later rising to two hundred. According to Livingston, Potach warned him if he wanted to get along in town he had better take care of him. Denying any acceptance of money or gifts, Potach stated that his dealings with Livingston were limited to visiting his cafe in 1928 and 1929. True, Potach did often come to his cafe was Livingston's rejoinder, but the stops were used for payoffs and presents of liquor which were wrapped in packages about a foot and a half square. In those packages, Potach maintained, was meat for his hunting dogs.

200

The trial lasted three days and after thirty minutes deliberation the jury returned a verdict of not guilty. Police Commissioner Henry Dunn announced that Officer Potach was entitled to remain on the morals squad, and commended him as an honest and conscientious officer, lied about by Livingston and Volker. A day later Dunn changed his mind and suspended Potach, along with a statement of confidence in his integrity. The suspension followed a bribery complaint against Potach filed by the county attorney after a conference with Mayor Metcalfe. Potach's bond of $1,000 was put up by Tom Murphy, and word soon circulated that Livingston and Volker, on grounds of self-incrimination, were not going to repeat their testimony of Potach accepting bribes.

At the preliminary hearing the two men duly proceeded to claim their rights against self-incrimination and the case was dismissed. Their reticence and the failure of any other witnesses to come forth cleared Potach and his suspension was lifted. Resolution of the case bears the imprint of men carefully, accurately, and quietly calculating the situation. Both County Attorney Henry Beal and Metcalfe were Dennison men; the former had announced after the jury's verdict that no bribery charges would be filed against Potach because Livingston and Volker were liars. But following his conference with the mayor, the county attorney initiated legal action.

A police officer on trial for three days had been identified as a taker of bribes, and his accusers were found not guilty of criminal libel. Given the publicity, some official action had to be taken against Potach and a shrewd one was decided upon: file the complaint thus doing one's duty, but relying on Livingston and Volker to refuse to testify on grounds of self-incrimination. In the libel trial itself, answers to questions about the purposes of the alleged payments had been evasive. Not even a hint issued from Livingston or Volker to the effect Potach had provided protection from criminal activities they might have been involved in. Another round in court and exposure of their operations would have been threatening to the two bootleggers.[51] Rather than take the risk, they evaded a return to the court and the city's official face was saved.

201

Potach was not the only collector in the organization; Johnny Marcell and "Toad" Riley took care of south side payments. One of their men, a detective, had his own method of selling protection to prostitutes. They bought subscriptions from him for magazines that never showed up in the mail.[52] Consequences of nonpayment to campaign funds (or failure to subscribe) where inflicted upon a madam who was approached by the owner of her house at 13th and Capitol and his attorney (a cousin of the chief of police). Pay us $300, she was instructed, or be raided; she refused and was raided that night.[53]

Gamblers, prostitutes, and bootleggers enjoyed security in Omaha so long as they paid their dues and were properly restrictive in their ambitions. Having purchased the permission to operate, they supplied those illicit services always in demand by people willing to pay the price. Buyer and seller functioned in a controlled market in Omaha, and crime was organized by Omahans not by outsiders. Representatives of syndicates came to Omaha as visitors, but the city was under Dennison's firm control. Omaha was a city for outside organized crime to cooperate with, not to dominate. Intercity illegitimate business transactions were conducted on the basis of agreements reached between the "Old Man" and his counterparts in other communities.

Various commentaries over the years about wide-open and sinful Omaha preceded the Harding Report, and those familiar with the city knew that all manner of diversions were available. A decade before Harding's account of vice, a former Omaha police officer had submitted his findings as a special investigator for the Committee of 5,000 (an anti-Dennison group) to a Nebraska legislative committee. Omaha was teeming with prostitutes, the legislators were told, and gambling flourished because authorities made no effort to enforce the laws. The committee witness related that when he became a member of the force, the chief of police advised him to keep his mouth shut, do as he was told, or be fired. The advice was not taken; following an unauthorized raid the officer carried off, the chief kept his word and the too zealous officer was fired.[54]

Two years after the legislative committee heard the ex-officer's commentary, an Assistant Attorney General in Washington, D.C., read in a letter from the U.S. Attorney in Omaha about the "gang's" carrying on a large-scale gambling operation in town: card players, crap shooters, horse players, all these and more were available. Gambling was estimated to be bringing annually from half a million to a million dollars profit to the Dennison organization.[55] When Roy Towl was on the city commission his second time, the only Dennison opponent elected in 1930, he asked Inspector of Detectives Benedict "Ben" Danbaum to name some of the more well known gamblers in Omaha. Danbaum, firmly in the Dennison camp, was unable to think of even one, adding he was under standing orders from the chief to arrest people caught gambling. Then he pointed out how difficult it was to secure evidence sufficient to obtain a conviction in court.[56]

At that very moment there were a number of gamblers operating in Omaha who were nationally known. Sam Ziegman and P.C. "Packy" Gaughan were operating the Baseball Headquarters at 413 South 15th Street, taking out full page advertisements in the *Police Annual*, reminding readers in large print of their direct wire on sporting events. Their Baseball Headquarters fell out of favor with the "Old Man" for a while one year and was frequently raided. Detective Sutton stated he several times warned Ziegman against gambling, arrested him at least six times, but kept finding racing forms and betting slips when he entered the Baseball Headquarters.[57] During one of these raids, three telephone calls were taken while the raiders were there. Sam House, another Omaha gambling figure, firmly denied between brief phone conversations any gambling was going on in the place. Answering one of the rings, Sam told the caller no dollar tickets were taken there, but they were available for two dollars. Returning the phone in its place, he explained to the officers the query was about airplane tickets. A police raider answered another call, and was instructed to put down "twenty to place on Francis."[58]

A number of other gamblers might have come to Danbaum's tongue, such as "Snorts" Weyerman at the Diamond Cigar Store (cigar stores frequently had more to offer than their cigars), "Whitey" Petit, Eddie Barrick, Lou Jackson, Charles "Clink" Clair, to name a few of the more prominent. Years later, when gambling was being cracked down on in Omaha in the late 1940s, several of these men moved to Las Vegas and helped build it into a U.S. gambling oasis.

Among the emigrants were Sam Ziegman and Eddie Barrick, who went on to fame in horse race betting. The Omaha gambling fraternity's influence in Las Vegas's earlier days was such that their new home was sometimes referred to as "Little Omaha." Visitors to "Vegas" from the town of Ziegman's long gone Baseball Headquarters still carry with them a message from those who remember: "Tell 'em you're from Omaha and they'll treat you right."

Mention of Las Vegas brings to mind images of rows of slot machines swallowing coins of all denominations, occasionally returning a few as a gesture of encouragement. Decades before the desert city became a tourist and gambling mecca, there were approximately 1,500 slots in Omaha by the estimate of one cigar store dealer. A profit of over $800,000 was the take for the Omaha slot machine industry in 1902, but from their profits the cigar store proprietor or whomever made campaign contributions to the "Old Man" for the privilege of operating the profitable machines.[59] The gentleman from the Texas House and the Arcade, the "Pick-handle" Tom of earlier days, was not content merely to graft the gambling dividends of others. Dennison abandoned his policy game in the early 1900s, but opportunities were abundant for keeping him involved and close to his trade. One of his ventures was into the Riverside with Nesselhous, Lynch, and Haskell. In the spring of 1914 Lynch had suggested to Nesselhous they take over the already established Riverside and agreement was reached. Soon the place was raided by county officials and the owners shortly thereafter were contacted by Nesselhous with an offer to buy it. They expressed little interest in selling until Nesselhous pointed out the difficulties of operating if frequently raided, and assured them they would be.

The selling price was $750, the bill of sale made out to Haskell. Dennison and Nesselhous spent four to five thousand more expanding and improving the Riverside into a fashionable late nightspot. When it opened in July it was in violation of at least three laws: no liquor license was secured, drinks were served after hours, and gambling took place. A license was deemed unnecessary because of the protection secured by Lynch's partnership in the venture, and the sheriff and his deputies were unconcerned with activities at the Riverside. Peak hours for the club were from midnight to four a.m., and alcohol was abundant despite the state's eight o'clock closing. To help entertain the two to three hundred people who drove out nightly from the city for food and drinks, slot machines were available. Those slots, recalled the Riverside's floor manager after the place was closed (in March 1917), were "plugged" to pay off even less than in other parts of town.[60]

The Dennison/Lynch split ended the Riverside's days, but Dennison and Nesselhous were not out of the gambling business by any means. After the Riverside, they ran a series of places at various locations, but their most successful was the Friar's Club. First they operated out of a basement on lower Douglas Street, under a billiard parlor, although the word basement does injustice to the elaborate gambling house they ran. During the reform government years their establishment was closed, but Dennison and Nesselhous opened another in a hotel at 13th and Dodge when their machine returned to power. By 1925 they had formed the Friar's Club and members and friends of the organization were signed on; other persons gained entry to the Club rooms only if they were known or invited. Located on the third floor of a structure known as the Old Elks Building on the east side of 15th Street between Farnam and Harney, the Friar's Club was a high roller place for serious gamblers. It closed down for the two weeks before and after elections, but otherwise was in profitable business until 1929.

Ben Danbaum was reputed to draw a $1,000 a month from the Friar's Club for his services, which were to hustle off to jail anyone getting out of line. A third partner (there were six) in the club was Frank Housky, for years Dennison's main card and dice man.[61] Customers were numerous and Nesselhous's businesslike operation and well calculated percentages paid off handsomely. The "gang" was estimated in 1925 to be making in the neighborhood of $20,000 a week from various gambling activities in Omaha, with the Friar's Club responsible for a considerable portion of the take. U.S. Attorney James Kinsler wrote his superiors in Washington, as an example of the stakes, that he had heard of a man who had lost $1,700 shooting craps in the Club. Bets well into the multiple thousands were placed by prominent and wealthy patrons.[62]

An estimated million dollars each was made by Dennison

and Nesselhous during the four or five years the Friar's Club operated.[63] Quietly it passed away and no obituary exists to share information on its demise. But even though Dennison and Nesselhous closed their gambling house, many other games of chance remained open, and bootleggers and prostitutes enjoying boom times. Dennison often boasted he never made any money from the city's prostitution, never taking a cent from any prostitute or landlady. In a 1930 interview Dennison avowed "I haven't been interested in gambling for a long time and never had anything to do with bootlegging. And I'd shoot myself before I'd fatten off the earnings of a woman."[64] His disavowal is true to the extent he did not personally make collections from the houses, and he kept himself distant from the trade by always having a lieutenant responsible for the red light district. Gambling he was personally involved in; he had no similar ties with prostitution. However, the protection money collected was in fact a tax payable to the shadow government of Tom Dennison.

Prostitution came early to Omaha as it developed into a trade and outfitting center. Six years after the city was founded, county census takers recorded harlot as the profession of several women (including two sixteen year olds), and their number grew as the city grew. By 1911 the estimated number of prostitutes (by now shirtmakers on census rolls) in the boisterous river city was 2,600, with the net income from the twelve largest brothels thought to be over half a million dollars a year.[65] Before the 1911 Albert Law dispersed prostitutes somewhat, Omaha had a well defined red light district, located east of 12th and between Douglas and Davenport Streets.[66] A short-lived but highly concentrated area of prostitution was located in 1907 within the square block formed by 8th and 9th Streets and Dodge and Capitol Avenue. Called the Arcade, the entire square block consisted of several alleys with rows of cribs built along both their sides. A former madam familiar with the Arcade wrote:[67]

> Each crib consists of two small rooms, about six feet high; a door and a window forms the whole front. Each crib has a projecting corner, and a casual glance down the line gives it a scalloped appearance, which is meant to be artistic.
>
> These alleys are paved, regardless of expense, and have heavy gates at each end. One of the alleys is covered by a fancy roof, the ceiling has a showy red design, embellished with many electric

lights.

The Arcade, sometimes called Dream City, operated for only one year, but its reputation has proved immune to time.

Women paid fifty dollars to get a key to a crib, then had to pay from one to five dollars a day to occupy it, paid in advance to E.F. Martin's collector. Martin owned several properties in the neighborhood, renting them out to madams and saloons. The fifty prostitutes in the Arcade had to buy all their liquor in a bar at 9th and Dodge, and all the food they bought had to come from the restaurant next door. William A. Sutherland, a Martin business associate, was proprietor of both. Known as the "king of the red light district," Martin had 140 to 150 prostitutes in his various houses, with his income during the year the Arcade was open estimated at \$75,000.[68] Martin's tenderloin district operated under the protection of "The king gambler" [Dennison]: "the political dictator of the lower ward, the go-between for the city official and graft and collectors of campaign funds."[69] Every month Martin sent a fifty dollar bill to both the day and night captains, and Chief of Police Donahue ordered the "king of the red light district" was to be left alone.[70] Nonetheless, toward the end of 1907 the Arcade proved to be too much to tolerate; two weeks after an exposing article on its activities appeared in a newspaper, the city prosecutor and police magistrate secured warrants and arrests followed. Padlocks were put on the gates and the cribs were shut down. Meanwhile, and thereafter, Martin's remaining extensive realm continued business as usual.[71]

After the 1911 Albert Law ostensibly shut down the disorderly houses in the red light district, many prostitutes became streetwalkers and several madams relocated their establishments. Three years after the statute went into effect, a robbery and murder in Hazel McVey's brothel on north 14th Street briefly focused attention on vice in the city (Dennison and Nesselhous both went to the police station when they heard Hazel had been arrested and Nesselhous put up her bail). Police Commissioner John Ryder when asked if prostitution existed in Omaha innocently replied, "Why, I don't know any more about it than you do." Mayor Dahlman said that "The place [Hazel's] should be closed at once . . . and so should other resorts of the same kind, if they exist . . . ."[72]

A little over a year later the Minister's Union set out to bring to the mayor's attention the fact they did indeed exist. In a report presented to the city commission, the Union called attention to thirty establishments where prostitution existed and drinking went on well beyond eight o'clock in the evening. A "surprised" mayor announced his firm opposition to brothels and streetwalkers and called for their eradication. No harm was seen by "Cowboy Jim," however, in a man taking a drink either before or after eight p.m. Commissioner Ryder, head of the police department and reponsible for enforcing the law, did not give a "snap of his finger" for the "hulabaloo" about drinking after hours. If a man wanted a drink he should have it, was the commissioner's opinion. The report indicated that the mayor and the police commissioner would have had little difficulty in finding either an after hours drink or prostitutes to eradicate. During the month of February 1915, representatives of the Minister's Union had circulated downtown and accumulated their evidence of violations of the laws. In the course of their walks in the lower third ward, the Union men were repeatedly solicited on the sidewalks and from windows, were illegally served drinks, and witnessed gambling.

One night they came upon a room, on a saloon's second floor, full of drinking men and women, dancing and singing (both labeled lewd and vulgar); business, they were told, was best after midnight. A bar a few doors away had no rooms available, but girls who were, ready to accompany a client to a hotel. A few steps more to another saloon and the researchers were solicited by eight prostitutes. Their task took them to the Mandarin Cafe, above the Budweiser, on a Sunday afternoon where they able to make an illegal purchase of beer; then they entered another saloon by an alley door, went downstairs and bought a bottle of beer and a flask of whiskey. On subsequent nights after hours, or on Sundays, they bought beer or were solicited, sometimes both, at the Alleyette Saloon, King Joy's Cafe, the Henshaw Hotel, Charles Lewis's bar, and in the basement of the Paxton Hotel.

At the Owl Club (on the third floor at 117 1/2 North 16th), gambling was added to their usual list of beer and whiskey available. Additional solicitations from windows were duly recorded as February turned into March, and the list of places illegally selling alcohol became longer. After the report was presented to city officials, A.C. Kugel, now police commissioner, exclaimed "I was surprised beyond words!"[73] He must have been one of the few surprised people in the city. Maybe the commissioner was reacting to the results of two fairly recent grand jury investigations, neither one of which was able to discern violations of liquor or disorderly house laws. One of them in its quest for information established a committee charged to spend an evening searching for vice and lawbreakers. They departed from the Budweiser, escorted by none other than Johnny Lynch, an individual well qualified to be a third ward guide. The committee reported it was unable to unearth either violations or witnesses to illegal conduct. [74]

A subsequent grand jury in a six week probe uncovered not a single incident of gambling, no prostitution, and no violators of the liquor laws in Omaha. Public officials were untainted with suspicion of wrongdoing, and civic and social conditions as well as the police department were adjudged excellent. Jury members did admit to having heard rumors about disorderly houses having spread all over town because the Albert Law crippled the red light district. It would be better for the city if those purported houses were all together in a segregated district the jurors' concluded.[75]

Prostitution not only flourished in Omaha but was another manifestation of intercity illicit business contacts. Prostitutes were organized into groups for traveling in a circuit, replacing one another in houses and thus offering customers a variety of selection over time. From Omaha the women traveled to Sioux City, Iowa; to St. Paul, Minnesota; to Chicago; thence south to St. Joseph and Kansas City, Missouri.[76] Within Omaha prostitutes were regulated as to where to eat and purchase clothes or other items. Neither circuit prostitutes nor those permanently in Omaha shopped openly as other women did. Madams kept accounts at organization sanctioned establishments and their inmates went only to these at specified times.[77] One madam was especially solicitous of her charges' well-being, and aware they were not welcome on the city's streets in the daytime hours made arrangements for them to enjoy some night air.

Lulu arranged for rented automobiles to appear at her place on south 16th, near Leavenworth Street, about three in the morning. The women then were treated to an early morning ride, with Lulu providing the service about three times a week.[78]

Throughout the Dennison era prostitution continued, madams and prostitutes paying protection for the opportunity to sell their services. Whether in the days of Martin and his Arcade or a score and four years later when Mr. Harding came to town to uncover vice for the state attorney general, collectors made their rounds of the brothels and streetwalkers. After a three month investigation, Harding announced Omaha was still wide-open for prostitution, with most of it centered in one part of the city. By Harding's time the locale for houses of prostitution had moved a few blocks west and north, to 13th and 14th between about Jackson Street and Capitol Avenue. The investigator reported in his "racy narrative," as the *World-Herald* called it, that many women in the houses told him they were protected by the police. One prostitute confided her landlady had been paying protection for a long-time and "We get our orders from the police department just what to do when there is any heat in town."[79]

Because of the Harding Report the heat did go on, and one night some forty arrests were made in raids. Bond was posted at $500 cash for keepers of disorderly houses and $25 for inmates, although it was to be withheld until they had a physical. Judge Neble soon appeared on the scene, however, and reduced the bond to $100 for the madams and instituted immediate bond for the rest. In court next morning Neble freed nineteen of the arrested women, fined fourteen (two keepers of disorderly houses fined $50, the others $10 to $25), and five forfeited bond.[80]

The close working relationship between prostitution and the legal system came into embarrassing view with the publication of the 1931 *Police Annual*. Accustomed to the advertisements which accounted for half of the publication, purchased by the city's largest firms and industries as well as the smallest, readers were taken aback by a host of startling ads in the 1931 edition. Among those giving their compliments to the police department was an unusually large number of women with addresses in suspect parts of the city. Rosa at 1316 Capitol reminded readers of her "Good Rooms"; Sylvia next door gave the compliments of her rooming house; Betty sent her compliments, as did Minnie, Edna, Sophie, Emma, and many more friends. A public outcry arose after the *Annual* appeared, and Mayor Metcalfe ordered the advertising money of persons under police surveillance to be returned. In a letter to the police chief, the mayor warned if his department did not comply the *Annual* would be suppressed. [81]

A final comment on the madams and their prostitutes is to note their civic obligations were well attended to by the machine. As soon as women gained the right to vote, prostitutes had added to their long established duty of contributing to campaign expenses the duty of voting, now ordered to register and vote as directed by Headquarters. Failure to fulfill their obligations as citizens and cast their ballot as instructed was injurious to their business.

In addition to the women who appeared in the *Police Annual*, there was also a host of speakeasies and gambling places who had paid their $30 to $100 to appear on its pages. Just like the gamblers and brothels, bootleggers needed exemption from law enforcement, and they well knew Tom Dennison was the conduit to protection. He had been in the business of helping alcohol vendors make illegal sales a long time before the 18th Amendment went into effect. For years the organization had served its clients by protecting them from the inconveniences of the state's eight p.m. and Sunday closing laws. Opportunity to perfect his protection system under conditions of all-out prohibition had arrived in 1917 when Nebraska went legally dry, thus the machine was well prepared when the nation ordered drinking alcohol was to cease.

Lawmakers soon discovered that neither state laws nor national amendment quenched the local or national thirst.[82] Where there was a market, there appeared sellers, operating in violation of the law but securing exemption from prosecution so long as they were "fixed." A simple transaction took care of the fixing; a bootlegger paid the organization's collector, sometimes a policeman, and bought from organization approved wholesalers. The magnitude of illicit liquor sales in Omaha gave birth to stories such as the one about a gentleman who came into town and asked a woman if she knew where he could get a drink. "Do you see that millinery store over there," she asked? "Yeah," he answered, "can I get a drink there?" "No, that's the only place in town you can't." There were others of course, but a listing of places the stranger might have patronized in 1932, confined only to a portion of the city (south of Leavenworth, east of 24th, exclusive of the Italian sector) contained the names of 132 soft drink parlors, cabarets, residences, hotels, coffee houses, or cigar stores where liquor was sold. Another listing limited only to soft drink parlors but city wide provided 174 names and addresses where liquor was available in violation of the law of the land.[83]

Retailers, and the wholesalers who supplied them, purchased protection, and if they did not, as with prostitutes or gamblers who were uncooperative, were soon raided. Payments were levied on wholesalers on a volume basis; for example, Rawley and Marcell offered a south side bootlegger protection for himself and his customers in return for one dollar for every gallon sold. Favored wholesalers had buyers directed to them by the organization, as Charles Hutter found out when he was informed he could continue to sell liquor and be taken care of if he bought from Frank Calamia.[84] Not to buy as instructed was to run the risk of being raided, as John Staskiewicz discovered. Visited by Stanley Ciurej, Staskiewicz was warned by Ciurej if he did not buy from him he had better watch out for Potach and Irwin (a federal prohibition officer)--"They'll be visiting you."[85]

As one individual in the trade put it, there was "not a chance of being caught because everything is fixed."[86] In fact, policemen might have provided the protection. A grand jury cited as an overt act that Joe Potach "on or about January 1, 1931, was present at 414 North 16th Street, affording protection while a quantity of intoxicating liquor was transferred . . . from the automobile of [Art] Colombo to that of William J. Maher."[87] Billy Maher's name was a familiar one among bootleggers and Dennison workers, referring to himself and his brethren similarly employed as "poor old honest bootleggers."[88] It also appears frequently in the 1932 conspiracy indictment against Dennison and his associates, wherein of 168 charges of overt acts, 145 specifically relate to selling intoxicating beverages. Maher was no small-time operator; in November 1931 in a shed behind a residence he and Lawrence Scavio had about 404 gallons of whisky and 188 of alcohol. A truck parked nearby had about 45 gallons of alcohol loaded on it. Two months later Maher and the Mardi brothers (James and John, alias Tatino) had stored 215 gallons of whiskey and 342 of alcohol in two locations.[89]

Frank Calamia, another recurrent name in the conspiracy trial, produced bootleg liquor on a farm in Sarpy County (known as the Carl Hofeldt farm). He had two stills going there, and in the spring of 1931 had on the premises 100 gallons of whiskey and 1,213 gallons of alcohol.[90] Calamia's stills were not alone in the business, and two large ones for a time were in downtown Omaha, one in a building that once housed the Farrell Syrup Company. It was called upon to make a different kind of liquid in the late twenties. Located on the northwest corner of 9th and Dodge Streets, the Farrell still and boilers reached through the first two of the building's four floors, the third floor used for storage and the fourth for packing and shipping. Ten vats were in the building, each about six feet deep and thirteen across.[91]

Gene Livingston had the still shipped in from Chicago, along with four Chicagoans to install it. They had difficulty in getting the operation started, however, and its life span was short. The protection Livingston thought he had acquired was arranged through an officer, Fred Palmtag, who was not a Dennison man.[92] Palmtag became impatient when his repeated demands for money were not met, difficult for Livingston to provide since his still was not yet functioning. Turned down once too often, Palmtag's patience deserted him and in a restaurant he hit Livingston with a pistol and knocked him out. Then he went to Council Bluffs where he informed on the still to federal prohibition officers and a raid followed.[93]

Undaunted, Livingston moved a few blocks to 1207 Howard and within a year the Howard Street still appeared, but again he was raided before he was hardly started. Officers entered an elaborate three story distillery, valued at $50,000, with a daily capacity of 1,000 gallons. Three stills were operating when the raiders arrived, but no operators were there to greet them. Livingston had purchased the building under the alias of Henry Landsman, with the avowed intent of establishing a mercantile jobbing company. A gold leaf sign was on the door and the windows were painted black half way up; anyone who tried to look inside had their view cut off by a heavy partition. Behind the partition was Livingston's shipping department; on the second floor there were three stills and condensers and on the third were fifty 500 gallon vats of mash, all full.[94] Out of business before he could get started, Livingston did little more than create problems for himself, both in Omaha and Chicago circles, as shall be seen later.

In the early winter of 1932, special federal agents were sent into Omaha thanks to the efforts of a small circle of men, including Roy Towl, who were determinedly anti-Dennison. Telephone tapping was one of their tactics in the attempt to uncover illegal activities in Omaha and secure evidence against the machine. Not surprisingly the listening agents' reports are replete with verbatim conversations about buying and selling bootleg liquor, and several days were taken up at the conspiracy trial while they were read. The records reveal Frank Calamia, for example, answering the telephone and hearing a caller say "30 gallon red, tonight," and Frank then agreeing to the transaction. Jim called one day and asked whether any of the aged stuff was still available. "You bet," Calamia answered and took the order for "five of that and ten of the green in a new keg." Interesting details appear; how many jugs fit in the back of a Ford standard coupe? The answer, after a moment's computation, was two dozen in four cases. Another caller to Calamia wanted to know whether there was any Golden Wedding in town; Frank had none and did not know if anyone else did. The two agreed something else would be substituted, but carry the Golden Wedding label. Delivering the Golden Wedding or other bootleg liquor called for automobiles with altered spring systems, a source of business for favored garages: "Frank, this is the garage. About the springs in your Willys, the coil springs will cost you $22.50 and I can put two extra leaves in your springs for $16.00." Frank wanted to know which was best and was told the coil springs, "because if you are using it for business when it is empty it won't be so noticed as much as the other, and besides it will make hard riding."

That customers were not confined to speakeasies and included drinkers from the top level of society as well as lesser, was recorded in a call to Jimmy Mardi's from Dave, who instructed Mardi to deliver a "gallon of white" to Room 501 at the posh Athletic Club. Mardi protested the desk man would not let him through. "Just mention Jack Algiere's name," Dave assured Mardi, "He is a big shot and you won't have any trouble."[95] Another opportunity for the more affluent to enjoy a drink without being bothered was offered in the tenth floor restaurant of the Brandeis Store Building. A bungalow home was on the eleventh floor where liquor was said to be on hand, although it was not sold or served in the restaurant. Diners brought their own liquor and served themselves. Two prohibition officers from the Minneapolis office in February 1925 spent five evenings dining in the Brandeis restaurant, and every time watched customers flout the drinking law.[96] Needless to say, prohibition never made its way to Billy Nesselhous's suite at the Fontenelle Hotel.

Under the machine's protection, bootleggers pursued thriving although illegal careers in Omaha. The situation as to narcotics is less clear since seldom even mentioned. Their presence in Omaha was long-standing, dating to opium dens run by Chinese around the turn of the century. One of these was in the basement of the Midway, and there were at least three others, two on 12th Street between Douglas and Capitol Avenue and one on Capitol between 10th and 11th Streets.[97] During the World War I years, a variety of drugs were available, one woman asserting she stayed in Omaha because it was easier to find dope there than elsewhere. Pool halls and peddlers along west Q street were mentioned as sources at that time.[98] Sam House, an individual linked with Dennison, was reputedly the largest and most notorious dope dealer in the Missouri Valley.[99]

While Dr. Van Camp and perhaps others involved in narcotics were sheltered under Dennison's protective shoulders, the number of persons arrested and sentenced for violations of the Harrison Act, for one period at least, suggest the "Old Man" did not much concern himself with protecting its transgressors. From July 1, 1921, to November 10, 1924, 196 persons were imprisoned for more than a year from the Omaha area judicial district on narcotics charges (average one year and eleven days), with another 138 receiving sentences of less than a year. Twenty-three dismissals were recorded and 32 fines levied.[100]

The nature of the narcotics trade and its secretiveness leaves little basis for a judgment as to its relationship to Dennison and his organization. All that seems possible to say is that the traffic existed, but in what context so far as the "Old Man" is concerned remains unknown. But gamblers, prostitututes, and bootleggers were clearly machine clients, and for all three profit and loss depended upon the protection Dennison supplied. To provide that protection, his organization carefully maintained a special relationship with Omaha's law enforcement machinery.

Chapter VI

[1]Leighton, *Five Cities*, p. 195.

[2]Letter, Towl to Wilson, February 3, 1932, Towl papers, Box 1, Folder 1932, February, City Hall. Others listed were "Gale at the Union Pacific, Jolly at Cudahy's, Tom Murphy, U.S. National Bank. . . , Tom Quinlan of Brandeis and Gould Deitz." See also Towl memo, n.d., Towl papers, Box 1, Folder 1932, January 1-14, City Hall.

[3]Maher interview, October 23, 1979.

[4]Report, "Activities on 15th Street, March 3, 1932," Towl papers, Box 1, Folder, 1932, March, City Hall.

[5]Zerbe interview, July 16, 1979. Mr. Zerbe worked at the stable as a boy and recalled these Sunday morning sessions.

[6]Scott interview, July 22, 1980.

[7]*Ibid.* Also Maher interviews, October 23, 30, 1979.

[8]Statement of Mrs. Grace Housky, p. 35.

[9]Larsen and Cottrell, *The Gate City*, p. 132, and see pp. 132-140; see also Sorenson, *The Story of Omaha*, pp. 642-644. Wattles's autobiography provides a quick overview of his life, merely sketching the highlights, revealing little about himself or his times. Gurdon Wallace Wattles, *Autobiography of Gurdon Wallace Wattles* (New York: The Scribner Press, 1922); on his business career see pp. 46-64, on public service pp. 65-113.

[10]Special Report, Kansas City Investigator #10, January 5, 1914, Rosewater Collection, Reel 3, Box 1927.

[11]Cornwell, "Bosses, Machines, and Ethnic Groups," p. 131. See also Chudacoff, *The Evolution of American Society*, p. 161; Holli, *Reform in Detroit*, p. 180; Orth, *The Boss and the Machine*, p. 90, and Fainstein and Fainstein, "The Political Traditions of the City: Machine and Reform," pp. 13-14. The assimiliation thesis was summed up by Tammany's Richard Croker: "There is no denying the service which Tammany has rendered to the Republic. There is no such organization for taking hold of the untrained, friendless man and converting him into a citizen. Who else would do it if we did not . . .?" Quoted in Riordan, *Plunkett of Tammany Hall*, p. xix.

[12]I am indebted to Edward Shafton for the concept of the boss as a "peoples lobbyist," Shafton interview, October 3, 1979.

[13]EOW-H, April 21, 1903.

[14]Quoted by William C. Pratt from *The Unionist*, September 6, 1935, in his "The Omaha Business Men's Association and the Open Shop, 1903-1939," unpublished paper, 1984. The BMA lasted until 1949 when it merged with another organization.

[15]EOW-H, January 31, 1906.

[16]Arvid E. Nelson, Jr., *The Ak-Sar-Ben Story* (Lincoln: Johnsen Publishing Company, 1967), following p. 390.

[17]Letter, Crawford to Irvin Stalmaster, Assistant Attorney General [Nebraska], September 9, 1932, Sorensen papers, Box 39, Folder 191.

[18]Maher interview, October 23, 1979.

[19]EOW-H, March 23, 1921.

[20]Letter, Crawford to Irvin Stalmaster, September 14, 1932, Sorensen papers, Box 39, Folder 191, and second letter to Stalmaster, same date; letter, Murphy to Dear Friend Irvin, September 15, 1932, *Ibid.*; Towl memo, n.d., Towl papers, Folder 1932, February, City Hall.

[21]Letter, Crawford to Towl, May 11, 1932, Sorensen papers, Box 35, Folder 65.

[22]Report, Kansas City Investigator, n.d., p. 1, Rosewater Collection, Reel 3, 1927. The investigator erroneously refers to W.J. McConnell [sic] as the "gang's" attorney in all important cases.

[23]*Ibid.*, and Shafton interview, October 3, 1979.

[24]Letter, Crawford to Stalmaster, September 14, 1932, Sorensen papers, Box 39, Folder 191; letter, Crawford to Stalmaster, same day, *Ibid.*

[25]Letter, L.C. Andrews, Assistant Secretary, Treasury Department, Washington, D.C., to The Honorable Attorney General, United States, December 21, 1925, National Archives, Department of Justice, Subject: Classified Correspondence, file 12-45-8. Cited hereafter as Van Camp file. Dismissal of charges in letter, O.R. Luhring, Assistant U.S. Attorney General to James C. Kinsler, September 9, 1928, Van Camp file.

[26]Letter, James C. Kinsler, U.S. Attorney, Omaha, to Mabel Walker Willebrandt, Assistant Attorney General, Washington, D.C., December 18, 1925, Van Camp file. Charges may be found in *No. 4140 Criminal, United States District Court, District of Nebraka, Omaha Division. The United States of American vs. Dr. Lee Van Camp. Indictment Violation Sections 1 and 2 Harrison Anti-Narcotics Act, As Amended,* Filed November 2, 1925, R.C. Hoyt, Clerk, by John Nicholson, Deputy.

[27]See letter, J.C. Kinsler to Colonel L.G. Nutt, Head, Narcotics Division, U.S. Treasury Department, December 16, 1925, Van Camp file; Radiogram, Kinsler to Nutt, same date, *Ibid.*

[28]Letter, Kinsler to The Attorney General, December 24, 1925, Van Camp file.

[29]Letter, Kinsler to Mabel Walker Willebrandt, December 18, 1925, Van Camp file.

[30]"Memorandum for the Solicitor General," by O.R. Luhring, Assistant Attorney General, December 23, 1925, Van Camp file.

[31]Steffens defined boodling as "Everything the city owned was for sale by the officers elected by the people." *Shame of the Cities*, p. 84, and see pp. 69-100 for Boss Edward R. Butler's highly developed boodling in St. Louis.

[32]Frost interview, October 30, 1979.

[33]EOW-H, August 25, 1931.

[34]Zerbe interview, July 16, 1979; and Towl memo, n.d., Towl papers, Box 1, Folder 1932, February, City Hall; Maher interview, November 6, 1979.

[35]EOW-H, February 15, 1934.

[36]I am indebted to Dr. John Ragan for this information. Ragan interview, September 22, 1979; also to Henry J. Walsh, a nephew of Dennison's, for his knowledge of Dennison's contacts with other cities and friendship with Pendergast. Interview with Henry J. Walsh conducted by Orville D. Menard, October 3, 1979, Omaha, Nebraska.

[37]EOW-H, February 5, 1931; see also Bee, January 3, 1937.

[38]For example, Ringwalt interview, August 7, 1939 (an insurance executive); Cathers interview, July 16, 1979 (retired high school teacher); Zerbe interview, July 18, 1979 (he operated a rent-a-car agency in his earlier years); Maher interview, November 6, 1979 (a Dennison worker and bootlegger); and interview with William Noyes conducted by Orville D. Menard, September 10, 1979, Omaha, Nebraska (Mr. Noyes was a former city official and political activist whose father had been a city commissioner in Dennison's last years).

[39]EOW-H, February 5, 1931.

[40]Willard, "The Machine Is Trimming the City."

[41]Ragan interview, September 22, 1979.

[42]Special Report, Kansas City Investigator #10, January 5, 1914, Rosewater Collection, Reel 3, Box 1927.

[43]Report, Palmtag to Towl, September 18, 1931, Towl papers, Folder 1931, September-December, City Hall.

[44]Deposition of George B. Burrier, ODN, April 19, 1907.

[45]Zerbe interview, July 16, 1979.

[46]Letter, Crawford to E.D. L'Sullivan [sic], April 2, 1932, Sorensen papers, Box 35, Folder 65.

[47]Memo, "Means of Collecting," attached to letter, Murphy to Edson Smith, July 5, 1932, Sorensen papers, Box 35, Folder 65.

[48]ODN, February 2, 1902, and April 24, 1907.

[49]Anonymous letter, n.d., Towl papers, Box 1, Folder 1931, September-December, City Hall.

[50]Memorandum, "Potach Bribery," January 13, 1932, Towl papers, Box 1, Folder 1931, January 1-14, City Hall.

[51]See MOW-H, March 12, 13, 14, 15, 1930; EOW-H, March 11, 12, 14, 1930; EOW-H, March 25, 1930; Bee, November 17, 1931.

[52]Anonymous letter, May 27, 1931, Towl papers, Box 1, Folder 1931, May-August, City Hall.

[53]EOW-H, March 23, 1903.

[54]MOW-H, March 8, 1923.

[55]Letter, Kinsler to Willebrandt, April 17, 1925, Van Camp file, 5-45-13-1.

[56]EOW-H, November 29, 1932.

[57]EOW-H, July 27, 1930, and October 25, 28, 1930; see letter, Crawford to Stalmaster, "Re: Sam Ziegman," July 19, 1932, Sorensen papers, Box 39, Folder 191.

[58]MOW-H, March 12, 1930.

[59]EOW-H, August 19, 1902.

[60]EOW-H, February 16, 18, 1918; ODN, February 15, 16, 18, 1918.

[61]Statement of Mrs. Grace Housky, Sorensen papers, Box 35, Folder 67. Also on the Friar's Club, Zerbe Interview, July 18, 1979; Frost interview, October 10, 1979; Maher interview, November 11, 1979.

[62]Letter, Kinsler to Willebrandt, July 1, 1925, Van Camp file, 5-45-

13-14.
[63]Letter, Towl to Wilson, February 3, 1932, Towl papers, Box 1, Folder 1932, February, City Hall.

[64]Florian Newbranch interview, EOW-H, January 3, 1930.

[65]Leighton, *Five Cities*, p. 197.

[66]The Albert Law provided "Whoever shall erect, establish, continue, maintain, use, own or lease any building, erection or place used for the purpose of lewdness, assignation or prostitution shall be guilty of a nuisance . . . and shall be enjoined and abated as hereinafter provided." A person found guilty of violation of an injunction by a judge empowered to "summarily try and punish the offender" could levy a fine of between $200 and $1,000 or imprison in county jail for three to six months, or both fine and imprison. *Laws of Nebraska 1911*, Chapter 63, "Ill Fame Houses."

[67]Washburn, *The Underworld Sewer*, pp. 45-46.

[68]*Ibid.*, pp. 47-50; Sunday W-H, December 1, 1907.

[69]Washburn, *The Underworld Sewer*, p. 56.

[70]Sunday W-H, December 1, 1907.

[71]EOW-H, December 12, 14, 16, 1907; Sunday W-H, December 15, 1907; Martin's interests were listed as the Arcade with fifty cribs; twelve cribs on 9th Street, Capitol Avenue to Dodge; fourteen on Dodge Street, 8th to 9th; ten from 9th to 10th on Dodge in a second row of houses; twenty on Capitol Avenue, 9th to 10th; and eleven on an alley opening on 9th between Dodge and Douglas. He was also given as the proprietor of several houses on 9th, stretching one block north and south of Dodge, where Blanche Wilson paid rent of $150, Mary Leonard $150, Anna Nelson $150, Frankie Edwards $125, and Cleo Weston $125. See also ODN, November 14, 1907; EOW-H, December 12, 14, 16, 1907, and Sunday W-H, December 15, 1907.

[72]EOW-H, January 16, 1914; see also EOW-H, April 22, 1912, and the judgment that the Albert Law was enforced about as effectively as in other cities of the state.

[73]EOW-H, March 3, 1915.

[74]*Ibid.*, June 14, 1911.

[75]ODN, March 14, 1914.

[76]Special Report, Kansas City Investigator #32, February 20, 1914, Rosewater Collection, Reel 3, Box 1927; and Zerbe interview, July 18, 1979.

[77]Creal interview, August 9, 1979.

[78]Zerbe interview, July 18, 1979.

[79]EOW-H, February 5, 1931.

[80]Disorderly houses were listed at Sylvia Hulett, 1314 Capitol Avenue; Rosy Mann, 1309 Capitol Avenue; Rosy Brown, 1316 Capitol Avenue; Jane Lewis, 1301 Davenport; Sadie James, 1509 Davenport; Goldie Wells, 414 No. 14th; Mary Fields 411 No. 15th; Mary Hunter, 416 No. 14th; Anna Smeall, 2522 N Street. EOW-H, February 6, 1931.

[81]*Omaha and Metropolitan Police Relief and Pension Fund Association, 1931*, published by the Omaha Police Department. And see the letter from Crawford to Stalmaster, March 24, 1932, wherein Crawford credits Officer Bert Thorpe for the idea of seeking contributions "in a big way" from madams and "various joints operating in the city." Sorensen papers, Box

35, Folder 66. See EOW-H, November 11, 1931.

[82]On Nebraska's prohibition law see *Laws of Nebraska 1917*, Chapter 187, pp. 425-451.

[83]Letter, Murphy to W.E. Nance, Special [Prohibition] Agent, March 24, 1932, lists attached. Sorensen papers, Box 35, Folder 66.

[84]Document 7025, Grand Jury Indictment, Overt Acts numbers 8, 9.

[85]EOW-H, October 25, 1932.

[86]EOW-H, October 20, 1932. Several days of the conspiracy trial were devoted to testimony on stills and bootlegging. Also Smith Interview, October 9, 1979; and letter, Mrs. Wood to Towl, August 14, 1931, on protection payments, Towl papers, Box 1, Folder 1931, May-August, City Hall.

[87]Document 7025, Grand Jury Indictment, Overt Act number 18.

[88]Maher interview, October 30, 1979.

[89]Document 7025, Grand Jury Indictment, Overt Acts number 57, 58, 59.

[90]*Ibid.*, Overt Act number 35.

[91]EOW-H, February 22, 1928.

[92]Memorandum, "Summary of Omaha Situation," Towl papers, Box 1, Folder 1932, February, City Hall.

[93]Maher interview, October 23, 1979.

[94]EOW-H, March 26, 1979.

[95]For transcripts of wiretaps see Document 7025. The vocabularly of bootlegging included: green meant raw moonshine whiskey; white meant ethyl alcolol; alky meant ethyl alcohol also; plant was a place where liquor was concealed; Golden Wedding was a brand name; Log Cabin another brand; tin meant a one gallon can of ethyl alcohol; stuff meant intoxicating liquor; thirsty meant a thirty gallon keg.

[96]Letter, J.C. Kinsler to E.C. Yellowley, Chief, Prohibiton Agents, Washington, D.C., April 17, 1925, Classified Correspondence, Department of Justice, National Archives, Records Group 60, file 5-45-13-1.

[97]Sunday W-H, October 27, 1901.

[98]EOW-H, March 11, 1918.

[99]Letter, Kinsler to Willebrandt, December 18, 1925, Van Camp file, no number; letter, Crawford to Mrs. Marling, July 14, 1932, Towl papers, Box 1, Folder 1932, June-July, City Hall.

[100]Letter, Joseph A. Manning, Narcotic Agent, Office of Agent in Charge, Minneapolis Division to J.C. Kinsler, November 12, 1924, Van Camp file, 5-45-13.

CHAPTER VII

Operations: Justice

*Reform administrations suffer
from a diarrhea of promises
and a constipation of performance.*
--James M. Curley

Of all the agencies and operations of local government, the most crucial to Tom Dennison's political machine were the police and legal machinery. Domination over the underworld and control of crime depended upon selective law enforcement by the police, compliant judges, and obliging juries. When a Dennison collector took a payment for protection, the buyer had confidence the brothel, speakeasy, or games now had sanction to satisfy customers. If someone in town became troublesome and needed "jamming," the police were called upon to harass the culprit through stringent application of the law. Occasionally a client or friend stumbled into difficulty with the authorities since control was never complete; now was the time for the "Old Man" to come to assistance by moving into judicial chambers and courtrooms to assure a favorable decision. Crimes committed with organization toleration or sanction received scant attention from the authorities and investigations were apt to be cursory. Since the organization in fact supervised crime it was in a position to apply its own code of justice to thief and victim, sometimes returning stolen goods to owners--usually for a price.

Rewards and punishments were staples of machine operations, and orders issued from the office in the Karbach Building to agents of the law demonstrated a host of techniques to take care of one's friends and punish the foe. Having those orders obeyed depended upon helping the right people win elections, and the crime machine became a political machine. Its primary ambition was to place Dennison dependent members on the city commission or in elected law enforcement posts such as county attorney or municipal judge. Third ward workers were keenly aware that electoral success meant renewal for another term of their unwritten contracts to continue in business.

Success at the polls confirmed the machine's dominant voice in selection of the police commissioner, the chief of police and other officers. For years these posts were occupied by Dennison men, and State Attorney General Christian A. Sorensen was accurate in stating in 1932 that "Tom Dennison has been in control of the department for ever so long . . . . It is such complete control that some of the highest ranking officers of the police department report at his office every morning."[1] Roy Towl, who at the time of Sorensen's comment was serving as police commissioner thanks to a Dennison scheme to discredit him, was questioned about Sorensen's remark. "Yes," agreed the police commissioner, "Tom Dennison controls the police department."[2]

In letters to Washington, D.C., Towl singled out the detective bureau as understood to be entirely under Dennison's direction, from Chief of Detectives Danbaum to plainclothesmen who reported to Dennison daily, some days several times.[3] A listing of officers sent to Irvin Stalmaster, Assistant State Attorney General, by Tom Crawford carried the names of seventeen officers closely aligned with Dennison and Nesselhous, including Chief "Gentleman Jack" Pszanowski, Bert A. Thorpe, Joe Vinci, Ben Danbaum, Joe Potach, Harry Buford, and Detective Paul Sutton. Then followed the names of 113 officers who could not be trusted because they were aligned (but not "closely") with Dennison, Nesselhous, Marcell, and Rawley. While many of them did not personally know the machine leaders, Crawford advised, they loyally carried out the orders of men in the first group.

Crawford added a long list of officers who were neither closely aligned nor aligned, but went along with the machine's dictates "chiefly because they know that to do differently would mean a 'Beat' out in the sticks--or one made to order for them to divert them from any interference."[4] The plight of policemen in this category is evoked in conversations between Assistant Chief George W. Allen and then Police Commissioner Towl, with the commissioner telling Allen he knew most of the officers were dominated by Dennison, including Inspector Thorpe and Chief Pszanowski. Towl confided to the assistant chief that the mayor and council would not permit him to touch Pszanowski. Even if he did move against the chief, said Towl, and advanced Allen the promotion would be short-lived. The uncomfortable assistant chief pointed out "I don't want to do anything but stay right where I am and keep out of trouble and get my pension."

Certainly officers have to be cautious, and Towl admitted he did not blame them. We have to be pretty careful Allen confirmed, adding it caused problems to become identified with either Butler or Towl or anyone opposed to Dennison. During a later discussion Towl informed Allen he was going to take him into his office for special work. Allen agreed to follow orders, but the next morning he and his wife came to Towl's office, both distraught. Mrs. Allen, sobbing, said "I am afraid you are getting us into a lot of trouble. We do not want to take any part in political differences . . . ."[5]

The only officer Towl identified as resisting the gang was Fred Palmtag, who had agreed to work closely with him. Soon thereafter Palmtag was demoted from his ten year detective rank to patrolman, and five months later he was suspended by Inspector Thorpe, an officer on Crawford's closely aligned group. An hour after Palmtag's suspension, Towl reinstated him and his case was quickly taken up by the city commission. Palmtag went to Joseph Koutsky, a commissioner who visited Dennison frequently, to discuss his situation and ask for help. You are in trouble with the powers that be, Koutsky informed him, and they were the ones to talk to. Palmtag protested he had unsuccessfully tried to talk to Dennison and was in trouble only because he had followed orders. His reward was Koutsky's admitting he also took orders from Dennison, because if he did not do as told his friends suffered; the commissioner added he had property in South Omaha to protect. Then Palmtag heard his case laid to rest by Koutsky:[6]

> I am sure that the charges against you are not right, but I have to vote the way they want me to, as there are lots of things that come in this council that I want and I don't want to get in bad with those people. I might want something myself. Fred, you made a great mistake when you went to work for Mr. Towl, out of his office.

When it came to a vote, Palmtag was dismissed by a count of

five to two (Towl and Arthur Westergard "no"). Nine months later Palmtag again became a sergeant when Towl was no longer police commissioner.[7]

While he still had the job, Towl's efforts to demote or fire policemen aligned with Dennison were as unsuccessful as his attempt to help Palmtag. First he tried to drop three officers on grounds of insufficient funds in the department. His fellow commissioners, over Towl's objections that the machine was dictating to them, quickly reinstated the three. When he issued orders demoting Sutton and Thorpe, Towl was again overridden and learned from the city attorney's legal opinion, requested by Mayor Metcalfe, that while the police commissioner could demote policemen they in turn could appeal to the city commission. And the commission, advised the city attorney, was given by the charter supreme authority over the fire and police departments. Therefore it held ultimate power over promotions, demotions, removal, and discipline.[8]

Not the only officer to run afoul of Dennison, Palmtag's removal from duty was not unique. Several years earlier three other officers were taken off the force on Dennison's instructions. Two gentlemen from Red Oak, Iowa, after selling cattle in Omaha, decided to see the glitter of downtown that evening. Rather late and after learning the third ward deserved its reputation, they were picked up by three policemen who took them off for jail. Before they made it to the station, the two were shook down and their remaining twelve dollars was taken. They were then released to make their way home as best they might.

Back home in Red Oak they shared with the sheriff the story of their night in Omaha. A friend of Dennison, the sheriff called Omaha's boss and asked "What the hell kind of a police force you got there?" After hearing the story, the "Old Man" called Henry Dunn, then police commissioner, and had him place in a line-up all officers on duty the night the Red Oak visitors were in town. Invited back to Omaha for the occasion, the two victims identified the three who had taken them and their money into custody. The officers were immediately fired.[9]

Offending one of Dennison's many friends or exhibiting political differences with him were sure ways to place a job in jeopardy. Denny O'Brien was a man who learned of the "Old Man's" distaste for unsanctioned candidates. O'Brien, a Democrat, while working as a city prosecutor had made Dennison uneasy, but thanks to Dahlman, O'Brien was allowed to stay on because the mayor wanted to keep fellow Democrats on the payroll. Nonetheless, when O'Brien had the temerity to file for county attorney, interpreted by Headquarters as a challenge to their choice, Henry Beal, he went too far. Metcalfe, now mayor, received a call from Dennison who instructed him to fire O'Brien, now working in the city legal department. It was agreed O'Brien would be kept on until after the election for the sake of appearances. True to the plan, Metcalfe fired O'Brien shortly after the election.[10]

Use of the police department to advance the cause of the machine and its friends--or deter the uncooperative-- came on many fronts. At one point in the late 1920s two adventuresome souls decided to put slot machines around the city, neither securing Dennison's approval nor dividing profits with him. Organization informers were instructed to report to Headquarters the location of every slot machine they came across. Then Sutton and Crawford were sent out to enforce the law, confiscating machines belonging to the challengers. Customers in the cigar stores, or wherever, were arrested when the unapproved slots were taken.[11] A clear message was delivered: illicit enterprises operated free of police interference only if cleared by the underworld's government.

On the other hand, Dennison was as quick to aid a friend as to punish a foe, as Billy Maher learned the night he was arrested for resisting arrest. In a soft drink parlor on North 16th Street, where the drinks were not so soft, Maher was campaigning for the Dennison slate by assailing Butler and his supporters. A fight broke out and Maher was taken to the police station: "What did they pinch me for," Billy wanted to know, "I worked for the Square Seven." Tom Dennison soon was on the scene to pay Maher's fifteen dollar bond (Maher had over $1,500 on him when searched) and the incident was forgotten, except by the arresting officer who was soon after reassigned to an undesirable beat.[12]

Dennison's personal links with the police are evident

not only in his police officer chauffeur (Buford) and secretary (Crawford), but also in his unofficial bodyguard one evening. Threats had been made against Dennison by an old enemy, but he decided nonetheless to attend a wrestling match. Spectators thought it curious that in one part of the audience there were about a dozen policemen, all in the same section as Tom Dennison. Police headquarters denied any bodyguard was provided for Dennison by the city, and said only one policeman was assigned to the match. All the rest were there on their own and just happened to sit around Dennison.[13]

The "Old Man's" underworld and police contacts kept him informed on crimes committed in the city, and given proper inducements at Headquarters (cash or as repayment for favors as in the case of the furrier) stolen goods were made to reappear. One victim robbed of a diamond ring was subsequently approached by a Dennison police officer and asked whether the ring was insured, and if so for how much. The response, an affirmative and for $3,500, was relayed to Dennison, who had the ring. Since it was insured, the "Old Man" decided to keep the ring; had it not been he planned on sending a negotiator to settle on a sum for return of the gem.[14]

A diamond not kept made its way back to the owner by way of Billy Nesselhous. Billy received a call one day from the brother of a man (both from northwest Nebraska) who had lost a five carat diamond ring during a night out in South Omaha with some prominent Omahans. "Don't worry," counseled Nesselhous, and advised that within an hour or two to expect someone to appear at the hotel room where the brothers were staying. Have a hundred dollar tip ready for services rendered said Nesselhous; an individual soon knocked and when the door was opened he asked, "Are you Quigley?" Following a "yes" reply, the messenger held out the ring with the explanation someone had found it. The ring and a hundred dollars then exchanged hands.[15]

The call to Nesselhous was made with the knowledge that every morning a report was delivered to the Karbach Headquarters listing events of the previous twenty-four hours: who had come to town, who left, what had happened in neighborhoods under organization jurisdiction. Costs were a business matter with little room for sentiment or concern for any personal relationship with the the management. Billy Doyle learned that being Dennison's keeper of the protection books did not provide immunity from being assaulted and robbed. When he appealed to the "Old Man" to recover his stolen watch and diamond, he was assessed a fifty dollar handling fee before the goods were returned.[16] Considerations other than cash or repaying favors occasionally prompted the "Old Man" to cycle stolen goods back to their owners.

One day a cattleman from Blair, Nebraska, made a big sale at the Omaha stockyards and he proceeded to celebrate his good fortune. Celebrating too much, he awoke the next morning with empty pockets. Back home in Blair he told an attorney, familiar with conditions in Omaha, of his escapade. A call was put through to Dennison's office and the attorney explained the situation, especially as it related to the family's borderline financial condition. Dennison wanted to know why he was called since he had nothing to do with the fellow's loss. "Mr. Dennison," came the voice from nearby Blair, "We think you run Omaha." For whatever reason, the boldness of the comment or maybe sympathy, the man's money was returned.

Motives were usually more clear, however, and a charge was the usual pattern for playing middleman between robbed and robber. Owners of a home furnishings company one morning opened their store to discover several valuable carpets had been stolen. A friend suggested Tom Dennison be contacted to see whether anything might be done about recovering their substantial loss. "The Old Man" was accordingly appealed to and a deal was worked out. Soon a marriage was going to take place, said Dennison, with the groom a member of the police department. It was insinuated that a couple of those fine rugs would make a fine wedding present. The store owner agreed and less the wedding present the stolen goods were returned.[17]

Advantages of Dennison's close relationship with law enforcement agencies were many and varied. Whenever a raid was being planned that was not machine ordered, loyal officers were relied upon to inform Dennison of time and place.[18] Targeted establishments were duly warned and raiders entered a brothel without prostitutes, a gambling den with neither games nor players, and soft drink parlors actually serving soft drinks. Allegations of suppressing evidence were sometimes lodged against the police, as materials disadvantageous to a Dennison ally mysteriously vanished. In the Van Camp case, Detective Sutton was pointed to as having removed marked money and narcotics that were being held for Van Camp's prosecution.[19]

Evidence also sometimes suddenly became insufficient, as happened in the case of a young man charged with larceny. He was employed in a hardware store near the county courthouse, and over a period of time stole goods from his employer. When he was arrested, police found in his home a gunny sack filled with knives, razors, and sundry other items taken from the store. The accused's father asked him why he had stolen the goods (which he had admitted in a signed statement). The boy replied he sold most of the items and used the money to pay for drinks at Pete Loch's saloon. Go talk to Loch, the father was advised by a friend, who knew of the saloonkeeper's relationship with Dennison, and explain your son's predicament. As suggested, the father went to Loch to plead his son's case: a young man with a family to support, spending his money in Loch's saloon instead of for home.

Loch agreed to see what he could do, then put out the word he wanted to talk with Chief of Detectives Steve Maloney. A call soon came through to Pete, and he and the officer talked the case over. Maloney appeared in the courtroom the morning of the preliminary hearing to have a brief and private conversation with the judge. To the courtroom and the defendant the judge announced Mr. Maloney had just informed him there was insufficient evidence to prosecute and the case was dismissed. On the sidewalk a few minutes later, Maloney urged the young man to stay out of trouble and strolled away.

The young man's case reveals the law being lifted from someone's shoulders by the organization, but for others it was brought heavily to bear. Tom Crawford had a brief falling out with the organization in the late 1920s, forcing his resignation from the police force. To support himself, he started a taxi cab company on the south side, but fares failed to materialize. Anticipating customers from the large number of people he had met as a policeman, he was surprised that instead of coming to him they avoided him.

Then he heard Dennison and Roscoe Rawley had instructed Joe Potach to pass the word that anyone who patronized Crawford's Nash Taxi Company would be raided.[20] Crawford retaliated by threatening to run for city commissioner and expose gang activities, ones he knew well and Dennison well understood he knew. A compromise was worked out and Crawford returned to the police force and the organization, abandoning his taxi company and political ambitions. His brief rebellion was not forgotten by Dennison, however, and Crawford was denied by the "Old Man" when he later came to him for help.

Dennison's controlled crime endeavors made him well placed to be informed about car thefts, and his office for some years was central to a leading racket. An Omaha police officer, A.C. Andersen, was sent to Iowa, in about 1919, to interview an imprisoned member of an organized gang of car thieves. Through the night Andersen listened and took notes. When he returned with his notes transcribed into a statement, the prisoner refused to sign, fearing if he put his name to his words he would be killed if he ever returned to Omaha. Andersen turned the unsigned statement over to the chief of police and never heard of it again. But he was put on Dennison's blacklist and eventually felt compelled to leave the force, although he was reappointed after Dennison was closed down. What was confessed that night, and made Andersen a threat to Dennison for Andersen was not a Dennison fellow traveler, was "that the plans for the stealing and disposition of cars were formulated in Dennison's office and under his direction."[21]

In later years the car racket involved three cities: automobiles stolen in Chicago were driven to Omaha where they were reconditioned and their serial numbers destroyed. With new paint and new serial numbers, they were delivered to Grand Island, Nebraska, to be sold. Whether Dennison was still giving directions from his office for the intercity automobile business is unclear; two other men, Wiley Compton in Omaha and "Speck" Brotherton in Grand Island were identified as the principals, but it is probable Dennison's tolerant hand was not far removed from the operation.[22] Had Compton been operating outside Dennison's purview, his business likely would have attracted great official attention. Independent operations did not fare well in Omaha.

Three police officers, George Summitt, Ben Danbaum, and Chief Charles Van Dusen learned that lesson when they decided protection collections made in Tom Dennison's name did not necessarily have to be turned over to him. Dennison, of course, found out. Calling Crawford in one day, Dennison told him the three officers were to be put in their proper place. Crawford received orders to raid Marie Studer's place on North 17th Street, not an accidental choice out of the many available to raid. First of all, she was known to have been paying protection to Summitt, who was posing as a Dennison collector, and second, Summitt was taking liquor confiscated elsewhere by the police department to Studer's, in a police car no less. With instructions to keep the plans secret to avoid a tip-off, Crawford secured a warrant and enlisted the help of Potach and another officer.

When the raiders charged in, Summitt and two other detectives were among the men drinking at Marie's. Crawford allowed all three officers to leave, with Summitt instructed to report to Thorpe and tell him what had happened. After the police wagon arrived and Marie's customers and liquor were headed for the station, Crawford called Dennison and was instructed to tell curious people Marie's was raided because neighbors had complained about a disorderly house in their neighborhood. Among the first to ask Crawford "why" were Van Dusen and Danbaum in a closed door session in the chief's office. Both men were irate at Crawford, with Van Dusen insisting it was his responsibility as chief for setting up raids. Then he threatened the officer with suspension, but relented when Danbaum nodded a negative. Crawford was ushered to the door by the chief, reminded on the way he was fortunate in being given a second chance. The last word was Crawford's who retorted the second chance was not his but the chief's. Had he been suspended, warned Dennison's secretary, a new chief of police would have been named within two weeks.

Marie was fined $150, as recommended by Dennison to the judge, and her attorney appealed the case to district court. Now Dennison sent a messenger to Studer (under instructions he was not to tell her he had been sent by the "Old Man") to suggest she send her lawyer down to Headquarters. Dennison was a good fellow willing to help people in trouble, he reminded her. Dennison feigned lack of knowledge of the entire affair when the lawyer appeared to request assistance for his client. Dennison said he would be happy to assist a loyal friend like Marie, and instructed the attorney to secure an affidavit from her. She was to state she had paid Summitt money, believing she was buying protection from Van Dusen and Danbaum. In return Dennison promised the attorney he would make arrangements with the court through an intermediary (Paul Steinwender, the county attorney serving as a conduit for messages from Dennison to judges) to take care of the case. Raider Crawford would not appear in court against Marie, promised Dennison, if the affidavit was delivered to Headquarters. The case would be dismissed for lack of prosecution.

All worked out as Dennison planned, with the document delivered the next day. Crawford did not appear when the case was called and it was dismissed. Marie was grateful for the "Old Man's" intervention on her behalf, and the "three thieves," as Dennison called the officers, were brought to heel by the paper now in his possession, secured through his manipulation of the legal system. That talent surfaced again following the Harding Report's appearance, which brought Chief Pszanowski a summons to the "Old Man's" private office. After the Boss and the chief conferred, Pszanowski returned to his station and ordered raids on all places mentioned in the report, and a few more besides. Not part of the official instructions issued were those given to the raiders to let it be loudly known that interference with business as usual in Omaha was the fault of state officials--Sorensen and Stalmaster. Chief Pszanowski and his men, let the record show, were doing their job in attacking vice. At the same time they were making a political statement about the threat to the well being of illicit business when reformers got out of hand.[23]

To prove organization protection was advantageous even in this time of adversity, Dennison arranged for Judge Neble, Crawford, and attorney Bernie Boyle to meet at the police station in the chief's office. There the Judge proclaimed that persons arrested in the raids were entitled to immediate bail, and it was his duty to levy such bonds as to restore their freedom. Crawford and Boyle then selected from the Day Book (a listing recording arrests) the names of individuals arrested who were friendly to Dennison and the organization. Neble then proceeded to reduce the initial bonds levied on the Dennison favored, with the bond money put up by Boyle, who had received the funds from Nesselhous. Criticized by Sorensen and Stalmaster for his action, the Judge grandiloquently defended himself:[24]

> Whenever I can come to the aid of unfortunate humanity who are what they cannot help being, I shall always be ready to rise to their defense in the rights guaranteed to them by the constitution of our state.

In an attempt to reduce the impact of the Harding Report and its descriptions of vice in Omaha, a copy was taken to the Omaha Printing Company where scores of reproductions were made and distributed to the desks of state legislators, ministers, and others throughout the state. As the copies spread so did word circulate by their distributors, carefully avoiding any indication Dennison was behind their work, that the filth and vice described was nothing but an indication of Harding's and Sorensen's perverted minds and morals. They had not only associated themselves with such lascivious activity, but had used public funds to do it.[25]

Raids for machine political ends were a well developed Dennison technique, and police raiders were put into service in city campaigns. To pacify "drys" and reduce their criticisms of the administration and conditions in the city, incumbents were prone to demonstrate their strict attention to duty and morals with crackdowns in the days just prior to elections. In the 1930 campaign Dennison gave orders to Police Commissioner Dunn to order Robert Samardick, who had a reputation as a raider deluxe as both a federal prohibition agent and police officer, to clean up the city. He was to raid and arrest whomever was breaking the law. Samardick proceeded to do exactly that. Then, in the wake of the raids, organization men made the rounds bemoaning the situation and promising even worse times if the opposition slate won the forthcoming election. Soon a stream of angry bootleggers stormed to Dennison's office, but he denied any control over Dunn, whom the "leggers" assailed for appointing a known and hated person like Samardick. Aware of the hostility against him, Dunn called Dennison and said the raiding tactic was hurting him more than the opposition. Dennison agreed, and an announcement was issued by Dunn that Samardick was being released from the force. The damage done was too great, however, and the sacrificial Dunn was the only member of the Square Seven not reelected in 1930. In the third ward he ran last among the incumbents, and was even behind machine apostate Dan Butler.[26]

Dunn suffered his loss, but Dennison's capacity to neutralize political opposition through legal mechanisms was undiminished and again demonstrated in the case of C.C. Galloway, editor of *The Omaha Guide*, a newspaper primarily of Omaha's black community. Galloway published an article stating Officer Tom Crawford had shot and killed an innocent black bellboy in the course of a raid. Buford brought the story to Dennison, who instructed Crawford to take it to Ben Baker for determination if there was grounds for a libel suit. Crawford returned to Dennison with Baker's opinion that it was a possibility. He then stood by while the "Old Man" called County Attorney Beal and made arrangements for filing a criminal libel charge against Galloway. Dennison's concern, however, was less on behalf of Crawford's reputation than over the fact the editor had been attacking the county attorney's office over another shooting.

On the morning of the preliminary hearing, Henry Beal appeared and talked at length with Galloway in the city prosecutor's office. When the conversation was over, Beal sought out Crawford and told him an agreement had been reached; in return for Crawford's dropping the libel charge there would be no more attacks on the county attorney and his office. The deal was consented to by Crawford, who had been instructed by Dennison and Nesselhous to comply with whatever Beal requested. The charge was dropped and Galloway promised to make no more trouble for Beal.[27]

Galloway fell victim to a threat of legal action; Roy Towl was victimized when the organization decided to make him police commissioner in 1931, a means to discredit him among underworld and upperworld figures alike. Towl was a native Omahan, born in 1881, who graduated from South High School and went on to become an engineer. After an assignment with a railroad in Mississippi, he returned to Omaha and established his own engineering firm, doing work for counties, railroads, and drainage districts. He ran successfully for the city commission on the reform ticket in 1918 and became head of the Department of Public Improvements. During his three year tenure he designed planned zoning for Omaha, pressed for residential paving, eased access to downtown Omaha, and headed the lowering of Dodge Street hill. Along with the rest of the reform ticket, he was defeated in his bid for reelection but remained active in politics. Professionally he concentrated on river behaviors in alluvial plains, often sought by railroads for his expertness.

Nine years after his first bid for reelection he was successful in returning to city hall, the only member of the reform slate to make it against the Dennison candidates. A strikingly handsome man, Towl was a determined opponent of Tom Dennison and the organization. They gave him the fire department as his initial responsibility in the spring of 1930 when he succeeded in being elected, but a resolution was introduced by Mayor Metcalfe the following January to transfer him to police commissioner. Only Towl voted against the change in duties, realizing the job was being forced upon him for political reasons and the department would not really be under his control.[28]

Surely Towl was aware a similar tactic had been used when the organization determined to put Dan Butler in his place after his defection from the ranks. Assigned the position of police commissioner, Butler became the target of abuse as law enforcement was twisted into a tool to embarrass the individual putatively in control of the police. For example, Butler, the police chief, and the head of the morals squad suddenly began to receive a spate of anonymous letters naming prominent Omahans as bootleggers. The letters not only identifed them, but reported these individuals were spreading the word they were protected by Dan Butler since he became police commissioner. Butler, known as being quarrelsome, reacted as Dennison anticipated and ordered raids on the putative bootleggers. Officers did as told but failed to expose any trace of bootleg activity, to Butler's dismay and the outrage of those raided. Policemen were next instructed by Headquarters to pinch people on the slightist pretext, and then, when they complained, to blame Butler's zeal for law and order. Drivers by the hundreds were ticketed in a surge of riveted police attention to traffic violations. Hapless citizens who telephoned the station were informed Police Commissioner Butler had issued the get tough orders and officers were only obeying.

236

Another trick played on Butler involved a church lawn social. His office received information that considerable liquor was going to be dispensed in addition to ice cream. The anonymous informants said bootleggers were going to operate from cars parked in the area when the social took place; that would be safer than trying to operate out of a nearby house or building. On the scheduled evening, Butler sent two officers to search all the cars in the church's neighborhood; people at the social were alerted by Dennison messengers to the mission Butler's "cops" had been assigned. The next day, Police Commissioner Butler suffered another barrage of criticism from innocent and much offended citizens.[29]

A few years later it was Towl's turn to discover the political pitfalls Dennison and associates had in store for Omaha's police commissioner. Not unaware of his plight, in a discussion with Assistant Chief Allen, Towl brought up what he considered to be a strange cooincidence. Mayor Metcalfe had announced he wanted a law-abiding city and bootlegging was to be suppressed. A special concern specified by Metcalfe were soft drink parlors and the police were called upon to close half of them. Seventy-two illegal parlors were named on a list handed over by the diligent mayor to the new police commissioner. Moving to carry out Metcalfe's shutdown order, one Towl little disagreed with, he requested Paul Sutton, an officer with much experience on the morals squad, to provide him a list of the worst offenders of soft drink parlor licenses. Towl figured about ninety per cent of the establishments were probably bootlegging, but if he was to close even half he wanted to make other than an arbitrary decision, hence his request to Sutton. A few days later Sutton obligingly handed over his list--containing the exact seventy-two places Towl had in hand from the mayor. "Now Chief," asked the police commissioner, "don't you think this looks fishy?" Realizing what he confronted, Towl then said to Allen, "Well, I just made up my mind that the gang wants me knock off these places and create disfavor toward me and build up favor for themselves."[30]

His assessment was accurate. As had happened under Butler, the city again experienced police officers with vigorous enforcement of the law their purpose in life, now attributing their zeal to Police Commissioner Roy Towl. Raids were one means to "jam" Towl, but bootleggers and panderers were not likely to admire Towl to begin with. More important as a means to discredit him were activities designed to harass ordinary citizens. Standing in a hotel lobby, or buying a newspaper or magazine in a cigar store became preludes to verbal abuse, arrest, and a ride to the police station. The police commissioner was responsible of course--after all, people were not treated this way when he was in charge of the fire department.

One cigar store owner complained that in the five months Towl was police commissioner his store was raided five times. He was charged each time with keeping a disorderly house and his customers were placed under arrest. In every instance the case was dismissed. The owner accused the police of entering his store in between the raids, ordering customers out and threatening to arrest them. Other times officers demanded to know what his customers were doing there, what their business was, and then warning them not to return. Testimony to the fact Towl was bearing the brunt of reactions to such police activity is expressed in a letter to Towl from the aggrieved cigar store owner, imploring him to restrain the police department "over which you are the Commissioner in charge."[31]

A dentist and several others were taken into custody one afternoon, taken to the station and put in the bull pen with telephone calls at first denied. An hour or two later they were released on bond, but never told what they had been arrested for. On occasion vagrancy was the pretext for arrest, as a visitor learned shortly upon leaving Towl's office. After buying a newspaper, he was entering the Henshaw Hotel when he was accosted by a detective who ordered him to come along. After a ride in the patrol wagon, the gentleman, who was in the landscaping and fertilizing business, was booked for vagrancy. Denied access to a telephone, he was delivered to a cell where he stayed some forty-five minutes before allowed his call. He was released after a friend responded and produced a fifty dollar bond.

One day in July three officers entered the lobby of the Boquet Hotel, looked over the twenty-five men standing or seated in the lobby, selected six and took them to the station on vagrancy charges. They spent an hour and a half in a cell before they were permitted to use a phone. Later, all filed affidavits attesting to their employed status, including among them a baker, a hatter with the same firm for ten years, and an operator of a brick and coal yard in Audubon, Iowa. Another individual one afternoon was standing just outside the Baseball Headquarters looking at the score board facing the doorway. A policeman shoved him inside and arrested him as an inmate of a disorderly house. For no apparent reason the Minden, Iowa, farmer was under arrest for the first time in his fifty-six years.[32]

Responding to the criticism directed his way, the embattled Towl wrote his chief of police he objected to having people arrested for reading a newspaper, and insisted no one was to be held incommunicado on a misdemeanor charge.[33] Within a month of his letter, Towl had made himself too much of a nuisance in a murder investigation and it was time for him to return to the fire department. At a special meeting of his city commissioner colleagues, just a few days after the anniversary of his unwanted appointment to the post, Towl was removed as head of the police department. His year had been a tumultuous one and it was widely acknowledged he had headed the department in name only, reversed and overridden on most matters he considered important, especially on personnel questions.[34] Omaha's machine had demonstrated its ability to turn law enforcement on and off as it suited its purposes. That capacity enraged men like Roy Towl, as did Headquarter's apparent ability to use its police department contacts to ensure certain crimes were not investigated as thoroughly as unrestrained police work might have procured.

A case in point is provided by Officer Joe Potach who killed two men in 1925, both in the line of duty according to coroner's juries. The September shooting of Earl Williams seems to have warranted exoneration, for Williams was a fugitive tracked down and fired on when Williams, said Potach, shot at him. While heading a shipment to Omaha, Williams had trouble with one of the two cars carrying a large supply of bootleg liquor from Chicago. Parking both automobiles not far from Logan, Iowa, Williams called from a farm house to a garage in Omaha for help. After Williams and his men left, the farmer, his suspicions aroused since help was available in nearby Logan, called the sheriff who responded with deputies. They came upon Williams and three other men and a shoot-out followed.

One of the sheriff's men was wounded in the exchange and two of the bootleggers were captured, Williams and another escaping. A week's manhunt followed, Potach searching South Omaha and circulating among bootleggers for information. His efforts paid off when he received a tip-off Williams was hiding at Frank Vopalka's house at 29th and Spring Streets. Vopalka's daughter had brought the fugitive to the home, after listening to him plead he needed a place to hide until nine that evening, when he was to be picked up for an escape to Mexico. Williams told her he did not expect to be taken alive, and that Potach would kill him for sure, just as he had killed Jimmy Griffin seven months before.

Disguised as a female, Williams was introduced to the family as Lizzie, a young woman hounded by the police who was going to stay just a few hours then be on her way. Forty minutes before the scheduled departure, Potach and three or four other officers arrived at the Vopalka home. While Potach stationed his men around the house, Williams fled into a bedroom and crawled under a bed. With orders to the other officers to get Williams no matter what happened to him, Potach entered the dark bedroom. As he stooped to look under the bed, Potach related, a bullet whizzed by his head. He in turn fired three times, heard a groan and Williams, his lips rouged, mascara around his eyes, was hit. "My God, you've killed a woman," exclaimed one of the other officers when he looked under the bed. But he was wrong; it was Earl Williams, age twenty-eight, who had boasted he would take a couple of coppers with him and accurately predicted Potach would kill him if they met. The next day Potach was cleared of any wrong doing, and the sheriff of Logan complimented him for having saved Iowa the cost of a trial and probably of a hanging.[35]

The killing of Jimmy Griffin, referred to by Williams, is more questionable as to line of duty, but there is little question Potach was protected. Griffin was a bootlegger convicted of manslaughter, free on bond pending appeal of a ten year sentence when he had his fatal meeting with Potach at George Kubik's home. Mrs. Kubik told reporters immediately after the shooting that Potach, who was with two other officers, had entered her home, gun in hand and un-

240

leashed a "tirade of abuse" on Griffin. Potach later testified he took Griffin into the Kubik's kitchen and when he
went to search Jimmy, the suspect stepped back and reached
for his hip pocket. Potach said he fired in self-defense
thinking Griffin was going for a gun.

When Mrs. Kubik testified for the coroner's jury, her
memory changed, and now she recalled there was no quarrel-
ing and Potach's revolver was in his pocket. Secretary to
Chief of Detectives Danbaum, William Gurnett, questioned
Mrs. Kubik about her earlier story and an angry Potach
brandishing his gun. She was asked whether she heard him
call Griffin any names. "No, sir," she replied. Then Gurnett asked if Griffin had talked back to the officer. "Yes,
he did," she responded, "Griffin appeared to be quarrelsome." Next question: "The officers appeared to be perfectly sober and they acted like gentlemen, just like officers
do when they are making an arrest of [sic] investigation,
did they not?" She answered, "Yes, sir."[36] Three others who
were present the night of the shooting, George Kubik, a
policeman, and another bootlegger, all testified in similar
fashion, and the jury determined Joe had fired in the line
of duty.

Kubik, according to Tom Crawford, had a different
story about the shooting, one not told to the authorities.
Griffin was murdered, Kubik informed Crawford, out of revenge for a bootleg fraud. A few days before being shot,
Griffin had sold Joe Teshnolidek several barrels supposedly
containing alcohol, but which were in fact false top barrels and contained ninety-nine per cent water. Potach had
stormed into Kubik's, also a bootlegger, found Griffin,
called him a rat and demanded money because his partner,
Teshnolidek, had been swindled. Griffin protested he had
not known Teshnolidek and Potach were partners, repeatedly
apologized and promised to return the money. Potach was not
satisfied, and Griffin, afraid of Potach, made a run for
it. Potach shot him, then turned on the Kubiks with the
warning they had better keep quiet if they wanted to continue in the bootlegging business. If they did as told he
would "fix it" with Marcell and Rawley. A few years later
George Kubik's name was added to the list of unsolved Omaha
murders.[37]

In the unlikely event a friend of Dennison was arrested and brought to trial, a favorable verdict usually issued from a jury in a courtroom presided over by a cooperative judge. An opponent of the organization, on the other hand, confronted more than legal problems if brought into an Omaha courtroom, as Frank Erdman was aware. Charged with having planted a bomb at Dennison's house, his summation of the situation was revealing: "I would feel sure of an acquittal with an honest jury . . . but a man can't tell what he is running up against when it comes to a jury" [in Omaha].[38] As he foresaw, Erdman was declared guilty by his jury, but his conviction was reversed by the state supreme court on grounds of insufficient evidence.

Dennison was known as a man able to fix any jury in Douglas County, and Pete Loch considered himself "one of the best little fixers of a jury you ever saw."[39] The first step in a fix was to secure a list of prospective jurors for a forthcoming session, some 150 to 170 names. Securing the list was no problem since the county attorney or one of his assistants made it available. Next a city directory was consulted, and after each name employer and occupation were duly recorded. That task accomplished, Dennison invited associates to his office and asked them to peruse the list, placing their initials in front of names of persons they knew well enough to contact should it become necessary.

When all or almost all of the names were thus initialed, the list was retyped in triplicate, one copy going to the county attorney, the other two kept by Dennison. When a case came up that was of interest to Headquarters, a cooperating attorney was assigned and presented a copy of the list. Therefrom he and the county attorney selected jurors identified as known to someone working with the organization. Names of the dozen selected were sent to Dennison who then telephoned the individuals whose initials appeared in front of the names, urging them to contact the juror in question, or their employer if friendly to the organization, on behalf of the accused. Once in court the county attorney presented his case, performing his job creditably, to jurors prepared to vote not guilty. They might even have been visited by a member of the organization if the case was important enough. Officers Crawford or Buford were sometimes sent on these errands to make a special plea and win a promise for a favorable vote.

Federal cases included prospective jurors living well beyond Omaha's city limits. Not to see the organization's brand of justice thwarted, Dennison then put into operation a system to reach jurors in other parts of Nebraska. Aware that banks were likely to have a wide range of contacts in small communities and their vicinity, Dennison asked his banker friends to make telephone calls to their local counterparts to secure information on summoned jurors. Friendly small town bankers received special appeals to deliver a favorably disposed juror. Another source of information the machine tapped was an officer of the Union Pacific Railroad, who was relied upon to acquire information about prospective jurors through local station agents spread widely in the state. With the information thus gathered, working through local figures or emisaries sent from Headquarters, Dennison was at best provided a pliant voter and at worst had a chance to make a case for the accused and perhaps influence a vote. Through these devices, also used for grand juries, the organization secured favorable verdicts for its friends.

Some trials were of interest enough to result in Dennison appearing in a courtroom. On these occasions he was an obvious figure, sometimes even seen within the judge's chambers.[40] A raid at the Midway in 1912 provides evidence of the difficulty in securing a verdict against Tom Dennison's friends. Owners Jack Broomfield and Billy Crutchfield were subsequently tried for selling liquor after eight p.m. and for keeping a gambling room. Their jury included Fred Elsasser and Edward Malone (the latter an office manager for Hayden Brothers), who just happened to be in the courtroom and were selected as substitutes when two jurors chosen the previous week were excused by the judge.

When the jury voted, the first ballot went three to three. On another try, guilty picked up another vote (in police court only six jurors were used and attorneys had no right of challenge), but Elsasser and Malone steadfastly held for acquittal and a hung jury resulted. A juror later told a reporter, "I am satisfied and so are the others that both he [Malone] and Elsasser knew before they reached the court that they would be on the jury."[41] A week later another jury failed to convict the two men from the Midway. As in the initial trial, there was a last minute change in the jury's composition; three jurors were found by the

court to have valid reasons not to appear and proper substitutes again just happened to be available. When the jury
considered the defendants' guilt or innocence, the vote was
a divided three/three.

A week later a third trial followed, and a substitute
juror, Sam Hoff, a former police officer and deputy sheriff
living at the home of then County Commissioner John Lynch,
hung the jury with his one not guilty to five guilty. Hoff
was selected from those in the courtroom by the court officer, and Tom Dennison and Lynch left the room when Hoff
joined the jury. After the trial one of the majority jurors
remarked there was no chance for a verdict since Hoff held
out from the very beginning of discussions, without ever
providing a logical reason for his insistence on acquittal.
In light of these proceedings, a letter to the editor of
the *World Herald* directed him to look up the law regarding
police juries, going on to say he would find therein that
the magistrate did not have to call upon people present in
the courtroom to fill vacancies on a jury. Furthermore he
was not obliged to use the court police officer to make
selections, a task properly delegated to the sheriff. In
the three Midway trials, the policeman on court duty had
selected the men who subsequently hung the juries. In a
fourth trial for the Midway's owners, again no verdict was
reached, amid unchanged proceedings.[42]

Opportunities existed in the courtroom not only for
taking care of one's friends, but also for the financial
advantage of organization insiders. To that end, in Marcell's south side he exercised his discretion to change
disposition of cases after daily adjournment. For example,
a bootlegger tried for possessing liquor might be fined by
the judge a hundred dollars and costs. Marcell dutifully
recorded the decision in the court docket--in pencil.
After everyone was gone for the day he returned to the
docket to erase his entry and change the record to read
"possession dismissed, reduced to keeper of a disorderly
house." Then the fine was converted to fifteen dollars
befitting the lesser charge and eighty-five dollars vanished from the city books.[43]

Justice for profit, justice and law enforcement for
rewards and punishments, justice as the mechanism for controlling crime were highly developed features of Omaha's

244

political machine. Vice flourished but was localized; crimes were committed but kept at what was apparently a tolerable level; widespread violations of the prohibition act were well known but as a *sub rosa* business network rather than anarchic. Under Dennison's watchful eye crime in Omaha was locally syndicated, and because highly structured was able to resist penetration by externally organized crime. Neither the civic consciousness of its law-abiding citizens nor the efficiency of the police department can claim credit for that achievement. Thomas Dennison was responsible for controlled crime in Omaha, doing so with the acquiescence and financial support of many of the city's leading citizens.

Tolerance wore thin, however, during the World War I period when Smith's reformers succeeded in taking over city hall with the messianic Ringer as police commissioner. Like Towl later, he had a position of leadership with few willing to be led where he wanted to lead. Word went out from the Karbach Building that "Lily White Ringer" was to be stymied at every turn and discredited in every way possible. A means to the end was to demonstrate uncontrolled criminals and crime were features of an Omaha under a reform administration, unlike when the organization was in control. To make the point, a sensational daylight holdup of a bank was executed to direct attention to Ringer's ineffectiveness. The Farmers and Merchants State Bank robbery, as well as others, were attributed by Crawford to Dennison's connections with nationally known criminals who were invited to Omaha by the "Old Man" to ply their trade and embarrass the Smith administration. The striking and daring dimensions of the bank robbery were heralded in a banner newspaper headline: "Greatest Haul Ever Made in Nebraska."[44] The robbery was attributed to "out-of-towners" and there were never any arrests made.

Omahans were alerted no one was secure in a city prey to daring criminals. The newspapers, especially the *Bee*, began running articles suggesting citizens had as much to fear from keepers of the peace as from criminal elements. Reports of police improprieties, brutalities, and ineffectiveness added to the city's woes, its inhabitants warned to fear their law enforcers as well as rampant lawbreakers. The *Bee* and Dennison's political organization appear to have shared the goal of discrediting the reform administration and demonstrating its inability to protect Omaha's citizens. Mayor Smith and Commissioner Ringer were particular targets of the *Bee*, "subservient to and part of the system," the journal that printed whatever the "Old Man" and Johnson wanted, playing a key role in undermining faith in the police department and exacerbating tensions in an increasingly uneasy community.

Abetting the machine's purpose of raising doubts about law enforcement under Ed Smith and Dean Ringer, the *Bee* through the summer and fall of 1919 printed sensational coverage of alleged assaults by blacks on white women in Omaha, and on racial strife elsewhere. Large-scale black immigration during the war years, and intense job competition as veterans returned from Europe, helped fuel rising discontent. Dennison seized upon a volatile situation to further the task of harassing the reformers, and the *Bee* attacked city administration, demanding Ringer's removal and blasting the police department for tyranny and abuse. From early June to late September 1919, twenty-one women reported assaults. All the victims were white and sixteen of the assailants were identified as black.[45] Comparison of stories about these and other incidents reflects the *Bee's* concentration on the racial issue. (Two other Omaha papers, the *Daily News* and the *Monitor*, a black community weekly, were similar to the *World-Herald* in their more subdued coverage.)

In early June a *Bee* story related the robbing, throttling, and assault of a young girl by a black male in Council Bluffs; the *World-Herald* briefly noted that a Council Bluffs woman had escaped an attacking black man.[46] Several days later the *Bee* wrote that a woman had been the victim of a black or Mexican who dragged her into some weeds, tore off nearly all her clothes, then assaulted her. The same incident was mentioned in the *World-Herald* without reference to race.[47] Racial strife in Ellisville, Mississippi, was front page news in Omaha, and both newspapers reported the lynching and burning of a black man there. The *Bee's* coverage was similar to that of its competitor, but the *Bee* added the comment that authorities in Ellisville had characterized the lynching as having been carried out in a "manner that was orderly."[48] A few days later Omaha had what the *Bee* called a near riot at a ball park when a black player (on an all black team) hit a white player (on an all white team), and spectators of both races surged onto the field. Off-duty policemen present as fans were able to prevent the spread of violence. While the *Bee* carried the story on page one, the *World-Herald* placed it in the sports section on page six, captioned as "Free-for-all-Riot" and not until the eighth of its nine paragraph coverage was race mentioned.[49]

Less than two weeks later the *Bee* reported that five blacks were lynched and burned in Longview, Texas; the *World-Herald* confined itself to noting a clash there which resulted in four whites being wounded with no mention of lynching or burning.[50] Race rioting in Washington, D.C., in July provided a banner headline for the *Bee*, followed by stories of whites retaliating for recent attacks on white women by black men. Mobs of whites were killing blacks according to the *World Herald*. A *Bee* editorial a few days afterward labeled the riots a national disgrace--understandable in light of the crimes that had been committed--but anger and race prejudice were not proper responses. Authorities in Washington were accused by the *Bee* of being lax and unable to handle a situation they should have seen coming, a message no doubt intended for Omaha's city hall.[51] Race rioting followed in Chicago within a week, and the *Bee* headlined there were seven deaths and the black belt was in a shambles. The Chicago mayor's request for troops to help restore order was emphasized by the *World-Herald*.[52]

Quickly the two papers returned to local news but different in the way they reported the story of a black man rescued from a white mob. According to the *Bee*, the crowd was infuriated and impelled to action by the accusation that the black, who allegedly was guilty of four previous attacks on young girls, had tried to assault a white woman. The incident was reported in the *World-Herald* without any mention of race.[53] Five days later *Bee* readers learned that a one-armed black man had criminally assaulted a twelve year old girl, first strapping his victim to her bed. A more restrained *World-Herald* carried a brief item about an assault by a one-armed man, identified as black, but without reference to the girl's age or other circumstances.[54]

During the summer, *Bee* editorials, sometimes carried on the first page, assailed Police Commissioner Ringer,

247

called for his removal, and blasted the police department for tyranny and abuse. In late August, for example, the *Bee* criticized Omaha law enforcement, complaining that "a carnival of crime" was being visited on the city, with assaults, robbery, and violence the consequences of incompetent police unable to protect citizens.[55] Just a day after these scorching words, race rioting broke out in Knoxville, Tennessee, and once more the *Bee* provided provocative coverage of violence and another banner headline. Whites had broken into nearby stores for arms and ammunition while attempting to take custody of a black man accused of murdering a white woman, the paper informed its audience. The *World-Herald* told in a short story without headlines about a Tennessee mob gone wild.[56] In early September the *Bee* resumed its attack on the city administration following the shooting of a young black bellboy during a police hotel raid. The youth's death was cast by the newspaper as the "crowning achievement" of the police department, reflecting its "disgraceful and incompetent management."[57] The culmination of the tirade came on Friday morning, September 26, 1919.

Bee readers opened to the headline "Black Beast First Sticks-up Couple," then went on to: "The most daring attack on a white woman ever perpetrated in Omaha occurred one block south of Bancroft Street near Scenic Avenue in Gibson last night."[58] Phrasing by the *World-Herald* was less inflammatory, as it had been all summer, as it said, "Pretty little Agnes Loeback was assaulted by an unidentified negro at 12 o'clock last night, while she was returning to her home in company with Millard [sic] Hoffman, a cripple."[59] Hoffman's name was Milton, not Millard, and he adamantly maintained throughout his life he was not a cripple. (When he was three years old he broke a leg which never properly mended and therefore was much shorter than the other. As a result, he wore a heavy metal brace and built up shoe.) He and Agnes (they later married) identified black Will Brown the next evening at the Loeback home, where police had taken their suspected robber and assailant. A mob of 250 people gathered outside the house, cornering Brown and three police officers. When police reinforcements arrived, Brown, who at one point had a noose around his neck, was spirited away by the officers, his clothes torn, his head and hands bleeding.[60]

He was first taken to the police station, but was soon moved to the fortress looking county jail for better security. On Sunday morning the twenty-eighth, word passed in the Gibson neighborhood that a lynching mob was going to form at Bancroft School for a march on the courthouse. Telephone calls from the vicinity began coming to police headquarters reporting that a mob was forming at the school "with the intention of hanging Will Brown."[61] About 300 people showed up, mostly young men and a few women. Milton Hoffman took the lead and he led his youthful crowd downtown, picking up an additional 600 followers along the way. They were met by two dozen officers waiting at the courthouse. The officers talked with members of the throng who seemed more in a bantering mood than dangerous. Word was sent to police headquarters the situation did not look too serious, but the report proved to be a serious error of judgment. A close friend of Agnes Loeback's, William Francis, was slowly circling the courthouse on a white horse, exhorting the mob to do its duty, a rope dangling from his saddle horn. Increasing in size as adults joined the melee, the crowd increased also in intensity and anger, urged on by Francis and others. Additional police were summoned, and by late afternoon 100 officers faced an estimated 4,000 people. About 5:00 p.m. a now aroused mob began physically attacking the police and storming the courthouse. An hour later Police Chief Marshall Eberstein arrived and tried to reason with the rioters, but he was shouted down. The mob began shattering windows in the building, breaking down doors, and fires were started.[62]

Pawnshops and hardware stores were looted and arms and ammunition were taken to the battle site. Gunfire broke out, and sixteen year old Louis Young, one of the mob's youthful leaders, was shot while trying for the elevator leading to the fifth floor, where Brown and other prisoners were being held. A block away from the courthouse, thirty-four year old businessman James Hiykel fell fatally wounded, two bullets in his body.[63] Firemen rushed to the burning building, but their trailing hoses were cut to pieces by the mob. Anyone attempting to help the authorities was chased down streets and alleys and beaten. At 10:30 p.m. Mayor Smith, who had been on the scene for several hours, came out of the courthouse. As he attempted to talk with the mob, a blow knocked him unconscious. He was dragged down Harney Street toward the intersection at 16th; three

249

times a noose was thrown around his neck, but a young man, Russell Norgaard, managed to remove it. When the rioters entered the intersection, the rope was thrown over the arm of a traffic signal tower, placed around the mayor's neck, drawn tight, and the "Mayor swung clear of the ground."[64]

What happened next is unclear because of varying accounts of the mayor's rescue. One version reported by the *World-Herald* credited the heroism of Detectives Charles Van Buren, A.C. Andersen, Lloyd Toland, and State Agent Benedict "Ben" Danbaum with saving Smith's life. The four officers were praised for having driven through the mob to the mayor, Danbaum at the wheel. "I drove the car right at the tower," Danbaum later explained. "Andersen stood up and cut the rope and pulled the mayor into the car. I gave her the gas and we drove out, knocking several men down."[65] Another story is that instead of Andersen cutting the rope, Norgaard untied the noose and led the unconscious Smith to Danbaum's automobile. The mayor was being pulled up and down, and during one of these cycles Norgaard and another fellow got their hands between the noose and the victim's neck. Smith collapsed, but the two young men helped him to his feet and walked him to the car Danbaum had driven to the scene. Smith was rushed to Ford's Hospital where he remained in serious condition for several days. Two months later, Norgaard was appointed to the police department as a chauffeur in recognition of his helping to save the mayor. Danbaum, a Dennison man and a detective under the Dahlman administration, had been dismissed from his duties by Smith and Ringer in February 1919 and had taken a job with the state sheriff's office. For driving to assist the mayor, whatever the particulars of his role, he was rewarded with reinstatement to the police force.[66]

At the courthouse events were nearing their climax. Flames were spreading, and Sheriff Clark led his prisoners and men to the roof where gunshots from higher neighboring buildings were soon added to the threats from below. Under what circumstances Brown ended up in the hands of his enemies is unknown. Clark reported that it was other prisoners who seized Brown, and in the smoke and confusion passed him over their heads to the mob. Beaten into unconsciousness, his clothes torn off by the time he reached the building's doors, he was dragged to a lamp pole on the south side of the courthouse at 18th and Harney Streets, shortly before

250

11:00 p.m. There his body was hoisted into the air and riddled with bullets. When brought down, his shattered corpse was tied behind a car, dragged four blocks to the intersection of 17th and Dodge where he was cremated. While his body burned, bits of the lynch rope sold for ten cents each. Later the charred remains trailed behind an automobile driven through the downtown streets. Shortly before he ended up in the hands of the mob, Brown had moaned to Sheriff Clark, "I am innocent, I never did it, my God, I am innocent."[67]

By 3:00 a.m. army troops were patrolling the streets and uniformed men behind machine guns greeted Omahans the next morning. The riot had cost the lives of Brown and two others; thirty-one individuals were injured as of 2:00 a.m.; thousands of dollars in damages blemished a building that had been the pride of the city, and irreplaceable records were destroyed. Pondering the riot's effects, the *World-Herald* earned a Pulitzer Prize with its "Law and the Jungle" editorial, drawing attention to the city's disgrace, humiliation, and the consequences of inefficient government. Reliance on the authorities to maintain order had been misplaced, said the editorial, and Omahans would henceforth seek a stronger police force and more competent leadership.[68]

The *Bee's* editorial page returned to the attack on police inefficiency and resulting lawlessness, observing that "ample warning was given of the approaching storm."[69] Damage to the courthouse and the loss of records were deplored, but there was no mention of Will Brown--only a reference to "lives lost."[70] In response to a question from a New York newspaper, Victor Rosewater returned to familiar themes to explain the riot's causes. Among them, said Rosewater, were resentment at the failure of authorities to punish blacks who had assaulted women, the atmosphere of lawlessness which had settled over the city, the lack of leadership in the police department, and lastly, the social unrest in the aftermath of the war.[71]

Thoroughly discredited by the lynching, the Smith administration was unable to recover from its effects, although some effort was made to redress the situation. Several people were arrested for complicity in the riot, but Hoffman, a long time associate of Dennison, was not among them, despite his leadership role at Bancroft School. Nor was he indicted by the grand jury convened to investigate the riot. Hoffman's first job was thanks to his cousin, Tony Hoffman, a ward worker for Dennison. The elder Hoffman introduced Milton to the "Old Man," who hired him when he learned the youth, a recent business school graduate, knew shorthand. Milton worked as Dennison's secretary for about a year and prospered. After traveling for a while, Milton returned to Omaha and helped Dennison during campaigns, including casting his first vote before he was twenty-one.[72] Efforts by Omaha police and the Douglas County Sheriff to locate Hoffman in the days after the riot were unsuccessful.[73] In fact, he set off for Denver immediately afterward, where Dennison's influential friend Vaso Chucovich held sway. Seven years later he returned to Omaha and a career in city government.[74]

The grand jury convened on October 8 and appointed John W. Towle as its foreman. After a six week session, it issued a report which strengthened the image of ineffective leadership in the city, and of police incompetence the day of the riot. Absence of the police chief and the police commissioner at critical moments was deemed unfortunate by the jurors. According to military witnesses called, proper leadership on the scene could have dispersed the mob any time between three and six without firing a shot. "Unmentionable crimes and assaults upon women and girls," contempt for law and authority, economic problems, and social unrest were contributing factors to the riot, the grand jury concluded. Among the immediate causes, the jurors included "undue criticism given to courts, police and public officials by the press of the city."[75]

The press, that is, the *Bee* was also condemned by church leaders for its sensationalism and attacks on the police. The Pastor of the First Christian Church, Reverend Charles E. Cobbey, said from his pulpit that "the yellow journalism of a certain Omaha newspaper" created the conditions for an outbreak of violence. "It is the belief of many," asserted Cobbey, "that the entire responsibility for the outrage can be placed at the feet of a few men and one Omaha paper."[76] Another church leader, Reverend Titus Lowe, traced the riot to attacks on the city administration and exaggerated reports of crime "made by a local newspaper." The next day, Reverend Lowe bluntly proclaimed the lynching

252

was the result of calculated planning by politicians of the "old gang."[77] Omaha's Ministerial Union concurred in a resolution adopted late in October, condemning the *Bee* for printing misleading and vicious statements regarding public officials. In the Ministerial Union's opinion, the riot was in large part "instigated by sensational, misleading and maliciously false statements published in the *Bee.*"[78]

Police Commissioner Ringer, a week after the riot, issued a statement in which he charged that Omaha's criminal elements were gratified by the turn of events. According to Ringer, the "gang" had demonstrated on September 28 how far it was willing to go to return to power.[79] A *Monitor* editorial likewise mentioned political motivations behind the riot, referring to the "hidden, but not wholly concealed hand, of those who would go to any extreme to place themselves in power."[80] Major General Leonard Wood, sent to Omaha to lead troops in restoring order, added his voice and accused the *Bee* and the "old criminal gang" as being responsible for the events of September 28, 1919. Omaha was a fine city, he said, except for a few men and one newspaper. The further his investigation probed, added the general, the more he was convinced of an organized effort, with alcohol distributed freely while "a regular taxi cab service was maintained to bring men to the scene of the riot."[81]

In 1921 the issue of the "gang's" role in the riot became a rallying point for the reform elements attempting to remain in control of city hall. Towle, who had chaired the grand jury investigation of the riot, said it was planned and launched by "the vice elements of the city." He was also quoted as saying, "I want to say to you that the riot . . . was not a casual affair; it was premeditated and planned by those secret and invisible forces that today are fighting you and the men who represent good government."[82]

Direct responsibility for what followed the attack on Loeback and Hoffman has often been attributed to the Dennison organization. In this view, the subsequent riot and lynching were dire consequences of well planned "gang" activity, including organizing the march on the courthouse and providing manpower to impassion the crowd. Rumors later circulated about hoodlums having been imported from Chicago to assist in funneling the riot to its proper violent course. According to Tom Crawford, Dennison's organization deliberately poisoned Omaha's atmosphere, carefully setting the stage for an outbreak. He recalled the "Old Man" himself boasting to his policeman secretary that most of the attacks on women were white Dennison men in black face.

The notion of disguised whites appeared publicly a month after the riot when a committee of black leaders met with city officials. They suggested answers to three questions would shed light on the unprecedented outbreak of assaults, supposedly by black men upon white women, during the months preceding the lynching. Were blacks actually committing those alleged attacks? If so, were they being paid by someone? Finally, were these crimes being committed at someone's direction by white men with blackened faces?[83] The questions went unanswered, but by Crawford's account of later conversations with Dennison, the "Old Man" and Nesselhous had indeed concocted the assaults to create racial panic for political reasons.[84]

Yet others have different recollections and deny Dennison and his organization had anything to do with the events of September 28, 1919. A member of the police force at the time states with conviction, "Dennison never had nothing to do with that riot. Positive of that. Just a bunch of punks got started down there on 16th Street and it kept growing and growing."[85] A nephew of the "Old Man" who served many years with the fire department maintained that the machine had no role in instigating the mob; it was kids who really were responsible for setting the affair in motion. "Maybe there was some help from the organization," he suggested, "but Tom didn't know about it."[86] When asked about Dennison's responsibility for the riot, Billy Maher said with characteristic bluntness, "That's the silliest thing in the world, for anybody to ever dream that." Dennison was not behind it, claimed Maher, because the sheriff was one of his best friends and he would not have imperiled his life with burnings and shootings. "Tom Dennison would have no more tolerated any of his outfit having anything to do with hurting Mike Clark than he would of putting a gun to his own head. There were no Dennison men up there," concluded Maher, "they were not leading anything."[87]

Were Dennison and his men behind the courthouse riot or not? Hoffman's role and relationship with Dennison are intriguing, but the answer remains equivocal so far as the incidents from Brown's arrest to his murder are concerned. There is no firm evidence the Dennison machine actually instigated the particular events of September 26-28, 1919. What does seem clear is that Dennison and the *Bee* were responsible for having helped create conditions ripe for the outbreak of racial violence. Will Brown was the victim of political machinations. Billy Maher well summarized Dennison's reaction to the riot. After denying the "Old Man" had anything to do with the day's events, the loyalist added: "I don't say he didn't get a kick out of it, the way it ruined the administration that was in, because naturally they were against him."[88] In the next election they were voted out, Omahans dismayed by what had happened to their city, just as planned by Dennison in his various displays of the impotence of the reform government.

For the next ten years the Dennison machine enjoyed renewed vigor, and it was business as usual for its many partners. But as the 1920s drew to a close, they did so with the sound of gunfire in Omaha's streets. Underworld differences began to break the calm surface of the city and it was earning the name "Little Chicago." Three murders in particular called attention to crime and vice in Omaha, and the long kept on lid was obviously slipping. Two of the murdered were gangland figures and their being shot was in a way tolerable. The third assassination was of a different dimension, for a prominent business man was the victim; his death set in motion events destined to bring an end to Tom Dennison's Omaha.

NOTES

Chapter VII

[1]Bee, January 6, 1932.

[2]*Ibid.*

[3]Letter, Kinsler to Wm. J. Donovan, Assistant to the Attorney General, December 17, 1925, Records Group 60, file no. 12-45-8-3; letter, Kinsler to Willebrant, *Ibid.*, no file number.

[4]Letter, Crawford to Stalmaster, August 27, 1932, Towl papers, Box 1, Folder 1932, June-July, City Hall.

[5]Memorandum, "Concerning Potach and Allen," *Ibid.*, January 1-14.

[6]Memorandum, n.d., Towl papers, Box 1, Folder 1931, May-August, City Hall. See also letter, Crawford to Stalmaster, September 13, 1932, Sorensen papers, Box 39, Folder 191, wherein Koutsky is referred to as a tool of Dennison.

[7]See EOW-H, March 19, 1931, August 8, 12, 1931; Bee, August 25, 1931; MOW-H, April 27, 1932.

[8]EOW-H, June 1, 1931, June 20, 1932; MOW-H, January 8, 1932.

[9]Maher interview, October 23, 1979. The names of the three officers were recalled by Mr. Maher as Felix Dolan, Victor Lundeen, and Peter Hagerman.

[10]Letter, Crawford to Eugene D. O'Sullivan, "Why Denny O'Brien was let out by Metcalfe," July 26, 1932, Sorensen papers, Box 39, Folder 191.

[11]Letter, Crawford to Stalmaster, September 2, 1932, *Ibid.*

[12]EOW-H, May 7, 1930; memorandum, "Situation in Omaha," Towl papers, Box 1, Folder 1932, February, City Hall.

[13]EOW-H, February 26, 1914.

[14]Letter, Murphy to Dear Friend Irvin, n.d., Sorensen papers, Box 39, Folder 191.

[15]Quigley interview, June 4, 1979.

[16]Special Report, Kansas City Investigator C.F.M.P., December 20, 1913, Rosewater Collection, Reel 3, Box 1927.

[17]Ringwalt interview, August 8, 1979.

[18]Investigator's Report, n.d., Rosewater Collection, Reel 3, Box 1927.

[19]Anonymous letter, May 27, 1931, Towl papers, Box 1, Folder 1931, May-August, City Hall.

[20]Letter, Murphy to Stalmaster, September 31, 1932, Sorensen papers, Box 39, Folder 191; letter, Crawford to O'Sullivan, July 26, 1932, *Ibid.*

[21]Letter, A.C. Andersen, Kansas City, to Towl, January 13, 1932, Towl papers, Box 1, Folder 1932, January 1-14, City Hall.

[22]Memorandum, "Potach Bribery," January 13, 1932, *Ibid.*

[23]Letter, Crawford to Stalmaster, September 13, 1932, Sorensen pa-

pers, Box 39, Folder 191.

[24]EOW-H, February 6, 1931; letter, Crawford to Stalmaster, September 6, 1932, Sorensen papers, Box 39, Folder 191.

[25]Letter, Crawford to O'Sullivan, July 6, 1932, Sorensen papers, Box 35, Folder 35; letter, Crawford to O'Sullivan, July 15, 1932, *Ibid.*, Box 35, Folder 66.

[26]Letter, Crawford to Towl, May 28, 1932, Sorensen papers, Box 35, Folder 65.

[27]Letter, Crawford to Alexander Jamie, Chicago, March 30, 1932, Towl papers, Box 1, Folder 1932, March, City Hall.

[28]Bee, January 21, 1931; MOW-H, January 21, 1931.

[29]Letter, Crawford to Stalmaster, "Dan B. Butler," September 12, 1932, Sorensen papers, Box 35, Folder 66.

[30]Memorandum, n.d., "Concerning Potach and Allen," Towl papers, Box 1, Folder 1932, January 1-14, City Hall.

[31]Letter, L.B. Lemahan to Towl, June 12, 1931, Towl papers, Box 1, Folder 1931, May-August, City Hall.

[32]See notarized affidavits by Carl Bolen, Dr. A.I. Hughes, James McLaughlin, R.A. Stewart, A. Sullivan, Michael Kerno, Carl Fiscus, B.F. Koch, Ed Smith, and Robert Albertson, all dated July 10, 1931, Towl papers, Box 1, Folder 1931, May-August, City Hall.

[33]Letter, Towl to J.J. Pszanowski, December 8, 1931, Towl papers, Folder 1931, September-December, City Hall.

[34]Bee, January 22, 1932; MOW-H, January 21, 1932.

[35]EOW-H, September 16, 24, 1925; Maher interview, October 23, 1979.

[36]EOW-H, February 2, 3, 1925.

[37]Letter, Crawford to Stalmaster, September 13, 1932, Sorensen papers, Box 39, Folder 191.

[38]EOW-H, May 23, 1910, and Sunday W-H, March 3, 1912.

[39]ODN, February 20, 1918.

[40]On jury fixing see EOW-H, October 19, 1932; Special Report, Kansas City Investigator #32, Rosewater Collection, Reel 3, Box 1927. Frost interview, October 30, 1979; letter, Crawford to Stalmaster, June 11, 1932, Sorensen papers, Box 35, Folder 65; letter, Murphy to O'Sullivan, May 25, 1932, *Ibid.*; letter, Crawford to Towl, April 19, 1932, *Ibid.*

[41]EOW-H, January 19, 1912.

[42]EOW-H, February 9, 1912; also *Ibid.*, January 8, 26, 1912, and February 3, 7, 8, 1912.

[43]Letter, Crawford to Stalmaster, September 9, 1932, Sorensen papers, Box 39, Folder 191; letter, Crawford to Towl, April 21, 1932, *Ibid.*

[44]EOW-H, December 31, 1919; and see letter, Murphy to Edson Smith, May 9, 1932, Sorensen papers, Box 35, Folder 65.

[45]ODN, September 27, 1919; MOW-H, September 27, 1919.

[46]Bee, June 4, 1919; MOW-H, June 4, 1919.

[47]Bee, June 20, 1919; MOW-H, June 20, 1919.

[48]Bee, June 27, 1919; MOW-H, June 27, 1919.

[49]Bee, June 30, 1919; MOW-H, June 30, 1919.

[50]Bee, July 12, 1919; MOW-H, July 12, 1919.

[51]Bee, July 22, 1919; MOW-H, July 22, 1919.

[52]Bee, July 29, 1919; MOW-H, July 29, 1919.

[53]Bee, August 12, 1919; MOW-H, August 12, 1919.

[54]Bee, August 17, 1919; MOW-H, August 17, 1919.

[55]Bee, August 29, 1919.

[56]Bee, August 31, 1919; MOW-H, August 31, 1919.

[57]Bee, September 2, 1919.

[58]Bee, September 26, 1919.

[59]MOW-H, September 26, 1919.

[60]MOW-H, September 27, 30, 1919; Bee, September 27, 1919.

[61]Grand Jury Final Report, District Court Journal, No. 176, Douglas County, Nebraska, p. 287; see also Bee, September 29, 1919.

[62]Material on the riot is incorporated from Orville D. Menard, "Tom Dennison, The Omaha Bee, and the 1919 Omaha Race Riot," *Nebraska History*, 68 (Winter, 1987), pp. 152-165.

[63]"Omaha's Riot in Story and Pictures," Omaha: Omaha Educational Publishing Company, 1919, unpaged; see also Bee, October 1, 1919.

[64]MOW-H, September 30, 1919.

[65]MOW-H, September 29, 1919.

[66]On Danbaum see EOW-H, April 12, 1930; Norgaard's role and reward, Bee, November 23, 1919, and MOW-H, December 17, 1919.

[67]Bee, September 29, 1919; see also Criminal Appearance Docket No. 21, Douglas County, Nebraska, pp. 64-65.

[68]MOW-H, September 30, 1919, "Law and the Jungle."

[69]Bee, September 30, 1919.

[70]*Ibid.*, and see Arthur Age, "The Omaha Riot of 1919," unpublished Master's Thesis, Creighton University, Omaha, Nebraska, 1964, pp. 68-70.

[71]Bee, October 1, 1919.

[72]Hoffman interview, November 14, 1979.

[73]ODN, November 20, 1919; see also ODN, October 1, 4, 1919, and EOW-H, October 4, 1919.

[74]See letter, Murphy to Roy N. Towl, April 18, 1932, which mentions the "cripple fellow" sent to Denver and Chucovich and concludes with "WILL THIS SHOW THE DENNISON HAND IN THE COURTHOUSE RIOT" (caps in the original), Sorensen papers, Box 35, Folder 65. See also letter, Murphy to Roy N. Towl, August 16, 1932, Towl papers, Box 1, Folder 1932, June-July, City Hall.

[75]Grand Jury Final Report, p. 285.

[76]*Monitor*, October 9, 1919.

[77]*Ibid.*, and October 10, 1919.

[78]Bee, October 21, 1919.

[79]MOW-H, October 8, 1919.

[80]*Monitor*, October 2, 1919.

[81]ODN, October 5, 1919.

[82]EOW-H, April 23, 1921.

[83]ODN, October 31, 1919.

[84]Letter, Murphy to Towl, August 16, 1932, Towl papers, Box 1, Folder 1931, June-July, City Hall; Smith interview, from his conversations with Crawford, April 1, 1974; Ringwalt interview, from recollections of the elder Dr. Harold Gifford, August 7, 1979; Frost interview, October 30, 1979.

[85]Interview with Herman J. Creal by Orville D. Menard, August 9, 1979, Omaha, Nebraska.

[86]Interview with Henry J. Walsh by Orville D. Menard, October 3, 1979.

[87]Maher interview, October 30, 1979.

[88]*Ibid.*

CHAPTER VIII

Assassination

Love and death, possessing and killing,
are the dark foundations of the human soul.
--Emile Zola

"STOP GANG WAR!---MAYOR." Metcalfe's February 1930 newspaper headline injunction was necessitated, he said, by the fact Omaha could not have men hunting each other down in its streets.[1] The night before, a Lincoln automobile owned by bootlegger Gene Livingston had been riddled with forty shotgun slugs and revolver bullets at 32nd and Farnam Streets. Three men in another car had pulled alongside Livingston's and opened fire; a man who fit Livingston's description jumped out of the Lincoln and ran to a third automobile. A man with many enemies, Livingston, the uninjured "alky baron," was later picked up by the police at a billiard parlor but claimed he knew nothing about the incident.

Livingston's criminal record began in May 1921 when he was arrested and convicted for burglary and served eighteen months in the penitentiary. From then on his life was a series of aliases and arrests, generally for violations of the prohibition act. Two of his better known enterprises that brought him into court were the Farrel and Howard Street stills. Another prohibition arrest was made when he and a partner, George Kubik, were picked up in March 1928 for possession of a carload of alcohol. In April two years later Livingston was sentenced in a federal court to ninety days imprisonment on the charge. Scheduled to begin his sentence on May 12, Livingston did not live to return to prison.

About three a.m. the morning of the first day of May, two and a half months after his Lincoln was shot up, the twenty-seven year old Livingston entered a speakeasy at 1432 North 17th Street. He asked if he could stay over because he had drank quite a lot, then requested a drink of water. Directed to the kitchen, he stepped to the sink, and then through a window came a hail of shotgun and pistol fire, from three men the police later estimated. Livingston died within an hour, his assailants never to be apprehended.[2] Among Livingston's enemies were competitors in Omaha, angered by his free agent, lone wolf method of operating, as well as people in Chicago he owed money. Was he killed by Omaha competitors or Chicagoans out to settle nonpayment of a debt? The answer is unknown, although a combination of the two is likely; that is, Livingston's execution was doubly desired and a cooperative effort probably was worked worked out: Chicagoans to be the executioners, protected while in Omaha to carry out their crime.

Two days before Livingston was murdered he had sent an emissary to Nebraska's assistant attorney general in Omaha, Irving Stalmaster. Stalmaster was informed Livingston was ready to tell the entire story of corruption in Omaha, involving federal, state, county, and city officials. If he talked, Livingston wanted immunity from prosecution in return. Stalmaster asked why Gene was willing to become an informer and was told, "Because they are threatening him."[3] Although Stalmaster revealed the visit and its substance, he refused to disclose the identity of the emissary, and either did not know or would not tell who "they" were. Grace Housky, wife of Frank who was a Dennison intimate in the machine and the Friar's Club, remembered Livingston's shooting and wondered aloud to her husband how it had happened, an accident or what? Frank laughed and said, "No, it was not an accident, he just talked too much."[4]

That Dennison knew Livingston was in danger is seen in an elaborate scheme to protect his enforcer, Joe Potach, from becoming a suspect. Arrangements were made for Potach to go with his family in late April to Los Angeles, a city where Dennison had many friends. Potach was instructed to visit them and establish his identity in case an alibi would later be useful. Moreover, a letter was to be sent from Los Angeles by Potach to Roscoe Rawley to further substantiate his west coast visit.[5] Potach testified during the conspiracy trial that the spring Livingston was shot, he had taken his family to California. He denied Dennison had anything to do with financing the trip, stated they returned five or six days after the murder, and recalled writing to Rawley from L.A.[6] But doubts are raised about Potach's presence in California on May 1; a woman who went to school with him said she saw him about seven p.m. that evening in Omaha. Potach's presence in town until after Livingston's shooting is suggested again in Grace Housky's answers to Eugene O'Sullivan's questions. The attorney received a "yes" from her when he asked whether Potach had taken a trip to California. Then he suggested that Potach really was not in California at all, at least until not after Livingston's death. "Well, I don't know about that," replied Mrs. Housky, "but there was something funny about it."

"Had she ever heard that Potach was really in Omaha until after Livingston was killed, and then went west?" asked O'Sullivan. "And mailed a letter?" Mrs. Housky came back, although O'Sullivan had not mentioned any correspondence. He repeated his question, and she answered "yes." Then he wanted to know whether the "letter was sent out there before he ever went there?" Again a "yes."[7] Whether Joe Potach was or was not in California at the time the "alky baron" was murdered cannot be determined, but the circumstances certainly imply Dennison and Potach knew something was in the wind and the "Old Man" wanted to have his faithful lieutenant covered. Gene Livingston's enemies were not merely local, since he also owed money to Chicago backers. In the Farrel and Howard stills he had Windy City partners and was an agent for them in Omaha, trying to operate independently of the local powers.[8] The day Livingston was shot the press circulated the theory he had been killed for failure to pay a debt to Chicago alcohol interests. According to an article, "One of the biggest dealers in the U.S." had told another Omaha bootlegger that Livingston had better pay off the $40,000 he owed or he would not live until May.[9]

Livingston was known in the Omaha underworld as having connections with Al Capone, and the still for the Farrel Building was shipped from Chicago as a result of a deal between Livingston and two of Capone's men. When the Farrel Building was raided, its contents were confiscated and Livingston's creditors added to his woes, demanding payment for their still. He tried to stay in business by opening the Howard Street operation, but again was raided and pressure mounted. Since Livingston did not have the money to repay his Chicago backers, they demanded their still in lieu of the money. A junk company had purchased the confiscated Farrel still from the government, and Livingston proceeded to buy it and arranged to have it sent in two box cars to Chicago. But his partners never received their merchandise, for the still was taken from the cars by federal agents, who had been tipped off by someone, down to the very car numbers.[10] Livingston with neither $40,000 nor the still became a man under a death sentence, carried out on May 1, 1930. The murder went down as unsolved.

A year and a half later George Kubik's name was added to the unsolved killing file. He was a large and powerful man, known as a leader and boss of a packing house gang. Kubik gained favor with the Dennison machine by informing it of stills, shipments, and names of competitors, information he acquired by being in effect an underworld detective. In due course he began "dealin" himself, and beginning in 1928 was arrested several times on bootlegging charges, working with Livingston for a period. It was in Kubik's place in South Omaha that Potach killed Jimmy Griffin, and Kubik and his wife were witnesses as Potach demanded money of the victim for having cheated on Joe's partner in a false top liquor sale. Assured by Potach of protection in return for his silence, Kubik thought he now had not only a green light as a bootlegger, but also had leverage on Potach and the organization because of what he had witnessed. While Kubik's knowledge did work to his advantage for a time, it was also reason for the organization to place little value on his life.[11]

Jack Dempsey fought Bear Cat Wright in Omaha the night of November 11, 1931, and Kubik went to the fight with his son. Afterwards they went to a soft drink parlor at 42nd and L, run by John "Yacki" Staskicwicz, and drank beer until the father said "Let's go." They drove to their outlet at 4410 South 27th Street, where the younger Kubik filled up some pints for morning delivery and put them in their Ford truck. George Jr. then drove off; a few hours later his father lay dying in a hospital of multiple gunshot wounds.[12]

Before he died, Kubik told what had happened to him. When his son left in the Ford, George Sr. drove to his home at 4004 So. 26th Street and parked his car in the garage.

As Kubik walked toward his house, three men he did not recognize appeared, all with guns. They took $500 from him, a diamond stickpin, and diamond ring. "Is that all?" asked Kubik. "Not by a damned sight. Get . . . in the car." Two men sat with him in the back seat while the third drove west to 60th Street, then turned a short distance north and stopped near F Street. Ordered out of the car, Kubik begged for his life, afraid to move. He was thrown and kicked out, then picked himself up and started to run. A couple of steps were all he made before shots caught up with him and he fell, mortally wounded but still conscious. One of his assassins saw he was still alive and ordered one of the other men "to give him the works." A gunman walked over and fired at Kubik's head, the bullet hitting him in the jaw (he already had one in his left side, one in a shoulder, and one in the abdomen). Satisfied their job was finished, the men sped off in their car. Their victim, "so full of lead they almost melted him down when they buried him," crawled 200 yards to S.P. Sorenson's home. They helped him inside and called the police. Kubik died a few hours later in the hospital after describing his ordeal, but unable to identify his killers. All he said of his assailants was that they were Italian.

Three weeks earlier Kubik had received an ultimatum, warning him to stop operating as an independent bootlegger. He ignored it and continued shopping around for the best deal rather than buying from approved sources. On the south side, the day before the shooting, word circulated in bootlegger circles someone was due "to get the works." Bolstering the story was the arrival in town of three strangers in a car with Illinois license plates. Most of the independents went into hiding, but Kubik went to the Dempsey prize fight.[13] A Buick sedan, bearing Illinois license plates, was located by the police in the rear of a garage in the Italian district near downtown within a day or two of the shooting. Four copper jacketed .38 bullets, the same type as killed Kubik, were found in the car. Its owner turned out to be in jail; he said he had recently come to Omaha, then nothing more was publicly said about the Buick. Detective Sutton's comment on the case was that Kubik was the victim of robbers because gangland slayers did not bother to take cash, rings, and stickpins.[14]

A newspaper reported three men were traced as having

arrived in Omaha a few days before the murder, checking in at the Harney Hotel. They told the clerk they were in town for the Dempsey fight. Two of them registered as from Kansas City and one listed Terre Haute. Until they went out early on fight night, they kept close to their rooms. Two of them rushed in at one fifty a.m. and asked for their bill, saying they were leaving immediately; Kubik had been shot less than an hour earlier. The third man did not appear and the other two took a cab to a bus station and asked when the next bus left, no destination mentioned, just when. Told there were no departures for several hours the men walked out, heading south on 16th Street. No more was said of the two men or of the third.[15]

Kubik's assassination was attributed to his refusal to cooperate with the proper south side liquor dealers, and it also was rumored he had been informing a straight federal agent on locations of protected operations. Several men remembered an argument that followed Calamia's storming into Kubik's about a month before the shooting, obviously convinced Kubik had been passing information about Calamia's stills to the "feds." "You bohunk son-of-a-bitch," Calamia shouted, "You had my still knocked off." Then came a warning: "You know what happened to Livingston for trying to run this town. And that will happen to you."[16] It did happen to Kubik but little more can be said with any surety about his murder or his murderers. Whatever Officer Sutton's appraisal, Kubik's assassination had all the hallmarks of a gang slaying, with clear motives: his alleged informing, refusal to go along (playing instead the dangerous game of independent), and the information he held over Joe Potach's head. His death was timely if not timed, welcomed if not planned by many of his associates.

Gene Livingston and George Kubik were racketeers, men of the underworld killed by men of the underworld in an internecine warfare. Their deaths made headlines for a day, but little threat seemed to confront Omahans far removed from the world of stills and the bootleggers' business methods and system of justice. The bullets entered few homes, and it was difficult to wax indignant about men being shot who were perceived as deserving of being shot. Cases closed, killer or killers unknown.

A little over a month after Kubik's murder, gunfire in

Omaha brought an end to another life. Whatever the degree of the machine's involvement in the deaths of Livingston and Kubik (most likely monitoring official disinterest), the murder of Harry Lapidus bears its imprint. It was also a massive error in judgment, because the target this night was not an underworld figure, but a prominent business and civic leader. Two theories provide motives for Harry Lapidus's death, either one sufficient for his removal by the Dennison organization. A gang like shooting, the means of removing Lapidus, demonstrates the machine's leadership had yielded, after all its years of success, to the arrogance of power.

On New Year's Day 1933, the *World-Herald* featured a listing of Omaha's biggest news stories of the just elapsed year as selected by the city editor and his assistants. "Liquor syndicate investigation and trial" was in first place with the "Lapidus murder investigation and subsequent shakeups" coming in second.[17] No text accompanied the selections, therefore no connection between these two top stories was intimated or suggested. Omahans easily recalled the liquor syndicate trial, daily front page news in the fall just past, and the Lapidus murder, brought into the trial, had not faded away. The "subsequent shakeups" was in reference to Roy Towl's being shifted from police commissioner back to commissioner of fire protection and water supply in the wake of his efforts to carry on an investigation of the Lapidus killing. The shakeup was far deeper than could be discerned from the city editor's list of events, because an intimate connection existed between Dennison's weeks in court and the murder of Harry Lapidus. A direct line may be drawn from the Lapidus assassination to the prosecution of the "Old Man" and fifty-eight of his associates for conspiracy to violate the National Prohibition Act, thence to the Dennison machine defeat in the spring 1933 city elections--the real shakeup linking the two stories.[18]

Unlike Livingston or Kubik, Lapidus, President of the Omaha Fixture and Supply Company, was a ranking member of Omaha's legitimate business community. He was noted for his philanthropic and service activities on behalf of the Jewish community (he served several terms as president of the Jewish Community Center), and as a man with a particular fondness for hospital work and charity.[19] Although known for his generosity, he was also reputedly greedy. Family and friendships bound him closely to men with politically sensitive positions by the time of his death. His son-in-law was Irving Stalmaster, assistant attorney general to Christian A. Sorensen, who, as state attorney general, vigorously opposed crime and corruption in Omaha. A close personal friend of the dead man was Robert Smith, prominent Republican and father of Edson Smith, assistant U.S. district attorney in Omaha. (The elder Smith was one of the pallbearers at his friend's funeral.) Contacts and reputation enveloping Lapidus assured his death would not go unnoticed, and he was eulogized in an editorial as:[20]

> . . . in every sense of the word a splendid citizen, one whose energy and interest were not confined to personal success, but ranged far in the field of human progress. Business, political reform, civic improvement, philanthropy knew him for a tireless, aggressive, positive worker, never too busy with his own affairs to take a lively and active part in affairs of public concern.

Harry Lapidus, successful businessman, public figure, forty-nine years old, was on his way home from the Jewish Community Center when he was shot at approximately 11:20 p.m., two nights before Christmas Eve. As he was driving down the street another car pulled alongside his and both autos stopped in front of 1915 Park Avenue, at the east edge of Hanscom Park near the lagoon. Two men left the second car and approached Lapidus, still seated in his, and words were exchanged for about three minutes, a nearby resident later told the police. Three quick shots were then fired, and Harry Lapidus died; the car motor continued to run with the gearshift in neutral. His killers ran back to their automobile and sped off into the night and obscurity. When the police arrived on the scene, a passing motorist having seen the body and notified authorities, "they found the LaSalle sedan, with Harry Lapidus slumped over the steering wheel DEAD, with one foot on the foot brake pedal, and the left foot dangling out the left front door which was open." Laconically the police report noted that when two officers and the police ambulance arrived, they "were not needed."[21]

Indeed they were not; all three shots hit Lapidus in the head. One bullet, fired three or four inches from his face, entered just to the left of his nose then coursed upward to lodge in two pieces in the right lobe of his brain. Fired about eighteen inches from the victim, another bullet passed from just below his left ear to exit in front of his right ear about eye level. It went on to hit the window of the right door, and police were puzzled when they were unable to find the bullet since the glass was not broken. They finally found the ricocheted bullet in Lapidus's left hand overcoat pocket. No powder burns were left by the third shot, which hit him in the lower part of the brain then traveled upward to the top of his skull.[22]

Two hours after the bullets ended Lapidus's life, Gerald Cunningham was arrested as a suspect. His stepfather, C.E. Weldy, had been killed the previous May in an automobile accident near Missouri Valley, Iowa, that had involved Lapidus. A grand jury at Logan, Iowa, saw fit to indict Lapidus for manslaughter, but the indictment was quashed. Another grand jury looked into the case and returned a no bill, although a damage suit was later filed against Lapidus with regard to Weldy's death. Another young man, Jack DePorte, was also arrested based upon information he once had threatened Lapidus for breaking up a romance between DePorte and the daughter of an employee of Lapidus. By Christmas Day, ten men and one woman were being held by the police, all of whom were soon released, including Cunningham and DePorte, when their explanations about their activities on the night of the murder were verified.[23]

Various theories circulated as to motives for the murder. Was it revenge, as suggested by the Cunningham and DePorte arrests? No, business competitors were responsible said Mayor Metcalfe, when he revealed he had information that firms losing bids to the Omaha Fixture and Supply Company had resolved to take extreme measures. According to the the mayor's undisclosed source, a large contract awarded to Lapidus's firm by the Marshall Field Company in Chicago might have angered other bidders and they took revenge on him. Between August 1927 and March 1930 Omaha Fixture and Supply did win four contracts with the Chicago business, the largest for $27,000 and the smallest $1,220. These were hardly sums to incite to murder any of the competitive bidders for the jobs, each checked out by a special investigator working for Roy Towl.[24]

County Attorney Beal added attempted kidnapping by amateurs to the list of causes, after a meeting between himself, Detective Sutton, and attorneys representing the Lapidus family. Beal announced there was agreement the killing was not by professionals, for professionals would not have stopped Lapidus, talked with him for three minutes, and relied upon revolvers (several residents in the area told police they heard the cars stop, loud voices, then the shots). Professionals, said the county attorney, used shotguns or machine guns and fired without warning. Amateur kidnappers probably killed Lapidus when he resisted, Beal went on, or persons holding a grudge shot him after a brief argument.

Inspector Sutton gave credence to a grudge theory, dismissing the kidnapping idea when he stated he was inclined to think "the killer was a personal or business enemy of Lapidus who killed in a rage."[25] Amateurs as the assassins became questionable when Attorney General Sorensen said he had learned (from "a very reliable source") a week before Lapidus's murder that gangsters from Kansas City or St. Joseph had entered Omaha and something big was going to be pulled off. "The assassination of Lapidus may have been the 'big thing'," Sorensen concluded.[26] Sutton now shifted to the gangland explanation and introduced a new perception of Harry Lapidus. The detective intimated Lapidus was shot because of his own dealings with bootleggers, and was a victim of organized crime. Killing him was perhaps "a belated aftermath" of Gene Livingston's murder. Sutton now recalled a letter from Chicago received during the investigation of that shooting, warning prominent Omahans, including Harry Lapidus, "might have trouble because of the Livingston case." Lapidus was murdered, it was implied, by out-of-town mobsters who had racket interests in Omaha.[27] By linking the names of Livingston and Lapidus, Sutton posited connections between the esteemed and reputable businessman and the underworld of bootleggers and their killers.

As theories and implications circulated about the Lapidus murder, the question of involvement of the machine headed by Tom Dennison was always close to the surface. There is evidence that Sutton's effort to direct attention to Chicago--thus away from Omahans--was but one of the Dennison organization's tactics to allay suspicion of its own involvement. Lapidus was a threat to the machine for one of two reasons, or even a combination of the two if both are given credence. First there is Harry Lapidus the civic minded good citizen, helping the authorities combat criminal activities in his city. But Sutton raised the possibility of another side to the man, one in the rackets himself through association with Gene Livingston, and tied in, or trying to be, with vice rings. From this perspective, Lapidus was a man not satisfied with his legitimate gains, murdered because he was a competitor trying to muscle in.[28]

Laissez-faire was not the preferred business formula for illegitimate enterprises, and controllers of crime and vice in Omaha had long taken a dim view of those who challenged the monopoly. Livingston had attempted to operate free of the organization, as had George Kubik, and the Livingston/Lapidus connection is set forth in a remarkable document written by Roy Towl. A long time enemy of the machine, Towl, convinced of its involvement in the Lapidus murder, had few illusions about what he was up against and took steps to ensure his words were safeguarded if something happened to him. On December 31, 1931, he prepared a statement "addressed to the Omaha World-Herald, the Omaha Bee-News, the Chicago Tribune, and the New York Times. Copies are distributed in two separate boxes in the Safety Deposit Vaults of the Omaha Trust Company," he advised, "in stamped envelopes addressed to the newspapers mentioned."

Cora Marling, Towl's secretary, notarized the statement the same day. Towl recorded that at noon on December 31, Jack Burbeck, employed by a second hand automobile company he had recently dealt with, came to his office and gave him facts not yet revealed to anyone:[29]

> He said that Anna Book at 516 South 26th Avenue was the Private Secretary of Gene Livingston; that all of the telephone calls to Chicago were made from her telephone and that Harry Lapidus was the financial backer for Livingston and Dutch Voker [sic].

If Towl's informant was correct, and there were other sources suggesting Lapidus had underworld connections, a possible motive for Lapidus's death was his involvement as a vice market rival.

But three months later a special investigator, Donald L. Kooken, brought to Omaha by the city commission under Towl's prodding, cleared Lapidus of charges of underworld activities in a report to Mayor Metcalfe:[30]

> Numerous reports had been received to the effect Lapidus had
> been at one time connected with the rackets in Omaha. This lead
> was carefully followed, but no indication of a connection with any
> racket operating in Omaha was disclosed. Various underworld char-
> acters were contacted as well as a number of racketeers now doing
> time in the penitentiary. These men were questioned with a view to
> establishing a possible racketeering connection. It developed that
> there was no foundation for the statement Lapidus was a racketeer.
> On the contrary, the general opinion of the underworld was to the
> effect that it was because of Lapidus's interest in fighting crime
> that he was killed.

Thus we return to citizen Harry Lapidus the crime
fighter, killed not as a competitor, but because he threatened operations by passing harmful information on to law
enforcement agencies at the state level. Two days after
Lapidus was shot, Attorney General Sorensen had announced
in Lincoln that Lapidus was well known for his anti-gang
activities. "There is no question," said the solemn Sorensen, "but that he was a thorn in the side of the gang . . .
. Records of my office here show that Lapidus was behind
most of the moves against the Omaha underworld for the past
20 years."[31] During the conspiracy trial *The New York Times*
reported the public spirited Lapidus had been "particularly
aggressive as a reformer with a penchant for meddling with
underworld affairs."[32]

Selling fixtures to restaurants, soft drink parlors,
and other bootleg outlets, the president of the Omaha Fixture and Supply Company had been well placed to become
intimately informed about underworld activities. Owners
complained to Lapidus about being forced into the "syndicate," that is, the local distribution organization. Locations, protection payments, personalities involved, all
became known to Lapidus and he was willing to share his
knowledge.[33] Dennison was reputed to be outraged at Lapidus
for passing information to Roy Towl. Lapidus also had his
close contacts in state government through his son-in-law.
That the fixture and supply dealer was courting danger with
his activities was made clear to Grace Housky in a conversation with her husband, Frank, shortly after Livingston's
murder. Gene had been shot, Frank told his wife, because he
talked too much. "'Now wait' he told me, he says: 'There is
some more going to get it too,' and he says, that is--he
named that fellow that was killed, that Jewish fellow?"
"Kubik?" asked O'Sullivan. "No, that big Jew, Lapidus."

When O'Sullivan questioned whether anything else was said about Lapidus, Mrs. Housky replied, "Well, of course he was in their way." "In what way?" O'Sullivan wanted to know. "Well, I don't know, it is a lot of politics." Mrs. Housky added Frank warned that if Lapidus did not keep his mouth shut and quit nosing in, he was going to be taken for a ride.[34] In a letter to the mayor, Don Kooken concluded the strongest motive he had uncovered was gang revenge for the victim's serving as an informer to the attorney general.[35]

The daring and ultimate act of murdering Harry Lapidus culminated a series of efforts to harass and discredit him. These failing, direct action apparently followed. For some time a campaign had been waged against him, directed from the Karbach Building. One of its tactics developed around C.E. Weldy, who died in the Iowa automobile accident Lapidus was involved in. Seeing an opportunity to damage Lapidus, Dennison sent Tom Murphy and Harry Buford to the Logan area immediately after the incident. They spread rumors and tales about Lapidus designed to create a bias against him, and negatively influence a grand jury. Murphy visited bankers in Missouri Valley and Logan, while Buford, acting as Murphy's chauffeur, went to garages, filling stations, pool halls, and cigar stores. Their message was that Lapidus had fixed the county attorney at Logan in order to secure a dismissal of his case, boasting he was going to get off. He had been in accidents before without penalty, the Omaha messengers asserted, and he considered the Iowans a bunch of easily fooled hoosiers.[36] In fact a grand jury did return a manslaughter indictment against Lapidus, but it was quashed; a second returned a no bill.

To spread the rumor Lapidus had previously injured people in other accidents, Dennison instructed Crawford to write an anonymous letter to the county attorney in Logan about a November 2, 1929, car/pedestrian accident involving Lapidus in downtown Omaha. The investigating officers had reported that the right front fender of Lapidus's car was dented just behind the front wheel, and it looked as though seventy-three year old John Fox had walked into the automobile, receiving lacerations, bruises, and a possible fractured skull. Anxious to discredit Lapidus, Dennison told Officer Crawford to remove the squeal (twenty-four hour report of duty) on the accident from files at police headquarters and substitute an altered version. Crawford did as requested, fabricating another squeal leaving out the portion saying John Fox apparently walked into the automobile, and entering one attributing responsibility to Lapidus. Under remarks the original report said Fox was crossing the street "when he was struck or walked into" a Hupmobile sedan driven by Lapidus, followed by the remark it "looked like this man walked into the car."

Crawford's altered version stated Fox "was struck by an auto, a Hupmobile sedan, that was driven by Harry Lapidus . . . who was driving west on Farnam Street, injuring him as above stated." Placing the new version in the police files, Crawford then wrote his anonymous letter to the county attorney across the river inviting him to request information from the Omaha Police Department about Lapidus's driving record. Falsification of the record is borne out by a copy of the original squeal sheet from another city file that bears a different form number than the altered version. The former was printed in December 1928 and the latter in January 1931. In addition, the true record bears in the upper right-hand corner a printed 192 followed by a typewritten "9." In the same place on Crawford's replacement report there is a printed 193 with 1929 typed over it.[37]

According to Crawford, the "Old Man" offered him $1,000 to kill the bothersome Lapidus while he was involved in business negotiations with a firm in New York City. Dennison suggested, said Crawford, that he should follow Lapidus and in either New York or Chicago eliminate him. Crawford later wrote he refused the mission, aware Dennison was not a man to take rejection lightly.[38] Although the secretary did not turn murderer, he did comply with Dennison's instructions to write a letter purportedly emanating from Chicago, implying gangland forces in that city were out to get Lapidus. Written in early February 1931 with the intent of diverting responsibility away from Omaha when something happened to Lapidus, the letter was dated the twentieth, and connected him with racketeers in Chicago. On the witness stand in 1932, Crawford testified Dennison told him that with the letter on file at the police department heat would be taken off Omaha "in case we have to rub him [Lapidus] out."[39] Here was the letter Detective Sutton mentioned to the press after Lapidus was killed, suggesting it revealed the dead man was mixed up with a Chicago gang responsible for shooting him. The letter, announced the Detective, was from Chicago; indeed it was, at least it was mailed from Chicago and in the month of February.

After Crawford wrote the false message, he sent it in a sealed envelope within an envelope to his sister-in-law in Chicago, along with instructions to mail the inner letter back to Omaha. In a signed statement dated August 20, 1932, Mrs. Thomas Trainor, Crawford's sister-in-law, acknowledged receiving the letters in February the previous year, the inner one addressed to the Chief of Police, Omaha. She had followed instructions and dropped the letter for the chief in a mail box within a few hours of receiving it.[40] Sent from Omaha to Chicago and back to Omaha the letter reads in part:[41]

> There is a little information that I have got that I think you should know. A friend of mine here who mixes up more or less with the gang overheard the following conversation. It seems several months ago there was a jew from your city who arranged for a still to be sent to Omaha and set up. The agreement was if the place was raided and still taken he would pay eight thousand dollars. They have never collected this money. They have been informed that several other jews were in with this man Livingston and they intend to held them responsible. A man named Milder, and another named Lapedus [sic]. . . . You can expect a visit from those people here anytime as they are determined to get this money or there [sic] lives. They plan on leaving here most any day.

Since no mention was made of the correspondence until after Lapidus's death, Towl asked Chief Pszanowski about the department's policy on threatening letters. Towl wanted to know whether it had been filed, or just what happened. Chief Pszanowski replied he had shown it to Sutton who put it in his pocket. Towl then asked how long Sutton had been carrying the letter around in his pocket, and was told "I can't say, I think he had it all the time."[42] Only after Lapidus was murdered, did the Detective apparently remember the letter in his pocket.

As police commissioner Roy Towl was the elected official responsible for law and order in Omaha, a city where a prominent man had just been murdered, but with a police department that was not an independent agency. Despite Towl and public concern, the likelihood of a thorough investigation that might point to Dennison and his organization was scarcely likely. Towl had long been an enemy of Tom Dennison, then his front seat as police commissioner and the treatment he received convinced him more than ever of the absolute necessity to break the "Old Man's" power. Even before the Kubik and Lapidus murders, Towl had contacted an organization known as the Secret Six, a group formed by wealthy Chicagoans to struggle against Al Capone. A November meeting with the organization's chairman brought Towl the promise a top flight investigator would be sent to Omaha at the proper moment. Just nine days after Harry Lapidus was killed the proper moment was at hand.

Having no trust in his own police department, Towl immediately after Lapidus was shot had asked his fellow commissioners to permit him to employ an outside investigator to work under his direction and be responsible to him alone. Apparently fearing adverse publicity if they failed to act, his colleagues agreed, with the proviso the investigator report to both Towl and the mayor. Towl protested but finally accepted the arrangement rather than being denied completely the opportunity to have outside help and a man he could trust. In a stormy session the council granted Towl his special investigator, but denied him the $25,000 he requested. A few days later $4,000 was appropriated for expenses, and Towl sent for Donald L. Kooken, the man recommended by his contacts in Chicago.[43]

The city commission promised Kooken full assistance and cooperation from all city agencies and access to information the police department had gathered about the case. A man characterized by Towl as a superior criminologist, Kooken came to the case with extensive experience in investigative work. His career as a detective started out during World War I when as a young soldier he helped his camp commander with a narcotics investigation. He served overseas as an intelligence officer, and was quickly hired by the Baltimore and Ohio Railroad as an investigator when the war ended. He joined the federal government in 1927 and was sent to Chicago two years later, establishing a record there within twelve months for arrests and convictions. When not tracking lawbreakers he attended the University of Chicago, taking courses in police administration and criminology. After the Secret Six was formed, Kooken was sought out because of his record and talents, and the federal government granted permission for him to become the group's assistant director.[44]

Kooken initiated his Omaha investigation on January 1, 1932, but soon discovered, assurances to the contrary, his efforts to secure assistance from the police department were not to be realized. In fact, from the very night of the killing, it was obvious Towl's fears that the police would work on the case with less than dedication were well founded. Neither the police chief, nor the head of the detective bureau, nor anyone from the police department called Towl to report the Lapidus murder. It was a newspaper reporter who informed the police commissioner. Towl then went directly to police headquarters, where both Chief of Police Pszanowski and Head of Detectives Sutton were unavailable. Pszanowski later explained he had been "under the weather" at home, and Sutton maintained he was at a friend's home that night and fell asleep on the couch; not until the next morning did he learn of the killing.[45] Towl's summation of the police department's immediate response to the crime was, "I have been absolutely discouraged as I look over the record of that night and the bungling manner in which the matter was handled from beginning to end."[46]

His review of what took place on the murder scene suggests no effort was made to preserve physical evidence: two detectives and a police reporter arriving in a Chrysler emergency vehicle drove alongside the Lapidus car, where the killer's car had been, and obliterated tire tracks; people were allowed to mill around the site and no attempt was made to hold them back or prevent the destruction of any evidence that might later have been obtainable. Police officers and newspapermen searched Lapidus's LaSalle, looking for a gun they said, but "No attempts were made to lift fingerprints from the car until the following morning, after it had been handled by innumerable persons."[47]

When Towl later asked Sutton, during a long discussion about errors committed at the murder site, whether tire tracks of the escaping car had been preserved the detective said they should have been. Then Towl wanted to know if a car turning at high speed, as the assassins' car had when it turned off Park Avenue, would leave distinct tire marks? Sutton replied marks were recorded of one car, but Towl interjected they were those of the Lapidus car coming to a stop. Reviewing the situation, the commissioner of police referred to the people gathered around the slain man's automobile as "a crowd at a circus," and regretted the failure to record automobile tracks of the escaping car.[48] "Do you think the men on the ground did their duty?" asked Towl. Sutton answered they had not. Towl called the police investigation the most "botched up" he had ever experienced. How could so many errors have been made the commissioner wanted to know. "There are mistakes made in every job," his head of detectives blandly replied.[49] Honest mistakes or the result of instructions from higher up Towl must have pondered. The fact Dennison man Paul Sutton appointed three faithful Dennison lieutenants to conduct the Lapidus murder investigation, Harry Buford, Joe Potach, and Joe Vinci, could hardly have consoled Towl.

His suspicions that the machine was not interested in permitting a genuine investigation were confirmed after Kooken arrived and attempted to do what the police had not. Botching their own investigation, at least in Towl's judgment, the police now proceeded to hamper Kooken's attempts to unravel the mystery shooting. Repeatedly he found himself at odds with police officers, despite the agreement providing for information availability and cooperation. Requests for reports on the case brought Kooken a one page synopsis and a general verbal description. When he asked to examine the death car, Sutton told him it had been reconditioned and returned to the family. Kooken located the auto the next day in the police garage in the same shape as when brought in.

Hearing about the Chicago letter, Kooken tried, without success, to get a copy from the police; finally he and Towl secured one through their own efforts. When they asked for the envelope the letter had been sent in, Sutton remembered throwing it away in February. Undercover men working for Kooken were told by policemen to leave town, and witnesses he interviewed were later queried by police as to what they had revealed. One witness questioned by Kooken was later picked up by the police and held for an hour, until the Chicago investigator found out about the arrest and secured his man's release. Several witnesses the police had examined went unquestioned by Kooken because the police refused to share their names.[50]

A policeman reported to Tom Dennison all of Kooken's movements, and in case the officer missed something a private detective also shadowed Kooken. An effort was made to quash Kooken's efforts when Dennison lieutenant Harry Buford contacted a close friend of the Lapidus family, asking him to use his influence with the family to have them request the special probing cease. A second visit by the same officer to the same person with the same mission came in due course.[51] Now came the time to transfer Towl back to the fire department, for he was proving too large a nuisance over the Lapidus case as police commissioner. Moving Towl was the final step in destroying Kooken's capacity to pursue successfully his investigation as frustration followed frustration. On February 25, 1932, he formally withdrew, telling Towl it was impossible to continue considering the handicaps placed in his way, increasingly worse since Towl's change in assignment.[52] Officially off the case so far as the city of Omaha was concerned, Kooken returned to Chicago but continued to follow it through Towl and Tom Crawford, who under the alias of Murphy went to Chicago.

Kooken wrote two reports after he resigned, one on March 2 addressed to Attorney General Sorensen, the second going to Mayor Metcalfe a day later. In the report to the mayor, Kooken traced his investigative efforts and complained about the lack of cooperation he had received. Denied assistance and information, especially from the police department, Kooken said he had no choice but to withdraw. Omaha's chief executive read that Lapidus was killed by someone who knew him, and the strongest motive was revenge for his opposition to Omaha's criminal gang. No mention is ventured as to who the assassins might have been.[53] More revealing is the report to Attorney General Sorensen. A copy was sent by Sorensen to U.S. Senator from Nebraska R.B. Howell with the advisement the report was highly confidential with the contents unknown to Omaha's police department.[54] In his report to the attorney general, Kooken reviewed the "hopelessly muddled" preliminary police investigation, and discussed his own thwarted efforts.

Kooken then went to the heart of the matter and wrote of persistent rumors and anonymous letters attributing the murder to three Dennison men, all police officers. Undercover Kooken men had all brought back the same story with the same three names. Donald Kooken concluded Lapidus was killed because of his anti-gang activities in Omaha, and he stated the killing was ordered by Tom Dennison. Those orders were followed, Kooken believed, by the three officers the murder was generally attributed to.[55] Since Kooken had no physical evidence to connect Dennison or his three men with the murder, he advised only a confession could actually resolve the crime in a court of law.

It remains unknown whether Tom Dennison did indeed order the murder of Harry Lapidus, or whether the men identified by Kooken were actually the killers. No one ever came forth to confess, and evidence never appeared to substantiate Kooken's charges. However, early efforts to discredit Lapidus, preparations to throw suspicion on figures in Chicago, the police mismanagement of the investigation subsequent to the murder, the blocks thrown at Kooken to despoil his progress, all indicate a machine blameworthy in the assassination of Harry Lapidus. If Dennison was responsible for leading members of his organization to such an act, it can only be judged a tremendous error of judgment in a career little given to error.

Perhaps therein lies an explanation. For three decades Dennison's life was charmed and he led his forces with guile and cleverness through years of victories. As time passed, the machine began to overestimate itself and underestimate its enemies, a major miscalculation the powerful and arrogant repeatedly succumb to despite a succession of fallen Goliaths. A direct line runs from the shooting beside the Hanscom Park lagoon, to a federal courtroom, and to the demise of the machine in the following spring election. At Lapidus's funeral Rabbi David A. Goldstein said in the eulogy that "No one asks for revenge in the death of Harry Lapidus . . . . But his death is a sign to us all, a command that this community be cleansed of those influences which brought about his end."[56] Few heeded the command at the time or in the year following, but the few who did were committed to fulfilling the sign the death of Harry Lapidus had imprinted upon them. Their motives varied but the goal was identical--defeat Tom Dennison.

About midnight a week after Lapidus was killed, Roy Towl received a telephone call asking him to come to Council Bluffs and bring Irving Stalmaster with him. Towl was unable to contact Stalmaster and about an hour later was telephoned again. He was informed the caller had been double-crossed and run out of town by the "gang." The yet unidentified fellow said he knew who killed Lapidus, adding that two prominent Omahans were behind the murder. Towl asked if it was "T" and "B" (Tom and Billy). "Yes," was the prompt reply, "those are the right people."[57] Towl now recognized the voice and identified the caller as Tom Crawford. From this point the two became allies, enlisting the dead Lapidus to serve in their small army to battle Tom Dennison. Few of the living had the temerity to join them, but those who did determined to bring Tom Dennison to trial, not for the Lapidus murder for which there was no evidence, but on other charges. Their goal was not a guilty verdict in the conventional sense--they sought the publicity of a lengthly and public courtroom contest, the means they adopted to weaken and finally destroy the "Old Man" politically.

Within a year Dennison and fifty-eight of his associates were in federal court thanks to the efforts of a small group around Towl. These political reformers and Dennison enemies were willing to resort to whatever means within the law they perceived as likely to bring defeat to their opponent. The instrument decided upon was a court of law turned to blatant political purpose.

Chapter VIII

[1]EOW-H, February 14, 1930.

[2]*Ibid.*, May 1, 2, 1930.

[3]*Ibid.*, May 1, 1930.

[4]Grace Housky Statement, Sorensen papers, Box 35, Folder 67.

[5]Letter, Crawford to O'Sullivan, April 22, 1932, Sorensen papers, Box 35, Folder 65; letter, Murphy to W.E. Nance, Special Agent, Federal Building, Omaha, April 4, 1932, Sorensen papers, Box 35, Folder 66.

[6]MOW-H, November 18, 1932.

[7]Grace Housky Statement.

[8]Testimony given by George Volker at hearing before the Board of Pardons, January 12, 1932, at State Penetentiary [Lincoln, Nebraska], Towl papers, Box 1, Folder 1932, January 1-14, City Hall. Volker worked for Livingston beginning in 1927 or 1928.

[9]EOW-H, May 1, 1930.

[10]*Ibid.*; Maher interview, October 23, 1979; Zerbe interview, July 6, 1979.

[11]"Analysis of the Crime Situation in Omaha," February 18, 1932, Towl papers, Box 1, Folder 1932, February, City Hall.

[12]Report to B.F. Danbaum, Inspector of Detectives, May 14, 1932, on report of conversation with George Kubik, Jr., Towl papers, Box 1, Folder 1932, May, City Hall.

[13]EOW-H, November 12, 1931.

[14]*Ibid.*, November 13, 1931.

[15]*Ibid.*

[16]Letter, Murphy to Smith, July 1, 1932; Reports to B.F. Danbaum, Inspector of Detectives, on conversations with John Kubik (George's brother), May 14, 1932; George Kubik, Jr., May 14, 1932; John Staskicwicz, May 7 [sic], 1932; John Repo, May 21, 1932, Towl papers, Box 1, Folder 1932, May, City Hall.

[17]*Sunday Omaha World-Herald Magazine*, January 1, 1933, p. 3.

[18]Document No. 7025.

[19]On Lapidus's activities see *The Jewish Press*; election as Jewish Community Center President, March 25, 1925, March 4, 1926, March 3, 1927, March 1, 1928. On his hospital work see July 5, 1923, January 31, 1924, May 29, 1924, January 27, 1927, February 8, 1929.

[20]MOW-H, December 24, 1931, editorial, p. 14.

[21]Responding officers report to the Chief of Police, December 22, 1931, 11:30 p.m., Towl papers, Box 1, Folder 1931, September-December, City Hall.

[22]Report, Don L. Kooken to C.A. Sorensen, March 2, 1932, Sorensen

papers, Box 39, Folder 191.

[23]MOW-H, December 23, 25, 1931. Letter, Don L. Kooken to Hon. Richard Metcalf, Mayor, March 3, 1932, Sorensen papers, Box 39, Folder 191, pp. 1-2.

[24]Letter, Kooken to Metcalfe, pp. 2-3.

[25]MOW-H, December 24, 1931.

[26]*Ibid.*, and December 25, 1931.

[27]MOW-H, December 24, 1931.

[28]Interview with Louis J. Pruch, conducted by Orville D. Menard, July 24, 1980, Omaha, Nebraska; also Zerbe interview, July 16, 1979, and Kurtz-Gordon interview, July 20, 1979.

[29]Statement, Roy Towl, December 31, 1931, Towl papers, Box 1, Folder 1931, September-December, City Hall, p. 1.

[30]Letter, Kooken to Metcalfe, p. 3.

[31]MOW-H, December 24, 1931.

[32]*The New York Times*, October 30, 1932, Pt. II, p. 6:1.

[33]Edson Smith interview, April 1, 1974.

[34]Grace Housky Statement.

[35]Letter, Kooken to Metcalfe, p. 5.

[36]Letter, addressed to "Dear Friend," n.d., Sorensen papers, Box 35, Folder 66.

[37]Copies of the two squeals may be found in Sorensen papers, Box 39, Folder 191. This incident is also written of by Crawford to Irvin Stalmaster, September 16, 1932, Towl papers, Box 1, Folder 1932, August-September, City Hall.

[38]Letter, Crawford to Robert Smith, May 9, 1932. See also Crawford to O'Sullivan, April 22, 1932, Sorensen papers, Box 35, Folder 65; MOW-H, October 19, 1932.

[39]EOW-H, October 18, 1932; and see Crawford to "Dear Friend," "Plotting to Kill Harry Lapidus," n.d., Sorensen papers, Box 35, Folder 66.

[40]Statement of Mrs. Thomas Trainor, resident of Chicago, dated August 30, 1932, Towl papers, Box 1, Folder 1932, August-September, City Hall.

[41]Letter, Anonymous to Chief of Police, February 20, 1931, Towl papers, Box 1, Folder 1931, January-April, City Hall.

[42]Record of conversation with Chief Pszanowski, n.d., Towl papers, Box 1, Folder 191, January 1-14, City Hall, p. 2.

[43]Statement, Roy Towl, n.d., Towl papers, Box 1, Folder 1932, January 1-14, City Hall; and MOW-H, December 29, 1931, January 5, 1932.

[44]Memorandum, n.d., Towl papers, Box 2, Folder 1933, June-July, Mayor.

[45]Statement, Roy Towl, n.d., Towl papers, Box 1, Folder 1932, January 1-14, City Hall. See also Record of conversation with Chief Psznanowski.

[46]Statement, Roy Towl, n.d., Towl papers, Box 1, Folder 1932, Janaury 1-14, City Hall, p. 4.

[47]*Ibid.*, p. 5. Also letter, Kooken to Attorney General Sorensen, March 2, 1932, Sorensen papers, Box 39, Folder 191.

[48]Record of conversation with Detective Sutton, January 7, 1932, Towl papers, Box 1, Folder 1932, January 1-14, City Hall, p. 6.

[49]*Ibid.*, p. 8.

[50]Statement, Roy Towl, n.d., Towl papers, Folder 1932, February, City Hall, pp. 6-8.

[51]Letter, Kooken to Sorensen, March 2, 1932, Sorensen papers, Box 39, Folder 191; also letter, Kooken to Metcalfe, March 3, 1932, *Ibid.*

[52]Letter, Kooken to Towl, February 25, 1932, Towl papers, Box 1, Folder 1932, February, City Hall.

[53]Letter, Kooken to Metcalfe, March 3, 1932, Sorensen papers, Box 39, Folder 191.

[54]Letter, Sorensen to R.B. Howell, May 14, 1932, Sorensen papers, Box 39, Folder 191.

[55]Letter, Kooken to Sorensen, March 2, 1932, Sorensen papers, Box 39, Folder 191.

[56]MOW-H, December 25, 1931.

[57]Statement, Roy Towl, December 31, 1931, Towl papers, Box 1, Folder 1931, September-December, City Hall, p. 1.

CHAPTER IX

Destruction

Ah, you too Vanity!
I knew you would overthrow me in the end.
--Cyrano de Bergerac

Several explanations have been advanced to explain the downfall of bossism, most the reverse side of factors that nurtured their growth and blossoming. Among the suggested causes was the broadening horizons of businessmen from local reliance and perspective to regional and national. Businesses no longer solely dependent on the immediate environment for their livelihood, and with decision making lifted beyond the municipal borders meant a political boss less and less necessary to their operations. And as time went on association with a boss became less savory as their reputations waned and a political gap joined the social gap. Another factor which weakened the bosses was the success of structural reformers who managed to install devices deliberately designed to sabotage political machines. Voter registration and the secret ballot helped to reduce election day frauds and the machines' ability to deliver the vote. Nonpartisan and at-large elections weakened the ward heelers and the bosses' party foundations. Civil service merit systems undermined a key cog in machine operations--patronage--and sealed bid systems became the means to combat boodle and corruption.

Emergence of the middle class as a potent political force signaled the appearance of a sizeable electoral sector the bosses had little influence over since it was not dependent upon the machine and its favors in return for votes. As the middle class increased in size and electoral potency, its newcomers assimilated the ethos of politics must be clean and businesslike, and turned their backs on machine politics. Another problem was the stemming of the immigrant tide in the 1920s, depriving the bosses of their ready made electors, for years a natural font for accumulating voters in return for the organizations' assistance. Adding to their woes, the machines watched a competitor in the welfare business emerge as the federal government entered the field. Favors which heretofore had earned gratitude and therefore votes were now provided compliments of Congress. Dennison left the scene before federal welfare became a feature of American life, but in any case welfare as *the* central feature in the end of bossism (Edwin O'Connor's "last hurrah" explanation) has been effectively challenged by the experience of at least two cities. In both Kansas City and Pittsburgh the federal government's entering the welfare and employment scene was turned to benefit by the local political machines rather than debilitating them.[1] But just as the business community had raised its consciousness beyond the local level, so did government become increasingly national in the course of the century. Washington's weight was brought more and more to bear on state and city governments, and a boss seemed less and less an essential feature of community life when important decisions were being made elsewhere.

All the above contributed to ushering political bosses from their positions of power. No single factor explains alone the demise of the machines, just as no single element bears full responsibility for their appearance. Taken together, explanations advanced for the rise and fall of bossism provide a panoply for understanding, and a sense of the interrelatedness of forces which contribute to alterations in our political landscape. But machine opponents in Omaha, Nebraska, in 1932 were impatient with or more likely unaware of historical currents later identified by scholars. Their concern was an immediate one and their focus was next year's city election.

Their problem was how to defeat Dennison; what tools, what methods could be invoked to transform repeated electoral defeats into a victory? Efforts to wrest power from the "Old Man" by the ballot box were doomed so long as his machine manipulated a mass of voters. How then to undermine Dennison's long entrenched position and foster voter disaffection, resulting in his defeat at the polls? The answer was in the judicial system, summoned not for justice but for political ambition. Towl and his associates did not invent the technique since machine opponents in several cities, confronting conventional political channels controlled and blocked, turned courtrooms into political forums as the means to discredit their boss and alienate the electorate. Reformers discovered courts paved the way to goals denied them when relying on traditional approaches. Their goal was political banishment, not a guilty verdict and imprisonment for the boss (seldom realized); these might be attractive sidelights but not crucial to the fundamental task.

Courts of law provided dramatic settings for extensive newspaper coverage. As trials progressed, the press relayed witness testimony of questionable, corrupt, and illegal machine activities, accomplishing for reformers what their good government campaigns did not. Revelations of machine inner processes and operations evoked voter disgust, and although acquittal might issue from a jury, at the polls many a boss subsequently was found guilty by the voters. Highlighting the reformers embracing the courts for political ends is not intended to provide a single causal explanation of boss defeats, for the demise of bossism is a complicated phenomenon. Calling attention to boss as defendant is merely an effort to take into account tactics which proved eminently suitable for machine opponents. While many studies of individual bosses have followed their subjects into the courtroom, it was always as a singular case, failing to note such a fate befell many of their brethren. Viewed comparatively rather than city specific, there is a striking similarity in the reformers' resort to courts for political purpose.

Even in one of the few studies that attempted to provide a cross section analysis of political bosses, the phenomenon goes unobserved, although the courts are much evident. When Harold Zink's 1930 study of twenty bosses was completed, two of his subjects were still politically active. Of the remaining eighteen, Zink attributed loss of power in all but seven cases to death or natural causes. Decline of that seven, Zink informs us, emanated from "causes so unlike that it is difficult to classify them."[2] But a common unmentioned element wends its way through Zink's presentation of the fate of these seven men. Professor Zink dutifully recorded indictments and trials of the seven, but failed to reveal the pattern underlying them: involvement in legal proceedings with electoral defeats not far behind. He came close in noting Edward Butler (St. Louis), George

B. Cox (Cincinnati), Abraham Ruef (San Francisco), and Albert A. Ames (Minneapolis), "All became involved in legal proceedings of a criminal character. But . . . ," he then asserts, "back of reform in each case some other factor really stood preeminent."[3]

True enough. However, the essential point is that to deal with the four bosses Zink mentions, the reformers turned to the courts as their means of protest and in each case the result was political ruin for their target--whatever factor was impelling them. In addition to Butler, Cox, Ruef, and Ames, Zink should have added to his list of bosses enmeshed in legal difficulties an additional six of his subjects: William Tweed, Charles Murphy, and Richard Croker of New York City, Chicago's Frederick Lundin, Israel Durham (Philadelphia), and William Flinn of Pittsburgh. For seven of these ten bosses their political eclipse was heralded by courtroom challenges. The other three, Croker, Murphy, and Flinn, politically survived their legal test and sustained power (Murphy finally surrendered his power to death; Croker and Flinn fell as victims of internal political battles). Only two of the seven whose careers were broken through the courts went to prison (Tweed and Ruef), but the political potency of the courts had been well demonstrated. Judicial punishment was not at stake; political power was.

What of the fate of bosses in Zink's study who avoided courtroom exposure? Death, illness, or internal organizational struggles ultimately took away their power. For the seven whose fate was not determined by these causes, the courts were the precursors of political change. Machine opponents throughout the nation, unable to defeat their enemies in the electoral arena so long as their organizations sustained voter support, turned to the law and to public disclosure in the courtroom's hallowed confines. The reformer's alarums, impotent in speeches and campaign rhetoric, achieved credence when filtered through judge, jury, sworn witnesses, and attendant newspaper coverage.

Tweed was taken to court following publication of materials gathered by a spy of the Democratic Reform Movement. Ultimately he went to jail, no longer the powerful leader of Tammany, although the institutionalized New York City machine was able to carry on without him.[4] In Cincinnati, Cox succeeded in quashing an indictment for perjury secured against him by his enemies, but "the tilt broke his spirit and he soon relinquished much of his political control and shortly thereafter he died."[5] A wealthy grand jury foreman spearheaded the campaign to rid Minneapolis of "Doc" Ames. After three trials Ames "emerged a white-haired stooped figure who few recognized as the magnificent politician of a few months earlier."[6] His reign was over even though his case was ultimately dropped. In Chicago, after a sensational trial for conspiracy to defraud the board of education, Lundin's attorney, the famed Clarence Darrow, secured an acquittal for his client. But "in spite of hopeful words to the effect that 'truth crushed to earth will rise again' Mr. Lundin found himself seriously crippled after his acquittal."[7]

Courtroom experiences of "Colonel" Butler, boss of St. Louis, broke his spirit and drove him into retirement. Zink tells us two trials (bribery charges with Butler once found guilty but reversed by a higher court, and once acquitted) weakened him physically and cost him his zest for political life.[8] Philadelphia's Israel Durham suffered the political consequences of his trial (for recovery of some five million dollars) with a "severe" defeat at the polls, and shortly thereafter he fell ill and died.[9] San Francisco's boss, Abe Ruef, like his counterparts in other parts of the nation, fell prey to the power inherent in the judicial process when adapted for political purposes. Traps and threats joined tactics of other suspect nature as the means to put Ruef in prison. The underlying political motive was expressed by Francis J. Heney (a federal agent on leave with President Teddy Roosevelt's permission), when he said Ruef's imprisonment would "have a wholesome effect upon other political bosses for the next decade at least."[10] Heney's broader vision of the court's mission and his political purpose are again revealed in his saying, "The greatest benefit which the city and the whole country would derive from the prosecution would be the insight which we will have given them into the causes of corruption in all large cities and into the methods by which this corruption is maintained."[11]

These words became a primer for similar undertakings elsewhere as the judiciary was recruited for political wars. The fate of many bosses after Zink's study follows a similar pattern: bosses taken to court soon thereafter experienced political defeat; those able to avoid courtroom confrontation held their power until voluntary retirement or death. In the latter group are Frank Hague of Jersey City, Edward Crump of Memphis, and in Chicago Edward Kelly and Richard Daley.[12] On the other hand, three bosses went to court: Tom Pendergast of Kansas City, Boston's James Michael Curley, and Omaha's Tom Dennison. Pendergast and Curley both went to prison, and though Dennison never went behind bars, he, like the other two, was bereft of political significance when he left the courtroom after weeks of testimony and exposure.

An intriguing division between the two groups, drawn by Lyle Dorsett (without reference to Dennison who was pre-FDR), was that those who went to court faced opponents availed of federal support. The four who avoided court contests enjoyed an ally in the national capitol who aided them in staying out of court and in sustaining their machines. So long as a boss was dependable in White House eyes--delivered the vote and was useful--as was true of the four in Chicago, Jersey City, and Memphis, administration succor was forthcoming; but if the boss did not deliver (Curley) or became an embarrassment (Pendergast), then court action was not far behind, aided and abetted by Washington, D.C.[13]

In the spring of 1939, Tom Pendergast pled guilty to two counts of income tax evasion and was sentenced to prison. Putative reformer Lloyd Stark, federal investigators, and courtroom and press coverage brought the Kansas City boss to ruin; elections the next year registered his organization's collapse. Pendergast's machine, which had survived the various alleged causes for boss downfall thanks to its skillful adaptability, did not endure long beyond the trial.[14] Boston's famous James Michael Curley was an early Franklin Roosevelt supporter, but he was not a boss in the manner of Hague, Crump, or Daley--he lacked the organizational base they controlled and thus was unable faithfully to deliver the vote. Therefore Curley was abandoned by Roosevelt, who turned to more reliable Democratic forces in Massachusetts.

Several years later Assistant Attorney General Tom Clark pressed for and secured an indictment against Curley for using the mails to defraud in a highly suspect case tried in Washington. "Despite the fact that there was not one concrete piece of evidence against him," he was found guilty and sent to prison.[15] Although Curley had been able to win the mayor's office (for the fourth time) the fall previous to his January 1946 conviction, perhaps in part because of his legal troubles in Washington and a defensive Bostonian reaction, he was never able to win another electoral contest.[16] Thrice more he ran for mayor (in 1949, 1951, and 1955), but thrice was denied another return to city hall by Boston's voters. A career that began in 1900 with election to the Boston Common Council was over.

Other factors and developments than FDR and courts played their part in Curley's political ruin, as well as for Pendergast. But the judicial connection, flowing from Tweed through so many others to Curley, unites them as a common element in their political destruction. That element usually is missing in the careers of bosses whose careers culminated in more favorable fashion. They may have come close or watched associates go to court and conviction, as did Daley, but so long as they personally avoided the docket their tenure held.

Several years before his colleague Tom Pendergast was broken via the courts, Tom Dennison was brought to the end of his career through the judicial system. Unable to break the "Old Man's" grip on city politics through the ballot box, his opponents turned to the courts in the early 1930s as the means to an end now familiar. In Omaha, as elsewhere, being a political boss was not a crime, consequently other activities had to be unearthed that did stand as statutory offenses. Indicted offense and verdict, were not, however, ends in themselves for many on the law's side. Their target was public opinion and engendering voter dissatisfaction with Tom Dennison and his rule. A small group of Dennison opponents were activated by the Lapidus murder, and they began working together soon after the killing to end the dominion of the political machine they held responsible. Roy Towl was the central figure, a man who feared for his city and scorned the machine which he saw as malevolently going directly or indirectly "into every home of the city with its influence."[17] His view was shared by others, but not many were willing to confront Dennison who after so many years of domination enjoyed power enhanced by reputation for power. Only a few entertained the thought or the hope on New Year's Day 1932, that the year had arrived for breaking Dennison's hold on the city. These few, differing in motives but united in the common desire to rid Omaha of the "Old Man" and his "gang," began plotting to bring Dennison to his political trial.

One of them, attorney Eugene O'Sullivan, in former years had been *personna grata* with Dennison and received business referred from the organization. For years he labored for machine candidates in elections, believing they were good-hearted liberals defending Omaha's oppressed and needy.[18] O'Sullivan eventually underwent a change of heart, and aligned himself with anti-machine sentiments. Word quickly was sent out from headquarters to Dennison allies to send no more legal business to O'Sullivan. In early 1932 Towl and O'Sullivan joined forces, the attorney adding his insider legal knowledge to Towl's passion. In addition to working with Towl's small group to bring Dennison to the court, O'Sullivan also appeared during the trial as a surprise government witness.

Two legal figures at the state level became privy to the maneuvers, Christian A. Sorensen and Irvin Stalmaster. Nebraska's attorney general had occupied himself since entering office in 1929 with opposition to crime and corruption in Omaha, but had little success given Dennison's entrenched position. Sorensen was willing to cooperate with O'Sullivan and Towl as his office and resources permitted. In addition to the impetus coming to him from Sorensen's office in Lincoln, Stalmaster had a personal stake in the situation in Omaha. Lapidus had been his father-in-law.

A local federal contact was provided by Edson Smith, assistant U.S. district attorney in Omaha, appointed to the position by U.S. District Attorney James Kinsler. Newspaper coverage of the appointment observed Smith was twenty-four years old and a recent graduate of Harvard Law School. His becoming assistant U.S. district attorney was attributed to the lifelong friendship between Kinsler and Robert Smith, Edson's father. The elder Smith, prominent for years in Nebraska Republican party circles and clerk of the district court, had been a close friend of Harry Lapidus. Another figure involved was U.S. Senator from Nebraska R.B. Howell, whose campaigns had been managed by Robert Smith. Elected to his second term in 1929, Howell was described by Billy

292

Maher as a "do-gooder" and bitter enemy of Dennison.[19] Howell's role was important as a Washington contact, and Sorensen and he corresponded about developments in Omaha, albeit circumspectly from the Washington end.

Donald Kooken, the imported and frustrated Chicago investigator, continued a close relationship with Towl after officially leaving the Lapidus case. He was a contact person for Towl with the Secret Six, and helped keep Crawford out of view until both of them appeared in Omaha for the conspiracy trial. When Towl became Omaha's mayor after Dennison was defeated in the trial's aftermath, he appointed Kooken superintendent of public welfare and coordinating officer for the mayor's office.

A key figure in the small circle's efforts to bring Dennison to a courtroom, Tom Crawford hid out in Chicago during the months of preparation, fearful of retribution from the "gang." Crawford had doubled as a police officer and secretary to Tom Dennison in the late 1920s, but the two had a bitter parting in the fall of 1931, the policeman feeling he had been framed by the "Old Man." In September of that year Crawford was sacrificed on behalf of Frank Housky, Dennison insider and partner in the Friar's Club, amid allegations of Crawford's having an affair with Housky's wife and stealing his car. Housky's car vanished from the Relay Garage one night, and the man on duty identified Tom Crawford to Ben Danbaum, from a picture in the *Police Annual,* as the man who took the car. Positive identification in person came shortly after in the police chief's office, and Crawford was charged with conduct unbecoming an officer and suspended. No charge of auto theft was lodged against him.

He learned Dennison had sent word to the department to get rid of him, and rather than wait for dismissal Crawford resigned. In a preliminary hearing for the Housky divorce proceedings, Crawford's name became involved with adultery intimated, but again no charges were filed (they came several months later when Crawford was indicted for wife and child abandonment, despite the fact his wife neither appeared nor raised any accusations against him).[20] In the midst of his September difficulties Crawford appealed to Dennison for assistance, but was abruptly turned down. He was waved off by the "Old Man" who said, "Housky has got so much on us that I've got to take his end of it." Crawford complained about being shabbily treated and then dared a warning: "Why put me up against it, I've got plenty on you too." According to Crawford's court testimony, Dennison responded, "By God, if you talk, we will give you what we gave Gene Livingston." Crawford retorted, "When I'm ready to talk I'll talk--and in the right time and place."[21] To initiate arrangements for the time and place he made his midnight telephone call to Towl on December 28.

Spirited away to hide in Chicago under Kooken's protection and the alias of Murphy, Crawford began corresponding with his Omaha allies. One of his February letters to O'Sullivan brings the group into focus:[22]

> Just a few lines which I ask that you convey to Roy Towl immediately. Tell Roy Towl, that I would appreciate an immediate meeting here . . . . We are completing plans this week, and whereas each of the following are involved to some extent, I would like to have them present . . . . Don't forget, I want Stalmaster, Robert Smith, C.A. Sorensen, Roy Towl and Edson Smith for this, the last conference before the big hit.

The "big hit" was reference to a pending federal grand jury, the first step in securing an indictment against Dennison. The direct link between the Lapidus murder, the grand jury, and the conspiracy trial is found in Kooken's report to Attorney General Sorensen. Lamenting the collusion of the city and county administrations with the Dennison organization, Kooken informed Sorensen an attempt to prosecute anyone in connection with the Lapidus murder would be fruitless. "For this reason it was determined that the only method to bring about a condition whereby a confession could be hoped for," said Kooken, "would be to first break up the control exercised by Dennison and his criminal organization."[23] To this end, Towl and Kooken went to Smith at the U.S. attorney's office and "mapped out a program" to combine information they had with that of federal special agents to secure an indictment against Dennison.

Desirous of political reform, synonymous with getting rid of the "Old Man," the small group set about its task, some impelled by concerns of illicit and illegal activities too long sanctioned in Omaha, and revenge a possible motive for others. Crawford viewed himself with dual motivation, telling the sheriff of Douglas County, "When they crossed me Charlie, they crossed the wrong man and . . . now they will have to pay the penalty." His overall purpose, however, was beyond the personal level because his goal, wrote Crawford, "was to awaken Omahans to the political-crime-liquor-vice-and gambling combine in their city."[24] Edson Smith alone seems to have been occupied with law enforcement for the law's sake, preparing and prosecuting a case wherein criminal activities, in his judgment, warranted a trial. The facts suggested overt acts amounting to a conspiracy for the government to prosecute; as far as Smith was concerned, politically desirable side effects would be a bonus, but certain political results were not his fundamental objectives.[25]

The degree to which these men confided to one another their plans and goals is unknown. It appears the group was informal, with an inner circle composed of Towl, Crawford, O'Sullivan, and Kooken. Others were willing to cooperate so far as their positions permitted; for example, Crawford told Towl that although he was providing the federal district assistant attorney facts, he was unable to explain to him his "greater purpose" because of Smith's official position.[26] Crawford was an indefatigable letter writer, sending most of his information on the Dennison machine to Towl and O'Sullivan, but also with Stalmaster and Edson Smith on his mailing list. Sorensen and Stalmaster followed the developing situation in Omaha to the point Crawford reported to O'Sullivan he had been informed the two state officers had talked together about arranging a fund to help support Crawford's family.[27]

Traffic was not all one way, however, and Towl occasionally wrote Crawford, and kept in contact with Don Kooken. A precious commodity because of his insider's information, Crawford was prized by both sides and he expressed fears of kidnapping of his family and attempts on his life should he be discovered. He recalled two shots fired at his car shortly before he left Omaha, taking them as a warning, and an intriguing letter was received by relatives and friends after he was hidden in Chicago. Purportedly written on behalf of "Sanctuary Ltd., Founded and Endowed 1918, 'To provide sanctuary and asylum in illness and distress'," the letter was an obvious attempt to track down Crawford by his Omaha enemies. The writers stated they were urgently trying to contact "Thos. B. Crawford" at the request of a Sanctuary patient; if the recipients knew where Crawford might be reached, they were asked to forward his address and phone number. Should they be unable to help, the name of someone who could was welcome.[28]

A last comment on the the men working in the early months of 1932 to bring Dennison to political trial is provided in an overheard remark of Ben Danbaum after Dennison and others were indicted. The long time Dennison cohort was not among them, despite the fact he was well known in the city for his faithfulness to the "Old Man." An informant reported he heard Danbaum say he had expected to be indicted along with the rest. But, Danbaum continued, he "outsmarted them by getting lined up with the gang that caused all this trouble, and by so doing, I kept within the good graces of them and avoided an indictment."[29]

A conviction the trial was basically political survived in the memory of organization member and worker Billy Maher, who was among the indicted. He was ready to plead guilty for selling liquor and "take the rap," but, he said, he and his fellows were not really tried for their retail and wholesale business endeavors. A conspiracy for the sale of intoxicants was brought against them: "But they didn't want us. They wanted the organization--the political organization."[30] Dan Gross, one of the attorneys for the defense in the conspiracy trial, absolutely agreed in his depiction of the proceedings as a political show, the stage set in the court to create an anti-Dennison atmosphere. Politics, argued Gross, were the motive for the trial, the "key to the whole miserable mess." In his closing statement, he returned to the political theme, observing the prosecution had accused Dennison of being involved in politics. In his estimation the case amounted to nothing more than showing that involvement. Gross admitted Dennison had been a participant in the city's political life, then he turned to the government prosecutors and asked how they received their jobs, except through politics. "I say," he concluded, "politics is the keynote to your entire case."[31]

The reference was a telling one in that U.S. Attorney and long time Omahan Kinsler had shortly before been removed from his position to be replaced by a gentleman from York, Nebraska. Senator Howell's influence and Washington's shadow over events are suggested here. (Kinsler nonetheless appeared in court during the conspiracy trial, but defending some of those under indictment instead of prosecuting them.) Newly appointed U.S. Attorney Charles E. Sandall complained it was unfair to talk about political motivations for the trial since he had legal residence in York, and he and his assistants did not care anything for politics in Omaha.[32]

The *New York Times* identified the underlying purposes at work during the days of courtroom exchange, and ran a story under the heading "Conspiracy Charges Against Alleged Liquor Ring Have Political Ramifications."[33] In the Assistant U.S. Attorney's trial summation a month later, those ramifications were made quite clear:[34]

> In an organization for monopoly of the liquor business, who logically would be its head? he asked. Who but a gambler who has found gambling not so profitable, and turns to the liquor traffic as a more profitable venture? And who but a man with political influence could operate and hold together such a syndicate, hold in line not only the members, but police officers as well?

Early moves in generating outside support against the organization, even before the Lapidus murder, were claimed by both Towl and Crawford, then operating independently. While on vacation in September 1931, Towl went to Chicago and contacted the Secret Six, explaining the "political criminal combine" in Omaha. Assured of Secret Six assistance, Towl went on to Washington, D.C., and the Department of Justice to tell his story and enlist support.[35] Two months later special federal agents were in Omaha setting up wiretaps. As a member of the city commission's waterways committee, Towl in late November attended the Mississippi Valley Association meeting in St. Louis. Also attending was Robert I. Randolph, chairman of the Secret Six, missed by Towl in his September visit because Randolph had been in Washington at the time. Now the two had the opportunity to discuss Omaha bootlegging and criminal activities, and Randolph pledged his best man to Towl "at the opportune time." That time arrived nine days after the Lapidus shooting when Kooken came to Omaha.[36]

Crawford too went to Washington in September, and both the Prohibition Bureau and the Internal Revenue Service promised their cooperation in cleaning up Omaha.[37] In February Dennison's ex-secretary told O'Sullivan he was in contact with federal authorities, searching for evidence to present the grand jury, and making arrangements for special federal agents to raid Omaha bootleggers.[38] Amos W. Woodcock, Director of the United States Prohibition Bureau, visited Crawford in Chicago in mid-March and was further enlightened on conditions in Omaha.[39] By this point, special federal agents were well into the investigation, for the conspiracy trial record contains wiretap transcripts covering the previous November and December, and federal search warrants issued on January 25 for entry into various bootlegging operations.[40] Maher recalled with annoyance that everybody's phone was monitored, from his mother to the mayor. "They got a lot of bootleg information," he admitted, "but Holy Christ they didn't try us for bootlegging, they tried us for everything from stealing doormats to murder."[41]

In a letter he wrote during the trial, Towl acknowledged the efforts of Woodcock's agents. After mentioning his service as police commissioner when their investigation began, Towl complimented the agents for their contributions and success.[42] The federal role in the case was recognized by Crawford when he observed "The United States Government had to be enlisted first for several reasons which would require too much space for me to set out herein."[43] Towl and Crawford were not alone in seeking and securing federal assistance, for C.A. Sorensen and R.B. Howell worked to the same end. Nebraska's attorney general sent the U.S. Senator Kooken's confidential report on the Lapidus killing, and asked the Senator to request the Justice Department to assign one of its best men to Omaha on grounds the murder was part of the conspiracy to violate the national prohibition law.[44]

Responding to Sorensen, Howell advised that Woodcock was temporarily out of town and recommended a delay until his return. The Senator noted Woodcock had known Lapidus, thought highly of him, and his advice was to ask Woodcock for assistance and then the attorney general.[45] A month after this exchange, Howell wrote an intriguing letter to Sorensen. It is not possible to determine from it the exact intention or what consequences may have followed, but as an example of the atmosphere surrounding the case and attending circumspection it is worth repeating in part:[46]

At last we have got a start in connection with the confidential matter respecting which you wrote me about the end of May. Someone will call on you shortly for a conference. I am in hope of results.

After you hear from the representative of the Prohibition Unit write me.

From late 1931 to well into the next year, Towl and his small group labored to bring Tom Dennison to trial. Their efforts were not in vain, for a federal grand jury filed an indictment against him and fifty-eight of his associates, including William E. Nesselhous, Roscoe Rawley, John T. Marcell, Paul Sutton, Joseph Potach, Harry Buford, Frank Calamia, and William J. Maher, for conspiracy to violate the National Prohibition Act, with 168 overt acts to effect the conspiracy. The charge in the case reads:[47]

> That on or about January 1, 1922, there was formed in the City of Omaha . . . a conspiracy which had as its objective the sale . . . of intoxicating liquors, and the maintenance of places where intoxicating liquors would be kept for sale and sold; that from time to time additional persons became members of the said conspiracy until a large number of persons were among its membership . . . ; that the said conspiracy became known as the Omaha Liquor Syndicate and it continued in existence until January 26, 1932 and thereafter.

Beginning on October 10, 1932, the trial went on for two months, until the judge declared a mistrial following a week of deadlocked juror deliberations. From the trial's opening days to November 10, the prosecution, with Tom Crawford as its star witness, placed before jurors and the people of Omaha its case against the defendants. Day after day testimony disclosed underworld activities in the city: bootlegging, the protection racket, and violence perpetrated by the organization. Fixing of juries, highjackings, political influence exerted over the police department by Dennison, were all vividly described by Crawford and other government witnesses.

Just a few days before the trial started, Don Kooken and Crawford appeared in Omaha. Kooken was seen at the federal building conferring with Towl, a federal prohibition investigator, and a city detective who had cooperated with Towl. Kooken refused to tell reporters what he was doing back in Omaha, and Towl blithely said it was his day off and he decided to drop by the federal building. The mystery of three beds placed in a grand jury room in the building was solved when it was learned Edson Smith had ordered them brought in. His star witness, Crawford, was to stay there for his protection. When a reporter went to the room and knocked, Crawford responded and in answer to why he was in Omaha said "I been in Dublin." The federal district attorney's office stated he was an insider of the Dennison gang who had been double-crossed and was going to provide valuable testimony in the forthcoming trial.[48]

An attempt by Dennison's attorney to secure a continuance for reasons of his client's health failed (the case had already been postponed once from September 3). In view of the fact Dennison had been seen on the streets in recent days conducting his affairs (he had been under surveillance by federal agents since the postponement), Judge Joseph W. Woodrough ruled the claims of hypertension of the retinal blood vessels, a partial paralysis from a stroke in June, and high blood pressure were insufficient to warrant further delay. On a fall Monday as the clock hands atop the federal building moved to register two in the afternoon, the "Old Man's" days in court began. A half hour earlier the courtroom had filled to its capacity, and another sixty curious people milled about in the corridors. Tensions were high as well known but seldom seen characters of Omaha's bootlegging scene entered the courtroom, accompanied by police officers who were not escorts but co-defendants.

Amid the excitement of the trial's first two days (Billy Maher during a recess exchanged blows with a former chief of detectives) jurors were selected, men of modest means from surrounding rural communities. In his opening statement, Federal District Attorney Sandall promised to bring evidence before the court demonstrating Dennison's interest and influence in having certain men elected to public office and appointed to posts within the police department. Sandall resurrected the Harry Lapidus murder, declaring details of a feud between Dennison and the victim were to be disclosed, the results demonstrating the "gang's utter lack of restraint when it came to protecting itself. He told Omahans that Dennison hated Lapidus because of his interfering in operations by seeking proper law enforcement. Dennison's efforts to discredit Lapidus by sending Murphy and Buford to Iowa were brought to public view, as was the falsification of police records, and the

300

phony letter from Chicago designed to throw an investigation away from Omaha.[49] It was not to be the only time the government attempted to connect the accused with the killing of Lapidus; the shooting made recurrent appearances throughout the trial. In his final arguments Edson Smith "roused a storm of protest" from defense counsel when he declared the evidence showed Dennison and his colleagues had an interest in the Lapidus assassination and the subsequent investigation.[50] Judge Woodrough instructed the jury the defendants were not being tried for murder, but Smith argued they had taken action to prevent Lapidus from giving information to authorities. Figuring prominently in the case, Harry Lapidus was brought back among the living to serve as an important element in attracting and swaying public opinion.

The government first called star witness Tom Crawford to the witness stand, "red-haired, bullet-headed," to share his knowledge of the Dennison machine. During his several hours over three days in the witness box, he recounted his career from the first meeting with Dennison in the Karbach Building in 1921 (seeking help on the advice of friends following a suspension from the police department) to their parting the previous year. He said he was Dennison's secretary from the mid-1920s on, and described how he and the organization protected bootleggers who paid their protection money and raided those who were remiss, how signatures were forged on bail bonds, how juries were fixed--the gamut of machine underworld activities.

Crawford strongly linked Dennison with the Lapidus murder, telling the packed courtroom about being offered a $1,000 by the "Old Man" to kill Lapidus, and his role in typing the letter sent to Chicago and then back to Omaha to deflect suspicion of local guilt. He remembered being told by Dennison it was going to be necessary to get Lapidus out of the way, because he was responsible for shutting off income. Soon there would be nothing left, Dennison was quoted as saying, and Omahans not in the courtroom read later that "The spectators, though prepared by District Attorney Sandall's opening statement for this testimony, received it in stunned silence."[51]

He brought Gene Livingston into the case with testimony about Joe Potach and his alibi letter mailed from California when the bootlegger was shot. And he recited Dennison's farewell words at the time of their break: if he talked his fate would be the same as Livingston's. Several days later other witnesses recited their recollections of George Kubik's lurid death. Omahans in their daily paper were reminded once again of violence in their city, and the organization was depicted as directly responsible. Then came the reading of endless pages of wiretap transcripts and an education into the vocabulary and methods of the bootlegging industry. W.E. Nance, who was a special investigator for the prohibition bureau during the wiretap period, divulged the authority for the taps had been given in writing by the U.S. Attorney General.[52]

As the trial made its way into November, a typewriter expert from Chicago testified the letter mailed from her city to Omaha with the purported threat to Lapidus was written on the same typewriter as two others from a machine used for Dennison's correspondence. The next day a former police officer reported that in 1924, just before the city elections, he had received a verbal order from Chief Pszanowski to assign Crawford to Dennison's office for special duty.[53] A Treasury Department chemical analyst took the stand to give Omahans a sense of dollars well spent as he reported liquor coming from Omaha was a "pretty good" grade and better than moonshine. A testimonial of sorts was provided by the witness, Charles Fulton, as he shared his research results. American Bourbon whiskey from Frank Kawa was cited as one of the better makes, and Gus "Curly" Fagerberg was complimented, as it were, for his grade of homemade whiskey. Clan Campbell whiskey, produced from the City Club Beverage Company, was a genuine product but probably "cut."[54]

Another government witness, Clifford Hill, traveled from the state penitentiary where he was serving a four year manslaughter sentence in connection with the slaying of a still tender. Hill told the packed courtroom about the 150 to 200 hijackings he had participated in and around Omaha. On every occasion but two, he recalled delivering the stolen goods to conspiracy co-defendant William Maher. Locating the stills or their trucks was a simple matter of keeping watch on known retailers until a shipment arrived, then following the truck back to its still.[55] Roy Towl was summoned to the witness box and narrated his travails as police commissioner, availing himself of his highly publicized public forum. Ironically, the day Towl's testimony appeared in the *World-Herald*, it was the first time since the trial began that the case was not page one news. It was relegated to page six as Franklin Delano Roosevelt's election as president ranked as the sole story that fall able to squeeze the conspiracy trial into inner pages.[56]

Local news recaptured the front page the next day as Judge Woodrough freed Harry Buford and six others with a directed verdict in their favor, announcing insufficient evidence had been entered to connect the men with any conspiracy. Defense attorneys attempted to secure a similar boon for the remaining accused but the Judge denied their requests.[57] Unable to secure release for their clients, given Woodrough's decision, the defense now came forth as the prosecution rested its case. Ben Baker and his colleagues took the offensive by discrediting Tom Crawford, and a series of witnesses challenged his assertions of having been close to the "Old Man." He was portrayed as just another worker, a man not to be trusted, certainly never Dennison's secretary nor in any way in a confidential relationship with him. Crawford was remembered by George Yeager as a fellow who hung around headquarters, "chewed out" on one occasion by Dennison. And the idea of Crawford being a secretary was silly--no one did secretarial work for Dennison, according to the witness, and he did not even have a typewriter in his office.[58]

One after another defense witnesses refuted Crawford's claims and recollections of conversations. Patrick Boyle, a former newspaperman, proprietor of the Cornhusker Cigar Store for the most recent three years, denied Crawford's assertion that Dennison had a private office in his store. He was prepared to admit Dennison had an office upstairs in the building, but no private office in his place. What had happened, he said, was an effort to discourage loafers who had a habit of hanging around a small room in the store. To keep the loiterers away he had "Dennison" printed on the door, but the "Old Man" quickly had Boyle remove his name. That, said Boyle, was the end of Dennison's so-called office in the Cornhusker.[59]

City Commissioner Henry Dunn, Chief Pszanowski, City Prosecutor Alex Brundgardt, Assistant City Attorney Bernard

Boyle, and others castigated Crawford and the government's case. Mayor Metcalfe showed up to inform the court he had asked Dennison for help in solving the Lapidus murder. One witness remembered Crawford borrowing a typewriter from a shoestore adjacent to the Cornhusker Cigar Store, and telling the loaner not to say anything to anybody about a letter to Chicago he wanted stamps for. Detective Paul Borowiak testified he had been doing stenographic work for Dennison the past five years, when not on police duty, and he had seen Crawford neither around the office nor ever using Dennison's typewriter.[60]

Dennison took the stand on November 15, smiling his narrow smile occasionally, but for the most part serious, wearing "his familiar fighting face, his cold gray eyes glittering." Guided by Baker's questions, he went into a series of denials of Crawford's statements. No, he had never met Capone and did not know anything about Capone's system. No, he had never talked to anyone about a liquor syndicate in Omaha. No, he had never tried to influence police commissioners, nor had he anything to do with marking jury lists. He continued to deny all of Crawford's assertions: no, he had never told Crawford that Buford was to be in charge of the black district; no, Buford's consent was not necessary for arrests on the north side; no, officers did not make raids on his suggestion or orders; no, Crawford had not written any correspondence for him--personal or anonymous--(he did not believe in anonymous letters he added); and no, Crawford had never done any clerical or stenographic work for him; no, he never told Crawford to report to Marcell or Rawley, and Crawford "Never made a report to me in his life." Dennison's testimony was a lengthly disavowal of Crawford, an individual the "Old Man" declared he had never associated with.[61]

Following Dennison came his co-defendants: Potach denying any knowledge of any liquor plot or having conversations with Dennison about killing Livingston ("Certainly not"), and dismissing point by point testimony against him from government witnesses.[62] Neither Nesselhous nor Rawley knew anything about a liquor syndicate. Crawford had told the court Rawley gave him a list of good and bad places, that is, ones which had or had not made their campaign contributions, and to be raided or not raided accordingly. The lists referred to, Rawley testified, were actually campaign rosters, distributed to organization workers. Rawley assured the court Dennison never sent any messengers to him on any kind of business, and surely he and Marcell had never attempted to influence appointments of police officers--known bootleggers--to the south side.[63]

When Marcell took the stand he stated he had never heard anything about good or bad lists until the trial started. He denied telling Crawford which bootleggers were behind in their contributions (he knew nothing about protection money), and instructing them they better go see the "Toad." In fact Marcell was unaware Roscoe Rawley had the nickname of "Toad."[64] Nesselhous denied any partnership with Tom Dennison, though he acknowledged his telephone number was for a phone in Dennison's office. Since having to close the Budweiser because of prohibition, Nesselhous had, he confided, occupied himself with taking care of his health. The jury learned he also dabbled in stocks and bonds, and was president of the W.E. Nesselhous Realty Company.[65]

The defense rested its case on November 23, and the next day, for only the second time since the trial started, it failed to be weekday front page news. Motions for dismissal were introduced over the next couple of days, and late on a Saturday afternoon Judge Woodrough admitted he was unable to remember what the evidence was as it applied to this or that individual. He concluded by saying he was going to declare mistrial on Monday morning for all those where he was not positive what the issues and facts were. If he turned an individual over to the jury where such doubts existed in his own mind, the judge said he would be remiss in his duties.[66]

Thirty-two defendants went free Monday morning when Woodrough declared a mistrial for them; only sixteen now remained on trial for conspiracy to violate the prohibition act, including Dennison, Nesselhous, Rawley, Marcell, Sutton, Potach, Calamia, and Maher. Final arguments began that afternoon and after listening to Lawrence Shaw, an assistant U.S. attorney, for over an hour, Woodrough interrupted him. The judge admonished Shaw by saying he was yet to hear a word about liquor or violations of the liquor act. Then he asked the prosecution to say something that actually applied to the indictment. "I would like to know," Wood-

305

rough demanded, "what evidence there is to connect these defendants with violation of the liquor law."[67]

For the first time Dennison was not in court when it resumed the next morning. His record of never being late, never leaving early--one not matched by his co-defendants-- was broken by a case of pneumonia. Edson Smith continued for the prosecution, taking chalk in hand and on a six by eight foot chalkboard drew a chart for the jury of the government's perception of the syndicate. Top center he wrote "Central Direction," and two names--Dennison and Nesselhous. A south branch directorate was added, and the names of Roscoe Rawley and John Marcell were printed there-in; William Maher was written in as heading the north branch. Enforcement, immediately under Dennison and Nessel-hous, was the preserve, according to the chart, of Paul Sutton, Joe Potach, and Thomas Crawford. Other branches, such as distributors, hijackers, and dealers were added to provide jurors and newspaper readers the prosecution's interpretation of syndicate operations and its key figures, Tom and Billy, at the top. In his summation to the jury, Smith returned to the theme of Dennison's political activi-ties, for only with influence in decision making and en-forcement circles, Smith stated, was the syndicate and conspiracy charged by the government able to exist.[68]

Defense final arguments returned to a favored theme, Crawford's credibility as a witness. Ben Baker led the attack, for starters calling the government's star witness "everything that is vile." Then he accused Crawford of breaking his oath as a police officer, who, on top of that, broke his vows to his God, his church, and his family. Finally, perjury was added to Crawford's list of misdeeds. Baker scorned him as a man who saw the light only after he had been double-crossed by the "Old Man," that is, the attorney caustically added, after Dennison's refusal to help him when he was accused of automobile theft. Turning to the jurors, the eloquent Baker proclaimed:[69]

> It was not the light of Moses, not the light from heaven that Crawford saw, because after he had seen the light he crept into another man's home, stole his automobile, his wife and furniture, and traveled over the country with another man's wife at her ex-pense. I am saying the only light he saw was the light from the flames of perdition.

306

His client, concluded Baker, was "not a liar and contemptible rat like Crawford."[70]

On December 5 Judge Woodrough gave the jurors their final instructions, telling them that in a case of the type before them it was necessary to have proof a conspiracy was actually put into operation, plus evidence of money transactions. There was no testimony of money paid to any defendant the judge reminded his jurors, and he impressed upon them the accused did not have to prove they did not receive money--it was the government's job to prove they had. Did the individuals involved know a conspiracy existed and make themselves a part of it, Woodrough asked. As to the murders brought into the case, the judge observed there was no competent evidence introduced to prove any complicity by any of the defendants.

Acknowledging his opinions were not binding on them, Woodrough warned the jurors that Crawford's testimony had to be scrutinized with "caution and hesitancy." Attention was drawn to his participation in actions perpetrated by the machine, and the judge raised questions as to the reliability of an accomplice turned witness, seeking to justify himself and elicit sympathy by heaping obloquy on former friends. An injustice was in the offing, Woodrough closed, if the jurors failed to subject Crawford's testimony to an exacting analysis. He reminded them of the man's own testimony about writing anonymous letters which, according to the judge, "exemplified to us an abnormally deceitful bent of mind, unscrupulous in concocting falsehoods."[71]

Thus enlightened the jury went into deliberation. On the fifth day the jurors sent word they had a report to make, and when court convened on Friday afternoon the foreman announced agreement was unattainable. Woodrough appealed to the jury to persist and its members again went into seclusion and discussion. All the weekend they debated and voted, but when the jury was summoned for a progress report, "hopeless disagreement" were the words heard in the crowded courtroom. A week from the start of the jury's consideration of the guilt or innocence of Tom Dennison and the remaining defendants, mistrial was declared. One of the jurors later said the only thing they agreed upon was they did not admire Tom Crawford; everything else was hopeless deadlock and inability to find any one, pair, or more of the defendants guilty. Dennison was not in the courtroom when the case came to an end; he was home peacefully sleeping.[72]

It seems there was reason for his repose. After the trial and its result entered history, Edson Smith was summoned by a few of the ex-jurors to a meeting at the Hill Hotel. They told him they were sure at least one of co-jurors had been fixed. The name of the suspected bribed juror was given to him and he recognized it as the same one as written on a note slipped to him by a prohibition agent when the jury was being selected. After the name the words "no good" were on the note. Smith was aware by virtue of pre-trial work that the man in question was anti-prohibition but knew little else. He made a judgment the individual in question was not a strong personality, one incapable of swaying others or holding out, and challenged more formidable appearing types.[73]

That jurors had been contacted and a fix made remained vivid in the memory of a widow whose husband had served on the jury. One day a relative through marriage, a man from Omaha with political aspirations, visited the couple's farm near Hartington. The men went outside to talk, and what appeared to be a serious discussion went on for half an hour. After the visitor left, the husband related the gist of the conversation and its connection with the forthcoming Dennison trial. His name was on the list of prospective jurors and he was assured the trial was going to be lengthly. Selected jurors would be fortunate, because a daily fee was to be paid in addition to room and board. Think of it, said the hard pressed farmer, money to help tide them over the coming long and financially difficult winter of 1932-33. How they could make it unless some extra income became available? He was among the summoned; when the time came he went to Omaha, served as one of the jurors for the two month trial, and was paid for his services.

His wife visited him once during the trial, but there was no mention of proceedings or the nature of the case. When it was finally over, she was surprised to see her husband enter their home and stagger from door to chair. "I never thought I'd make it," he mumbled, "I never thought I'd make it." She asked what he meant and he told her the full story of the Omahan's visit. If selected as a juror, in return for serving and receiving his fee the visitor from Omaha had exacted a promise from the farmer--a vote of not guilty. Depression poor the farmer accepted the proposition, but as the days and weeks of the trial bore on he became convinced a "not guilty" was impossible. "I couldn't see voting for Tom Dennison as innocent," he told his wife, "he was guilty as hell." His oath had to take precedence over his promise. During the week of jury deliberations he became convinced others had been similarly contacted, but unlike himself stuck to an innocent vote and hung the jury. As for the farmer from Hartington, "I thought I'd get shot before I got out of town. I really did. I didn't think I'd ever see you again." For months thereafter the couple lived in fear of retribution, but events belied their anxiety and they went unharmed. Nonetheless, near a half century after the trial, the widow insisted upon anonymity.

There was no retrial; the federal government decided not to pursue the case since it was widely understood prohibition was soon to end. Dennison and his associates had been taken to court but not to jail. No matter--the trial had served its political purpose, the machine was irreparably damaged. When the mistrial was declared an editorial expressed disappointment, saying the outcome was unfortunate because it left open the question of guilt or innocence. But there were benefits, the writer went on, for "it has contributed to arousing the civic spirit. It has tended directly to put the city and all of its people more vigilantly on guard."[74] Towl and his comrades had succeeded. Their point was made and in a few months proof of their victory was registered at the polls.

There were no convictions, but Towl, Crawford, Kooken, O'Sullivan, Sorensen, Stalmaster, and Howell shed no tears when the mistrial was declared. Their mission was accomplished, as recognized by one of the accused when he looked back to the trial's consequences: "They hurt us politically. They hurt Dennison politically."[75] The "Old Man" and his men, their organization and methods, were front page news for over two months. Day after day activities previously either quietly rumored or tacitly accepted since so long established were transformed into notoriety and what became one of the two major stories of the year.

The accuracy and truthfulness of what passed from the

lips of Crawford and other prosecution witnesses were decried by the defense, but Towl's larger ambition was fulfilled regardless of witness veracity. An image was created, an image of machine evil emanating from offices in the Karbach Building and entering city hall, the police department, and eventually citizens' lives and homes. The courtroom inspired image supplanted tolerance, sympathy, or esteem for the "Old Man" in those lives and homes. In late October, well before the trial's end, Roy Towl wrote to an associate in Chicago to tell him the Omaha case was proceeding satisfactorily. He conveyed his thanks for assistance received from the Secret Six, then expressed the haunting loneliness of the challenger: "I regret that other officials and citizens of Omaha have not joined me in this fight . . . ." Then he forecast a return to more traditional political methods than he had been following for a year: "we expect by next spring that we will have a good organization in the open and for our cause."[76]

As the 1933 city election approached, an open organization did appear, the Independent Voters League. Formally constituted on the 12th day of January at the Elk's Club, the IVL promised "a new deal for the voters and taxpayers and a general change at City Hall." Officers and an executive committee were selected, and the civic reaction Towl and Crawford had anticipated was underway.[77] Homage to the conspiracy trial for laying the foundation for the successful advent of the IVL was made by a founder and member of the executive committee. He and the others recognized a strong factor in their winning the next election was the trial's exposure of machine machinations: Dennison was ripe for plucking "because of the feeling from that conspiracy trial."

In composition the IVL, the founding member recalled, was dominated by middle class people: no big names, no big monied figures. Many came to the organization because they needed jobs, and jobs were filled by "ins." And it looked like the IVL was going to provide the next incumbents for city hall, thanks again to the preceding fall's much publicized events in a federal courtroom. Little change was outwardly evident among Dennison's upper class supporters, for those in the higher circles who had been pro-Dennison remained so. But another IVL supporter carried the memory of many businessmen who were willing to contribute to the effort confidentially, they too cognizant of change in the offing and seeking to preserve a place in the corridors of power.[78]

Roy Towl was willingly recruited into the IVL, and in an address to the group returned again to the Lapidus case, branding it the darkest page in Omaha police history. After providing a recap of his city department transfers thanks to the Dennison dominated commission, he captioned the campaign's paramount issue as ridding the city of organized crime and vice.[79] As the election headed toward the primary, the *World-Herald* editorialized that the city's temper was for change and new blood in the city council.[80] For the first time in the memory of many Omahans, a primary was held without a certified Dennison slate. A Blue ticket did surface, touted as Dennison selections, but the candidates listed disclaimed any connection with or knowledge of it. Commissioner Koutsky, long a compatriot of the "Old Man," was one of the disclaimers and added a political epitaph: "I honestly don't think Dennison's taking any part in this. He left for California the other day, and I think he'd stay if he had anything to do with it. He's a sick man."[81]

Dennison did return from the west coast a couple of days later, to a city where disagreement reigned as to whether he was or was not participating in the election--or even could. As early as January the press was serving notice in the trial's aftermath that the machine and Dennison were broken. Malcolm Baldrige, a one term second district Congressman (1931-1933), almost a month to the day after the trial ended, was depicted in an editorial cartoon with a rope over his shoulder, towing a broken down automobile ("The old Dennison machine") from a political dump, with the caption "I can make a new one out of it I Betcha."[82]

Baldrige had been contacting people in Omaha, claiming the backing of businessmen, and asserting his desire to "in fact play the role of a well known political arbiter of many years standing."[83] He called a confidential meeting of members of the organization and told them he had gone to see Tom Dennison and asked him right out if he was going to be head of the ring anymore. Dennison replied "no," his aspirant successor reported, and the "Old Man" said he was leaving Omaha for good. Baldrige then asked if he could take charge and Dennison gave his permission. Endowed with a privately secured right of succession, Baldrige informed the men he had gathered he was now head of the organization. He was going to run Omaha and take care of men who needed jobs. All that was necessary was for his selections to be elected and he would then take care of Towl and Butler.[84] But his choices were not elected and Mr. Baldrige's short tenure as Dennison's successor was over. The election shattered his Omaha political ambitions as well as what was left of the machine.

On election day only two incumbents were elected, John H. Hopkins and Towl. The other five were Towl's companions on the IVL slate; all six of the IVL candidates had won. Their victory was complete and Roy Towl was selected by his fellow commissioners to become Omaha's new mayor.[85] For the first time since 1918, and only the second time since the turn of the century, the machine's opponents dominated city hall. And this time there was no return. Long time workers looked into the debris of their machine and wondered who might be able to restore it. Nesselhous was ill, wealthy, and uninterested. Others approached had diminished zeal for political combat because of their now comfortable station in life or advanced age. Billy Maher attributed the failure of leadership to two factors: men who might have taken over were too old, and others did not have "guts enough to get out front."[86]

Dennison's loyal ally failed to note that his leader, like his counterparts in many other cities, had run a highly personalized machine but deficient since one part, the "Old Man's," was crafted as irreplaceable. A system providing for succession was unthinkable when the ambitious were perceived as challengers to destroy rather than heirs to groom. When Dennison's personal power and will left him (and neither had in 1918), his creation, without substructure or blueprint for succession, was unable to carry on. Machine politics in Omaha were over.

By now history had claimed the great waves of immigration, and a growing and politically conscious middle class was on the scene, prepared to legislate reforms in city politics when given, or taking, the opportunity. Increasingly national in outlook, the business community was shedding its predominately local and regional orientation. Aged and ill, the "Old Man," a power for so long, was increasingly California's guest. Nationally and locally change was beckoning in the early 1930s as the depression spread discontent, and incumbents at all levels of government were threatened because they were "ins." The designs and timing of Towl and his associates were favored by the environment.

Dennison's encounter with the court does not provide the sole explanation for his downfall since the above forces were gnawing at machine politics in America. But it does expose the immediate impetus to his defeat, the crucial factor in the interplay of currents characterizing Omaha in the early 1930s. His opponents proved the more skillful in his final contest as a small group of willful people, blocked in the more conventional channels of political battle, effectively used the legal system to realize political ambitions. Courtroom and attendant news coverage provided the means to alienate the machine's long faithful voters. The fall conspiracy trial was the prelude to last rites administered in the spring elections.

Dennison returned to California and Omahans never again saw him outside the Karbach Building, feeding the pigeons. Their final farewell came the following February when his body came home for burial at Forest Lawn Cemetery, next to Ada and their two infant sons. Dennison was injured in an automobile accident near San Diego in late January 1934 while being driven to a horse race track. His driver later said another car caused a collision; a family version said Dennison's car swerved to avoid hitting a dog in the road. On February 14, 1934, Thomas Dennison died of a cerebral hemorrhage. Over a thousand people attended his funeral, among them leading personalities of Omaha's political and law enforcement communities. The monument at the grave site is large and imposing, like Tom was, and only one word appears: "Dennison." For those who know him and his times, nothing more is necessary.

Chapter IX

[1]O'Connor's *The Last Hurrah* thesis has been effectively challenged by Lyle Dorsett, *The Pendergast Machine*, and in his *Franklin D. Roosevelt and the City Bosses*. See also Stave, *The New Deal and the Last Hurrah: Pittsburgh Machine Politics*; Roger Biles, *Big City Boss in Depression and War: Mayor Edward J. Kelly of Chicago* (DeKalb: Northern Illinois University Press, 1984). On decline of political machines see Banfield and Wilson, *City Politics*, pp. 121-127, 263-265, 330-331; Gosnell, *Machine Politics Chicago Style* (Chicago: University of Chicago Press, 1937), pp. 183-186; Tarr, *A Study in Boss Politics, William Lorimer of Chicago*, pp. 67-68; Salter, *Boss Rule: Portraits in City Politics*, pp. 242, 258; Harvard, "From Bossism to Cosmopolitanism," pp. 84-94; Cornwell, "Bosses, Machines and Ethnic Groups," pp. 27-39; McKitrick, "The Study of Corruption," pp. 502-514; Fuchs, "Some Political Aspects of Immigration," pp. 10-31.

[2]Harold Zink, *City Bosses in the United States* (Durham: Duke University Press, 1930), p. 56. Zink's book is one of the few in the vast literature on bossism that takes a comparative approach to the subject.

[3]*Ibid.*, p. 59.

[4]*Ibid.*, pp. 100-111. Alexander B. Callow, Jr. points out that in Tweed's case "the crusade against the Tweed Ring won the battle and lost the war." Callow, "The Crusade Against the Tweed Ring," from his *The Tweed Ring* (New York: Oxford University Press, 1966), reprinted in Callow, *The City Boss in America* (New York: Oxford University Press, 1976), pp. 194-214; the quotation is from p. 212.

[5]Zink, *City Bosses*, pp. 57-58. See Miller, *Boss Cox's Cincinnati*, pp. 205-240. Cox's legal problems drew bitter reaction from President Taft and the GOP brought pressure on Cox to resign. He refused one week and quit the next.

[6]Zink, *City Bosses*, p. 349.

[7]*Ibid.*, p. 289.

[8]*Ibid.*, pp. 316, 57.

[9]*Ibid.*, pp. 58, 56, 34.

[10]Bean, *Boss Ruef's San Francisco*, p. 204.

[11]*Ibid.* See Zink, *City Bosses*, pp. 354-361.

[12]In 1929 a New Jersey legislative committee became intrigued by the fact Hague was able to live as an obviously wealthy person on but an $8,000 a year salary. Three hundred thirty-five witnesses provided 8,200 pages of testimony and it appeared Hague was in serious trouble. However, he marshaled his forces and never was even indicted. See Steinberg, *The Bosses*, pp. 37-40. Reformers challenged Daley's machine and in the 1972-74 years he saw several associates indicted and convicted for

an array of offenses. But it appears it does not suffice to convict underlings as a reform tactic, at least not in Chicago. See Len O'Connor, *Clout* (New York: Avon, 1975), pp. 4-5, and 238-257.

[13]See Dorsett, *Franklin D. Roosevelt and the City Bosses*, pp. 48, 97; according to Steinberg, "Roosevelt played along with Hague through most of his first two presidential terms because the boss controlled the state's delegation to the national convention and the presidential electoral vote." Steinberg, *The Bosses*, pp. 62-63.

[14]Dorsett, *The Pendergast Machine*, p. 121. Lloyd Stark's break with Pendergast, who had helped make him governor, was motivated by political ambition; limited to one term in the governor's mansion, Stark set his sights on the U.S. Senate seat held by Harry Truman, who was backed by the Kansas City boss. Therefore, Stark separated himself from Pendergast and became a reformer with the avowed goals of exposing the machine's corruption and thereby embarrassing Truman. See *Ibid.*, pp. 77-79. See also Maurice Milligan, *Missouri Waltz* (New York: Charles Scribner's Sons, 1948). The book's subtitle is "The Inside Story of the Pendergast Machine by the Man Who Smashed it." Milligan asserts his book "is a true account of how the Federal Government closed in on Pendergast and rocked his political machine to its foundations." *Ibid.*, p. 169.

[15]Dorsett, *Franklin D. Roosevelt and the City Bosses*, p. 34. See also James Michael Curley, *I'd Do It Again* (Englewood Cliffs, New Jersey: Prentice-Hall, 1957), pp. 327-328.

[16]According to Joseph F. Dineen, "If Boston wanted to get rid of Curley it would do so very handily. It didn't care to have anybody in Washington do it for them." Dineen, *The Purple Shamrock* (New York: W.W. Norton, 1949), p. 291. For additional reading on bosses and their courtroom problems see Samuel P. Orth, *The Boss and the Machine* for brief but useful portraits of Tweed, McManes, Butler, Cox, Ruef, and Ames. See also Tarr, *A Study in Boss Politics: William Lorimer of Chicago*. In Lorimer we find another boss whose political influence dwindled after being charged with, among other things, unlawful use of funds (he was acquitted).

[17]Memorandum, Roy Towl, "Concerning Potach and Allen," n.d., Towl papers, Box 1, Folder 1932, January 1-14, City Hall.

[18]EOW-H, April 18, 1933. Also letter, Crawford to Stalmaster, September 13, 1932, Sorensen papers, Box 39, Folder 191.

[19]Maher interview, October 23, 1979.

[20]Letter, Crawford to Edson Smith, April 19, 1932, Sorensen papers, Box 35, Folder 65; also MOW-H, November 12, 1932, and letter, Murphy to "Dear Friend Gene," May 30, 1932, Sorensen papers, Box 35, Folder 65, and letter, Crawford to Edson Smith, April 18, 1932, Sorensen papers, Box 35, Folder 65.

[21]EOW-H, October 18, 1932, and letter, Crawford to Gene, March 16, 1932, Sorensen papers, Box 35, Folder 65.

[22]Letter, Murphy to O'Sullivan, February 18, 1932. Sorensen papers, Box 35, Folder 65.

[23]"Report on the investigation of the murder of Harry Lapidus," Don L. Kooken to C.A. Sorensen, March 2, 1932, Sorensen papers, Box 39, Folder 191.

[24]Letter, Murphy to Charles B. McDonald, April 1, 1932, Sorensen papers, Box 35, Folder 66.

[25]Edson Smith interview, October 9, 1979; Shafton interview, October 3, 1979.

[26]Letter, Murphy to "Dear Friend Roy," April 19, 1932, Sorensen papers, Box 35, Folder 66.

[27]Letter, Murphy to O'Sullivan, March 18, 1932, Sorensen papers, Box 35, Folder 65; and letter, Murphy to Towl, June 1, 1932, *Ibid.* Crawford frequently lamented about his financial condition in his letters and appealed for help from O'Sullivan and Towl.

[28]Copy of the letter, dated May 9, 1932, is in *Ibid.*

[29]Bulletin, Towl, "Liquor Syndicate," n.d., Towl papers, Box 2, Folder 1933, November-December, Mayor.

[30]Maher interview, October 30, 1979.

[31]EOW-H, October 13, 1932; MOW-H, December 2, 1932.

[32]MOW-H, December 6, 1932.

[33]*The New York Times*, October 30, 1932, Pt. II, p. 6:1.

[34]MOW-H, December 1, 1932.

[35]Memorandum, "Liquor Syndicate," n.d., Towl papers, Box 2, Folder 1932, November-December, Mayor.

[36]*Ibid.*

[37]Letter, Murphy to O'Sullivan, March 18, 1932, Sorensen papers, Box 35, Folder 65.

[38]Letter, Murphy to O'Sullivan, February 18, 1932, *Ibid.*

[39]Letter, Murphy to O'Sullivan, March 30, 1932, *Ibid.*

[40]Document 7025 contains several search warrants and some thirty pages of wiretap transcripts. These are apparently but a sampling of the "endless pages" presented during the trial, taking from Thursday, October 27, to the following Thursday to read into the record, with two days out for the weekend. See EOW-H, October 28-November 3, 1932.

[41]Maher interview, October 23, 1979.

[42]Letter, Towl to Amos Woodcock, October 31, 1932, Towl papers, Box 1, Folder 1932, October-December, City Hall.

[43]Letter, Murphy to O'Sullivan, June 10, 1932, Sorensen papers, Box 35, Folder 65.

[44]Letter, Sorensen to Senator R.B. Howell, May 14, 1932, Nebraska State Historical Society, R.B. Howell Collection, Box S, Correspondence, "Son-Sou."

[45]*Ibid.*, Letter, Howell to Sorensen, May 19, 1932.

[46]*Ibid.*, Letter, Howell to Sorensen, June 28, 1932.

[47]Document 7025.

[48]EOW-H, October 6, 7, 8, 10, 11, 12, 1932.

[49]*Ibid.*, October 12, 1932.

[50]MOW-H, November 30, 1932.

[51]EOW-H, October 18, 1932.

[52]*Ibid.*, October 28, November 1, 2, 3, 4, 1932; Nance's testimony was on November 3.

[53]*Ibid.*, November 7, 8, 1932.

[54]*Ibid.*, November 9, 1932.

[55]*Ibid.*, November 7, 1932.

[56]*Ibid.*, November 9, 1932.
[57]*Ibid.*, November 10, 1932.
[58]*Ibid.*, November 11, 1932.
[59]*Ibid.*, November 12, 1932.
[60]*Ibid.*, November 15, 1932.
[61]*Ibid.*, November 16, 1932.
[62]*Ibid.*, November 18, 1932.
[63]*Ibid.*, November 22, 1932.
[64]*Ibid.*, November 23, 1932.
[65]*Ibid.*, November 22, 1932.
[66]Sunday OW-H, November 27, 1932.
[67]MOW-H, November 29, 1932.
[68]*Ibid.*, November 30, 1932.
[69]*Ibid.*, December 1, 1932.
[70]*Ibid.*
[71]*Ibid.*, December 6, 1932.
[72]*Ibid.*, December 13, 1932.
[73]Smith interviews, April 4, 1974, and October 9, 1979.
[74]MOW-H, December 13, 1932.
[75]Maher interview, October 23, 1979.
[76]Letter, Towl to Alexander G. Jamie, Chicago, October 26, 1932, Towl papers, Box 1, Folder 1932, October-December, City Hall.
[77]MOW-H, January 13, 1933. Bernard R. Stone, attorney, was elected president and chair of the executive committee; William H. Campen, head of Omaha Testing Laboratories, became secretary, and Max Barish was vice-president. Members of the executive committee were: Seymour Smith, Dennis E. O'Brien, C. Ray McKay, C.J. Southard, Richard Meissner, Sam Beber, Frank Frost, Harold Linahan, H.J. Lindeman, John Martig, Nelson Thorson, and Bernard Stone, chairman.
[78]Frost interview, October 30, 1979.
[79]EOW-H, March 14, 1933.
[80]*Ibid.*, April 6, 1933.
[81]*Ibid.*, April 4, 1933.
[82]MOW-H, January 12, 1933.
[83]Sunday OW-H, January 8, 1933.
[84]Report to Towl, n.d., Towl papers, Box 1, Folder 1933, January-April, City-Hall.
[85]EOW-H, May 3, 1933.
[86]Maher interview, October 23, 1979.

317

CHAPTER X

Conclusion

We are just a little part of the cosmos,
and a part can't know the entirety.
A period, a comma, can't understand the sentence.
--Georges Simenon

Percy Shelley's "Ozymandias" imparts both the arrogance and the transience of power. Vain and self-confident words hurl from the pedestal of Ozymandias's once glorious statue, celebrating the years he and his monument were vital and fearsome, possessed of immortality: "Look on my works, ye Mighty, and despair!" Today nothing but the pedestal, lightened of most its load, remains. Ozymandiases come and go, kingdoms and nations rise and fall, one political organism replaces another within the permanent context of survival, struggle, and power. Over the centuries humankind has sired a host of political forms, shaping diverse arrangements to determine who should rule and why they should be obeyed. Forms have changed, but ruled and rulers endure.

Political machines emerged in American cities in response to a confluence of forces in the late nineteenth century. Having made their appearance, the boss and his organization became formidable political organisms, spreading amoeba-like to flow into all levels and segments of society. Able to swing elections with the aid of his loyal workers, the boss became a city's power broker, the man sought by all who courted favors from city hall. The bosses were men who well understood the essential nature of political power. Their machines in their multifarious activities were constantly engaged in exercising it.

Those generous of their loyalty, time, and money were well rewarded. From the boss's cornucopia flowed jobs, recognitions, and rewards, both material and immaterial. Since the boss controlled the flow he was also able to punish by withholding his largess, and given his control of the police was able to inflict penalties varying from minor harassment to incarceration. Reliance upon the gift of reward and the weapon of punishment earned the boss a double image. One side of him was open pocket generosity, tendered by a man of his word to be turned to and trusted in a time of adversity. His beneficence won gratitude and loyalty. But the same man was feared for his powers of retribution, applied as necessary to keep "someone in line" or "jam" him. The boss had tremendous economic strength at his behest, thanks to his business allies, in addition to his political influence and sheer physical muscle. Opponents feared and hated him for his raw power. Shed of his generous facade, he was drawn as a corruptor of citizens, an enemy of morality and probity because of his fraudulent political activities and tolerance of vice.

Thomas Dennison ran a quintessential political machine, one with an enduring legacy. One seeking to understand contemporary Omaha's political institutions need search little further than the Dennison years, for to examine those years is to learn that what was hitherto taken for granted merely because it was there is transformed into a consequence of our heritage. Mayors and city councilmen are elected on nonpartisan ballots, seen by reformers as basic to breaking a boss's political influence by separating party from city government. It did not work out that way in Omaha; Dennison continued to win because of his superior organization, but nonpartisanship remains nonetheless a strong value at the city level. For many years elections for the city council were on the reformer favored at-large system, designed in response to the days of bossism to reduce the power of the ward heeler and ward based politics. Whenever Omahans were given the opportunity to revert to a district system by referendum, the majority said "no," a collective distrust demonstrated against the old politics. Only by its advocates going to the state legislature did district elections return to Omaha.

Every time an Omahan deals with a city or county civil servant who is under the merit system, reads about or participates in the bidding system for city contracts and construction, or registers and casts a secret ballot, the "Old Man" is alongside. Even though many in the city have never heard of him, Tom Dennison is part of their lives because he is part of their city's past. Since Dennison physically left the scene, Omaha has known steady growth albeit unspectacular. The Karbach Block which housed his office and the post office building where he was tried are long gone, replaced by structures embarked upon making their own history. Dennison's mentor, Edward Rosewater, had a public elementary school named after him (for his work in education--not in honor of his relationship with the "Old Man"); it lasted for many decades but was closed in 1983. In memory of the "Perpetual Mayor" Omahans have done little. There is brief Dahlman Avenue in South Omaha, just north of the Livestock Exchange Building and the stock yards where he worked when he first came to the city. A small park, easy to miss, just a few blocks south of the old third ward likewise bears his name, but few people know it exists.

Rosewater earned a school, now closed, and Dahlman garnered his two minor public mementos. No statue or public building reminds people of Frank Johnson, the very silent partner, but his Omaha Printing Company is large and prosperous. Johnson's creation is no longer downtown, having moved to spacious quarters in energetic south central Omaha. For Dennison there are neither streets, parks, schools, nor private enterprises. Cities are not wont to grant public recognition to bosses who ruled from behind the mayor's chair rather than in it. He founded no company to carry on his entrepreneurial spirit because his business was politics and his heritage must be sought in that domain. No buildings or statues for the "Old Man," but his monuments, sculpted by reformers, are in our political processes.

An autopsy of the political organism called the Dennison machine reveals intricacy, complexity, pervasiveness, and capacity for good and for evil. People from all walks of life contributed to and profited from its existence, not out of perverseness or admiration of machine politics, but because it was there, because it was the means to satisfy a goal. He was convenient given the political order of the times and for a price he delivered. It was the way business was done and neither apology nor guilt weighted down participants. The goal may have been keeping a brothel or a speakeasy open, or a retail business seeking a favor from city hall. The means was cooperating with Tom Dennison who, for a price, oversaw realization of those goals. Omaha's two worlds, the legitimate upperworld and the criminal underworld, converged on Tom Dennison as they sought his remedial powers but they did not merge. Two separate cities co-existed within the city limits, each with its own spatial and psychological territory. Dennison inhabited and was important to both.

He moved among the city's financial elite, and he also knew the gamblers and thieves. He was the middleman, the power balancer, helping to run a steady city, a safe city, satisfactorily providing for the upperworld a milieu where stability and financial security took precedence over rapid change. Stability and financial security were also assets for the underworld and Dennison here too delivered stability and thereby financial security. Working through Rosewater and later Johnson, he serviced the needs of one of his communities; alone or with Nesselhous he served the second. Through the interrelated, interconnected mechanisms of his machine he delivered elections and gained the influence to fulfill his promises. Stability was coveted by the two cities and Dennison responded by "keeping the lid on." He helped maintain a community proper for business as usual, whatever the business. In general he made possible a city where anything was available for the pleasure seeker, but controlled the elements providing the pleasures. Both illegitimate and legitimate businesses generally found arrangements satisfactory.

Omaha has a reputation as a conservative place, steady and stable, not prone to dramatic or sudden shifts in its way of life. It is a city where the words "average," or "nice" are used to describe it rather than extremes one way or the other. It is a city of neither delicate beauty nor great ugliness, neither far behind nor ahead of the times. It is a working city and "moderation" is its motto. Once more Omahans find in the Dennison years explanation for an important condition of their lives. During their city's years of adolescence a political machine cooperated with powers in the community who stressed the very characteristics said to characterize the adult: stability, moderation, caution, and orderliness. The formative years were the Dennison years and he and his allies established modes of thought which continue to prevail.[1]

The machine is long gone, but the quest for survival

and power continues in Omaha as elsewhere. Context alters but not the nature of the contest. Many changes have come to pass, evident in population increases and the city's growth both up and out. A mayor-council form of government was approved by voters in 1956 (with nonpartisan, at-large elections of course), abandoning the commission style familiar for so many Dennison campaigns. Political equality at the ballot box is more of a reality today than in Dennison's era, but the fact some persons exercise political influence well beyond their individual vote through profession or family political background is obvious.

What does not remain is any semblance of a political machine. Influentials and persons seeking influence, yes. Political conflict, differences over who should rule and how and do what, certainly. Political candidates accusing one another of having a political machine, oh yes, betraying another heritage of the Dennison years. In an electoral contest the temptation is great to brand the opponent with leading a political machine, a throwback to bygone days when the boss flourished. But an organization operating as the "Old Man's," structured like his, enjoying the loyalty that was his, able to deliver votes and reward its partisans and punish its enemies as he did--no.

When he abandoned the organization he had led so long he left nothing behind. In three decades of leadership he made no provision for succession, made no effort to institutionalize his machine. His was a common failing among the bosses. Their organizations were highly personal structures, cults of personalities, and they suffered no improvisations suggesting they could be replaced. Irreplaceable, there was no need to be concerned with replacement. After Pendergast, after Crump, after Hague, and after many other bosses, host cities became absent of political machines as their central figures left the scene. Rather than establishing permanent structures and means of political succession, they had personalized their power. In only two cities did political machines defy for many years the waves of changes used to explain the end of bossism. In New York and Chicago the machine became larger than its human parts, and despite changes and challenges that helped dismantle other political machines these endured. A succession of bosses came and went in the two cities, testimony to their institutionalizing means to transfer power and adapt.

323

Dennison's machine, like most others, was personal, and the loyalty and fealty built over so many years was to him alone. His workers became his survivors, not his successors. When a monarch dies the line of succession ensures the transfer of power (as elections provide for succession in a democracy or in Vatican City) and loyal subjects raise their glasses to toast "The King is dead, Long Live the King." When Dennison left the scene, the toast was only to the first phrase. From Nebraska and Iowa farm lad, to laborer in the southwest, thence to gambling palaces in several states, finally to Omaha where he captured political power and acquired financial security, Thomas Dennison was a colorful man who helped his city progress steadily and cautiously from frontier town to gateway city. Thousands of people responded with devotion and loyalty to the "Old Man's" helping hand. A lobbyist of sorts, he was a representative of ordinary people who had little political voice and less influence. They went to him or his lieutenants with their problems, and the organization secured redress. When Dennison left the scene, so did the peoples' lobbyist.

His Irish charm was well known, and like his ancestors he understood that official governments and office holders are not always the most powerful or attended to. He realized that behind the facade of government, unofficialdom is often more potent and there he placed himself. He was a keen student of humankind, well informed by his experiences as gambler and politician on its foibles and weaknesses. Thomas Dennison political boss and Thomas Hobbes political philosopher had no disagreement on human motivations: fear and self-interest. Tom Dennison was long good at what he did, very good, and earns admiration for his years of political astuteness and organizational skills. However, there was a dark side to him which mitigates admiration for he was a man "with mud on his shoes." There is a temptation to rationalize and say it was the nature of his trade to be sullied by the underworld city, that he was a man of his times and acted accordingly. But he was drawn too far from his preserve of pragmatic political leader, transforming into a man led by his own hubris and thence into error and underestimation of his foes. A complex mixture of contributions toward peoples' well being and actions dismally detrimental to the lives of others gathered in Tom Dennison. He would not claim great credit for the first, given his motivations, nor plead guilty to the latter, circumstances being what he understood them to be.

Political leaders trod a narrow path intersecting with beguiling byways. Depending upon their personal background and character, their interpretation of reality, leaders make decisions determining which byways they will follow. In the lofty domain of leadership, choices are made amidst the ever present peril of tragedy. Elevated beyond the restrictions of their inferiors, leaders initiate actions or issue commands their followers cannot. On one side of the leader's path are byways leading to enoblement, decisions made in the rarified atmosphere of power to enhance the human condition. On the other side are those which debase, misuses of power wherein distinctions between self-interest and general interest have vanished. The byways of abuse are especially likely to be chosen when power is challenged. Thus the phenomenon of fear of the loss of power leading to the power holder's corruption.

The tragedy of leadership is of two dimensions, one forgiving the other condemning. A leader enters the first compelled by his followers' collective well being, on their behalf making decisions sometimes violative of personal ethics and general standards of morality. Conscience suffers and someone suffers, a tragedy, but the consequences are deemed worthy by the led and by history and the leader is forgiven although personally wounded. The second dimension is the preserve of those who suffer from the arrogance of power. The tragedy here is power abused for self-serving purposes, and actions initiated which are demeaning and condemning. Tom Dennison was a political leader who took byways into the second dimension. Gifted with high native intelligence, shrewdness, and charm, he also possessed the capacity for both kindness and cruelty necessary for leadership. He chose a profession proper to his talents and it proved to be one he excelled in and he prospered. It also proved ultimately to be a costly one.

Three decades of leadership earned him both loyal followers and adamant opponents, the fate of any person long in a position of power. He was both loved and hated with reasons for both in ample measure. In the late 1920s his power was greater than ever and his opposition was near impotent. The less than mighty had good reason to look and despair. Yet power is elusive and what appears substantial is difficult to sustain, a condition leaders better realize than followers. Challengers are magnified and means to combat them are magnified--the second dimension beckons. The leader, Tom Dennison, arrogant in his power and fearful of seeing it taken away responded.

He was a potent force in Omaha for over three decades and finally reached the point where he called upon the mighty to despair and prudential leadership gave way to vain adventurism. No evidence exists to render a guilty verdict against Tom Dennison for any heinous crime. But considering his control of the underworld and his dominion over the "guns," he stands as implicated in the murders of Gene Livingston, George Kubik, and Harry Lapidus. The two racketeers were disposed of without fear of punishment or public consternation, paving the way for a third victim's death warrant. Success engendered success. But Lapidus's execution was the step too far, taken by men and led by a man who thought there was no longer any limits on their power. They learned differently. In the midst of the trans-formations overcoming the nation and foreshadowing the end of bossism, Roy Towl and his associates delivered a fatal blow to the Dennison machine. The conspiracy trial stands not alone as responsible for the 1933 final defeat, for general historical currents were at work reforming the political contours and Dennison was now an elderly and ill man. Voters went to the polls in a depression wracked economy, not an advantageous situation for incumbents. Nonetheless, the trial provided a key impetus and justification for voters to desert the organization, as Dennison himself did even before the votes were cast.

NOTES

Chapter X

[1]On Omaha's conservatism and one man's efforts to foster change, see Harl A. Dalstrom, *A.V. Sorensen and the New Omaha* (Omaha: Lamplighter Press, Douglas County Historical Society, 1988).

Appendix

The limited nature of Thomas Dennison's formal education is evident in his letters. Two examples are provided here, one from him to Victor Rosewater, dated April 9, year unclear but pre-World War I; the second to Homer Morris, dated March 9, 1901, one of three letters reproduced on a first page of the *Omaha Daily News* in 1904.

Dear Mr. Rosewater

Your welcome letter came are all and it was just what I wanted all the news all thoe I get the Bee every day do you think they can sadisfy the Governor office with Fedral apointments _?_ will not have?

I am getting posted on machine _?_ they are quite a few hear from Tammany Hall and I am getting posted up all thoe the way they runs Politicts hear in the Springs discounts Tammany or any where else. after you leave Omaha and find out what they do all round the country I have come to the conclusion that Omaha is the bannor city as far as Honesty is concerned in the hole country The Doctor will not let me go for two weeks yet that will put me all most to the first of May. This last few days I have been feeling splendid I see I J Dunn is doing that will gain them nothing one thing I have we will have to elect our county attorney this fall I hear Dunn has been playing poker in the Jacksman Club in the last couple of weeks it will not be outlawed when [no name provided] goes out of office. hoping you have a fine time ect. with best wishes I will close yours

TD

Source: Letter to Victor Rosewater, April 9, 190 _?_ , from TD at L the Arlington-Histman Hotels, Hot Springs, Arkansas. Rosewater Collection, microfilm, Reel 2, Box 1924. Omaha Public Library.

Omaha, Nebraska March 9, 1901

Mr. Homer Morris, Melbourne, Iowa:

   I thought I would drop you a line to hand to Sherman
or as we have all ways called him the Kid since he has
seene fit to keepe my watch and pistels which he has dilib-
erate stolen I will put him in mind of what I have done for
him and how ungrateful he is and how much he owes me.

   the money he got in cash from me was in the fall of
1892 Including money sent to him to Seattle to put up for a
bond that he jumped and money I sent him to jump out with
all so money I sent him to Calofornia all in the fall of
1892 was $3075.00 then in 1893 his trial cost $2,874.00
All so Charley Prince got $425.00 and afterward Hooker got
$295.00 this all was paid out by me and it was to his
freends and to protect him You hand him this all so the
folowing statement that is all moneys paid out as neere as
I can recolect and this is not puting in any thing for my
time and truble.

Tom Dennison

Source: Omaha Daily News, June 11, 1904.

BIBLIOGRAPHY

Newspapers

Chadron Record.
Denver Post.
Denver Republican.
Denver Times.
Examiner.
Jewish Press.
Leadville Chronicle Annual.
New York Times.
Omaha Bee.
Omaha Daily News.
Omaha World-Herald.
Red Oak Weekly Express
Rocky Mountain News.

Public Documents

Abstract of Votes Cast. Dawes County, Nebraska, Elections, Vol. I, II.
Chadron City Hall, Box 1895-1896.
City of Chadron, Boards and Personnal [sic] *1894-1903.*
City of Omaha, Council Chamber 1919.
City of Omaha Elections. Election Commissioner's Office, State of Nebraska, County of Douglas, City of Omaha.
(Dennison.) *The State of Iowa vs. Tom Dennison, The State of Iowa, County of Montgomery, In the District Court for Montgomery County, Documents 6122, Indictment for Robbery, 6123, Indictment for Receiving Stolen Property.*
Dennison Probate. County Court, Douglas County, Nebraska, in re Estate of Thomas Dennison, #21861, Fee Book 48, Page 296, Special.
Dennison, Thomas. File 5-45-13, Classified Subject Files of the Department of Justice, National Archives and Record Service.
Document No. 7025--Criminal, the U.S. of America vs. Thomas Dennison, et. al. Indictment: Conspiracy to Violate the National Prohibition Act. Signed: Earl D. Mallery, Foreman. Filed August 5, 1932, signed R.C. Hoyt, Clerk of the District Court.
General Index, Deeds. Dawes County, Nebraska, Vol. A.
Laws, Resolutions and Memorials Passed at the Regular Session of the First General Assembly of the Territory of Nebraska Convened at Omaha City, on the 16 Day of January, 1855. Sherman & Strickland, Territorial Printers, 1855.
Laws, Joint Resolutions and Memorials Passed at the Sixth and Seventh Session of the Legislative Assembly of the State of Nebraska, Begun and Held at the City of Lincoln, February, 17, 1870. Des Moines: Mills & Co., Printers and Publishers, 1871.
Minute Book, City of Chadron, 1894-1903.
Nebraska, Douglas County, "Criminal Appearance Docket," Vol. 21.
Nebraska, Douglas County, "District Court Journal," Vol. 176.

No. 4140, Criminal, United States District Court, District of Nebraska, Omaha Division. The United States of America vs. Dr. Lee Van Camp. Indictment Violation Sections 1 and 2 Harrison Anti-Narcotics Act, As Amended, Filed November 2, 1925, R.C. Hoyt, Clerk, by John Nicolson, Deputy.

Nesselhous Probate. County Court, Doublas County, Nebraska, in re Estate of William Nesselhous, Fee Book 53, Page 353.

Omaha Metropolitan Police Relief and Pension Fund Association Annual, 1909, 1925, 1926, 1931.

Record, Leadville City Council, 1885-1889.

The Revised Ordinances of the City of Omaha: also the City Charter, Former Charters of the City and Amendments thereto: Together with all State Laws Relating to the City. Omaha: Omaha Herald Steam Book and Job Printing House, 1872.

The Revised Ordinances of the City of Omaha, Nebraska, Embracing All Ordinances of a General Nature in Force April 1, 1890, Together with the Charter of Metropolitan Cities, the Constitutions of the United States and the Constitution of the State of Nebraska. Omaha: Gibson, Miller & Richardson, 1890.

Revised Ordinances of the City of Omaha, Nebraska, Embracing All Ordinances of a General Nature in Force August 1, 1905, Together with the Charter for Metropolitan Cities. Omaha: Klopp & Bartlett Co., 1905.

Thomas Dennison vs. The Daily News Publishing Company, In the District Court of Douglas County, Nebraska, Document 89.

Thomas Dennison vs. The Daily News Publishing Company, In the District Court of Douglas County, Nebraska, Document 91.

United States vs. Dr. Lee Van Camp (1925). File 12-45-8, Classified Subject Files of the Department of Justice, National Archives and Record Service.

Unpublished and Archival Material

Age, Arthur. "The Omaha Riot of 1919," unpublished master's thesis, Creighton University, 1964.

Bitzes, John G. "The Anti-Greek Riot of 1909--South Omaha," unpublished master's thesis, University of Omaha, 1964.

Collins, Milford Greta. Letter to author, March 30, 1979, in author's possession.

Dahlman, James. Papers, A/MSS, Nebraska State Historical Society.

Dahlman, James. Scrapbooks, Omaha Public Library.

Deutsch, A.P. Letters to author, July 16, August 2, and one in August undated (nine pages), 1980, in author's possession.

Hitchcock, Gilbert M. Papers, MS 3640, Box 2, Nebraska State Historical Society.

Howell, R.B. Collection, Nebraska State Historical Society.

Kerns, James Harvey. "Industrial and Business Life of Negroes in Omaha," unpublished master's thesis, University of Omaha, 1932.

Lindsey, Elizabeth, J. "A History of Woman Suffrage in Douglas County 1900-1920," unpublished typescript, Omaha Public Library.

Muir, Harold T. "The Formation and Adoption of the 1956 Omaha Home Rule Charter," unpubished master's thesis, University of Nebraska at Omaha, 1969.

Peterson, Garneth, O. "The Omaha City Council and Commission: A Profile, 1858-1930," unpublished master's thesis, University of Nebraska at Omaha, 1980.

Pratt, William C. "The Omaha Business Men's Association and the Open

Shop, 1903-1939," paper delivered at the 1984 Conference of the Organization of American Historians.

Rosewater Collection. Omaha Public Library.

Schmidt, William F. "Municipal Reform in Omaha from 1906 to 1914 as Seen Through the Eyes of the Omaha Press," unpublished master's thesis, University of Omaha, 1963.

Sorensen, Christian A. Papers, MS 2951, Box 35, File 65, Nebraska State Historical Society.

Towl, Roy. Papers, MS 3534, Box 1, Nebraska State Historical Society.

Zike, Irene S. "Some Aspects of Territorial and State Legislative Control of the Municipal Government of Omaha, 1857-1875," unpublished master's thesis, University of Omaha, 1946.

Select Books and Articles

Aeschbacher, W.D. "Development of the Sandhill Lake Country." *Nebraska History.* 27 (July-September, 1946), 205-221.

Aeschbacher, W.D. "Development of Cattle Raising in the Sandhills." *Nebraska History.* 28 (January-March, 1947), 41-64.

Bander, Edward J. *Mr. Dooley on the Choice of Law.* Charlottesville: The Michie Company, 1963.

Banfield, Edward C., and James Q. Wilson. *City Politics.* Cambridge: Harvard University Press and M.I.T. Press, 1963.

Bean, Walton. *Boss Ruef's San Francisco.* Berkeley and Los Angeles: University of California Press, 1968.

Biles, Roger. *Big City Boss in Depression and War: Mayor Edward J. Kelly of Chicago.* Dekalb: Northern Illinois University Press, 1984.

Blair, Edward and E. Richard Churchill. *Everybody Came to Leadville.* Gunnison, Colorado: B & B Printers, 1977.

Boorstin, Daniel J. *The American Democratic Experience.* New York: Random House, 1973.

Bryce, James. *The American Commonwealth.* Vol. II. New York: Macmillan and Company, 1891.

Burns, Robert H. "The Newman Ranches: Pioneer Cattle Ranches of the West." *Nebraska History.* 34 (March 1953), 21-32.

Callow, Alexander B., Jr., ed. *The City Boss in America: An Interpretive Reader.* New York: Oxford University Press, 1976.

------------------------------. *The Tweed Ring.* New York: Oxford University Press, 1966.

Capra, Fritjof. *The Turning Point: Science, Society, and the Rising Culture.* New York: Simon and Schuster, 1982.

Carey, Fred. *Mayor Jim: An Epic of the West.* Omaha: Omaha Printing Company, 1930.

Chudacoff, Howard. "Where Rolls the Dark Missouri Down." *Nebraska History.* 52 (Spring 1971), 1-30.

----------------------. *Mobile Americans: Residential and Social Mobility in Omaha 1880-1920.* New York: Oxford University Press, 1972.

----------------------. *The Evolution of American Urban Society.* 2nd ed. Englewood Cliffs: Prentice-Hall, Inc., 1981.

Coletta, Paolo E. "The Patronage Battle Between Bryan and Hitchcock." *Nebraska History.* 49 (Summer 1968), 121-137.

Cornwell, Elmer E., Jr. "Bosses, Machines, and Ethnic Groups," *The Annals of the American Academy of Political and Social Science.* 353 (May 1964), 27-39.

Curley, James Michael. *I'd Do It Again.* Englewood Cliffs: Prentice-Hall, Inc., 1957.

Dahlman, James C. "Recollections of Cowboy Life in Western Nebraska."

Nebraska History. 10 (October-December, 1927), 335-343.

Dalstrom, Harl A. *A.V. Sorensen and the New Omaha*. Omaha: Lamplighter Press, Douglas County Historical Society, 1988.

Davis, John Kyle. "The Gray Wolf: Tom Dennison of Omaha." *Nebraska History*. 58 (Spring 1977), 25-52.

------------------. "Jim Dahlman, Cowboy Mayor: Has Omaha Forgotten Him?" *Magazine of the Midlands*. April 3, 1977.

Dineen, Joseph F. *The Purple Shamrock: the Hon. James Michael Curley of Boston*. New York: W.W. Norton, 1949.

Dorsett, Lyle W. *The Pendergast Machine*. New York: Oxford University Press, 1968.

---------------------. *Franklin D. Roosevelt and the City Bosses*. Port Washington, New York: Kennikat Press, 1977.

Dustin, Dorothy Devereux. *Omaha & Douglas County: A Panoramic History*. Woodland Hills, California: Windsor Publications, Inc., 1980.

Fainstein, Norman I, and Susan S. Fainstein. *Urban Political Movements*. Englewood Cliffs: Prentice-Hall, 1974.

Filler, Louis. *The Muckrakers*. University Park: The Pennsylvania State University Press, 1968.

Frisbie, Mark. "The Fair That Put Omaha On the Map." *Magazine of the Midlands*. May 30, 1976.

Fuchs, Lawrence H., ed. *American Ethnic Politics*. New York: Harper Torchbacks, 1968.

Gosnell, Harold F. *Machine Politics Chicago Model*. 2nd ed. Chicago: University of Chicago Press, 1968.

Gottfried, Alex. "Political Machines." *International Encyclopedia of the Social Sciences*. Vol. XII. New York: The Macmillan Company and Free Press, 1968.

Greenstein, Fred I. "The Changing Pattern of Urban Party Politics." *The Annals of the Academy of Political and Social Science*. 353 (May 1964), 1-13.

Havard, William C. "From Bossism to Cosmopolitanism: Changes in the Relationship of Urban Leadership to State Politics." *The Annals of the American Academy of Political and Social Science*. 353 (May 1964), 84-94.

Hays, Samuel P. "The Politics of Reform in Municipal Government in the Progressive Era." *Pacific Northwest Quarterly*. (October 1964), 157-169, reprinted in Alexander B Callow, Jr., ed., *American Urban History*. New York: Oxford University Press, 1969, pp. 421-439.

Holli, Melvin G. *Reform in Detroit: Hazen S. Pingree and Urban Politics*. New York: Oxford University Press, 1969.

Killian, Margaret Patricia. *Born Rich: A Historical Book of Omaha*. Omaha: Assistance League of Omaha, 1978.

Koonig, Louis W. *Bryan: A Political Biography of William Jennings Bryan*. New York: G.P. Putnam's Sons, 1971.

Larsen, Laurence H., Barbara J. Cottrell. *The Gate City: A History of Omaha*. Boulder, Colorado: Pruett Publishing Company, 1982.

Lawson, Michael L. "Omaha, a City of Ferment: Summer of 1919." *Nebraska History*. 58 (Fall 1977), 395-418.

Leighton, George. *Five Cities: The Story of Their Youth*. New York: Harper and Bros., 1939.

McKitrick, Eric L. "The Study of Corruption." *Political Science Quarterly*. LXXII (December 1957), 502-514.

Menard, Orville D. "Tom Dennison, the Omaha Bee, and the 1919 Omaha Race Riot," *Nebraska History*, 68 (Winter 1987), 152-165.

-----------------------. "Imbibing in Elegance," *Persimmon Hill*, 15 (Winter, 1987), 26-33.

-----------------------. "The Rogue Who Ruled Omaha," *Omaha Magazine,*

March, 1978, 13-20.

Merton, Robert K. "The Latent Functions of the Machine: A Sociologists View." Reprinted in Alexander B. Callow, Jr., ed., *The City Boss in America: An Interpretative Reader.* New York: Oxford University Press, 1976, pp. 23-33.

Miller, Zane L. *Boss Cox's Cincinnati: Urban Politics in the Progressive Era.* New York: Oxford University Press, 1968.

Milligan, Maurice M. *Missouri Waltz.* New York: Charles Scribner's Sons, 1948.

Moscow, Warren. *The Last of the Big-Time Bosses: The Life and Times of Carmen De Sapio and Rise and Fall of Tammany Hall.* New York: Stein and Day, 1971.

Moynihan, Daniel Patrick. "The Irish of New York." Lawrence H. Fuchs, ed. *American Ethnic Politics.* New York: Harper Torchbacks, 1968, 77-108.

Murphy, Joseph P. *Wray M. Scott: His Life, His Times, and His Business.* Omaha: The Wray M. Scott Co., Inc., 1980.

Nelson, Arvid. *The Ak-Sar-Ben Story.* Lincoln: Johnson Publishing Company, 1967.

O'Connor, Edward. *The Last Hurrah.* Boston: Little Brown, 1956.

O'Connor, Len. *Clout.* New York: Avon, 1975.

"Omaha's Riot in Story and Picture." Educational Publishing Company, 1919.

Orth, Samuel P. *The Boss and the Machine.* New Haven: Yale University Press, 1919.

Ostrogorski, Mosei. *Democracy and the Organization of Political Parties.* Vol. II. Edited and abridged by Seymour Martin Lipsett. New York: Doubleday Anchor Paperback, 1964. "The Politicians and the Machine" reprinted in Alexander B. Callow, Jr., ed., *American Urban History.* New York: Oxford University Press, 1969, pp. 301-329.

Pagel, Al. "Omaha's Mind-Numbing Show of Shows." *Magazine of the Midlands.* September 21, 1980.

Rickard, Louise E. "The Politics of Reform in Omaha." *Nebraska History.* 53 (Winter 1972), 419-446.

Riordan, William L. *Plunkitt of Tammany Hall.* New York: E.P. Dutton & Co., Inc., 1973.

Roosevelt, Theodore. "Machine Politics in New York City." *The Century Magazine.* XXXIII (November 1886), 74-82.

Rosenbaum, Jonathan and Patricia O'Connor-Seger, eds. *Our Story: Recollections of Omaha's Early Jewish Community, 1825-1925.* Omaha: Omaha Section of the National Council of Jewish Women, 1981.

Rosewater, Victor. "Municipal Government in Nebraska." *Publications of the Nebraska State Historical Society.* 6 (1884-1895), 76-87.

Salter, John Thomas. *Boss Rule: Portraits in City Politics.* New York: McGraw Hill, 1935.

Sandoz, Maria. *The Cattlemen.* Lincoln: University of Nebraska Press, 1978.

Savage, James W., and John T. Bell. *History of the City of Omaha Nebraska.* New York and Chicago: Munsell & Company, 1894. Reprinted, Evansville: Unigraphic Inc., 1974.

Scott, Dial. *The Saloons of Denver.* Fort Collins, Colorado: The Old Army Press, 1973.

Sheldon, Addison E. *Nebraska: The Land and the People.* 3 vols. Chicago: The Lewis Publishing Co., 1931. II.

Showalter, John F. "James C. Dahlman, Mayor of Omaha," *Municipal Review*, XVI (1927), 111-117.

Smith, Zay N., and Pamela Zekman. *The Mirage.* New York: Random House, 1979.

Sorenson, Alfred. *The Story of Omaha from Pioneer Days to the Present Time.* Omaha: National Printing Co., 1923. 3rd ed.

Stave, Bruce M. *The New Deal and the Last Hurrah: Pittsburgh Machine Politics.* Pittsburgh: University of Pittsburgh Press, 1970.

Steffens, Lincoln. *The Autobiography of Lincoln Steffens.* New York: Harcourt, Brace and Company, 1931.

----------------------. *The Shame of the Cities.* New York: Peter Smith, 1948.

Steinberg, Alfred. *The Bosses.* New York: Mentor, 1972.

Sylvester. B.J. *West Famam Story.* np. nd.

Tarr, Joel Arthur. *A Study in Boss Politics: William Lorimer of Chicago.* Urbana: University of Illinois Press, 1971.

Washburn, Josie. *The Underworld Sewer.* Omaha: Washburn Publishing Company, 1909.

Wattles, Gurdon Wallace. *Autobiography of Gurdon Wallace Wattles.* New York: The Scribner Press, 1922.

Weinberg, Arthur and Lila, eds. *The Muckrakers.* New York: Simon and Schuster, 1961.

Wilhite, Ann L. Wiegman. "Sixty-Five Years Till Victory: A History of Women's Suffrage in Nebraska." *Nebraska History.* 49 (Summer 1968), 149-163.

Wolfinger, Raymond E. "The Development and Persistence of Ethnic Voting." Lawrence H. Fuchs, ed. *American Ethnic Politics.* New York: Harper Torchbacks, 1968.

Yost, Nellie, ed. *Boss Cowman: The Recollections of Ed Lemmon 1857-1946.* Lincoln: University of Nebraska Press, 1969.

Zink, Harold. *City Bosses in the United States.* Durham: Duke University Press, 1930.

337

338

339

341

343

CPSIA information can be obtained at www.ICGtesting.com
Printed in the USA
BVOW02s1245151013

PP5461700001B/1/P